CHINA'S ACCESSION TO THE WORLD TRADE ORGANIZATION

China's accession to the World Trade Organization (WTO), formally approved in December 2001 after 15 years of negotiation, will have a profound impact not only on the country's domestic situation, but also on the international community. This volume offers valuable insights into the consequences of this historic event, both from the perspective of China and of its European partners.

The book brings together expertise from scholars, policy-makers and representatives of corporate business, presenting a systematic examination into the interlocking nature of international and domestic forces. Insight into the complex dynamics of the accession process is offered by EU and Chinese representatives with hands-on experience of the international negotiations. Representatives from key economic sectors and social scientists discuss the domestic impact of China's membership of the WTO, analyzing the economic challenges and opportunities as well as the political, social and legal implications. Differing from most Western analysis of China's accession to the WTO which has tended to highlight the implications for China-US relations, the present study focuses on the consequences for future relations between China and the EU.

Rich in statistics, this volume will be of particular interest not only to experts and policy-makers involved in China's current affairs, but also to members of the business community, who need to better gauge the risks and opportunities arising out of China's further integration into the global economic framework.

English-language Series of the Institute of Asian Affairs, Hamburg

DÜI

VERBUND STIFTUNG
DEUTSCHES ÜBERSEE-INSTITUT

The Institute of Asian Affairs forms, together with the Institute of Comparative Overseas Studies, the Institute for Ibero-American Studies and the German Oriental Institute, the Foundation German Overseas Institute in Hamburg.

The objective of the Institute of Asian Affairs is to promote research on contemporary political, economic and social developments in Asian countries.

In so doing, the Institute endeavours to encourage the expression of various opinions. The reader should note, however, that the views expressed are those of the authors and not necessarily those of the Institute of Asian Affairs.

EAST ASIA BY THE YEAR 2000 AND BEYOND
Edited by Wolfgang Pape

CHINA'S ECONOMIC SECURITY
Edited by Werner Draguhn & Robert Ash

FRENCH AND JAPANESE ECONOMIC RELATIONS WITH VIETNAM
Henrich Dahm

TOURISM AND LOCAL ECONOMIC DEVELOPMENT IN CHINA
Gang Xu

CHINA'S LEGAL REFORMS AND THEIR POLITICAL LIMITS
Edited by Edward B. Vermeer & Ingrid d'Hooghe

CHINA'S COMMUNIST REVOLUTIONS:
FIFTY YEARS OF THE PEOPLE'S REPUBLIC OF CHINA
Edited by Werner Draguhn & David S.G. Goodman

ASIA-PACIFIC ECONOMIC COOPERATION (APEC)
THE FIRST DECADE
Edited by Jürgen Rüland, Eva Manske & Werner Draguhn

CHINA'S ACCESSION TO THE WORLD TRADE ORGANIZATION
NATIONAL AND INTERNATIONAL PERSPECTIVES
Edited by Heike Holbig & Robert Ash

CHINA'S ACCESSION TO THE WORLD TRADE ORGANIZATION

National and International Perspectives

Edited by Heike Holbig and Robert Ash

IFA

RoutledgeCurzon
Taylor & Francis Group
LONDON AND NEW YORK

First published 2002 by RoutledgeCurzon
2 Park Square, Milton Park, Abingdon, Oxon, OX14 4RN

Simultaneously published in the USA and Canada
by RoutledgeCurzon
270 Madison Ave, New York NY 10016

RoutledgeCurzon is an imprint of the Taylor & Francis Group

Transferred to Digital Printing 2006

Publisher's Note
This book has been prepared from camera-ready copy provided by the authors.

British Library Cataloguing in Publication Data
A catalogue record for this book is available from the British Library

Library of Congress Cataloging in Publication Data
A catalog record for this book has been requested

ISBN 0-700-71661-0

Contents

List of Contributors

Prof Dr Robert Ash
Chiang Ching-kuo Professor for Taiwan Studies, School of Oriental and African Studies, London/Chairman of ECAN

Dr Hans-Friedrich Beseler
Former Director General for Trade, European Commission (retired in May 2000), Special Adviser to the European Commission, Brussels

Prof Dr Sarah Biddulph
Associate Director, China, Asian Law Centre, Law School, Unversity of Melbourne

Dr Flemming Christiansen
Senior Lecturer in Chinese Studies at the Department of East Asian Studies, University of Leeds

Dr Newman M.K. Lam
Assistant Professor, Faculty of Social Sciences and Humanities, University of Macau

Ms Françoise Lemoine (DEA)
Senior Economist at the Centre d'Études Prospectives et d'Informations Internationales (CEPII), Paris

Dr He Liping
Professor of Economics, China Institute of Finance and Banking, Beijing

Dr Heike Holbig
Research Fellow at the Institute of Asian Affairs, Hamburg

Prof Dr Peter Nolan
Sinyi Professor of Chinese Management, Judge Institute of Management Studies, Univerity of Cambridge

Dr Jürgen Oberg
Executive Director, Siemens AG, International Operations Asia/Pacific, Munich

Dr Martin Posth
President, Asia Pacific Forum Berlin e.V.; former Member of the Board of Management, Volkswagen AG, in addition Chairman and President of the Group's Regional Headquarters, Volkswagen Asia-Pacific Ltd., Hong Kong

Mr Hans-Jörg Probst
Head of Allianz Group Governmental Liaison Office Berlin; served as Chief Representative of Allianz Group in Beijing 1997–2000

Dr Margot Schüller
Senior Research Fellow at the Institute of Asian Affairs, Hamburg

Ms Deniz Ünal-Kesenci (DEA)
Economist at the Centre d'Études Prospectives et d'Informations Internationales (CEPII), Paris

Dr Wang Yong
Associate Professor, School of International Studies, Beijing University

Prof Dr Michael B. Yahuda
Convenor, International Relations Department, The London School of Economics and Political Science, London

Preface

China's accession to the World Trade Organization (WTO) has been delayed for longer than many had expected. There is, however, a strong likelihood that its membership of the WTO will have become a reality by the end of 2001. The present volume seeks to offer valuable insights into the consequences of this historic event, both from the perspective of China itself and from that of its international partners.

For reasons that are readily understandable, most Western analysis of the broader impact of Chinese membership of the WTO has tended to highlight the implications for China–US relations. By contrast, the present volume focuses explicitly on the consequences of Chinese accession for relations between China and the European Union (EU). The various chapters reflect a variety of professional perspectives, as seen through the eyes of scholars, government policy-makers and representatives of corporate business in EU Member States (as well as in China itself). The volume also deliberately embraces not only the economic impact, but also the political, social and legal implications of Chinese membership of the WTO. By such means, the book makes available an unusually comprehensive picture of the potential challenges and opportunities arising out of China's further integration into the global economic framework.

With the benefits of hindsight, the protracted nature of negotiations following China's original application, in 1986, to join the General Agreement on Tariffs and Trade (GATT) – the predecessor of the current WTO – suggests the existence of a cyclical pattern of development. This cycle has been characterized by long periods of stagnation and inertia, punctuated by unexpected breakthroughs and progress – these, however, merely giving rise to further cycles of the same kind.

From one perspective, this cyclical rhythm appears to reflect the inherent nature of international trade negotiations, as these are embodied in the WTO process. The nine years of negotiations associated with the Uruguay Round, which encountered many setbacks before suddenly and unexpectedly reaching a successful resolution, provide one example of the innate obstacles. Another is observable in the pursuit of the Seattle Round, which, having been frequently postponed, was eventually rescheduled as the Doha Round. Underlying this halting and often erratic progress is the reality that no other single policy area is subject to so many different and potentially conflicting interests as those embodied in the formulation and implementation of trade policy. Indeed, such policy is perhaps unique in terms of the care with which the costs and benefits of new policies are calculated, as well as in terms of the transparency with which any positive and negative effects are attributable to the policy initiatives themselves. Nor is there any other area of economic negotiation in which representatives of corporate business and various social groups undertake such vigorous bargaining. All these factors help explain the protracted nature of China's WTO negotiations.

But from another perspective, it is possible to discern more distinctly individual reasons for the length of time that it has taken to bring China to the threshold of WTO membership. Not least, the continuing transformation, since the early 1980s, of the Chinese economy from a dirigiste, centrally planned system to one increasingly approximating a market – in official terms, 'socialist market' – system has given rise to fluid conditions from which to negotiate accession. In particular, existing WTO members have found it difficult to come to terms with a negotiating partner, whose very nature has been constantly changing. In addition, China's integration into international trading regimes has itself impacted on domestic policy and decision-making patterns and behaviour. Few would doubt that China's comparative international economic performance in recent years has enhanced the prestige of the leadership in Beijing. At the same time, the opening up of the country to the outside world has widened the spectrum of those who see themselves affected by Chinese membership of the WTO. Some of these welcome China's further integration into the global trading regime, but others have sought to challenge the authority of the central leaders. This tension between centre and region has further complicated the negotiation process.

In an awareness of the interlocking nature of domestic and international forces, this book seeks to analyze the consequences of China's WTO accession through a systematic examination of the ways in which all these forces have impinged upon one another. To this end, it is organized in four parts, as follows:

Part I adopts an international perspective in an attempt to analyze the stakes and stumbling blocks inherent in the accession process. Its embodiment of the hands-on experience of both EU and Chinese representatives engaged in the on-going negotiations, makes the analysis notable for the insights it provides into the complex dynamics of the negotiation process.

Part II is specifically concerned with domestic developments, its principal focus being the economic impact of China's accession to the WTO. Here, the chapters point to the existence of both challenges and opportunities. On the one hand, a pessimistic assessment of state-owned enterprise (SOE) reform predicts a further decline in the competitiveness of the state-owned economy. On the other hand, separate investigations of four major economic sectors – automobiles, telecommunications, insurance and banking – offer room for a more optimistic view of the domestic impact of Chinese membership of the WTO.

Attention has already been drawn to the importance of the non-economic dimensions of WTO accession, and Part III seeks to analyse some of the major challenges likely to face the political, social and legal systems. Here, there is general agreement that WTO membership will pose new problems in all three areas, although there is also a common recognition that widespread forecasts that such problems are likely to be reflected in the widespread breakdown of social and political order may be premature.

The final section of the book (Part IV) returns to the international dimension. It seeks to assess the implications of Chinese membership of WTO for global trade by examining possible future changes in trade and capital flows, especially within and between the EU and East Asia. An attempt is also made to analyze likely changes in the *modus operandi* of the WTO, following China's accession to it.

This volume is the product of revised papers, originally presented at the Fourth Annual Conference of the EU–China Academic Network (ECAN), held in Berlin on 1–2 February 2001. ECAN owes its existence to a grant made available by the European Commission. Since its inception in 1997, ECAN has each year organized an Annual Conference, as well as two Private Policy Workshops. The Fourth Annual Conference was co-organized by the Institute of Asian Affairs (Hamburg, Germany) and ECAN in cooperation with the Association of German Chambers of Industry and Commerce (DIHT). The event attracted more than 300 participants from many EU Member States, representative of the academic, diplomatic and business communities, thereby fulfilling one of ECAN's fundamental objectives, which is to foster a community of interest among all those professionally engaged with China.

The Editors

Part I

Stakes and Stumbling Blocks in the Process of China's WTO Accession

1

The EU–China Negotiations Breaking the Deadlock

*Hans-Friedrich Beseler**

Introductory Remarks

We are not yet there. Good progress has been made on all sides but certain impasses have still to be resolved. The bilateral agreements have now been concluded, the one with the USA in November 1999 and the one with the EU on May 19, 2000. Other WTO members, with the exception of Mexico, have also achieved agreement at the bilateral level. The results have been widely publicized and will be known by most of the readers (for the details of the EU–China agreement, see Annex 1). The US has given the green light and granted permanent normal trade relations (PNTR) treatment to China, at least for this year.

At the multilateral level, progress was made in the WTO Working Party sessions of November–December 2000 and January 2001 in Geneva; however, it was not possible to conclude. A new Working Party session has to be held but its precise date, and result, are uncertain. Given these circumstances, this article will concentrate on the following aspects:

1. The motives, difficulties, strategy and process of the negotiations;
2. the latest developments in the multilateral process in Geneva;
3. the implications for the EU–China trade relationship.

---

* Dr Beseler, Director General of Trade (retired) of the European Commission, served as Chief of the China Negotiating Team until May 2000. The opinions expressed here, however, are those of the author and not necessarily those of the European Commission.

Motives, Difficulties, Strategy and Process

Why this accession?

The European side has favoured China's WTO accession essentially for two reasons:

1. The EU counts among the strongest proponents of the multilateral trading system of the WTO, and we want to strengthen it. With China becoming, in the next years, one of the major players in the world, the system will not be able to work with China outside. We need the world's major economic powers in, and we need them to abide by the rules, enforceable under the mandatory dispute settlement system of the WTO.
2. China is in a delicate phase of transition from a state trader to a market economy. In this situation, we have to strengthen the liberal forces behind the present government for commercial, political and also for humanitarian reasons.

China, at least the liberal forces behind Premier Zhu Rongji, must have opted for accession for very similar reasons:

1. China has no alternative: the country had isolated itself for centuries, up to the tragic events in the middle of the 19th century. The communist experience, a hundred years later, led nowhere. Faced now with the challenge of globalization China has to open up to the outside and to liberalize inside.
2. WTO accession makes internal and external liberalization irreversible, at least the economic liberalization needed so urgently, as the country will have to abide by the liberal rules of the WTO.
3. The WTO system now governs trade relations between all major players. The system will continue to evolve (creation of an inbuilt agenda, start of a new round, initiation of other negotiations). China has to jump on the train if it does not want to be left behind the rest of the world.
4. For China, these liberal rules of the WTO will constitute the shelter needed to protect itself against protectionist tendencies of its competitors.

Why was it so difficult?

For the EU and other Western countries, there were three major preoccupations:

1. Ensure a level playing field for our industry. The EU market is very open already (with some 'minor' exceptions), and we are willing to open up further to the Chinese, but this has to been done on the condition of reciprocity: the Chinese 1.2 billion customers market should open up too, at least progressively.
2. The accession, much as we want it to happen, should not result in a dilution of the international trading system. China has to abide by the rules of the game, if not immediately, then at least after reasonable transition periods, and their termination should be determined clearly.
3. The danger of creating a precedent: China's WTO accession will not be the last one. Russia and others are waiting to join, too. If we create bad precedents now we shall regret them later.

For the Chinese side, there were also major difficulties:

1. The political problems which had to be tackled in the course of internal reforms: bureaucracy and state intervention are still very wide spread. After all, state-owned enterprises (SOEs) are still contributing about 40 per cent of China's GDP, 60 per cent of government revenue and 70 per cent of urban employment.
2. The fragile situation of the Chinese economy, half way between a less developed and an industrialized country.

The US–China agreement

Many countries, and especially China, had expected that the US–China agreement would pave the way for China's accession. The US deal which, after the unfortunate breakdown of talks between President Clinton and Premier Zhu on April 4, 1999, was finally concluded by Charlene Barshefsky on November 15, 1999, in Beijing indeed constituted a major breakthrough.

The US obtained significant concessions which have considerably simplified our own negotiations as, under the WTO most favoured nation (MFN) rule, concessions negotiated by one partner are automatically applicable to all other WTO partners. For us, this was particularly important in the following sectors:

- Tariffs, where US negotiations resulted in significant lowering of rates; for example, a tariff of 25 per cent for cars was agreed on, while Japan had only obtained a reduction to 50 per cent.

- Telecommmunications: the monopoly situation which has existed up to now was broken up: 50 per cent ownership for value-added services and paging, particularly for internet services.
- Banking: the US obtained an elimination of all geographical restrictions and internal branching within the same city within five years, as well as the right to deal in local currency with Chinese enterprises and individuals.
- Distribution rights: a first breakthrough was reached in this field.

But the US deal had also major shortcomings for the EU:

- The 'Euro specificity' problem: the US had been fighting – which of course is a natural thing to do – for their own interests: for oranges, where we grow mandarins, for bourbon whiskey, where we want to sell Scotch and Cognac, and for plastics where, we are more interested in cosmetics.
- Protectionist features of US agreement: the US insisted on and obtained a series of excessive safeguard clauses:
    - A general special safeguard clause for twelve years;
    - a special safeguard clause for textiles up to the year 2008, while the Multi–Fibre Agreement (MFA) expires in 2005;
    - anti-dumping: special rules for state trading which will be applicable for another 15 years.

It was evident that the specific concessions reached by the US did not satisfy the European Community which had other interests, in other sectors, for other products, to defend. Worse, it was evident that US insistence on excessive safeguard and anti-dumping rules had precluded them from insisting on more substantial concessions in sectors important for the future evolution of our China trade. The EU therefore risked bearing the costs of the US concessions if it did not manage to improve the US–China deal on substantial points.

The EU's strategy

Following the US deal, our main goal in the negotiations therefore has been

- to fight for 'Euro specific' concessions, particularly in the field of tariffs: for all spirits, cosmetics, ceramics, leather, textiles, footwear, machinery, marble and stones etc.;

- to improve the US deal on those points where we had a particular interest and where Washington might have obtained more if they had not concentrated on the negotiation of the excessive regulations mentioned above.

Commissioner Pascal Lamy attempted to reach a first breakthrough in March 2000. Unfortunately, he had to realize that there were certain cast iron principles on the Chinese side, which it proved were impossible to overcome:

- The ownership restrictions of 49 per cent in the mobile telephony sector (where the EU is the world leader, covering 90 per cent of the Chinese market) and of 50 per cent for life insurance;
- the 25 per cent duty for cars and the 50 per cent joint venture requirement in the same sector.

It was evident that a decision had been made at the highest level of China's political hierarchy which meant that any deviation from these principles would be a breaking point for the negotiations. In addition, there was of course the argument that, as President Clinton had accepted the Chinese position on these issues, why should what had been possible to the US be impossible to the European Community?

Thus, Commissioner Lamy and the Council of Ministers had to decide whether to break or compromise. The result of the Council's deliberations was that the European Commission could compromise if it obtained sufficient compensation in exchange for a more flexible position on these principles. Only after this compensation was granted by the Chinese was the breakthrough finally reached on May 19, 2000.

The negotiating process

Negotiations started more than fourteen years ago, proceeding through an endless number of sessions. There was broad involvement on both sides:

On the EU side, the main actors were:

- The European Commission holding the mandate to negotiate for the entire Community in all trade related matters. Within the Commission, the Directorate-General for Trade took the lead, with intensive participation of all other interested services, such as External Relations, Industry, Internal Market, Telecommunications etc. Up to the very end, the negotiations were held in close contact with all member states and interested sectors (cars, telecommunications, banking, insurance, brokers etc.).

- EU member states were following closely. While they all favoured China's accession, most of them had largely diverging interests and stakes in different sectors:

  - All bigger member states: banking, insurance, telecommunications, distribution, trade-related aspects of intellectual property rights (TRIPS);
  - Belgium: dredging;
  - Germany: machinery;
  - France, Spain and Italy: wine;
  - Italy: ceramics;
  - Portugal: textiles, olives, banking (especially in Zhuhai)
  - United Kingdom: spirits (with France), insurance brokers, lawyers.

- European industries shared many common goals (liberalization, privatization etc.) but each of the various sectors was, of course, defending its own interests. Some sectors were even split within themselves, most visibly in the automobile sector: Volkswagen, Audi and Citroën, all of them already well established on the Chinese market, were praising the virtues of high import tariffs, while BMW and others, still waiting to be let in to China, asked for reductions, a position shared by the Commission.

On the Chinese side, a multitude of ministries was involved in the negotiations which often made coordination of interests very difficult. The Ministry of Foreign Trade and Economic Cooperation (MoFTEC) took the lead, with the Ministry of Foreign Affairs and the State Administrations of various industries, agriculture, telecommunications, transport, banking, SOEs and others following. It soon became evident that all final decisions were taken at the highest level. In particular, Prime Minister Zhu Rongji was extremely well informed, even about minor details, and highly committed personally, especially since the experiences of his visit to Washington in April 1999. In the end, it was Zhu Rongji's final negotiation with Mr Lamy which led to the conclusion of negotiations on May 19, 2000.

The Multilateral Process in Geneva

Where are we now? The Working Party of November and December 2000 made good progress on questions such as:

- Rule of law problems:
  - Transparency, i.e. the publication by China of its draft laws and regulations before their coming into force as well as the provision for a certain period during which comments can be made, as this is the case in the EU, the US and other WTO member countries.
  - Judicial review: Administrative review bodies should now be independent, and in order to allow for legal action to be taken against their decisions, judicial review by independent tribunals should be introduced.
  - Uniformity in the application by China of all its laws and regulations.
- Transition review mechanism in order to regularly monitor China's implementation of its WTO obligations.
- Administration of agricultural tariff rate quotas: the two-tier approval process for importers shall be harmonized between Beijing and the provinces.

During the January 2001 Working Party session five major issues were under discussion:

- Technical barriers to trade, standards and certification: at present, China has a dual system: one, quick and simple for Chinese companies and another, long and complicated system, for foreign companies. The EU, and the US, too, have insisted on the elimination of this kind of discrimination. They demanded that the same standards, technical regulations and conformity assessment procedures should be applied to both domestic and imported products. China should also adopt internationally agreed standards.
- Licensing and trading rights: China requires that foreign traders, like Chinese traders, before starting commercial operations are not only are registered in the trade register but also fully incorporated and capitalized on the Chinese market. This requirement is rejected by the EU, the US and other WTO partners who

insist that this is an unnecessary burden for traders and not justified under WTO rules. Registration therefore should be required for fiscal and customs purposes only.

- Services:
  - China frequently restricts the choice of partners for joint ventures. We insisted, and so did the US, on the freedom of choice, demanding that joint venture partners may also be chosen in other sectors.
  - In the distribution sector, liberalization will start three years after accession and majority shares will be allowed after two years, except for chain stores – a precise definition of which has yet to be found.
  - Insurance brokers' activities will be progressively admitted on the Chinese market for large commercial risks. But what is a large commercial risk? A dividing line has to be found which should not be so high as to effectively shut down the Chinese market.
- Industrial and agricultural subsidies: China requests the right to invoke special LDC flexibility provisions of the subsidy code.

Good progress was made on most of these questions in the January 2001 Working Party session. It has not yet been possible, however, to reach a final conclusion. Now Mr. Ravier, Chairman of the WTO China Working Group, seems to intend to convoke the next, hopefully last, meeting of the group as soon as the constitution of the new US administration has made sufficient progress.

The next stage will then be the ratification of all bilateral and multilateral results by the different WTO countries. In the EU's case, the Council of Ministers' approval is required after consultation of the European Parliament (procedure under Article 300 of the Amsterdam Treaty). Beforehand, member states will want to scrutinize the precise texts negotiated with the Chinese side, and other countries will want to do the same. It is only after the conclusion of all these procedures that China's – and Taiwan's – accession will become effective.

Implications for the EU–China Trade Relations

In recent years, the Chinese economy has demonstrated extremely dynamic development. Growth rates were impressively high at between 7 and 8 per cent, and the tenth five-year-plan covering the years 2001 to 2005 supposes that this rate will be maintained during the period. Chinese exports have been booming, with those to the EU growing by 42 per cent in the first six months of the year 2000, bringing the Chinese trade surplus with the EU up to 40 billion Euros for the year 2000.

The WTO accession will open up new chances for China:

- China can avail itself, de jure, of the totality of liberalization measures accepted by the WTO since the foundation of GATT in 1948, be it in the area of customs duties, quotas, non-tariff barriers, goods or services. Usually, this implies an end to all special restrictions against the member countries' exports. In case of violation of trade rules by any of its partners China shall be entitled to invoke the WTO dispute settlement mechanism in order to protect its rights under the WTO treaties.

- The MFA will expire in 2005 and China, already the world champion in textiles, will be free to take advantage of this situation.

- Quotas still existing in the EU for shoes, porcelain and ceramic tableware will be abolished, and so will all other quotas in the US and other WTO countries.

- Anti-dumping legislation, already revised by the EU in order to take account of China's special situation, will have to be revamped by other WTO countries, too. This will alleviate the pressure on Chinese exports from that side.

- There will be increased foreign investment in China due to the opening of the Chinese market, a more attractive, predictable business environment and, last but not least, a modernized banking sector.

- Technical know how, new management practices and working methods will increasingly flow into China.

- Allocation of resources will be improved which will, in turn, support economic growth in China.

All this will open up new opportunities to the Chinese economy. However, China must also open its market. In particular, China will have to implement the following WTO commitments:

- The overall average tariff for industrial goods will go down from the current 17.8 to 9.2 per cent; for spirits from 65 to 10 per cent, for cosmetics from 30 to 10 per cent, for most machinery and appliances from 35 to about 10 per cent.

- On the agricultural side, tariffs for pasta will go down from 25 to 15 per cent, for butter from 30 to 10 per cent, for wine from 65 to 14 per cent, and for wheat gluten from 30 to 18 per cent.

- On the service side, the right to distribute will now be gradually opened at every level from wholesale to retail, except for a very limited number of products.

- EU and US banks will be able to establish and conduct local currency business with Chinese companies and individuals.

- Access for foreign insurance companies will be significantly improved.

- Operating licences for these companies will be granted on the basis of transparent prudential criteria. Firms will have access to the major cities within two or three years and to the whole country within five years of accession.

- China has also accepted opening a significant part of its telecommunication market.

- The right to provide telecom services in China's major cities shall now be accompanied by the right to provide services between these citites.

Thus, competition will increase. China will particulary suffer from the heavy burden of its SOEs. Although much has been done to reduce their number, the large enterprises in the 'strategic' sectors remain, with many of them making heavy losses. Moreover, there is tremendous overcapacity in certain sectors and regions.

The conservative forces and the hard liners, all those who have profited from the old system, will be tempted to resist the liberalization drive and to preserve the monopoly of the party not only over politics but also over the economy. There will also be growing pressure on the labour market at a time when a new social security net, once provided for by the SOEs, is still in the making.

Already now, unemployment is spreading through China. It is estimated by some to be around 20 per cent in the cities and much higher in the rural areas where approximately half of the Chinese work force is located.

Of course, China will not be exposed to these kinds of problems overnight. The market will be opend progressively and over long transition periods, most of them ending in 2005–06. Thus, China will have the time to adapt, to benefit from its normal comparative advantages, and to reallocate its resources to labour intensive industries. However, the challenge will be enormous. It will require a new relationship at all levels of government and business.

Need for a New Relationship

The European Commission shall monitor the implementation by China of its WTO commitments, and so will the US and other countries' governments. The Commission will do this with its own expertise and resources, and with the help of European governments and of European business. The latter will not hesitate to inform the Commission of problems they may identify. This does not mean that the EU will drag China into formal WTO dispute settlement procedures at every hint of a problem. The Commission clearly prefers a more consultative approach. Yet, in the last resort, it would certainly not hesitate to formally defend the European industries' rights under WTO rules.

But more will have to be done: we have to help to build a new relationship with China based on technical assistance and cooperation at governmental level and on dialogues between business representatives. The process is already under way and problems arising have been discussed at the EU–China Joint Committee meeting at the end of the October 2000 summit (for the details of this meeting, see Annex 2).

Annex 1

Results of the EU's Bilateral Negotiations as of May 15, 2000

Industrial Goods

- Import tariffs:

  The specific EU priorities not covered by China's previous bilateral Agreements were concentrated on 150 specific products varying from gin to building materials. On these EU-specific priorities, an additional reduction of 40 per cent on top of earlier offers was obtained (the average tariff for these products falling from 18.6 to 10.6 per cent, with the overall average tariff falling from 17.4 to 9.2 per cent).

- Quotas:

  In general, quotas will be progressively eliminated up to 2005. In addition, Since the US obtained the immediate liberalization of DAP fertilizers and urea, China's quota on Europe's fertilizer exports (NPK) will be liberalized upon accession, and restrictions in place this year will be immediately relaxed. In a parallel move, the EU shall also eliminate its quotas on Chinese products: shoes, porcelain and ceramic tableware.

- State Trading:
  - Liberalization of import monopolies on oil (refused to the USA) and fertiliser – China has agreed to open the market to private traders through a process of gradual liberalization. This means that firms will no longer be obliged to go exclusively through China's state importers when shipping oil and fertilizer to China. The oil and fertilizer sectors are the most significant domains where a state import monopoly has been in place.
  - Liberalization of export monopoly on silk – EU firms will be able to buy raw silk directly from Chinese producers (who produce 70 per cent of the world total). Until now all purchases had to go through state export channels. This will bring substantial benefits to the EU's numerous manufacturers of ties, scarves and other high value silk garments and accessories.

- Motor vehicles:

  China was not ready to lower its tariff beyond the 25 per cent agreed with the USA nor to renounce the mandatory 50 per cent joint venture requirement. However, it made compensatory concessions which are important for EU companies producing cars, vans and trucks in China. There are three key points:

  - All restrictions regarding the class and models of vehicles produced will be lifted within two years, leaving the car producer free to make such decisions on a purely commercial basis.
  - Provincial authorities alone will be able to approve investments in the sector up to $150 million (ceiling raised from $30 million), substantially reducing red-tape in the car industry.
  - For the manufacture of engines, China's joint venture requirement will be removed, allowing wholly foreign owned production.

Agriculture

- Market access (tariffs and tariff quotas): the US had pushed the overall duty level for agricultural products of 17 per cent down to 14.5 per cent for US priority products. For the EU, further improvements have been made for products of particular interest to the Community.

- Sanitary and phytosanitary (SPS) measures: the EU and China signed an SPS agreement that will provide for compliance by China with the WTO's SPS Agreement, as well as resolving a number of bilateral SPS trade frictions.

Services

- Telecommunications:

  China maintained its 49 per cent ownership restriction imposed on the USA. But, as compensation to the EU, the telecommunications offer has been considerably enhanced. China will open its mobile telephony market two years ahead of schedule, which is a crucial change in this fast-developing industry. For the first time, foreign operators will be permitted on the market with a 25 per cent share starting from accession. This will rise to 35 per cent one year and to 49 per cent three years after accession. China has also agreed to allow operations between Chinese cities (where the biggest business is located, covering more than 75 per cent of current usage) and not to restrict them to activities within each city.

The liberalization of domestic leased circuit services will allow joint venture and foreign telecom operators to create their own network (independent from the existing network) and to sell their capacity to clients in China.

- Insurance:

  - Seven new licences, five for life and two for non-life business, will be provided to EU companies immediately, and two more companies will be able to establish two sub-branches each in another city. This will substantially increase the EU presence in China, as only four companies are presently in the market.
  - Effective management control has been negotiated for foreign participants in life insurance joint ventures, through free choice of partner and a legal guarantee of freedom from any regulatory interference in privately negotiated contracts, on a 50:50 equity basis.
  - Foreign insurers will see their scope of business advanced by two years in life and non-life activities, selling the same products as their Chinese competitors.
  - Geographically, access of foreign insurers to Shenzen and Foshan has also been accelerated.
  - Brokers (insurance intermediaries) will have access to the Chinese market through cross-border and local establishment for the first time.

- Distribution:

  China has agreed to progressively eliminate the specific 50–50 joint venture restriction applicable to large retail stores (removing the 20,000 m^2 size limit), as well as that for virtually all retail operations with more than 30 outlets in China.

- Banking:

  The banking sector is already relatively open. International branching was allowed. The US obtained the elimination of geographical restrictions within five years and internal branching within the same city. Under the EU–China deal the offer has been further improved:

  - Distributors and other non-financial institutions will be able to give credit facilities for the purchase of all motor vehicles, including trucks, buses, tractors, motorcycles etc., rather than just cars.
  - China has also agreed to allow foreign banks in the city of Zhuhai to advance their operations in local currency. Zhuhai, which is just off Macao, holds several EU banks.

Horizontal Issues

- Government Procurement: China has agreed to full transparency and non-discrimination (MFN) in government purchases.
- Trade-distorting investment-related measures: the EU and China have agreed on commitments similar to those included in the Sino–US agreement, but also incorporating an obligation to eliminate industrial export subsidies and to offset requirements in the civil aircraft sector.
- National treatment: this is a basic GATT obligation. China has now made specific commitments to phase out legislation that gives unfair advantages to domestic producers in the field of pharmaceutical pricing, after-sales services of imported goods, chemical import registration requirements, control of imported boilers, and retail of imported cigarettes and spirits. In some cases China will be allowed one or two years to adjust her legislation to WTO rules.

Annex 2

Assistance, Cooperation, and Contacts

Technical Assistance

In order to support China's integration into the world economy, the EU has established a series of capacity building projects with a budget totalling over 20 million Euros. Some are already under way, others will start soon.

- A framework programme in support of WTO accession for Chinese officials dealing with the implementation of WTO commitments who will receive training in a wide range of areas.

- Assistance will also be offered in the following fields:
  - The reform and restructuring of the financial services sector;
  - the provision of statistics; a project was started in 1998 and has produced good results already;
  - the development of a transparent and non-discriminatory public procurement system: a project is now coming to an end and has proven very successful;
  - legal cooperation: a five year project has now been launched to train a first group of selected lawyers, judges and prosecutors;
  - Establishment of a modern and efficient system of intellectual property rights (IPR) protection. There has been an important project under way since 1999.

For the future, further projects can be envisaged on other WTO related subjects.

Intergovernmental Cooperation

On a broader scale, EU–China cooperation projects, financed with 60 million Euros or more every year, have been committed successfully over the last five years. They are part of the EU's overall cooperation programme with China, designed to support the country's wide-ranging social and economic reforms.

These projects have covered:

- education and training;
- science and technology, with a bilateral agreement now in force;
- energy and environmental issues;
- agriculture;
- civil aviation;
- telecommunications;
- legal cooperation and public administration training;
- village governance;
- human rights.

Further cooperation is now expected in new areas such as combating illegal immigration. Premier Zhu and President Prodi agreed on this point when they met in Brussels in July 2000 and during the October 2000 summit in Beijing. Their meeting followed the tragic events in Dover when 58 Chinese illegal immigrants lost their lives.

Premier Zhu has also proposed a seminar on the 'Society of Growth' and a conference on the 'Information Society'. The Fourth EU–China conference on energy will take place in 2001 in Beijing. Both sides will intensify their contacts under their customs cooperation treaty and there should be negotiations soon on subjects such as maritime transport and the use nuclear energy for peaceful purposes.

Business to Business Contacts

The EU China Business Dialogue was launched in 1998 as agreed between Premier Zhu and President Prodi. It will promote European investment in China. A meeting of top EU CEOs (lead by Vivendi) and high level Chinese business leaders took place on the fringes of the October 2000 summit. Moreover, the EU Chamber of Commerce in China (ECCC) launched in October 1999, now has more than 180 European members and 14 sectoral working groups. It will facilitate the integration of EU business and promote EU investment in China.

2

China's Stakes in WTO Accession

The Internal Decision-making Process

Wang Yong

Introduction

Negotiations on China's accession to the General Agreement on Tariffs and Trade (GATT) and its successor organization, the World Trade Organisation (WTO), have lasted for over 14 years, the longest accession process on record. The Chinese side jokes that the long wait has turned black hair to white and accuses some WTO members of trying to impose unacceptable conditions on China.[1] In contrast, developed nations – most prominently the United States – claim that what they want are only 'commercially viable' terms, and that China has dragged its feet in opening markets.

Since early 1999, however, negotiations have appeared to make great progress. In the agreements on WTO accession with the US, EU and other countries, China has committed itself to unprecedented liberalization and to settling remaining issues as soon as possible. As many correctly point out, Chinese concessions in the past two years far exceeded those made over the last five years. If the negative effects of the Asian financial crisis on China's economy and the political crisis caused by the NATO bombing of the Chinese embassy in Belgrade are taken into account, the concessions seem even more astounding.

Thus, two key questions present themselves to most observers: first, why was China's WTO bidding process, previous to early 1999, so slow? And second, why has China now become so eager to speed up the negotiations? The answers to these questions undoubtedly have implications not only for the debate on China's WTO membership in WTO member countries, but also for the prediction on China's performance of implementation of treaty commitments.

Much of the research to date has focused on explaining the sluggish pace of China's accession negotiations, placing much of the blame on the impact of the end of the Cold War, the crackdown in Tiananmen Square, and rapid economic growth in China. Before 1989, the strategic interests of the United States vis-à-vis the Soviet Union, combined with the perception that China's reforms indicated a move toward capitalism, prompted the United States and other Western countries to look favourably on China's membership of GATT. But the events of the late 1980s fundamentally changed the tenor of China–US relations. Moreover, as China has grown into a major trading power, Western countries have come to see China's bid for WTO membership as a key opportunity to extract market access concessions from the country.

Yet research into China's WTO policy-making process has been relatively thin, especially research into the bureaucratic politics surrounding the negotiations. In fact, personal interviews with Chinese economic officials reveal that bureaucratic politics goes a long way toward answering both of these questions.

This paper will address the following issues: what were the features and problems of the pre-1999 decision-making process on GATT/WTO? Why did the top leadership determine to speed up negotiations? What are the characteristics of the new policy coordination process arising from 1999, and what implications does this new policy-making mechanism have for China–US and China–EU negotiations?[2]

Scattered Power Structure

China's traditional power structure, established during the central-planning era, divided administration of all aspects of the economy among different agencies. Liberalizing trade regulations thus requires depriving these economic agencies of their powers and interests, or at least reducing their authority substantially. The GATT Uruguay Round agreements, especially the General Agreement on Trade in Services (GATS) and the Agreement on Trade-Related Investment Measures (TRIMs), require liberalization not only in the trade of goods but also in services and investment. As a result, an even larger number of economic agencies in the Chinese central government have found themselves drawn into the negotiations for WTO membership.

The PRC bureaucracy is characterized by overlapping jurisdictions, a result, in part, of its sheer size. Before the launch of government restructuring in 1998, there were more than 40 ministries, commissions and agencies, and more than half were directly related to economic and industrial affairs. For example, the State Council Commission on Tariffs (affiliated with the State Economic and Trade Commission, or SETC) and the General Administration of Customs together took responsibility for tariffs, but they had to consult with other agencies when setting new rates. In other words, they had to deal with pressures from other government agencies that wanted to protect domestic industries. The power to determine quotas was divided between the Ministry of Foreign Trade and Economic Cooperation (MoFTEC) and the State Planning Commission (SPC). MoFTEC was in charge of export quotas, while SPC took care of import quotas.

But these were only the agencies concerned with trade in goods – trade in services is even more closely protected and has proved to be the most difficult area of negotiations. The negotiations over market access in telecommunications services, for example, involve the industry's traditionally protectionist regulator, the Ministry of Information Industry (formerly the Ministry of Posts and Telecommunications) and other relevant agencies.

The way in which industrial policy was formulated presents another obstacle to bureaucratic agreement. To harmonize industrial policy on automobiles with WTO norms would affect the interests of the now downgraded Ministry of Machine-Building Industry's Department of Automotive Industry (in charge of project approval and production planning); the SPC's Department of Machinery, Electronics, Textiles, and Light Industry (which had project approval authority and was responsible for the biggest state-owned auto makers); the Ministry of Finance; and other ministries and local governments in charge of smaller auto factories. Even within the same agency, there could be several departments with disparate views. For instance, within the SPC, the Department of Long-Term Planning and Industrial Policy had different views and interests from the Department of Machinery, Electronics, Textiles, and Light Industry.

MoFTEC is the country's chief negotiating body on WTO, but only a few issues fall under its direct authority. Thus, the ministry has had no choice but to focus first on policy coordination with other economic agencies. Of course, the various relevant economic agencies do not have an equal say in the negotiations because they hold different administrative ranks. Among them, the SPC (now known as the

State Development Planning Commission [SDPC]) and the SETC enjoy a higher rank. Both of them are supra-ministerial agencies assigned to oversee, coordinate, or even direct the other agencies. With such a scattered and unbalanced power structure, China's pace in accession to the WTO would be understandably influenced, if not determined outright, by whether the supra-ministerial agencies – mainly SDPC and SETC – support the trade liberalization measures, and whether they are both able and willing to coordinate policy among those industrial ministries.

Coordination Difficulties: Loss of the Centre

In the labyrinth of bureaucratic politics in China, one routine bureaucratic process is the building of consensus among agencies with different policy agendas, known as policy coordination (*xietiao zhengce*). Some Chinese officials who have experienced such efforts have called this process ineffective, joking that 'coordination' means nothing.

Nevertheless, Chinese officials have attempted policy coordination regarding the WTO accession process. In 1986, China established a GATT policy-coordination body, the State Council Inter-ministerial Coordination Group on GATT Negotiations (*Guowuyuan guanshui ji maoyi zong xieding tanpan buji xietiao xiaozu*). State Councillor Zhang Jingfu was the first director of this group. The vice directors included the Minister of Foreign Trade, the Minister of Foreign Affairs, and the General Director of Customs. The group members included vice ministers or vice chairmen of other relevant ministries and commissions. In 1988, the group was renamed the State Council Committee on Inter-ministerial Coordination on GATT (*Guowuyuan guanshui ji maoyi zong xieding buji xietiao weiyuanhui*), with Vice Premier Tian Jiyun as chairman. In this committee, there were several vice-chairman-level agencies (*fuzuzhang danwei*); representaties from the SETC (established in 1993) were subsequently added.

The member agencies of this committee included the Ministry of Finance, the Ministry of Machine-Building Industry, the Ministry of Posts and Telecommunications, the Ministry of Electronic Industry, the Ministry of Textile Industry (restructured as the General Association of Textile Industry in 1993), the State Council Office of Import and Export of Mechanical and Electronic Products, and other relevant agencies. A vice minister from each agency was present at committee sessions.

According to its mandate, this inter-ministerial coordination committee was to coordinate policy on issues related to GATT/WTO. Prior to its dissolution in late 1998, the committee found itself unable to play this role, for several reasons. For one, it was not a standing agency but only a temporary vehicle for consultations, and as such lacked a secretariat with staff support. Because of the difficulties involved merely in calling a meeting, its sessions, if they occurred at all, were usually brief. As a consequence, the committee was unable to serve as a platform for consensus-building among the various agencies.

Second, it was remarkable that the SPC, at the time the most powerful supra-ministerial player, was excluded from the list of vice-chairman-level agencies. One explanation for the SPC's absence is that as the institutional representative of China's central-planning tradition, it foresaw that adjustment to GATT norms would result in the loss of its regulatory power over the economy. But without the participation of SPC, coordinating policy was extremely difficult.

Third, the other supra-ministerial agency, SETC, was weak in both reputation and bureaucratic power before the 1998 government restructuring. Established with the support of then Vice Premier Zhu Rongji, the SETC was assigned to oversee the routine operation of the economy. The SETC represented Beijing's efforts to macro-manage the developing market-oriented economy.

As a relatively new agency, however, the SETC found it difficult to play the role of policy coordinator. Senior leaders thus suggested a new mechanism under which the SETC would coordinate policy on trade in services (non-tariff items), while MoFTEC would build consensus on goods trade (tariff items). This new mechanism did not work well either. Some analysts have said that other agencies did not respect the SETC and instead complained that it was a duplicate and unnecessary institution. For most of the time, therefore, the SETC was in charge only of the reform of state-owned enterprises (SOEs), and thus was derided as the 'ministry of SOE reforms'. Under such circumstances, MoFTEC took the risky step of arranging its own policy-coordination mechanism.

MoFTEC: Coordinator in Action

As China's chief representative in the WTO negotiations, MoFTEC has been one of the most important forces in promoting trade liberalization. Though frequently accused of being motivated by self-interest,

MoFTEC insists that it is working in China's long-run national interests. Its commitment to early WTO membership is based primarily on the following points.

First, the international community is wary of China's rising international stature. A commitment to the WTO will send a strong political message that China is willing to play the trade game by international rules, and it will help persuade the world that China's rise is an opportunity rather than a danger.

Second, agreements among WTO members regarding trade liberalization will multiply and expand in coming years no matter what the Chinese attitude toward membership is. If it does not join the trade body, the country will be left out of the mainstream of the global economy. Without liberalization, China will not fully share the benefits of the free capital movements of multinational corporations. Therefore, MoFTEC argues, it is imperative for China to become a WTO member as soon as possible.

Third, protectionism in the form of high tariff and non-tariff barriers benefits specific industries, but imposes high indirect costs on the economy as a whole. These costs are reducing the country's ability to catch up, much less keep pace, with accelerating globalization. The country's industrial monopolies and only recently reduced high telecom rates are often cited as evidence of these high costs.

Fourth, only after WTO entry can China effectively protest the protectionist measures and unfair dumping charges frequently imposed on Chinese exports by its trading partners. Some experts who argue for a delay in WTO membership say that the country can gain the benefits of WTO membership through bilateral most favoured nation (MFN) arrangements. The MoFTEC team counters that only the WTO multilateral trade dispute mechanism can help China fight discriminatory treatment, and only membership can qualify the country for the benefits of phased-in textile trade liberalization.

Fifth, China's pervasive smuggling problem actually makes the country's high tariffs ineffective. Thus, to assess accurately the costs of lowering tariffs in specific industries, smuggling must be taken into account. For example, though 40,000 passenger cars are smuggled into China every year, the automobile industry has not only survived but also has improved its competitiveness. This shows that lower tariff rates are not necessarily destructive.

In multilateral negotiations with the China Working Party in Geneva, MoFTEC went to great lengths to put at ease otherwise wary participants from other PRC agencies, hoping that they would improve their offers at the negotiating table. Despite these efforts, however, progress on China's WTO accession remained slow.

One reason for the failure of MoFTEC's coordination efforts was the large gap that exists between MoFTEC and other PRC economic agencies at the level of a basic understanding of trade-liberalization issues. MoFTEC is exposed to the latest trends in the international economy and world trade, and hopes the country can adapt to these developments. But the industrial and economic agencies face the domestic problems of import competition and unemployment. These agencies inevitably expect greater protection from international competition. In the end, policy coordination was so slow that it seemed that only intervention by top leadership could break the deadlock.

Intervention of Top Leadership

In the complicated world of Chinese bureaucratic politics, support for policy changes from the highest levels of leadership is often critical. The Chinese top leadership presently supports greater concessions in exchange for gaining WTO membership as soon as possible. Views represented by MoFTEC appear to have the upper hand.

After 1994, a general consensus to delay WTO membership had formed across different industrial sectors and in public opinion. Difficulties in reforming the SOEs and popular worries about the consequences of large inflows of foreign direct investment made the top leadership reluctant to oppose this consensus. Despite some progress, China's WTO policy floated on a sea of bureaucratic politics. After the onset of the Asian financial crisis in 1997, some analysts concluded that China must be cautious in opening its markets because of the risks of greater international exposure. The prospects for China's WTO membership seemed to dim.

But to the surprise of many, the top leadership decided to intervene directly in the negotiations in early 1999. Because of changes in a number of political and economic circumstances, Beijing decided to change course, setting a schedule for certain market-oriented reforms. As these reforms progress, the leadership has recognized, WTO commitments will be helpful in pushing them along. In addition, the PRC government restructuring altered the major economic agencies' positions on WTO membership. There was also a change in the priorities on the leadership's agenda of economic issues as the need to boost exports and foreign investment became urgent. International pressures also played a role.

Though Premier Zhu Rongji is most visible in the WTO negotiations, the decision to speed up negotiations has obviously been supported by the entire leadership. China's change of heart reflects calculations based on several foreign relations considerations, including:

- By the end of 1999, the WTO planned to launch a new round of multilateral trade negotiations. If China did not enter then, review of China's application could be delayed until 2005. If China re-entered negotiations only after a new round of WTO trade talks, China would pay a much higher admission fee in terms of economic adjustment.

- Taiwan as an independent tariff territory has almost completed its negotiations with WTO members. Though China insists that it should enter the WTO before Taiwan, it seemed very likely that Taiwan would obtain membership first. This would imply a 'Two China' reality, and make the reunification question even more complicated than it is already.

- Faced with a pending presidential election, President Clinton hoped to wrap up the bilateral WTO membership negotiations. The conclusion of WTO negotiations would help to diffuse a trade war due to the huge trade imbalance but would also set conditions favourable to a significant improvement of China–US relations. On this issue, China emphasized that it was President Clinton who, in two letters of November 6, 1998, and February 8, 1999, took the initiative and requested that President Jiang Zemin conclude the bilateral negotiations by the first quarter of 1999.[3] The Chinese leadership recognized that it was imperative to grasp the opportunity to close the negotiations with the US before the election year started.

Fundamentally, however, considerations of domestic developments dominated as motives for an intervention of the top leadership:

- At the 15th Party Congress in 1997 and the People's Congress meeting in 1998, guidelines for SOE reforms and institutional restructuring were drafted and approved. These market-oriented reforms included gradually depriving government institutions of their direct power over enterprises, restructuring the ownership of SOEs, and kicking the military and police out of business. But the opposition of special interest groups has been much stronger than expected by reformers. By early 1999, the leadership came to a consensus that a commitment to WTO concessions would help to break the deadlock of reforms caused by special interests. Here we see a logic similar to that which has shaped two decades of reform, that is, to push forward reforms by the open door policy.

- China was experiencing an economic downturn triggered both by the Asian financial crisis and declining domestic demand. China's promise not to devalue its currency, though politically advantageous and widely praised for ensuring Asian regional stability, placed additional strain on already struggling PRC exporters. More importantly, foreign direct investment has slowed, and measures to stimulate the economy were less effective than expected. According to some estimates, China's economy must grow at least 6 per cent annually in order to cope with unemployment pressures. Chinese leaders are hoping that a WTO deal would raise foreign investors' confidence in China as a destination for investment, thereby giving a much-needed boost to the country's economy.

- The reforms in the first year of Zhu Rongji's premiership strengthened his power base. One of the most important of these was the restructuring of the central government, aimed at crafting a government structure more suited to a market economy. This restructuring has greatly reduced institutional opposition to further trade liberalization. Half of all central-government cadres were laid off, and the lucky survivors had to relinquish many of their regulatory powers. The number of State Council ministries, commissions, and agencies was reduced from 41 to 29. Almost all of the industrial ministries became state administrations within the SETC, the economic supervisory agency. Former ministries covering the machinery, metallurgical, coal, petroleum, chemical, textile and light industry, the Ministry of Internal Trade, as well as four specialized state-run companies, were subsumed under the SETC. The SDPC's competence has been relegated to a focus on mid-term and long-term macro-management; it no longer covers the regulation of trade quotas. Though it will take a long time for traditional economic and industrial agencies to give up all the powers they hold, their role has been greatly reduced.

In theory, there are at least four factors by which to judge whether the top leadership can make a political determination to intervene in WTO negotiations or not. These factors include the following questions: Is there any consensus among the members of the top leadership? How well will intervention serve the most important domestic objectives? Is it a good timing to extend intervention? And, does the top leadership believe that they have adequate power to realize intervention? In early 1999, the domestic and international developments perfectly satisfied these four elements for top leadership intervention. The intervention of early 1999 fundamentally changed the old pattern of bureaucratic politics characterizing the WTO policy coordination process.

The Rise of a New Policy Coordination Mechanism

A new policy coordination mechanism claims to have brought about the successful completion of China–US and China–EU negotiations. As we mentioned, government restructuring was one key to the formation of this new policy coordination mechanism. The government restructuring initiated in 1998 has lead to at least two significant consequences:

First, it greatly reduces the resistance of economic and industrial agencies to WTO accession. In accordance with the restructuring plan, more than half the central government civil servants were laid off and transferred to other non-government institutions. For example, about 45 per cent of cadres at the SDPC were retired or found positions in non-governmental institutions including state-owned companies. More significant to implications for WTO policy coordination is the fact that the responsibility and power of the surviving agencies has been redefined, limited to industrial regulation and macroeconomic management rather than direct management of SOEs. Specifically, all nine industrial ministries are restructured and become state administrations within the SETC, as suggested before. Moreover, this restructuring plan is only a transitional one. By the end of 2000 all nine state administrations had been dismantled, and their industrial macroeconomic functions are to be concentrated into one or two departments – mainly the department of administration of industries – with much less independence within the SETC. This phased-in restructuring plan reminds industrial leaders of who the real boss is. Like a nightmare, this pre-set fate has kept most industrial cadres of state administrations nervous about their own futures. As a result, these uncertainties obviously give leverage to leaders when they intervene in WTO policy coordination.

Second, the power of managing SOEs, discarded by industrial ministries, goes to a newly formed party apparatus called the Central Working Committee on Large Enterprises (*Zhongyang daxing qiye gongwei*) established in 1998 and renamed the Central Working Committee on Enterprises (*Zhongyang qiye gongwei*) in late 1999. The most important function of this committee is to appoint SOE managers and dispatch inspection councils (*jianshihui*) to these state firms. The nation's 167 largest SOEs fall under the specific jurisdiction of this special agency, the rest of them are left to the control of local governments. Premier Zhu Rongji plays a key role in the Central Working Committee on Enterprises, which obviously is an advantageous position for him to defuse complaints and concerns about WTO accession from state-owned enterprises.

Since early 1999, a new policy coordination mechanism has developed, continuing to dominate China's negotiations on WTO matters up to the present. This new coordination process has the following characteristics:

The top leadership, especially CCP General Secretary Jiang Zemin and Premier Zhu Rongji, take the helm at the negotiations with foreign partners. They also make final decisions in internal policy coordination. In key issues including agriculture and China's cultural market access, the top leaders themselves presided over the coordination meetings to determine which concessions the country should offer. On the other hand, the leaders intervened in bilateral negotiations at critical points, as they did in the talks with the US and the EU.

Supervised by the top leadership, the State Council established a new policy coordination organ in 1999, the State Council WTO Work Leading Group (*Guowuyuan WTO gongzuo lingdao xiaozu*), directed by State Councillor Wu Yi who reports directly to Premier Zhu Rongji.[4] As suggested, the State Council decided in late 1998 to dismantle the 12 year old ad hoc institution, the State Council Committee on Inter-ministerial Coordination on GATT. The dismissal was then justified by the explanation that international trade negotiation should be the proper function of MoFTEC. With this directive, the policy coordination power of MoFTEC has improved slightly, but it seems clear that MoFTEC alone is not powerful enough to successfully coordinate policy with so many agencies of equal rank. The China–US negotiations made the top leadership recognize the necessity of establishing a more powerful policy coordination body. In reality, the new Leading Group can be seen as the successor of the State Council Committee on Inter-ministerial Coordination on GATT/WTO. One difference between the two committees is that members of the Leading Group are composed solely of ministers of the central government. More important, Madame Wu Yi, well known for her strongman style, is claimed to be much more effective at coordination than her predecessors. Undoubtedly, Wu Yi has played a key role critical to the progress of WTO negotiations.

MoFTEC, the SETC and the State Council General Office together play a role as policy planning unit and secretariat of the State Council WTO Leading Group. With government restructuring, the MoFTEC Department of International Economic and Trade Relations is assigned the position of negotiator as well as coordinator of the policies of the various ministries and agencies. Obviously, its coordination ability has been strengthened. At the same time, the division of power suggested by senior leaders in 1996 is still partially effective. The suggestion was that MoFTEC take care of policy coordination regarding trade in goods while the SETC is responsible for trade in service related policies. Considering the fact that the SETC has incorporated nine old industrial ministries and the authority of industrial policy transferred from the SDPC, the SETC plays a key role of coordination in issues of trade in goods as well. To some extent, the SETC represents the views and opinions of streamlined industrial ministries, and sometimes invites complaints from them. As a result, the power of the SETC and MoFTEC in terms of coordination is partially overlapping. They have a relationship of cooperation and competition. Therefore, the State Council General Office, especially the No. 2 Bureau thereof, comes to play an important but often ignored role in the policy coordination process. The General Office often hosts policy coordination meetings for different ministries and agencies. Generally speaking, the three institutions, MoFTEC, the SETC and the State Council General Office, play the role of coordinator in the internal policy-making process.

The number of agencies necessary to consult has been greatly reduced, and the focus of coordination has concentrated on a small group of ministries and agencies. Before 1999, it had been an informal routine to engage almost all industrial and economic agencies in the coordination process. Now, the SETC stands for the interests of different industrial state administrations. Moreover, the SDPC's power is limited to macroeconomic planning, including drafting annual and five-year development plans. Due to the shift of function,

SDPC interests in WTO affairs have been reduced to the trade of grain and vegetable oil, and the pricing of important industrial products. The Ministry of Information Industry still seems to be a tough agency, more doubtful about the benefits from market liberalization. The financial sector including banking and insurance is more prone to influence by the opinion of Premier Zhu Rongji. Other ministries and agencies relevant to trade in services such as the State Tourist Administration, the Ministry of Justice, the Ministry of Finance, the Ministry of Construction, the Internal Trade Administration, and so on, appear not to be big obstacles in the policy process. On balance, the ministries and agencies sympathetic to market liberalization are now more powerful than ever.

The new policy coordination mechanism, however, has not yet changed the nature of central government bureaucratic politics. What has been changed the balance of forces surrounding WTO accession, but the role of actors outside the central government, including experts, opinion leaders, business community and local governments has not improved much.

The policy making process and the results of negotiations have been kept completely closed to the public. They are still top secret. For example, only a small group of people has the privilege to access detailed information about the China–US bilateral WTO agreement. The policy transparency has not yet improved even after the US government released the English version of the agreement on the internet.

Consultation with business interests has been limited. Under the domestic pressure following the NATO bombing, the MoFTEC briefed negotiation results to important industries and enterprises. For example, they consulted with automobile companies, petrochemical industries and electronics manufacturers. However, according to representatives from various industries, consultation with the business community is still not satisfactory.

Local government has been ignored in the internal policy process. This might create some unexpected problems when implementing WTO commitments.

Surviving the Bombing Storm

The chance coincidence of President Clinton's refusal to sign the bilateral WTO agreement and the NATO bombing of the Chinese embassy in Belgrade in 1999, all of a sudden threw Premier Zhu Rongji, the symbol of WTO negotiation, into the eye of a domestic political storm.

Struggling cautiously, however, the premier, and with him the new policy coordination mechanism, have successfully survived the crisis. On November 15, 1999, China and the US struck the bilateral agreement. For the conclusion of US–China negotiations, undoubtedly, the political unity and determination of the major leadership members was the most important factor. However, the tactics of damage control adopted by Zhu Rongji are another factor deserving of research. The survival through the storm itself proves that pro-liberalization forces remain powerful, assuring that the Chinese government will continue to honor its WTO commitments.

Chinese government representatives insist that domestic political pressure made President Clinton reluctant to sign the WTO bilateral agreement with China when Zhu Rongji visited Washington. They argue that they had already known it would be impossible for President Clinton to strike the deal before Zhu Rongji embarked on the trip to the United States in April 1999. Notwithstanding, what they attempted during the visit was to show the American public the fruits of the Chinese reform and open door policy and to allow a better understanding of China especially by the Congress and public opinion. Before the Chinese delegation left the US, the White House released the list of Chinese WTO commitments on the US Trade Representative's website in order to mobilize political support for the US–China deal.

This unexpected publication of Chinese commitments actually precluded the authority of MoFTEC to disclose a special presentation in its own form. MoFTEC usually keeps its agreements as classified documents. The revolution of communications created by the internet is seriously challenging the relationship between state and society in China. The action of the Clinton administration caused a serious political backlash against Chinese WTO negotiators. The tragic incident of NATO's bombing of the Chinese embassy triggered nationwide anti-US sentiments in China, fuelling the criticism of WTO commitments. Emotional opponents even labeled the Chinese delegation 'national traitors', and attacked the Washington commitments as the contemporary version of the 'Twenty-One Demands' – the most notorious treaty in Chinese modern history, imposed by the Japanese imperialists in 1915.

The critics focused on three major issues including: (1) whether the Washington commitments had received central authorization beforehand; (2) whether the commitments came out of the inter-ministerial coordination process; and (3) whether MoFTEC's negotiating style was appropriate to the situation. The MoFTEC team was accused having been too naïve in dealing with US negotiators.

Faced with mounting pressure, the leadership adopted a damage control strategy which could be defined as a strategy oriented toward economic self-interest. Later developments have proved that relieving political pressure by economic means has been quite successful. This strategy seems to have been composed of the following acts:

- Clarifying the misunderstandings of the Washington commitments. On the one hand, MoFTEC publicly announced that the White House version of China's WTO concessions was not accurate, with some clauses presenting only the US position. The list, for example, ignored the role of Chinese economic sovereignty; that is, all foreign direct investments require approval from the Chinese government. Also, to address the situation more specifically, the State Council circulated an internal memorandum of explanation to clarify public misunderstanding about China–US relations, especially regarding the WTO commitments made by the Chinese side in April 1999.

- Relieving concerns about China's industrial interests. The State Council encouraged enterprises in key industries to consolidate themselves into 'big group' companies. For example, the SETC raised the suggestion of building the nation's three largest automobile manufacturing bases in Changchun, Shanghai and Wuhan. The State Council quickly approved public listing programs for SOEs, most of which were believed to be at risk under the rules of WTO accession. 'Going Global' in the domestic and international stock markets presents an attractive option for Chinese enterprises because it is believed that the process of implementation itself encourages greater efficiencies and the introduction of innovative management techniques. At the apex of the political storms in 1999, China Unicom (the second largest telecommunication service company), China National Offshore Oil Corp, China National Petroleum Corp., and China Petrochemical Corp. obtained licenses to go public on the Hong Kong and New York securities markets.

- Promoting the potential of stock market investments. Chinese stock markets have played an important role in SOE reform and economic development. However, since the beginning of the Asian financial crisis, they have performed quite poorly. The

State Council adopted measures such as cutting interest rates, as well as expansive monetary and investment policies. Predictably, these policy options helped to calm complaints from stock holders.

- Enhancing social security coverage. The prospect of rising unemployment on WTO accession was (and continues to be) the biggest concern of the Ministry of Labour and Social Security, as well as local governments in particular. Through SOE reform, management functions and responsibilities are actually devolved from the central to local governments. As a consequence of the decentralization process, local governments are feeling more and more pressure to provide social security benefits directly. At the same time, the State Council decided to allocate more state funds to raise the minimum living standard and compensate both unemployed people and laid-off workers.

- Developing western China. The policy of developing western China had been discussed for a long time, but was apparently sped up in 1999. With this policy, hinterland provinces could obtain more Central government funds including preferential treatments extended to foreign enterprises located there. This measure could be regarded as partially continuing the 'political logic' of 'playing to provinces', which it was claimed was used by Deng Xiaoping in his reform and open door policy. [5]

With the assistance of these policies, the leadership succeeded in overcoming the political difficulties of 1999. And most meaningful to the WTO negotiations, the new policy coordination mechanism has been kept intact.

China–EU Negotiations

After the China–US WTO agreement had been signed in November 1999, Chinese negotiators expected that China could complete its negotiations with the EU quickly and enter the WTO before summer 2000. However, it took another six months for China to strike a bilateral deal with the EU. The Chinese negotiators were surprised by the intensity of pressure the EU put on China to push through European interests, especially in the areas of telecommunications and insurance. China's surprise seems to originate from two factors: (1) Though they had talked to their EU counterparts for a long time about WTO accession, it seems that they did not have an adequate knowledge of the EU trade decision-making process. The Chinese expected the EU to be satisfied with the same package that they had offered to the United States. This judgment proved wrong. (2) The lack of knowledge of specific interests of the EU was also a reflection of the fact that in the past they put too much emphasis on the US who were regarded as the main barrier on the path to WTO accession. On the other hand, the EU's flexible and sophisticated diplomatic manoeuvering – playing off negotiations between China and the US, for example – which made the European position appear sympathetic to the Chinese WTO position, was one of the factors leading to Chinese misjudgment. Chinese negotiators might well remember that for this supposed sophistication, the EU was accused by some US State Department officials of 'taking cover under a cloak' while the US aggressively negotiated with China.

Some people even have complained that the unduly prolonged negotiations forced China to lose half a year, and that, as a consequence, the US gained time to make a full review of their bilateral agreement. The result was for the US to press for further concessions – which they could not gain in bilateral negotiations – in additional multilateral talks. To others, the EU and the US appear to be working together closely to extract more concessions from China at the last minute. Because of this, the US and EU have now turned the multilateral process of drafting the Protocol of Accession and Working Party Report into another round of substantial negotiations, which should have been completed in bilateral negotiations already.[6] For example, the US has worked hard to redefine the specific terms of Chinese commitments, including the standards associated with large-scale insurance services and the local content of automobile production related to import quotas.

Other observers, however, may share the view that the EU has not exploited its holdout position to the fullest to pressure China into further concessions, which appears true if compared with the Mexican case. Moreover, the conclusion of the EU–China bilateral agreement was regarded as demonstrating good timing, right before the US Congress voted over China's permanent normal trade relations status.

Over the past several years, a consensus has been building among leaders and the public that state monopoly must be broken, that more competition will strengthen the country's economy and bring better services to consumers. Specifically, they criticize the finance, telecommunication and distribution industries as the least reformed sectors. State monopoly, the say, leads to a high proportion of bad debts in banks and low efficiency in telecommunication services. In order to change this situation, the government has encouraged more competition in these industries, including domestic as well as foreign companies. The first priority, however, is to encourage competition from domestic sources of capital – for instance, by allowing the introduction of share-holding companies.

It is still a politically sensitive policy issue to have majority equities for foreign banks, insurance companies and automobile manufacturers in China's domestic market, as was pointed out by Premier Zhu Rongji to EU trade negotiators in March 2000.[7] Elites as well as the general public are still influenced by ideas of economic nationalism. On the other hand, industrial interests play a very important role in deciding the direction and pace of liberalization in certain industries. For example, telecommunication services have been a focus of complaints from consumers, but the Ministry of Information Industry emphasizes that – as a state carrier of telecommunication services – China Telecom is required to subsidize the loss-making national postage service, from the earnings of its telecommunication services. More critical to the progress of reforms and economic growth for the whole of China, the Ministry maintains that it will be in a disadvantageous position to compete against foreign companies (which are only interested in providing services to China's lucrative urban markets) because it alone has the responsibility for supplying universal service to every corner of the country, especially to rural areas. The Ministry of Information Industry also cites national security as an additional reason to oppose the pressure of market access by foreign investors. With regard to foreign ownership of life insurance services, a 50–50 equity joint-venture was the bottom line for Chinese insurers, though in the end they succumbed to the added term 'possibility of effective control' by foreign insurers.

A lack of confidence is another factor contributing to China's cautious approach in allowing entry to its domestic markets by international investors. This reluctance is usually disguised in an argument which concludes that due to the limited economies of scale associated with most Chinese domestic firms it is too difficult for them to compete with international investors.

The Wal-Mart corporation is the most favoured example used as evidence to support this pessimistic approach. This view argues that, as the biggest retailer in the US, Wal-Mart had a total value in sales revenue of $132.2 billion with a profit of $4.1 billion in 1998 (equivalent to 1,093.5 billion RMB yuan). During this same time period in 1998, the total value in sales revenue of all the Chinese retailers in the entire country only reached 2,915.25 billion RMB yuan. A lot of people are shocked when they realize the fact that one company like the Wal-Mart corporation has a domestic market in the US that is equivalent to 37.5 per cent of the China's national retailing revenue. While Wal-Mart corporation is a US company, some large EU retailers can compare with it – with similar implications for China's domestic retailers.

In the area of insurance, some 'radicals' even argue for a policy of an 'upside down opening of the market', which means, insurance licenses may be granted only to medium-sized foreign insurers rather than to the largest international insurers. They maintain that, on the one hand, medium-sized insurers could play a role similar to the largest international insurers in disseminating advanced insurance technologies to Chinese firms, while, on the other, their competition would be moderate and fairer to Chinese insurers. Taking this view into account, it is easier to understand the high degree of pressure put on the Chinese insurance regulatory authority, and hence, its reluctance to issue new licenses to EU insurers. Therefore, Chinese industries usually request a transitional period for as long as they can get.

We have argued that even though, with the attention of top leadership, a new policy coordination mechanism has gained importance, China needs to consider not only the political feasibility of concessions requested by the EU but the opinions of certain domestic industries as well.

Final Remarks

China tried to finish the negotiations about all substantial issues before the swearing in of the new US president in late January 2001. But China will have to wait longer to finish the multilateral as well as bilateral talks before accession to the WTO. In the meantime, China is looking forward to a new round of opening up to the outside world. At the same time, China is preparing for a potential negative impact on its domestic industries. During the reform era of the last two decades, China's opening up has been based on its own standards and practices. Now, with WTO accession imminent, it will have no choice but to abide by international standards and practices. This is a completely new challenge for China.

Through an examination of the process of China's bid for GATT/WTO accession, we have found that the Chinese strategy of reform has set the pace of China's bid for the multilateral trading regime. During this process, the nature and transformation of bureaucratic politics has played a very important role. The recent rapid progress of WTO negotiation can be attributed to the market economy strategy of reform which China has chosen, that is, the path toward market-oriented reform and government restructuring in the spirit of a smaller government coupled with a stronger civil society.

International scholars tend to compare China's economic liberalization with the process in Japan and India. It is widely believed that with WTO accession, China has used or will use a much shorter time to open up than Japan and India did. This perception is a great tribute to the strength of the World Trade Organisation. While trade negotiators inspect China's pace in adopting rules and norms of the WTO regime, historians, with their usual critical perspective, will judge this new opening as China's 'great leap' forward into a more complete international community. To that end, some researchers of Chinese behavior in international relations support the argument that, driven by its own interests, China will make great efforts to meet its WTO commitments.[8]

Notes

[1]This joke was made by premier Zhu Rongji in his press conference of National People's Congress, March 1998.

[2]This article is mainly based on the author's interview with Chinese economic and trade officials, undertaken during the period from December 1998 to January 2001. Part is rewritten from the author's essay, 'Why China Went for WTO', *China Business Review*, July–August 1999, pp. 42–45.

[3]As for the two letters from President Clinton to President Jiang Zemin, see Joseph Fewsmith, 'The Politics of China's Accession to the WTO', *Current History*, September 2000, p. 269. The author's interview confirms Fewsmith's findings, which were gained from his interview with Chinese officials in 1999.

[4]For the latest description of the relationship between MoFTEC and the Leading Group, see the MoFTEC website http://www.moftec.gov.cn/moftec_cn/moftecjs/bjgjj/gjs.html.

[5]These concepts are raised in the book by Shirk, Susan L., *The Political Logical of Economic Reform in China*, Berkeley: University of California Press, 1993.

[6]Shao Zongwei, 'Nation to carry out pledges faithfully', *China Daily* (New York edition), Oct 24, 2000.

[7]For the recent heated debates between economic nationalists and economic liberals in China, see Wang Yong, 'China's Domestic WTO Debates', *China Business Review*, January–February, 2000, pp. 54–62.

[8]For one example of this research, see Pearson, Margaret M., 'China's Track Record in the Global Economy', *China Business Review*, January–February 2001, pp. 48–52.

Part II

The Challenge of International Competition to China's Economy

3

China and the WTO: The Challenge for China's Large-scale Industry

Peter Nolan

Introduction

China's impending entry to the WTO is an event of historic significance, comparable to the country's opening up after the Opium Wars. This article does not evaluate the possible impact of China's entry on agriculture, on the small and medium enterprise sector, on the level of foreign direct investment or the impact on the balance of payments. It examines a single issue, namely the impact of China's entry upon its large-scale state-owned enterprises.

The WTO agreement with the US is 250 pages long, with a detailed account of the steps that China agrees to take in order to implement the WTO rules. This is not just an 'agreement on paper'. The minute details will be taken very seriously by the high income countries. It is the most detailed agreement yet signed by any country on its entry to the WTO. It is far more specific than that signed by India, for example. Under the terms of the WTO agreement, China must cease to provide special support for large state-owned enterprises. Within China, the WTO rules require the whole country to become an internal free trade area.

For almost two decades the Chinese government experimentally charted its own independently-constructed reform programme. With the entry to the WTO under such detailed, internationally-set conditions, China has voluntarily given up a wide area of autonomy in charting the complex path of economic reform. The US-China WTO agreement 'in itself constitutes a massive programme of economic system reform'.[1] Chinese businesses will be forced to abide by the sanctity of contracts once they are signed: 'There should be no illusions that there will be a smooth ride over the next decade.'[2]

China has been granted only a five year adjustment period before it must implement in full the rules of the WTO. Many important changes will have effect from the day that China joins the WTO. Moreover, there will be strong incentives for multinational businesses to push their participation in the Chinese economy beyond that which is permitted legally in anticipation of a future more liberal regime which will retrospectively sanction the quasi-illegal advances they have made.[3]

Many commentators, both within and outside China, believe that entering the WTO will invigorate Chinese large-scale industry: 'Competition from abroad will help the Chinese to raise their level of efficiency, just like the US auto industry did in the 1980s in the face of Japanese competition.'[4]

This article argues that such a view is far too optimistic. In the course of two decades of struggle, China's large enterprises have changed substantially, gradually undertaking evolutionary institutional change in key aspects of their business organization.[5] During the same period, the world's leading businesses have undergone revolutionary transformation. As the epoch of the 'global level playing field' moves ever closer, it becomes increasingly necessary for China's reforming large enterprises to benchmark themselves realistically against the global giants. Since the mid-1980s China's large-scale industries have comprehensively failed to catch up with the world leaders. Indeed, they have fallen much further behind than they were just a decade or so ago. China's large-scale industries will face immense difficulties on the 'global level playing field' which is about to arrive in China. The intense problems that confront these firms are likely to have wide-ranging socio-economic and political repercussions both within China and its international relations, especially with the US, whose large firms have dominated the global business revolution.

China's Policy Goal

China began liberalizing the post-Mao economy in the late 1970s. The early versions of the contract system in industry were introduced in 1979, of which that at the Shougang steel company was the most important and symbolic. Therefore, one can say that China's industrial policy has been in operation for two decades.

A consistently stated goal of China's industrial policy has been to construct globally powerful companies that can compete on the global level playing field:

> In our world today economic competition between nations is in fact between each nation's large enterprises and enterprise groups. A nation's economic might is concentrated and manifested in the economic power and international competitiveness of its large enterprises and groups. International economic confrontations in reality show that if a country has several large enterprises or groups it will be able to maintain a certain market share and hold an assured position in the world economic order. America, for example, relies on General Motors, Boeing, Dupont and a batch of other multinational companies. Japan relies on six large enterprise groups and Korea relies on ten large commercial enterprise groupings. *In the same way now and in the next century our nation's position in the international economic order will be to a large extent determined by the position of our nation's large enterprises and groups.*[6] (italics added)

In pursuit of this objective, China's stated goal of industrial policy has been to construct a group of large-scale powerful industrial firms that can challenge the global leaders. These include

- Chinese Aviation Industry Corporation (AVIC) in the aerospace industry;
- China Petrochemical Corporation (Sinopec) and China National Petroleum Corporation (CNPC) in oil and petrochemicals;
- Sanjiu, Dongbei, and Shandong Xinhua in pharmaceuticals;
- Harbin, Shanghai Electrical, and Dongfang in power equipment;
- Yiqi, Erqi, and Shanghai Auto in automobiles;
- Shougang, Angang, and Baogang in steel;
- Datong, Yanzhou, and Shenhua in coal mining.

China's chosen global giant corporations were supported through a sequence of industrial policies, including

- general support through international protection via tariff and non-tariff barriers;
- selection as the joint venture partners for major international joint venture projects; preferential loans from state projects;
- preferential loans from state banks;
- privileged access to international stock markets with listing in Hong Kong and New York.

The Japanese Example

During a similar period in Japan's development, from the 1950s to the 1970s, Japan's industrial planners supported the growth of a series of oligopolistic companies that developed into globally powerful firms. After two decades of industrial policy in Japan, the country possessed a whole corps of globally competitive companies. By the late 1980s, it had twenty of the largest one hundred corporations in the *Fortune 500* list, including Toyota, Hitachi, Matsushita, Nissan, Toshiba, Honda, Sony, NEC, Fujitsu, Mitsubishi Electric, Mitsubishi Motors, Nippon Steel, Mitsubishi Heavy Industry, Mazda, Nippon Oil, Idemitsu Kosan, Canon, NKK, Bridgestone, and Sumitomo Metal. These companies developed through extensive support from state industrial policy, including

- tariff and non-tariff barriers;
- restrictions on foreign direct investment;
- preferential purchase policy by state-owned utilities;
- government defence procurement contracts;
- government-subsidized Research and Development (R&D);
- government-sponsored rationalizations of different industries;
- a 'flexible', pragmatic competition policy which allowed the growth of oligopolistic competition.

China's Success

China's gross domestic product has grown at an officially reported rate of 10.2 per cent per annum from 1980 to 1990, and 11.1 per cent from 1990 to 1998. Industrial value-added grew at an officially reported rate of 11.1 per cent in the 1980s and 15.4 per cent from 1980 to 1998.[7]

After twenty years of industrial policy in China, using many similar measures to those used by Japan, and with a similar explicit policy goal, major changes have taken place in China's large, state-owned enterprises. They have

- grown rapidly in terms of value of sales;
- absorbed a great deal of modern technology;
- learned how to compete in the marketplace;
- substantially upgraded the technical level of their employees;
- learned wide-ranging new managerial skills;
- gained substantial understanding of international financial markets;
- become sought-after partners for multinational companies.

Under these policies, China's large state-owned enterprises have avoided the industrial collapse of the former USSR. This not a small achievement, and the possibility of system collapse in China still needs to be taken very seriously indeed.

Under these policies also, China has attracted huge amounts of foreign direct investment (FDI). Throughout most of the 1990s, China was the largest recipient of FDI after the USA, regularly accounting for around 10-12 per cent of total world FDI and around one-third of total flows of FDI into developing countries.[8] Increasingly, global corporations have viewed China as central to their long-term strategy.

China's Failure

Despite important progress, none of China's leading enterprises has become a globally competitive giant corporation, with a global market, a global brand, and a global procurement system:

- China has just five companies in the *Fortune 500*;[9]
- China does not have one company in the world's top 300 companies by R&D expenditure;[10]
- China does not have a single company in the *Financial Times* 500 companies ranked by market capitalization;[11]
- China does not have any representatives in Morgan Stanley's list of the world's top 250 'competitive edge' companies.[12]

The competitive capability of China's large firms after two decades of reform is still extremely weak in relation to the global giants. This is extremely marked in the high-technology sectors, such as aerospace, complex equipment such as power plants, pharmaceuticals, as well as in 'mid-technology' sectors such as integrated oil and petrochemicals and auto components. However, even in sectors with apparently less advanced technology, such as steel and coal, there is a significant gap with leading global companies in the high value-added segments of the market. By the simplest of measures of sales revenue, profits and R&D, China's vanguard of leading firms that are intended to 'compete on the global level playing field', are still far behind the global leaders.

If the leading firms in each sector are compared with the global leaders, then it must be acknowledged that, despite significant progress, *China's leading firms are further behind the global leaders than they were when the industrial policies began almost two decades ago.* The China Big Business Programme undertook case studies of a number of leading Chinese firms and benchmarked them against the global corporations in the respective sectors.[13] The following is a brief summary of some of the main conclusions:

Aerospace: Chinese Aviation Industry Corporation (AVIC)

From the outside AVIC appears a giant to challenge the world's leading aerospace companies. Prior to its split into two units in 1999, it had around 600,000 employees. It had produced around 6,000 jet aircraft for the Chinese military, a four engine large passenger jet and a twin-engine indigenously-designed turbo-prop. Several of its subsidiaries were floated on the international stock market.

However, on closer inspection, AVIC is desperately weak. In the late 1990s, AVIC was almost insignificant in terms of the world's aerospace industry (cf. Table 1). Its pure aerospace revenues totaled less than $1 billion. The bulk of its revenue came from making a vast array of non-aerospace products, from dustbins to motor cycles, almost all in small-scale, globally uncompetitive quantities. If it adopted the manning levels of the global giants firms, it would employ less than 10,000 compared with several hundreds of thousands to-day. If AVIC were divided up into separate companies making airframes, engines, and avionics, it would be miniature compared to the global giants. The uncompetitiveness of AVIC is sharply illustrated by the fact that Chinese airlines refused to buy China's domestically-made large passenger plane, the Y-10, and placed hardly any orders for the turbo-prop Y-7. It is even more starkly illuminated by the fact that the core of China's airforce consists of planes bought from the former USSR. China has so far placed orders for around 200 Su-27s and 50 Su-30s.[14]

Pharmaceuticals: Sanjiu Pharmaceutical Company

Sanjiu made great progress in the 1990s, rapidly developing its marketing and branding skills, making highly intelligent product choices, modernizing its production facilities and developing a genuinely modern management capability. By the late 1990s, it was China's leading pharmaceuticals company.

However, Sanjiu's ability to compete directly with the multinationals is virtually non-existent (cf. Table 1). Its R&D is negligible compared to the multinational giants. A single modern drug costs around $500 million to develop, equivalent to the total sales revenue of Sanjiu.

The leading multinationals not only spend billions each year on R&D. They also spend even larger sums on marketing (in 1998 Merck spent $4.5 billion on marketing and administration).[15] Sanjiu has tried to avoid head-on competition with the multinational giants by focussing on traditional Chinese medicines. However, Sanjiu has found it very difficult to grow in China apart from its main product, *Sanjiu Weitai*, a stomach medicine. On international markets, despite passing the US food and drugs administration health requirements, it is also difficult for it to grow. The overseas Chinese community is not sufficiently large to provide for sustained long-term growth. The extent of prescription by Western doctors is still small. Moreover, lacking a patent, there is nothing to stop Western pharmaceutical companies producing the product and using their massive marketing structure to sell traditional Chinese medicines such as *Sanjiu Weitai*. Sanjiu would find it hard, or simply impossible, to compete with such a strategy. Moreover, there is nothing to prevent them from adopting such a strategy even within China, if they find the profit margin sufficiently attractive. In sum, Sanjiu's ability to compete directly with the multinationals is virtually non-existent.

Complex electrical equipment: Harbin Power Equipment Company (HPEC)

Compared with other developing countries, at the end of the 1970s China had a relatively advanced power equipment industry. It had three major producing units, with around three-quarters of the domestic market shared between them. At the beginning of the reform process, these three entities were under a single central source of control. If the three main Chinese producers had been able to effect a merger, they would have formed a genuinely large-scale entity, even in global terms. In fact, Harbin remained independent, as the 'national champion', while its two major domestic competitors formed joint ventures with multinational giants. Harbin was given considerable support from the state, especially through a centrally-negotiated technology transfer arrangement with Combustion Engineering. It was allowed also to raise capital by floating in Hong Kong. Harbin made great technical progress in the 1990s.

However, by the end of the decade it still lagged very far behind the world leaders in the sector (cf. Table 1). The power equipment divisions of the world leaders had a sales revenue and profits that were vastly greater than Harbin's. They possessed a mighty R&D capability that was able to ensure high-speed development of their technology, including increases in fuel efficiency, improvements in reliability and reduction in pollution. They possessed a global market and a global 'external firm' supplying them with components from plants across the world. They possessed powerful sub-divisions that were able to obtain long-term streams of high quality earnings through service contracts achievable through large-scale investment in information technology and human skills. By the mid-1990s, multinationals were taking around one-third of the domestic market and the entire first tranche of Three Gorges turbines was awarded to multinational companies. Harbin was almost incapable of competing in international markets.

Oil and petrochemicals: CNPC and Sinopec

During the reform years large institutional changes have taken place. The industry has absorbed modern management techniques. It has raised substantial capital on international markets through a series of H-share flotations of individual enterprises. A sequence of huge, multi-billion dollar international joint ventures has been agreed. With greatly increased autonomy for the production units, real competition began to develop among domestic producers. At the end of the 1990s, massive institutional change produced two huge vertically integrated firms, CNPC and Sinopec, that are both large enough to join the *Fortune 500* list of the world's top 100 companies. In addition, the China National Offshore Oil Corporation (CNOOC) has developed into a modern, large-scale offshore oil enterprise that superficially rivals Statoil of Norway. To outward appearances China has succeeded in establishing modern, globally competitive oil and petrochemical giants that can compete on the global marketplace.

However, the reality is very different (cf. Table 1). At the institutional level, the industry remained torn by the tension between, on the one hand, trying to support powerful, autonomous enterprises and, on the other, trying to construct globally competitive, giant multi-plant firms. The central government faces a huge task in trying to construct genuinely centralized businesses in which operational units are closely monitored and rewarded for business performance. The institutional structure of CNPC and Sinopec is still far removed from the 'business unit' structure that is the norm in the world's leading oil and petrochemical firms.

Apart from the institutional issue, major technical problems still exist for the industry. China's reserves have not proved as prolific nor as well-located as was once hoped. Offshore oil reserves have proved disappointingly small and are typically located at considerable depths. China's onshore oil reserves are mainly located in relatively distant areas in China's central Asian republics, notably Xinjiang. These are of uncertain amount and typically are at great depth. Both the cost of raising and transporting the products are high. By comparison, the global giants have a portfolio of high quality, low cost reserves. In the downstream part of the industry, China's major companies have a proliferation of high-cost, small-scale refineries. They have only a relatively small share of petrochemical output from high value-added, high profit margin products. The downstream distribution system is extremely backward compared to the global giants, lacking high value-added products, such as environmentally-friendly varieties of petrol, lacking modern logistics systems, and lacking a high quality global brand.

The sales revenue of CNPC and Sinopec places them in the middle ranking group of oil and petrochemical firms. These are generally thought to face great difficulties in competing with the global leaders. The profit level of CNPC and Sinopec are tiny compared with the global giants. The global leaders have much higher levels of R&D. They have the technical capability to develop reserves in areas that are beyond the technical capability of CNPC and Sinopec. They possess powerful positions in the production of high value-added petrochemicals and oil products.

The weakness of the Chinese industry on the global level playing field was sharply revealed by the disaster of the industry's flotation hopes. It had been hoped that the flotation of CNOOC, CNPC and Sinopec would together raise around $15-20 billion. The attempt to float these entities has in fact been an embarrassing disaster. CNOOC's attempted float was simply withdrawn when it became obvious that, instead of raising $2.5 billion, the initial public offering (IPO) would only be able to raise a much lower amount. Consequently, the flotation was shelved in October 1999 after the completion of the road show. CNPC had originally hoped to raise $10 billion from the flotation of PetroChina. The ambitions for the float were steadily reduced. In fact the flotation of CNPC raised only around $3 billion. Sinopec originally hoped to raise around $5 billion from its IPO. In view of the poor performance of the CNPC flotation, it seems likely that the Sinopec flotation will be postponed indefinitely. The main reason for the failure of these offering is the investors' perception of the institutional weakness of China's oil and petrochemical companies in the global competition, from a technical, a managerial and, especially, a corporate governance perspective.

Automobiles and auto components: Yiqi, Erqi, Dongfeng and Yuchai

China's leaders have made clear their intention that China should, like Japan, create a small group of world class auto assemblers and components manufacturers. After almost two decades of industrial policies, China's leading auto assemblers remain extremely small in a global perspective (cf. Table 1). The unit output of each of the top three Chinese producers amounts to less than one-twentieth of that of the top five global leaders. Even if the top three Chinese firms were combined into a single entity they would still not amount to more than a medium-scale producer, around the size of Volvo, which considered it was too small to survive in the global competition. Even together, they lack the necessary scale to benefit from global procurement systems that each of the global giants possesses. Moreover, the value of output per unit is far below that of the global leaders. Consequently, in terms of value of sales revenue, China's leading auto assemblers are even smaller compared to the global leaders, and their profits are miniscule, reflecting far lower value-added per vehicle. China's leading auto producers lag far behind the global leaders in terms of R&D expenditure. They lack the financial resources to develop new models and to invest in modern IT systems that can link suppliers to the core assemblers. They are far behind the global leaders in terms of marketing and brand development. China's auto manufacturers lack the capability to compete in export markets.

Yuchai is one of the most successful Chinese auto components companies. It rose from relative obscurity to become the largest medium duty truck engine producer in China. Its growth was due to a number of astute management decisions. These included the purchase of second-hand equipment from abroad, clever product choice and development, a keen sense of the importance of brand and advertising, including a deep understanding of the importance of product reliability and product guarantees, and early development of a sophisticated, national marketing system. Yuchai was a pioneer in all these developments and reaped the benefits of first mover advantage. Yuchai's ambition was to form a pillar of the development of the Chinese components industry. Its chief executive officer hoped to develop Yuchai into a Chinese version of the giant US companies Detroit Diesel or Cummins Diesel Engine, both large-scale global diesel engine makers.

By the end of the 1990s, Yuchai was still a tiny player in a global perspective (cf. Table 1). Its revenues were a small fraction of those of the leading global players, Caterpillar, Cummins or Detroit Diesel. The R&D expenditure of the leading players, Caterpillar and Cummins Diesel Engine, was far greater even than the annual sales revenue at Yuchai. These firms made steady progress in developing diesel engine technology, producing more reliable, more economical and less environmentally damaging engines. Each of them developed around them a network of global production centres and a global network of high quality suppliers. Both Caterpillar and Cummins expanded fast in China. Cummins established a joint venture with Dongfeng, which had been Yuchai's main customer during its phase of rapid growth in the 1990s. By the end of the decade Yuchai was virtually bankrupt.

Steel: Shougang

China's steel industry boomed during the economic reforms. During this period, Shougang rapidly increased its output. It undertook a wide-ranging programme of modernization, technical upgrading, and diversification into activities that might support its further expansion. It developed a significant export capability in both steel and steel plant construction. Its computerization skills developed sufficiently for it to win an important competitive contract to design and install the control systems for a leading US steel maker. Both Shougang's plans for expansion and its management style bore a close resemblance to those of South Korea's Posco steel company.

Despite these important advances in Shougang's institutional and technical capability, Shougang faced severe limitations on its capability to compete on the global level playing field. In the first place, although its output grew rapidly, a large part of the growth was in low value-added, low quality steel, such as construction steel. In the late 1990s, after two decades of rapid growth, high quality steel still accounted for only 15 per cent of its total output. Shougang's sales value in 1997 amounted to $2.2 billion, compared with $11 billion for British Steel, $12 billion for Usinor and $25 billion for Nippon Steel (cf. Table 1). All four of China's top producers together, namely Shougang, Angang, Baogang and Wugang, had a sales revenue of $9.0 billion, still well below that of each of the main European and East

Asian producers, reflecting, to a considerable degree, their high proportion of low quality, low value-added products. The low value-added in China's steel industry is reflected in the fact that in the late 1990s, the country still imported one-half of its consumption of car sheets, 70 per cent of its tin sheets, and 80 per cent of its cold rolled stainless steel sheets.

Shougang found it hard to extricate itself from a vicious circle. The fact that it mainly produced low quality steel meant that it was mainly in competition with small-scale local producers competing with them for local markets. The low value-added produced low profit margins, which in turn limited Shougang's capacity to modernize through investment in R&D and new products. In sharp contrast, the world's leading steel producers, including Arbed, Thyssen-Krupp, Usinor and Corus (the merger of British Steel and Hoogovens) had global reach, with plants across the world, and a high capability in specialist, high quality, high value-added steel. They were able to supply the global needs of large firms in such industries as packaging, automobiles, complex machinery, high quality construction, and white goods. The leading companies established close ties with their customers in order to meet their global needs for high quality steel.

Baogang (Shanghai) is the only large Chinese steel company that, by the late 1990s, had established a capability to compete on the global level playing field with the world's fast-transforming steel companies. Its greenfield site, strongly supported by the local Shanghai government, without a large body of existing employees and with the benefit of a booming local market for high quality steels, had developed into a potentially competitive firm able to compete on the global level playing field. In contrast, other leading steel firms in China remained heavily dominated by low quality products. However, even Baogang remained relatively small-scale in terms of global competition, with annual revenues of just one-quarter or less that of the world's leading steel firms.

Coal: Shenhua

In the midst of a vast sea of coal producers, the Chinese government has strongly supported the construction of a potentially globally competitive large coal company. The government has used powerful measures of industrial policy to help support the growth of a large modern 'high-quality coal company'. A primary objective is that this company can supply Chinese power stations with high quality coal that can reduce the environmental damage of burning coal to generate electricity. A subsidiary, but also important, goal is to create a firm that can compete with the global giant corporations in this sector, especially in supplying the fast-growing markets of northeast Asia, but also in supplying large modern coal-fired power stations on the Chinese coast. It has supported Shenhua's development through the grant of property rights to the vast coal reserves under the Ordos Plateau, as well as through the direction of large preferential loans. Following closely the model of the world's leading coal producers, Shenhua is building a dedicated railway line to ship coal 800 kilometres from Shenhua to a dedicated port facility on the coast. Starting from scratch, Shenhua has very low manning levels compared to old-established state-owned mines, which gives it a large advantage compared to domestic competitors in relation to wage costs, welfare burden and ability to organize a highly qualified and highly motivated workforce.

Despite these extremely positive aspects of Shenhua's development, it confronts many difficulties in battling with the global giant companies. Shenhua's property rights over the associated railway and port facilities are ambiguous. It is uncertain how secure Shenhua's long-term right to use the facilities exclusively will be. Nor is it clear how the long-term charge for using the facilities will be set. Shenhua operates in a fundamentally different environment from that of the multinational coal companies. The main source of domestic and international competition for the latter is other modern coal companies. However, Shenhua faces a fierce battle with other domestic producers as well as an increasing battle with the multinationals. Shenhua must compete with small-scale local producers that pay subsistence wages to workers in conditions that have not been seen for over 100 years in the advanced economies. The small producers are heavily supported by their local governments in their battle for survival with the large coal companies. Shenhua must also compete with heavily subsidized state-owned enterprises. Not only does Shenhua face severe domestic competition. It has also had to accept a major reorganization of its business structure, being forcibly merged by the central government with five large state-owned enterprises. This drastically altered Shenhua's character. Three of the mines are in a terminal state of decline and heavily loss-making. Instead of being a company with 7,000 employees, Shenhua overnight became a company with 80,000 employees.

Alongside the rise of the Chinese coal industry has gone a powerful re-shaping of the coal industry in the outside world. A powerful group of modern, high quality coal companies has emerged. They are supplying the modern coal-fired power stations in the USA and East Asia. Increasingly, they are supplying the power stations of developing countries, as the power generation industry is privatized, and operators seek the lowest-cost source of high quality coal. The emerging global giants, such as RWE, Billiton, BHP and Rio Tinto, are able to compete successfully in these markets by benefiting from having large deposits of high quality, mainly open-cast mines, through the provision of coal that is washed and graded, through centrally purchasing large amounts of modern large-scale equipment, and through supplying coal reliably through a tightly integrated transport system. Shenhua's capability to compete with these companies is weakened greatly by the problems it faces in domestic competition and by the enforced merger with the five state-owned mines.

In these fundamental senses, China's industrial policy of the past two decades must be judged a failure. The reasons for the failure of China's industrial policy are partially internal and partially external.

Internal Reasons for China's Failure

On the internal front, China's industrial policy encountered a number of peculiar problems which substantially differentiate the Chinese environment from that which Japan and Korea faced during their comparable period of catch-up at the firm level:

Where is the firm? China's industrial policy suffered from a lack of consistency in identification of the 'firm'. A great deal of China's economic reform process focused on increasing the autonomy of large 'enterprises', ultimately granting them rights as legal persons. This path of reform viewed the large plant as the core of enterprise reform. Based on the foundations of the contract system, the reform period witnessed an evolving struggle by former state-owned enterprises to increase their autonomy from the central authorities in Beijing. They did this through the following methods:

- independently using their retained profits to modernize and grow;
- struggling to become joint venture partners of the major multinationals and acquire modern technology;
- struggling to list on international markets and raise capital for modernization;

- taking over or investing in second and third tier enterprises. This path of reform led to a situation in which it was almost impossible for strong state-owned enterprises to merge with other strong enterprises. Whereas in the world outside China, 'strong' were merging with 'strong' at high speed, in China, the strong enterprises remained substantially independent of each other. When the state turned its attention towards attempting to merge large strong enterprises into large multi-plant companies, it proved extremely difficult to rebuild central control over the large subordinate companies.

Impoverished economy. China's attempts to construct large modern firms took place within the confines of a still extremely poor economy. China's income level and level of urbanization was far below that of Japan in the 1950s or 1960s, or Korea in the 1970s and 1980s, during the comparable periods of their industrial policy. This meant that China's aspiring globally competitive firms had to face a 'struggle on two fronts':

- A large fraction of domestic demand is still for relatively simple, low value-added products. In this market, China's aspiring large firms had to confront a sea of domestic small and medium-sized competitors, competing on price, often protected by local government policy and by a poorly developed transport system.

- In the relatively small market for high value-added products, China's aspiring large firms increasingly had to confront severe competition from imports and local production by multinationals. China's aspiring global giants were basically unable to compete in global markets, and remained confined to producing for the domestic market, caught in a vicious circle of limited scale in high value-added production, further restricting their capability to invest and grow in these areas of the market.

Local protectionism. China's huge size and strong traditions of relatively autonomous local government created a strong basis of regional support for emerging large firms. This is advantageous for firm growth in some senses. However, in an epoch of explosive globalization, it is not feasible for a single country, even one of China's size, to support several major players in each sector. In Europe, the governments of France, Italy and Germany have been extremely reluctant to allow the process of cross-border merger to grow rapidly. However, it has been hard for them to resist this process where the government does not have an ownership share. A major fear has been the possibility that a given country may be the main loser in downsizing and rationalization. This issue is even more acute in China, given the massive over-manning. Consequently, local governments have strongly resisted the merger of large local firms with large firms based elsewhere in the country.

Inheritance from the planned economy. China's reforms began from an existing body of large-scale state-owned enterprises, with large numbers of employees. As in the former USSR, the core of China's industry was a small number of large-scale plants. Under the Maoist system, and possibly influenced also by a distinctive East Asian cultural approach, China's large firms were constructed as a 'large family', with cradle-to-grave social support, and a deep sense of social commitment to employees and their families. Only after two decades of reform were China's large enterprises seriously attempting to downsize their workforce.

The retention of such a large number of employees on the payroll not only affected costs. It also drastically affected the possibility of creating a modern, competitive system of labour organization. A combination of government policy and the huge numbers of employees placed severe constraints on the growth of real wages. Moreover, the surrounding sea of poverty has meant that it is politically extremely difficult to implement such remuneration measures as stock options. Instead, the most successful large enterprises have allocated a large fraction of their disposable income to expanding welfare facilities which are provided reasonably equally for all employees, rather than reinforcing material incentive-based remuneration. This has stimulated a large number of highly qualified personnel to leave large state enterprises to work in better-rewarded jobs.

Incentive to diversify. Several factors interacted to cause a powerful incentive to diversify:

- limited capability to compete in export markets;
- constraints on mergers and acquisitions among large firms;
- commitment to the 'large family';
- high transaction costs consequent upon the undeveloped nature of the infrastructure.

These forces created a powerful incentive for diversification into unrelated businesses in order to provide channels for growth, profits, and employment. This approach was legitimated by the central government's support for the idea of a 'business group' with a core firm at its centre. In an even more extreme way than in Korea or Japan, the typical large Chinese firm constructed a wide network of diversified second and third tier businesses in which it invested. Only a small fraction of these were able to benefit from economies of scale.

Lack of focus in bureaucracy compared to Japan. The bureaucratic apparatus with which China was attempting to implement industrial policy was very different from that in Japan (or South Korea). Japan relied on relatively small professional civil services. It was powerfully imbued with a commitment to achieve economic progress following a massive military defeat. China's bureaucracy is vastly greater absolutely and larger even in relative terms. It lacks the intense commitment to national development of its neighbours in northeast Asia. Despite great advances in its technical capabilities and important successes in aspects of industrial policy, it has been unable to truly separate itself from the operations of the leading enterprises. Even after twenty years of reform, the Party remained deeply imbued with corruption, which seriously inhibited its efforts to implement a consistent, effective industrial policy.

Ideological commitment to state ownership. In sharp contrast with Japan and South Korea, China's policy-makers remained committed throughout to maintaining the commanding heights of large-scale industry in state ownership. Large state enterprises were allowed gradually to expand the absorption of capital from non-state sources, including Sino-foreign joint ventures, and flotation on domestic and international stock markets. However, even after two decades of enterprise reform, the government remained committed to substantial public ownership of large enterprises, providing a continued channel for bureaucratic intervention in large firms' management, despite persistent attempts to 'separate ownership from management'. This was in sharp contrast with Japan and South Korea during their catch-up.

This approach also ran counter to the trend in the advanced economies in which a string of global leading firms evolved out of privatized state enterprises. These included Usinor, Arbed, Corus (formerly British Steel), Posco and China Steel (Taiwan) in the steel sector, Elf Aquitaine, ENI, Repson/YPF and BP Amoco in oil and petrochemicals, Rolls Royce, British Aerospace and Aerospatiale-Matra in aerospace, and British Telecom, Deutsche Telecom, France Telecom, and Telecom Italia in telecommunications. By the year 2000, not one of the world's top 300 firms by R&D spending, and only a tiny handful of the world's top 500 companies by value of sales, was in the public sector.

Whereas Japan and South Korea had a relatively simple non-ideological goal of building globally competitive giant corporations, China's industrial policy remained suffused with ideology intertwined with the objective of building global giant corporations. The ideological objective provided a justification for central bureaucratic intervention to limit the expansion of ambitious and increasingly autonomous large enterprises such as Shougang, Shanghai petrochemical corporation and Daqing, and for the persistence of bureaucratic interference in the management of technically autonomous large enterprises.

External Reasons for the Failure of China's Industrial Policy

At least as important as the special difficulties that confronted China on the internal front in implementing a successful industrial policy, is the fact that China's attempt to build large globally competitive firms coincided with the most revolutionary epoch in world business history, possibly even including the Industrial Revolution. The period during which Japan and South Korea were putting into place their industrial policy to build global giant corporations was a much less dynamic one, albeit that the international economy grew strongly. China's efforts to support the growth of competitive global corporations has taken place at a time of unprecedented change in the international business system and in technical progress. By the end of the 1990s, large firms based in the advanced economies massively dominated the global economy (cf. Table 3). There were a number of aspects to the global business revolution:

Liberalization of world trade and capital markets. The period since the late 1980s has witnessed for the first time the opening up of a truly global market place in goods, services, capital and skilled labour. The only market which still remains bound firmly by nationality is the vast sea of unskilled labour. The integration of the global market place has been facilitated by the dramatic transformation in information technology (IT). It has been facilitated also by the comprehensive change in the impact of the international institutions. It is no longer practically feasible to benefit fully from trade with and investment from the developed countries without agreeing to extensive economic liberalization of international economic relations, especially those implemented by the WTO (including TRIPs and World Telecoms Agreement).

Explosive mergers and acquisitions (M&A). This period has witnessed the world's most explosive period of M&A. Global M&A rose from $156 billion in 1992 to around $3,300 billion in 1999. This process seems to be far from over, and already massively exceeds, in real terms and in terms of its significance, previous merger booms. Instead of an epoch of national champions and conglomerates, the advanced economies' business structures have been revolutionized. In almost every sector (including such diverse sectors as aerospace, IT, pharmaceuticals, autos, auto components, petrochemicals, complex equipment, fast-moving consumer goods, packaging and power equipment) (cf. Table 4) a small number of focused global producers dominates the world market. Not only have the core businesses experienced this explosive process of concentration. The deepening interaction between core companies and supplier companies has created an explosive 'cascade' effect that is rapidly leading to concentration and focus among the first tier suppliers and spilling over even into second and third tier suppliers.

Dramatic growth of business capabilities of leading global firms. The leading firms are able to benefit from large expenditures on focused R&D. The resulting technical progress has been comprehensively dominated by the global giant corporations. In 1998, the world's top 300 corporations spent around $250 billion on R&D, providing an explosive propulsion to the world's stock of applicable knowledge: 'MNCs [multinational corporations] are the world's chief repositories of economically useful knowledge and skills. All the screaming in the world will not change this.'[16] The leading firms are able also to benefit from massive expenditure on marketing and brand-building, of which advertising is just one component. The leading firms are able to attract the world's most able workers. They are able to benefit also from massive cost savings consequent upon global procurement systems and large gains from deep, constant interaction with supplier companies, facilitated by the revolution in information technology.

A veritable 'external firm' of global dimensions is being created in sector after sector. Increasingly, leading firms in all sectors are being distinguished by their capability to undertake systems integration stretching across the value chain. The most dramatic recent illustration of this process is the announcement by Ford, General Motors and Daimler-Chrysler that they are to establish a joint internet procurement network.[17] A large fraction of the world's auto components procurement will therefore flow through this unified system. The world's total auto components procurement amounts to $1,780 billion. The central co-ordination of a large fraction of the world's auto components makers through a single system represents a highly significant step in the growth of the 'external firm' that stretches across the entire value chain.

US Dominance of the Global Big Business Revolution

Not only is there a massive imbalance between the 'starting points' in the great globalization race on the global level playing field, but there is also a deeply uneven distribution of business power within the advanced capitalist economies in the big business revolution. The large firms of the USA dominate this process:

- ***R&D.*** The leading US-based companies have led the way in the resurgence of big business investment in R&D. The IT sector (hardware plus software) is by far the most important category of R&D expenditure,[18] with 74 of the top 300 companies by R&D spending in 1998. Of these 53 were US-based companies. No less than 16 out of the top 17 software firms by R&D spending were based in the US.

- ***FDI.*** The USA's share of total world FDI outflows rose from 14 per cent in 1986-91 to 27 per cent in 1997.[19]

- ***Fortune 500.*** By 1998, North American firms accounted for 37 per cent of the *Fortune* 500 ranking of the world's leading firms, ranked by sales value.

- ***Competitive edge.*** In 1998 Morgan Stanley identified a total of 238 companies that were 'world leaders'.[20] Of these 134 were North American.

- ***Market capitalization.*** In 1998 North America had 254 of the FT 500 companies (ranked by market capitalization).[21] At one point early in the year 2000, just two US-based firms, Microsoft and Cisco had a combined market capitalization of no less than $750 billion.

The Dilemma for Industrial Policy in China

The tortoise and the hare. If China had not opened itself to the international economy through trade and foreign investment after the 1970s, the progress in its large enterprises would not have been anything like as great as has been achieved. However, the pace of change in global big business has massively outpaced that of China's large enterprises. As the global level playing field is further and further established within China after it enters the WTO, few Chinese enterprises are in a position to compete with the world's leading companies in each sector. Given the differential rate of change in business structures and technological capability, it is hard to imagine that even a much greater length of time under current industrial policies could enable China to produce firms that could challenge the global giants. Would a further ten years of government industrial policy using the same measures as in the past two decades, or using any other industrial policy measures one can imagine, be able to ensure that China's large firms caught up with the global leaders? Is it possible that after a further ten years China's large firms might be even further behind than they are today?

Is catch-up at the level of the large corporation possible for any developing country in the new international environment? Chinese industrial policy is caught between the devil and the deep blue sea. On the evidence of the past twenty years, to remain relatively isolated and supported by government industrial policy, even if the policy is more focused, more realistic and more consistently applied, is unlikely to lead to the construction of globally competitive large firms. The pace of progress in the business capabilities of the world's leading firms is so great that it is hard to imagine any strategy that could lead to successful catch-up at the level of the large firm on a widespread basis. It is extremely difficult for many people to accept this. However, this is the blunt reality. It may no longer be possible for industrial policy to build powerful competitive large firms based in even the largest and most powerful of the developing countries. It requires immensely subtle international relations to accommodate this new reality. It requires a radical re-drawing of the ambitions of large developing countries, especially, but not only, China. It requires separating the goal of catch-up at the firm level from the goal of advancing national output, structural change, wage employment and the standard of living.

Great subtlety is required in international relations to cope with the new reality. Even for advanced European countries, it is very difficult to accept that 'national champions' may be unable to compete on the global level playing field as individual players. However, whereas individual European countries may have to accept the demise of their national champions, the continent as a whole is breeding a group of regional champions and transatlantic champions. For China, a huge civilization with a proud economic and political history, it is very difficult to accept that it may be unable to emulate Britain, the US, Japan and Korea in building national champions through industrial policy.

Is there an alternative? For there to be an alternative, there has to be a coherent realistic strategy. It is hard to identify what such a strategy could be in the face of the incredible pace of global change in the nature and business capability of large firms. It is better to 'seek truth from facts' than to live with illusions. There is no point in trying to fight a battle that cannot be won. The heroic age of building national champions through state-supported industrial policy may be over. The idea has not been defeated by the triumph of small-scale perfectly competitive firms. Rather, it has been defeated by the full flowering of global oligopolistic capitalism.

Can China cope with US dominance? US-based firms are by far the most powerful force in the global business revolution. Individual US-based large corporations are desperate to expand their activities in the 'new frontier' for global capitalism in China. The central position of large US-based firms in the global big business revolution will enable its firms to take the lead in the defeat of China's large corporations. Dealing with this reality will be a large policy challenge.

Nowhere is their dominance more pronounced than in the industries of the Third Technological Revolution, which will be at the centre of global business revolution in the early twenty-first century. The USA's representative at the World Telecoms Agreement negotiations was in no doubt as to the significance of the Agreement for US corporations: '[The World Telecoms Agreement] is a triumph for the American way. [...] US companies are the most competitive telecommunications providers in the world; they are in the position to compete and win under this agreement.'[22]

China's accession to the WTO has a wide significance for US foreign policy. In Charlene Barshefsky's view: 'The [WTO] Agreement has potential beyond economics and trade [...] Opening up China's markets will put enormous competitive pressure on China's beleaguered SOEs – bulwarks of political conservatism and socialist economics. Opening China's IT market will increase the flow of information among Chinese and between China and the outside world, in ways and in such volumes that no amount of censorship can control. *This cannot but promote the right kind of change in China.*'[23]

Afterword

There is a mounting chorus of opinion that supports high-speed Chinese integration with the world trade and investment system. There are many who argue: 'More pain, more gain', and 'If major surgery has to be undertaken, its best to do it all at once'. A leading commentator in Hong Kong has written: 'Regarding the numerous challenges that China will face on its entry to the WTO, including SOE reform, foreign exchange, banking, information technology, foreign trade, and human rights, China should take this one-shot gamble in relation to these challenges that result from the country's complete opening up to the outside world. No matter what, China must take this gamble.'[24] These sentiments echo in eerie fashion the comments a decade earlier on the need for dramatic system change in Russia and Eastern Europe. At that time there was wide support for the notion of the 'big bang': 'We argue in favour of an approach which we have christened Sbig bang'. [...] The essential feature is comprehensiveness, immediacy, and irreversibility with the objective of establishing a democratic, capitalist society that has a human face.'[25]

In the late 1980s and early 1990s, commentators were almost unanimously optimistic that radical system change would be followed by rapid improvement in Soviet economic performance and human welfare. In 1990 the World Bank, IMF, EBRD and OECD strongly supported radical economic change in the former USSR, predicting that such reform would be followed by a brief fall of national output: 'A recovery of national output should be able to get under way within two years or so. [...] Further strong growth of output and rising living standards could be expected for the remainder of the decade and beyond.'[26] Their predictions were to prove very wide off the mark. The Soviet economy collapsed and shows little sign of recovery a decade later. Human welfare deteriorated drastically, with a massive increase in death rates and rise in poverty.

In June 2000, a senior Russian official commented: 'Our reforms failed and the US is partly to blame for interfering unnecessarily in Russian development. But we should also blame ourselves that their stupid advice was accepted.'[27]

Notes

[1]US businessman R. Cooper speaking at the 'China Development Forum' held in Beijing in March 2000.

[2]*Ibid.*

[3]This has already been widely observed in the shape of the large-scale entry of foreign capital into the Chinese telecoms industry through the 'China-China Foreign' formula.

[4]US businessman R. Cooper speaking at the 'China Development Forum' held in Beijing in March 2000.

[5]Nolan, Peter and Wang Xiaoqiang, 1999, 'Beyond privatisation: Institutional innovation and growth in China's large state-owned enterprises', *World Development*, vol. 17, no. 1, pp. 169–200.

[6]Wu, Bangguo, Chinese State Council, quoted in *Economic Daily*, 1 August 1998.

[7]World Bank, *World Development Report*, New York: Oxford University Press, 1999, pp. 250–51.

[8]UNCTAD, *World Investment Report*, 1999.

[9]*Fortune*, 2 August 1999.

[10]Department of Trade and Industry (DTI), UK R&D Scoreboard, Edinburgh, DTI, 1999.

[11]*Financial Times*, 28 January 1999.

[12]Morgan Stanley Dean Witter (MSDW), *The Competitive Edge*, New York, MSDW, 1999.

[13]The following analysis is based on various case studies by Peter Nolan, all published between 1997 and 1999 in the series: China Big Business Programme Case Study, University of Cambridge, Judge Institute of Management Studies. The titles of the publications are: *Challenging the Established Large Enterprises: The Case of Yuchai Diesel* (1997); *Economic Reform and Institutional Change in the Chinese Petrochemical Industry, with special reference to the Shanghai Petrochemical Company Limited* (1998); *The Battle for the Chinese Power Equipment Market: The Case of Harbin Power Plant Equipment Group Corporation* (1998); *The Chinese Army's Firm in Business: the Sanjiu Group*, (1998); *AVIC: Internationally competitive aircraft manufacturer, diversified East Asian conglomerate or global sub-contractor?* (1998); *Large Integrated Steel Companies in China's Economic Development: the Case of Shougang* (1999); *Strategic Choices in the Development of the Chinese Coal Industry: the Case of the Shenhua Group* (1999); *Restructuring CNPC and Sinopec: feudal fiefdoms or modern corporations?* (1999).

[14]International Institute of Strategic Studies (IISS), *The Military Balance*, London, IISS, 1999, p. 175.

[15]Merck, *Annual Report*, 1998, p. 40.

[16]Wolf, Martin, quoted in the *Financial Times*, 17 November 1999.
[17]*Financial Times*, 27 March 2000.
[18]DTI, *op. cit.*
[19]UNCTAD, *World Investment Report*, 1998, p. 367.
[20]MSDW, *op. cit.*
[21]*Financial Times*, 28 January 1999.
[22]Charlene Barshefsky, US trade representative designate, quoted in *Financial Times*, 18 February 1997.
[23]Cf. www.ustr.gov.
[24]Zhang, Wuchang, mimeographed speech, 2000.
[25]Steinherr, A., 1991, 'Essential ingredients for reforms in Eastern Europe', MOCT-MOST, No 3, quoted in Nolan, P., *China's Rise, Russia's Fall*, Basingstoke, Macmillan, 1995, p. 56.
[26]IMF, World Bank, OECD and EBRD, *The Economy of the USSR: Summary and Recommendations*, Washington DC, World Bank, 1999, pp. 18-19.
[27]Karaganov, Sergei, Chairman, Council for Foreign and Defence Policy, quoted in the *Financial Times*, 3 June 2000.

Table 1:
Some indicators of the competitive capability of selected leading Chinese companies and selected leading global companies at the end of the 1990s

Company	Revenues $billion	Post-tax profits $million	Employees '000s	R&D $million
Aerospace				
Boeing ('97)	45.8	-178	239	1,830
Lockheed-Martin ('97)	28.1	1,300	190	1,060
BAe ('97)	10.4	681	44	690
AVIC ('97)	*3.1*	*72*	*560*	*n.a.*
Pharmaceuticals				
Merck ('97)	26.03	8,069	54	2,760
Novartis ('97)	22.34	6,166	87	2,620
Glaxo Wellcome ('97)	17.38	4,626	53	1,870
Sanjiu ('97)	*0.67*	*[98]*	*13*	*n.a.*
Power equipment				
Siemens ('98)	57.95	990	376	5,008
power division	6.39	n.a.	n.a.	n.a.
ABB ('98)	29.72	2,500	208	2,368
General Electric ('98)	100.47	9,296	293	1,930
power division	8.47	1,306	n.a.	n.a.
Harbin (HPEC) ('98)	*0.35*	*9*	*27*	*3*
Oil/Petrochemicals				
Exxon/Mobil ('97)	182.36	11,730	123	720
Royal Dutch/Shell ('97)	128.14	7,760	105	770
BP Amoco ('97)	123.30	8,540	123	390
CNPC ('98)	*32.6*	*[107]*	*1,540*	*n.a.*
Sinopec ('98)	*34.0*	*[194]*	*1,190*	*n.a.*
Autos				
GM ('98)	161.3	2,960	600	7,800
Ford ('98)	171.2	23,160	364	7,500
Daimler-Chrysler ('98)	154.6	5,660	300	5,800
Yiqi ('98)	*4.4*	*[21]*	*156*	*n.a.*
Erqi ('98)	*2.6*	*[-5]*	*134*	*n.a.*
Shanghai ('98)	*4.8*	*[594]*	*60*	*n.a.*

cont.

Auto components				
Bosch ('98)	28.61	446	n.a.	2,020
Denso ('98)	13.76	461	57	1,350
Caterpillar ('98)	20.98	1,513	86	838
Cummins Diesel Engine ('98)	6.27	-21	28	255
Detroit Diesel ('98)	2.16	30	7	98
Yuchai ('98)	*0.14*	*[15]*	*9*	*n.a.*
Steel				
Nippon Steel '98)	21.59	90	28 ('95)	n.a.
Posco ('98)	9.72	680	23 ('94)	n.a.
NKK ('98)	14.15	849	18 ('95)	190
Usinor ('98)	10.65	373	58 ('95)	180
Shougang ('98)	*2.16*	*[25]*	*218 ('97)*	*n.a.*
Baogang ('98)	*3.12*	*[265]*	*35 ('97)*	*n.a.*

IT Hardware (1998)			
Company	Revenues $billion	Profits $million	R&D spending $million
IBM ('98)	78.4	10,200	5,100
Hitachi ('98)	71.8	2,000	4,400
Hewlett-Packard ('98)	45.3	4,200	3,200
Lucent ('98)	29.1	2,500	4,900
Legend ('98)	*1.0*	*(28)*	*1*
TCL ('98)	*1.3*	*(49)*	-
Huawei ('98)	*0.7*	*(156)*	*120*

Note: Figures in [ ] indicate pre-tax profits

Source: The above tables are all from Nolan, P., *China and the global business revolution*, Basingstoke, Palgrave, 2001.

Table 2: Some indicators of the competitive capability of selected leading Chinese companies and selected leading global companies in the banking and insurance sector at the end of the 1990s

Institution	Revenues ($m.)	Profits ($m.)	Assets ($billion)	Equity ($m.)	Employees	Profit per employee ($'000)
Commercial banks, 1999						
Citigroup (US)*	82,005	9,867	716.9	49,700	176,900	55.8
Deutsche Bank (Germany)	58,585	2,694	841.8	23,200	93,232	28.9
Bank of America (US)	51,392	7,882	632.6	44,432	155,906	50.6
Crédit Suisse (Switzerland)	49,361	3,475	451.5	20,378	63,963	54.3
Industrial and Commercial Bank of China	20,130	498	427.5	21,918	549,038	0.9
Bank of China	17,632	534	350.7	17,921	208,792	2.6
Agricultural Bank of China	14,127	-110	244.1	16,273	500,000	-0.2
China Construction Bank	13,392	598	265.8	12,907	324,000	1.8
Investment banks, 1998						
Merrill Lynch (US)	33,962	1,259	299.8	10,132	63,800	19.7
MSDW	31,126	3,281	376.0	17,014	45,712	71.8
Goldman Sachs	22,478	2,428	217.4	6,310	13,033	186.3
J.P. Morgan**	18,110	2,055	260.9	11,439	15,512	132.5
Guotai	*325*	*75*	*1.5*	*192*	*2,800*	*26.7*
China South	*288*	*10*	*1.9*	*171*	*2,500*	*4.0*
Shenyin Wanguo	*258*	*44*	*2.1*	*265*	*3,000*	*14.7*
Insurance companies, 1998						
AXA (France)	87,645	2,155	508.6	16,395	92,008	23.4
Nippon Life (Japan)	78,515	3,405	23.3	10,559	71,434	47.7
Allianz(Germ.)	74,178	2,382	383.7	28,854	113,584	21.0
PICC***	3,858	101	5.3	972	84,657	1.2
Pacific	2,832	19	2.0	366	9,690	2.0
Ping An	2,409	42	3.4	446	110,595	0.4

Notes:
* The table puts Citigroup, which was grouped in diversified financials, in this group.
** The table puts J.P. Morgan, normally regarded as a commercial but actually an investment bank now, in this group.
The data is based in 1999.
* * * People's Insurance Company.

Source: The above tables are all from Nolan, P., *China and the global business revolution,* Basingstoke, Palgrave, 2001.

Table 3:
Dominance of firms based in high income countries of the global big business revolution

	Population		GNP, 1997 (1)		GNP, 1997 (2)	
	billion	%	$b	%	$b	%
HIEs	926	16	23,802	80	21,091	57
L/MIEs	4,903	84	6,123	20	15,861	43

	Fortune 500 companies (1998) (3)		*FT 500* companies (1998) (4)		Top 300 companies by R&D spend (1997)		Stock market capitalization (1997)	
	No.	% No.	%	No. %	No.	%	$b	%
HIEs	474	95	484	97	299	99	18,452	91
L/MIEs	26 (5)	5	16 (6)	3	2	1	1,725	9

Notes:
(1) at prevailing rate of exchange
(2) at PPP dollars
(3) ranked by sales revenue
(4) ranked by market capitalization
(5) of which: Korea = 9, China =6, Brazil =4, Taiwan =2, Venezuela =1, Russia =1, India =1, Mexico =1, Malaysia =1
(6) of which: Hong Kong =7, Brazil =2, Taiwan =2, Singapore =1, Mexico =1. India =1, Korea =1, Argentina =1
HIEs=High Income Economies
L/MIEs= Low/Middle Income Economies

Sources: *Financial Times*, 28 January 1999; World Bank, 1998: 190-1, and 220-1; *Fortune*, 2 August 1999 DTI, 1998: 70-80.

Table 4: Global oligopoly in the business revolution

Company name	Sector	Global market share (%)
Aerospace		
Boeing	Commercial aircraft orders over 100 seats	70
Airbus	Commercial aircraft orders over 100 seats	30
Rolls-Royce	aero-engine orders	34
GE	aero-engine orders	53
Pratt & Whitney	aero-engine orders	13
IT		
Lucent	internet and telecoms equipment	17
Intel	micro-processors	85
Microsoft	computer systems	90+
Cisco	computer routers	66
	:high end routers	80
Corning	optical fibres	50
Hyundai Electronics	DRAMS	21
Samsung Electronics	DRAMS	20
Sony	electronic games	67
Nintendo	electronic games	29
Ericsson	mobile phones	15
Nokia	mobile phones	23
Motorola	mobile phones	20
Pharmaceuticals		
Glaxo-Wellcome /SKB	prescription drugs:	7
	central nervous system	12
	anti-infection	17
	respiratory	17
	anti-asthma	31
	anti-herpes	49
Merck	prescription drugs:	5
	statin anti-cholesterol	40
	angiotension converting enzyme inhibitors	30
Medtronic	Implantable/interventional therapy technologies:	45
	pacemakers	50+
		cont.

Company name	Sector	Global market share (%)
	Autos	
Ford/Mazda/Volvo	automobiles	16
GM	automobiles	15
Daimler-Chrysler	automobiles	10
VW	automobiles	9
Toyota	automobiles	9
Renualt/Nissan	automobiles	9
	Auto components	
Pilkington	auto glass	25
GKN	constant velocity joints	40
Tenneco	shock absorbers/car exhaust systems	25
Lucas	brake systems	25
Bosch	brake systems	31
Bridgestone	tires	19
Michelin	tires	18
Goodyear	tires	14
	Petrochemicals	
BP Amoco	PTA	37
	acetic acid (technology licenses)	70
	acrylonite (technology licenses)	90
	Complex equipment	
Invensys (BTR/Siebe)	control/automation equipment	11
Siemens	control/automation equipment	10
ABB	control/automation equipment	9
Em erson	control/automation equipment	8
Fanuc	Machine tool controls	45
Schindler	lifts	25
Otis	lifts	18
Mitsubishi	lifts	13
Kone	lifts	9
	Fast moving consumer goods	
Coca-Cola	carbonated soft drinks	51
Chupa Chups	lollipops	34
		cont.

Company name	**Sector**	**Global market share (%)**
Proctor and Gamble	tampons	48
Gilette	razors	70
Fuji Film	camera films	35
Nike	sneakers	36
	Packaging	
Toray	polyester film	60
Sidel	PET plastic packaging machines	55
Alcoa/Reynolds (merger pending)	aluminium	24
	Power equiment	
GE	gas turbines (1993-98)	34
Siemens/Westinghouse	gas turbines (1993-98)	32
ABB/Alstom	gas turbines (1993-98)	21

Sources: Morgan Stanley Dean Witter (MSDW), *The Competitive Edge*, New York: MSDW, 1998, 1999; *Financial Times*, 19.1., 8., 21.5., 22.7., 11.9., 28.10., 1996, 6.3., 15.5., 24.11.1998, 8.2., 7., 10., 24.3., 15., 27.10., 15.11.1999, 18.1., 29., 31.3.2000; Glaxo-Wellcome, *Annual Report* , 1999; Merck, *Annual Report*, 1998; BP Amoco, *Annual Report*, 1998; Coca Cola, *Annual Report*, 1998; Sidel, *Annual Report*, 1998.

4

The Automobile Sector

Martin Posth

Introduction

At the time of writing, at the beginning of 2001, China is on the threshold of joining the WTO. At the same time the automobile sector expects the most far-reaching changes since its formation in the late thirties. However, before these structural changes actually take effect, the present situation can be described as follows.

More than 130 car factories, supplied by more than 3,000 companies delivering parts, components and spare parts, have produced and, as a general rule, distributed, approximately 1.83 million vehicles. One-third of these were automobiles. With these numbers, China is now the tenth biggest vehicle manufacturer in the world, and with regard to automobiles alone, it ranks fourteenth on the global scale. The total idle production capacities of all manufacturers may reach 50 per cent of all installed capacities (over 1.2 million units).

External tariffs of up to 80–100 per cent are protecting the domestic car market. Purchase prices of imported cars are 250–300 per cent higher than comparable prices abroad. Even for domestically produced cars one has to add up to 70 per cent to the average purchase price (Santana 2000: 26,500 US$, Audi A6: 60,000 US$, General Motors Buick: 34,000 US$) for value-added, sales, street and consumption tax which accrue when the car is actually operated. Furthermore, possession of a car is subject to a license.

Within the automobile sector, nine companies produce in alliance with a foreign investor on the basis of licensing agreements or joint ventures, e.g. Volkswagen (VW)/Audi, DaimlerChrysler, PSA/

Citroen, Daihatsu/Toyota, Honda, General Motors (GM), Suzuki, Fuji H.I. In addition, foreign cooperation exists with Ford, Volvo, Iveco, Isuzu, Nissan, Hyundai, DaimlerChrysler, Toyota and GM for light commercial motor vehicles, vans and trucks.

Almost all of the leading fifty Western auto industry suppliers are present on the Chinese market. The Volkswagen Group alone has initiated hundreds of joint ventures, direct investments or further co-operation in the supply sector. The American Delphi Company, the biggest supplier in the world, represents fourteen joint ventures and a total investment volume of about 400 million US$. The American Group ASIMCO, which is financed through American pension funds, has initiated more than twelve joint ventures. The South Korean manufacturer Daewoo Motors has invested about 1 billion US$ in component production in Shandong province. Together with other suppliers, local content production has reached between 40 per cent (minimum rate at start of production in joint venture) and over 90 per cent (Santana, Shanghai Volkswagen).

Since the start of production in 1985, Shanghai Volkswagen (SVW) has been the market leader in the automobile sector. Together with the second joint venture of the VW Group, FAW–Volkswagen (FAW–VW), the company represents a total market share of about 54 per cent (1999).

Both producers and suppliers are highly fragmented. The companies are scattered over the whole country, with only a few reaching the necessary economies of scale. In automobile production, these would imply the production of 200,000–300,000 units per year, and in engine or gear production, depending on production structures, of 1,500–2,000 pieces a day. With some exceptions, productivity and costs structure of the supplier side (80 per cent of the net value-added in automobile production) have reached 50–80 per cent of international standards. Concerning quality, only a few producers such as SVW and FAW–VW are meeting international requirements in their assembly sites. Furthermore, substantial progress is still to be made in the fields of marketing, distribution and services. Thus, it is not surprising that only a few companies actually do work profitably, among them the joint venture between the VW–Group and the Tianjin Automotive Group.

Due to exaggerated concerns surrounding China's WTO accession, consumers are now tending to put off the purchase of cars. As a result, sales are slackening, prices slumping (mostly in the compact and mid-range class car segment) and stocks growing.

In order to evaluate the entire market (2000: about 640,000 automobiles) more realistically in terms of potential demand and absorption capacities, one has to add to the officially approved imports the illegal imports of automobiles, mostly in the luxury segment (so-called 'grey imports'). The latter amounted to 30,000 automobiles per year. It was not until recent years that public authorities started to successfully tackle the wide-spread smuggling activities. Thus, the number of illegally imported automobiles should by now have decreased to less than 10,000 units per year.

The total number of automobiles is approximately 14 million units, among them about five million cars. Hence, automobile density has grown from a 1985 figure of 1:10.000 to 1:210 today – in other words, 210 Chinese share one car. If China reached an automobile density of 1:2 one day (why not?) the total number of cars alone would increase to 600 million units. This would easily excede the numbers in the rest of the world – surely an ecological apocalypse. More realistically, however, the number of Chinese automobiles should find its level between today's 5 million and 10, 50 or 100 million cars in the future.

According to a recent study conducted by China Mainland Marketing Research Co. in 14 larger provinces and cities, 7.8 per cent of families possessed a private automobile, 4.2 per cent of them were car owners. Other estimates give even higher numbers and indicate ratios of up to 25 per cent. However, in view of an average income of less than 1,000 US$ per year, such estimates seem to be exaggerated, even if a higher purchasing power parity is conceded. To buy a Santana, Chinese still have to pay at least ten times their annual income.

There are also 200 million bicycles, 30 million motorcycles, 15 million agricultural vehicles and 13 million tractors. The Peoples Republic of China possesses a road network of overall 1.3 million km, of which 2,700 km are highways. There are plans to expand these in the short term to a total of 10,000 km.

These are some incomplete snapshots of China's automobile industry. Before raising questions on the implications of the WTO accession for the Chinese automobile industry, including the specific consequences arising for European investors in this sector, it might be helpful to give an overview of the past. In the following, therefore, the historical development of the Chinese automobile industry as well as the role of government control of the development of an automobile industry will be briefly outlined. Only if we take these aspects into consideration will it be possible to see which conclusions can be realistically drawn from China's WTO accession and which scenarios are likely or unlikely to happen. Although the various segments of automobile production (trucks, commercial vehicles, buses, cars) share some common features, they are very distinctive. Therefore I will, in the following, concentrate on the car sector, which will be the most important sector in the future.

The Historical Development of China's Automobile Industry

Wherever the automobile industry has been introduced to a less developed country and became part of its industrial development, this process has always been accompanied by transfers of technology, know-how, and, as a general rule, foreign investment from developed countries. This is because the automobile, as a final product, reflects a representative cross-section of the industrial and technological capacities of the whole economy. Usually, it initiates an economic boost and supplementary spin-off effects. The beginning of the Chinese automobile industry can be traced back to the thirties. Starting with Soviet and later Japanese assistance, commercial vehicles and trucks have been manufactured at locations in Shanghai, Changchun, Tianjin and Nanjing. It was not before the 1950s that the production of cars started. The 'Red Flag' in the North and the 'Shanghai' (the replication of a Mercedes) in the South were produced at the First Automotive Works (FAW) in Changchun (Jilin Province), and at the Shanghai Tractor and Automobile Industry Corporation (STAC, predecessor of today's SAIC).

Major changes appeared in 1978 as a reaction to the new 'open door policy' introduced by Deng Xiaoping which initiated a slow opening up of the country towards the West. This was the starting point of the modern automobile history in the People's Republic of China. Very soon, the Chinese government began to focus on developing the automobile industry, declaring it as a pillar industry. This far-reaching objective was to be achieved by:

- modernization of domestic automobile and supplier industries and the introduction of locally manufactured products conforming to international technology, quality and pricing standards;

- access to and systematic acquisition of know-how in product and manufacturing technology; management and administration, together with training and vocational education in the broadest sense, at home and abroad;

- creation of competitive export structures, aiming at securing for China a world market position similar to that of Japan or South Korea.

This strategy was regarded as feasible and promising only if Western partners supported China. Consequently, the government started to search for suitable foreign automobile companies, though they were not to be allowed majority equity in the intended alliances. It was China's objective, first, to avoid dependency in automobile development, and second, and even more important, to prevent probable takeover bids. Typically enough, the first attempt to apply such a strategy took place in Japan, but Toyota refused, a strategic mistake which the company has been regretting until this very day. A similar thing happened in the USA with General Motors. Again, the Americans might still regret this lost opportunity, all the more so as the alliance finally launched in the late 1990s between 'Shanghai GM' and the VW–Partner SAIC (50:50 equity) was achieved only at the cost of a 1.3 billion US$ factory purchase in Pudong/Shanghai – supposedly the most expensive strategic investment in the company's history.

Eventually, the Chinese found their partner more or less incidentally in Wolfsburg in 1978. Volkswagen agreed in principle to enter a long-term partnership with the Chinese. The basic considerations for this commitment have been:

- to get a foothold in China and gain early access to a market with significant long-term sales opportunities;

- the prospect of increasing the commitment level in terms of product program and capacity in successive stages and in response to market requirements and potential sales;

- the creation of a 'VW bridgehead' in the Southeast Asian region, with the option of delivering to markets currently dominated by competitors.

After six years of negotiations, Volkswagen started the joint venture Shanghai Volkswagen Automotive Company Ltd. (50:50 equity) with the production of the Santana, a mid-range car. Simultaneously, other major automobile companies entered the Chinese market: American Motors (today DaimlerChrysler) with Beijing Jeep Corporation Ltd. (product: Jeep Cherokee) and Peugeot with Guangzhou Peugeot Company Ltd. (product: Peugeot 405 and pick-ups). Like Volkswagen, the American and French initiated joint ventures with a number of partners.

Subsequently, the challenges lying ahead were very much the same for the Americans, French, Germans, and their respective partners:

- construction of prefabricated assembly lines for, initially, SKD (semi knocked-down) and later, CKD (completely knocked-down) vehicle sets which were delivered and packed by the parent company, and organization of related material handling systems;
- modernization of the newly acquired factories (Volkswagen), factory parts (American Motors) or the complete construction of new assembly lines in a greenfield site (Peugeot);
- successive attainment of international production standards;
- successive creation of a country-wide service network (service, after-sales service);
- assistance in modernizing the outdated supply industry;
- formation of efficient company structures (management and organization);
- qualification and training for Chinese employees;
- balancing foreign exchange flows.

The Chinese emphasized that they expected state-of-the-art solutions (scientific management) from their foreign partners. They wanted to close technological and economic gaps in order to catch up with Western countries and, if possible, leapfrog phases of economic development – a wish that can and should be acknowlegded.

Against this background, the three pioneers – American Motors, Peugeot, and Shanghai Volkswagen – apparently started off with similar chances and options in the Chinese market:

American Motors only kept a minority equity of 31.3 per cent (about 16 million US$) in Beijing Jeep. When Chrysler took over the equity in 1987, the post of Director General on the US side had already been filled by the third person in a row, after his predecessors had worn themselves out in management disputes with the Chinese partner ('laying in the same bed and having different dreams'). Furthermore, the Americans were eager to obtain cash returns from the very beginning and without any considerations for the company's record. The Americans wanted to realize their return on investment, which was modest anyway, as quickly as possible. A lack of foreign exchange urgently needed to purchase CKD parts brought the company to the brink of disaster. It was only owing to the then Deputy Chairman of the State Economic Commission and today's prime minister, Zhu Rongji, that a creative solution was found. However, the following years did not bring about much success, either.

Peugeot, too, started with a minority share (34 per cent). Besides Peugeot, the municipality of Guangzhou (capital of Guandong Province) and a Hong Kong based company were stockholders of the company. Compared to the other two pioneers, Peugeot has been facing further challenges in addition to typical China-specific problems:

- Peugeot did not invest in an established automobile company but had to construct new assembly lines in a greenfield site.
- An experienced workforce familiar with automobile production, even if insufficiently trained, was not available.
- A nearby supply industry was lacking.
- Although the central government had approved the project, it did not support it.
- The product did not meet the demands of the Chinese market.
- Last but not least, the project never seemed to be a priority for the Paris head office – this may be indicated by the fact that Peugeot CEO, Mr Calvet, visited China for the first time in 1994, indeed only to sell his shares to Honda. Since then the Accord, an upper mid-range car, is produced in the same plant and has been introduced to the market successfully. As far as is generally known, the company never worked profitable with the French as a participating party.

In contrast to Peugeot and American Motors (Chrysler), Shanghai Volkswagen has, using a different framework, proved a success:

- SVW was declared a symbol for Chinese–German co-operation by both governments (and has been treated accordingly).
- Both sides agreed on basic objectives ('laying in the same bed and having the same dreams').

- In Shanghai, VW met a partner with some experience in automobile production.
- The 'parents', VW and three Chinese partners (STAC, CNAIC, BOC), were truly commited and wanted long-term success.
- Despite a financial interest amounting to 120 million US$, and although the company has been profitable in double figures from the first business year onward, VW avoided extracting any money as dividends during the first years.
- This policy benefited both partners and has created resources for a steady enlargement of the project. Due to cash-flow investments, capacities increased from 30,000 to 60,000, then to 120,000, and today to even 300,000 units. Also, the product range was broadened.
- At the same time, SVW established a country-wide after-sales network (with 500 stations).
- In the end, it has been the progress in local content production, reaching, after some difficulties, 93 per cent in the Santana production, which brought about the real break-through for the company. Again, it was Zhu Rongji, who in 1987 as successor to Jiang Zemin became mayor of Shanghai and who gave highest priority to the further development of Shanghai Volkswagen and its supply industry. In the same year, this led to the foundation of the 'Shanghai Santana Localization Community'. From that, Volkswagen created a solid structure for a successful future development of the VW project which the competing pioneers were not able to match any longer.

In analyzing the reasons why Shanghai Volkswagen became the market leader in China's automobile industry, the following key points can be mentioned:

- Although the Beijing government did not regard the joint venture as a project of the central government, it supported SVW from the very beginning. Naturally, the municipality of Shanghai strongly backed the project wherever possible. In retrospect, it might be telling that those who represented the Chinese partners in the early phase of the project were no less than today's President of China, Jiang Zemin, (until 1987 mayor of Shanghai,

1987–89 party secretary of Shanghai) and today's prime minister Zhu Rongji – both are still today accompanying 'their' former corporation.

- In contrast to Beijing Jeep and Guangzhou Peugeot, SVW never ran into any serious foreign exchange problems. Bound by contract, the partners were in charge of sales and marketing, and in return Volkswagen obtained a guaranteed market. Furthermore, the Chinese government provided a so-called foreign exchange quota amounting to 800 million DM for the whole project including funds to obtain the necessary CKD parts.

- The municipality of Shanghai focused on the quick modernization of its existing but decayed supply industry (again different from the situation in Beijing and Guangzhou). As a consequence, the city invested billions of RMB in this sector, bringing about increases in net product and, above all, employment.

- In return, Volkswagen had to do its homework properly, namely, the modernization of assembly lines and the introduction of modern management approaches. At the same time, VW had to nationalize the production and to create a country-wide service network, of course without cutting back on quality. This could only be achieved through a prudent personnel policy. For a start, Chinese staff to the tune of 1200 man-months were trained in VW plants in Germany and Brazil and prepared for production work in Shanghai.

- Another important distinction between VW and its competitors has been the fact that VW was never reluctant to share the company's know-how whenever necessary. By request, VW agreed to produce the Santana – in 1984 the most sophisticated mid-range car produced by Volkswagen, and not an out-dated product as frequently stated.

- Moreover, to quell another repeatedly formulated accusation: it is simply for economic reasons that the Santana is still being produced today after sixteen years of operation – a decision which is not related to any refusal on the side of VW to offer a new model: 80 per cent of the value added is produced outside SVW in the supply industry which had to cope with high investments (partly to be financed with foreign exchange) and a modest output. Bearing in mind the size of the Chinese market of about 650,000 units, one simply cannot expect the supply industry to become competitive and to meet international standards overnight. This is a crucial aspect which has to be considered when one looks at China's WTO accession.

- Discussing the success of SVW, some further points have to be mentioned: right from the start, the joint venture put emphasis on 'cross cultural management' approaches. Mutual trust, mutual understanding and mutual benefit were more than hollow phrases, but were decisive factors in daily routine. Maybe this has been the real key to success.

During the late 1980s and early 1990s, further competitors entered the apparently lucrative Chinese market:

- Although Shanghai Volkswagen had already started in 1985 to successfully produce the first five hundred Audi 100 on SKD basis, which were sold mainly to public agencies and government organizations, the Chinese partners of SVW did not show any interest in producing the Audi on a regular basis – a strategic mistake in retrospect. Thus, the Volkswagen Group agreed with the First Automobile Works (FAW) Changchun, in the northern province Jilin, upon a licensing agreement to produce the Audi 100 in 1988.

- In 1990 FAW–Volkswagen was founded with a 60:40 equity. A plant was set up with a capacity of 150,000 units per year and, in addition, engines and gears. It was decided to start the production with 30,000 VW–Jetta cars. The Audi production was been integrated into this joint venture in 1995.

- Citroen established an automobile factory of similar size together with the Second Automobile Works (SAW) in the new joint venture Dongfeng Citroen in Wuhan, Hubei province, on a greenfield site.

- In the small car segment Tianjin Automobile Works has been approved to produce the Charade under Daihatsu license. It proved to be a product which, due to its price rather than to its quality, quickly competed against the Santana. Today, Toyota participates in a joint venture founded in 2000 and maintains more than two dozen companies in the supplying segment.

- In the meantime, another two small car producers from Japan have entered the market with some help of clever local government authorities, but without any approval from the central government: Fuji Heavy Industry produces the Subaru in Guizhou province (licensed construction) and Suzuki produces the Alto in China's largest city Chongqing (licensed construction in the beginning, since 1995 construction in the Chang'an Suzuki joint venture).

The partly uncontrolled development has led to excess capacity in the automobile industry. This trend has deepened as state authorities base their five-year plans on fixed quantities rather than on actual demand. In addition, since the mid-1980s they have had to deal with millions of 'grey imports', mainly from Japan. The value of these cars was about three times higher than the overall investment of all automobile producers and suppliers together. With the exception of Shanghai Volkswagen and their respective suppliers, the remaining companies in the beginning generated hardly any profits. The siutation was similar in the production of buses, commercial vehicles, and trucks, again with some exceptions (e.g. FAW). Too many companies, old technology, bad quality and poor services impeded the sector's healthy development.

The Role of Government Control in the Development of the Automobile Industry

Right from the start, central and local authorities exerted influence on all projects with foreign participation. In particular, they focused on capacity, investment and project upgrading, finance and foreign exchange, product range, export and import, local content, ex works and retail pricing. Hence, they established a tight net of licensing procedures and general provisions at national and province levels – a highly opaque bureaucracy for outsiders. Nevertheless, projects which were not officially approved and, in most cases, not even economical, spread all over the country, with or without foreign participation, in the production and the supply industries. Some were simply set up as 'forger businesses', seeking their profits particularly in the grey spare part market by using brand names such as 'VW' or 'Audi' illegally. It should be mentioned here that, contrary to frequent citations, the so-called 'Little Red Flag' by FAW does not belong to these fake products; it is a contractual production of the Audi 100 after the phasing out of the licensing agreement. Audi even supplies CKD parts to the project.

On the suggestion of the Ministry of Mechanical Engineering (MMI), which at the time was in charge of the automobile industry, the central government felt obliged to react in 1994. The 'Industrial Policy for the Automotive Industry' (issued by the State Planning Commission on 19 February, 1994, and approved and published by the State Council on 3 July, 1994) has been the first attempt to formulate a comprehensive policy framework for a specific sector. It contained the following objectives and measures:

- developing China's automotive industry and turning it into one of the pillars of the national economy by restructuring the sector and improving the research and development (R&D) capacities of the manufacturers;
- achieving at least 90 per cent market share for locally manufactured cars by 2000;
- concentration on and consolidation of the national industry in two steps: first, by 2000, to support two to three companies to grow faster and become competitive 'large' groups and to support six to seven companies to become 'backbone' companies, and second, before 2010, to encourage 'large' and 'backbone' companies to link up and form three to four groups with international competitiveness;
- balancing foreign exchange (exports);
- giving high priority to developing local content successively reaching 40, 60, 80 per cent within three years;
- supporting companies with R&D facilities;
- providing protection for national car manufactures against SKD assembly (limitation) and FBU (fully built-up) imports (quotas);
- promoting private ownership of cars;
- extending maximum equity to 50 per cent for foreign partners in automobile joint ventures.

Although these policy guidelines brought some improvements, e.g. progress in local content production, a further expansion of the supply industry and a stronger commitment towards R&D activities within the companies (for example the R&D centre of Shanghai Volkswagen including a test track, or the Pan Asia Technical Automotive Centre Shanghai GM), the main policy objectives could not be implemented efficiently. This was largely due to conflicting interests at the central government level, and even worse at the local level. Regional and local egoisms (however understandable) led to a concentration of supply industries close to the manufacturers' locations. The policy as stipulated in the guidelines thus failed. It did not encourage investment in companies with a reasonable output. As a result, they were not able to supply as many producers as possible with parts, components or spare parts as originally intended. Even the projected co-operations, e.g. between SVW and FAW–VW for engine production, which aimed at preventing the creation of two indistinguishable factories producing the same engine, never came into being. Investments of 100 million DM could have been saved. Daimler Benz experienced a similar fate when it planned to put up a family-van production plant in South China. As two locations in two different provinces (Guangdong, Hainan) were taken into consideration, a clash of regional interests was predetermined which even the central government was unable to solve.

Furthermore, the central government changed its principles and respective responsibilities over and over. At the end of 1994 the Ministry of Mechanical Engineering invited the world's leading automobile producers to a well organised exhibition ('Family car, World Development & China's Strategy Presentation Seminar and Exhibition') to get hold of the latest information on automotive development in Western countries. In the end, however, the attending managers, with most of them having presented expensive project-cars for the Chinese market, were disappointed as they had misunderstood the event as an international bidding for the production of a family car.

Later on, and supposedly under the impression of the costs of private car ownership which was still ten times the average annual income, the government presented a new slogan: 'housing before (buying private) cars'. The slogan implied that former experiments with financing private cars (loans, leasing) were being brought to a halt again. Also, from 1997 to 2000, priority was given to urban public transport development.

In spite of state regulations, provinces and large municipalities such as Shanghai or Chongqing continue to attract new automobile projects, no matter whether these might contradict existing regulations or the five year plans or not. Hundreds of new companies with foreign participation have been put up, partly without government control. Even worse, cities and provinces with automobile production have started to protect their industries by means of special fees.

Last but not least, administrative responsibilities for the automobile industry have changed repeatedly. Since the last round of reorganizations, the central government and the 'State Administration of Machine-Building Bureau', a subdivision of the 'State Development Planning Commission' – itself a result of a merger between MMI and further former ministries – are now in charge of the sector.

Due to this development, the central government was again forced to react. Surprisingly, it did so in accordance with all relevant central commissions (planning, economy and trade), ministries (MMI, foreign trade and economic co-operation, public security) and public authorities (customs duty, industry and trade). They agreed on a directive for subordinate public departments (so-called *Guofa* 1997, No. 24) which brought into force 'Suggestions on Tightening the Administration of the Automotive Industry Project'. In addition, a revised version of the '1997 National Catalogue of the Manufacturers of Cars, Civil Specialized Vehicles and Motorcycles and their Products (General Catalogue)' was issued in early 1998. With these measures, the government wanted – at least on paper – to close the loopholes that had caused the fragmentation of the automobile industry. Without approval from the State Planning Commission or the State Economic and Trade Commission, nothing could be decided any more, even in the supply industry. For strategically important projects, even permission by the State Council was required. These measures might have been implemented with regard to WTO accession, whenever it eventually occurs. However, it was realized that billions of US$ of investments in the automobile sector would be lost if spent in an uncontrolled and vaguely targeted manner. Such a waste of money had to be prevented.

Summing up, one can say that, in comparison to other countries which entered automobile mass production after World War II such as Brazil, Mexico or South Africa, China has, with foreign assistance, developed its automobile sector as no other country has done within the last fifteen years. However, China has not succeeded – and maybe could not succeed in this rather short period – in establishing a powerful and competitive automobile industry meeting international standards in terms of price/cost relations, productivity/profitability as well as quality and service. Besides other factors, modest growth rates and the limited domestic market can be regarded as the main impediments. However, a few producers and suppliers have reached international standards with regard to productivity, technology, quality and profitability. This might be an encouraging sign for the future of China's automobile industry. The formation of the supply industry shows remarkable results, even if it might have been even more impressive without the local egoisms and the resulting tendency towards fragmentation. Producers as well as suppliers are only now starting to attempt to build comprehensive R&D facilities. Confronted with the protectionist and self-centred interests of the provinces, a thorough implementation of an over-all industrial policy and control of all automobile-related activities by the central government eventually had to fail.

These detailed facts have to be born in mind if one seriously wants to discuss the scope of and the need for action in China's automobile industry at the brink of WTO accession.

The Impact of WTO Accession

After bilateral negotiations between China and the USA in November 1999, the agreement reached with the EU in May 2000 and the approval of the US House of Representatives in May 2000 as well, China's way into the WTO is paved. The ongoing negotiations with Mexico and the discussion on the so called final protocol are merely technicalities and should not hinder the formal accession which is planned for the first half of 2001.

Like no other event since the 'open door policy' in 1978, China's WTO accession, the so-called second reform, will change the country and the national and international consequences can not yet be predicted.

In the following, the impact of WTO accession on the automobile sector is examined in some detail, focusing on the following questions: Which are the relevant WTO arrangements? What is the present situation of domestic competitors? What are the prospects for new competitors?

Relevant automobile agreements regarding China's WTO accession

The main provisions relevant for the automobile and supply industry were reached in the US–China agreement, while the EU–China agreement achieved only some minor improvements:

- Import duties on automobiles will decrease from the current 80–100 per cent to 25 per cent by 1 July, 2006.
- Import duties on automobile supply will decrease from the current 35 per cent or so to an average of 10 per cent by 1 July, 2006.
- Automobile quotas will be phased out by 2005. In the interim, the base level quota will be 6 billion US$ (the level prior to the start of China's industrial auto policy), and this level will grow by 15 per cent annually until elimination.
- Restrictions on trading rights (import and export) and on distribution (wholesaling, retailing, maintenance and repair, transportation) will be phased out over three years.
- Non-bank foreign financial institutions will be permitted to provide automobile financing upon China's accession.
- Restrictions in product policy (type, category, model) on automobiles produced in joint ventures will be phased out within two years of accession.
- The compulsory formation of joint ventures in engine production will be abolished and wholly foreign ownership permitted.
- The value level for automobile joint venture projects that is subject to approval will increase from the current 30 million US$ to 150 million US$ within two years of accession.

These are the formal arrangements which will create the basic framework for the automobile industry. Generally, they will lead to increasing price pressure and competition for producers and suppliers and, thus, to a consolidation of the fragmented and mostly inefficient market structures. Of course, this will not happen overnight, but only in the middle and long run. The necessary adjustments will be constrained by limited capacity to implement WTO rules. All in all, 170 economic rules, the entirety of commercial law, need to be adjusted to international standards. Although the Chinese government is committed to such changes one should not, as past experiences tell us, overestimate its capacity to put structural changes into practice. Furthermore, the process will imply a difficult and even dangerous balancing act between compliance with WTO rules on the one hand, and the need for control of the social impacts of WTO accession in the country. No government in the world would survive millions of redundant labourers released in the automobile industry. Hence, the West should not demand too much of China, as this would not be to anybody's advantage. Rather, we should attune to a longer transitional period as envisaged in the WTO rules. There is no reason why the Chinese should abandon something they have achieved through hard work and billions of dollars of investment in automobile and supply industries. This cannot even be in the interests of foreign investors. Looking at examples such as South Korea or Malaysia one can get an impression of how the future might look. Despite its twenty year membership of GATT/WTO, South Korea is still restricting automobile imports through non-tariff barriers. Also, Malaysia still refuses to open up its market for cars and car components in order to protect its industry, despite the arrangements made in the Asia Free Trade Agreement (AFTA). Of course, this is not a call for protectionism, but for a realistic overall assessment of probable future trends.

What is the present situation of domestic competitors?

Those producers who are already well-established in the Chinese market have to analyze how to secure their market position in a changing environment along the value-added chain from product development to sales. Probable changes in monetary policy are a crucial factor here. On the one hand, one cannot eliminate the possibility of a (gradual) devaluation of the Renminbi (RMB), particularly so as the Chinese government stabilized the currency's external value against the US dollar during the Asian crisis. On the other hand, it is likely that the Chinese currency will become fully convertible after a few years. In economists' terms, the RMB is convertible on the current account but not on the capital account. Imports and exports as well as investment will be affected by these factors. However, suitable measures will differ between producers:

- Market leader Volkswagen can claim that both joint ventures, Shanghai Volkswagen and FAW–Volkswagen, are basically producing according to world market conditions with regard to production technology, quality and productivity (2000: more than 250,000 cars in SVW, 90,000 VW Jetta and 17,000 Audi A6 in FAW–VW). The same is true for engine and gear production. FAW–VW is already exporting its products.

  In the middle car segment SVW performs with the Passat. The VW top model has been specially lengthened for the Chinese market. New investment worth 1.6 Billion Euro has been announced for the period until 2005 (Bora, Polo). By then, the car market may have grown to 1.2–1.5 million units. Especially in the fast growing small car segment, VW wants to participate with a product specially designed for the Chinese market, probably based on the 'Lupo' model. This should happen through extensive utilization of the existing joint capacities. However, one will have to wait and see to what extent private demand will boost the market. According to a recent study by the 'China National Consumers' Association', 10 per cent of the urban population wish to purchase a private car in 2001, 16 per cent in 2002 and 70 per cent have plans to do so between 2002 and 2005. Of course, not every plan becomes reality, especially in China.

The main challenges remain in the supply industry. VW expects and demands from its suppliers a 30 per cent cost decrease within the next five years. This will not be easy, because Chinese suppliers still have to import more than two-third of the technology needed for new product development. This requires huge investments to be allocated in foreign exchange. At the same time the market will continue to grow, but the output quantities – looking at economies of scale – will remain modest. Additionally, the supply industry has to switch to a production process which does not supply single parts or components but ready sets (like doors or seats) and modules. This means that considerable efforts will have to be made with regard to product development, quality and logistics. It remains uncertain whether producers will be able to switch to alternative international suppliers to purchase at low costs wherever possible. It cannot be expected that the Chinese government will suspend its local content requirements (40/60/80 per cent) overnight – the domestic supply industry would not survive such a sudden step. It seems more likely that local content regulations will be phased out gradually in order to facilitate a profound structural change. VW estimates that only 40 per cent of today's suppliers will meet the required standards in the future. As a consequence, mergers, insolvencies and new formations will remain on the top of the agenda. Therefore, it might be helpful if producers provide global delivery and service systems to their Chinese suppliers – as VW has announced it is to do with its 500 suppliers. Only in this way will supplier companies have a realistic chance to reach the quantities necessary to produce competitively.

Besides, after WTO accession the protectionist Chinese tax system will have to be modified. This could lead to a downward trend in prices, too. With regard to Shanghai, for example, this will mean the loss of a 15,000 RMB (about 5.500 DM) surcharge for every car not produced in the city.

Moreover, additional efforts will be necessary in sales, marketing, service and distribution. Here, WTO accession will offer new opportunities for which VW is well prepared: An independent marketing organization is on its way, and a financial service facility promoting financing and leasing is available through a representative office located in Beijing.

- Similar efforts can be attached to Audi which is part of the VW group with a 10 per cent interest in FAW–VW (VW: 30 per cent). Audi produces a lengthened version of the A6 for the Chinese market. Within the premium segment, which is also covered by GM's Buick and Honda's Accord, Audi has a market share of more than 30 per cent. This year, Audi wants to sell over 20,000 cars, and sales should increase to reach 30,000 cars per year in the near future. As this market segment is less sensitive to price changes than the middle range segment and will grow further in the years to come, the future prospects seem very promising here. Optimistic expectations might indeed be reasonable as, even after a reduction of import duties to 25 per cent, comparable foreign products will still be more expensive than domestically produced cars (as long as the importing companies insist on their profits). The prospects are less certain for imported Audi top models such as the Audi A8 and the sports car Audi TT.
- Peugeot, too, will try to readjust its product range. There are plans to offer the well-known Xantia in a lengthened version in the price segment between 35,000 and 40,000 US$ on the Chinese market.
- General Motors, jointly producing with the Volkswagen partner SAIC Buicks and sharing a joint platform for a passenger van, intends to enter the apparently profitable lower segment. The company plans to launch a compact car based on the Opel Corsa and named 'Sail' priced around 100,000 RMB (12,000 US$), quite below the price of the Santana, the car sold most at present. This would mean, to produce a third car in the same Shanghai factory, a difficult manufacturing challenge. A

newly announced plan to buy a 34 per cent share of the 'Liuzhou Wuling Automobile Co' based in the southern province Guanxi seems more promising as this would allow GM to get into the mini-van and small truck market, which is one of the major growth segments.

- Ford Motor company which at present only participates in a minor light commercial vehicle production (Transit) in Jiangxi province, also wishes to enter the lower market segment. However, one has to wait and see whether the plan of the compact car 'Ikon' which Ford launched as a small car for Asian markets can be realized. The preferred partner for this project, Chang'an Motor Corporation in Chongqing, already produces a small car together with Suzuki – Suzuki, in turn, is a partner of GM.

- Concerning the plans of Mazda, an affiliate of Ford Motor Co., it is also too early to make any assessments. Mazda wants to produce the mini-van 'Premacy' in cooperation with the First Autoworks Hainan from 2004 onwards, with a starting capacity of 20,000 units. It is questionable whether Mazda will be more successful than Mercedes Benz who tried to break into Hainan and Guangdong simultaneously in 1995.

- Daewoo is prepared to start the production with the car 'Matize' priced around 133,000 RMB (16,000 US$).

- Last but not least, Toyota deserves some attention. As has been announced, the company wants to compete in the lower market segment, too, and is preparing to produce the subcompact car 'Vitz', known as 'Yaris' in Europe, from 2002 onwards in cooperation with their joint venture partner, the Tianjin Automotive Industry Corporation (TIAC) in Tianjin. Toyota is well experienced in joint engine production (joint venture) in Tianjin and has rarely started something which was not crowned with success

- Wholly Chinese products, such as the 'Zhonghua' offered by the Shenyang Gold-Cup Auto-Making Company in the lower price segment (18,000–24,000 US$), stand little chance of success. From an international perspective, cars are far too complex products to be competitively introduced to the market offhand. This situation will not change over the next six to ten years, as we know from experiences with Chinese partners.

We tend to forget that most of the value added within automobile production is generated by the supply industry and not by the producers. Both are tied in a kind of risk community. If one part fails the other faces hardship, and vice versa. This is especially true for China. The obstacles surrounding WTO accession can only be solved collaboratively.

Opportunities and risks for new competitors

Given the existing overcapacity, the prospects for new competitors in the automobile market are linked with considerable risks. This is true especially because both Chinese partners and Chinese authorities usually support well-established companies in a different way from that with which they treat possible newcomers – in particular in a difficult environment such as the automobile sector. Of course, producers like Daewoo, Kia or even Ford who have already conducted some preliminary work in the supply industry, will be able to count on Chinese support. Yet, the quantitative development of the automobile market does not invite anybody to build up new production capacity, even if one takes the most optimistic data of 1.5 million units in 2005. In addition, anticipated attacks against the VW hegemony will hardly create any new room for manoeuvre. However, this scenario will without doubt change after 2005 if a stronger middle-class with a higher spending power boosts demand for automobiles.

The situation is completely different for car importers from neighbouring countries. With WTO accession, they expect a decrease in import duties and an increase in import volumes. As already mentioned, this practice would have hardly any impact on the price development in the luxury segment unless single importers abandon their present price policy and start to 'buy' market share. Of course, this would lead to difficulties for domestic suppliers. It is not clear how much of a price increase the customers are willing to accept. Will they buy a Mercedes, BMW, Audi, Jaguar, Lexus or Porsche 'whatever the price'? The Hong Kong market at least, where prestige and luxury are more important than prices, may underline more optimistic assessments.

The real battle will be fought in the medium and small car segment as the decrease in import duties to 15 per cent could lead to a situation where Chinese customers will prefer imported rather than domestic products, even if the imported car is slightly more expensive. Here, it will be crucial whether and how quickly domestic producers and suppliers manage to produce at comparable prices and quality. It is doubtful whether this can be done by 2006, the more so as tried and tested Korean dumping practices against China are likely to continue. This is especially true for parts and components. The outcome of the battle fought on the import market is not predictable, and even less so as it will very much depend on the literal interpretation of the WTO rules. One assumption, however, seems obvious: the Chinese government will not let those projects down which it has hitherto supported or tolerated, above all, because of the social and political costs that would be likely to follow.

However the development of the Chinese automobile industry looks, it certainly will rely on additional inflows of Western technology and know-how. Market liberalization in the segments of financial services and distribution will provide further opportunities for foreign investment.

Conclusion

China's WTO accession will enhance the long-needed structural consolidation of automobile production and supply. The necessary – sometimes profound – adjustments will not be based on government decisions derived from individual cases but on indirect market-induced developments and on market forces in general. As long as international competitiveness of the existing companies remains unattained, protectionist measures will continue. However, this seems to be tolerable. In contrast, protectionism within China will be phased out shortly after WTO accession. The nominally slow growth of demand, lack of efficiency and existing overcapacity, will not entice further foreign producers to enter the Chinese market until the middle of the decade.

Noticeable turbulence might appear in the lower car segment, because here foreign importers could position themselves quite easily. New opportunities appear 'around the car', with some prospects for domestic factories and companies. Regarding foreign investors, market entry under WTO rules will be more predictable and more reliable. Of course, the China specific risks will remain. However, the greatest risk might be *not* to be in the biggest market of the future.

Appendix

Figure 1: PR China - Locations of Chinese car producers with foreign partners

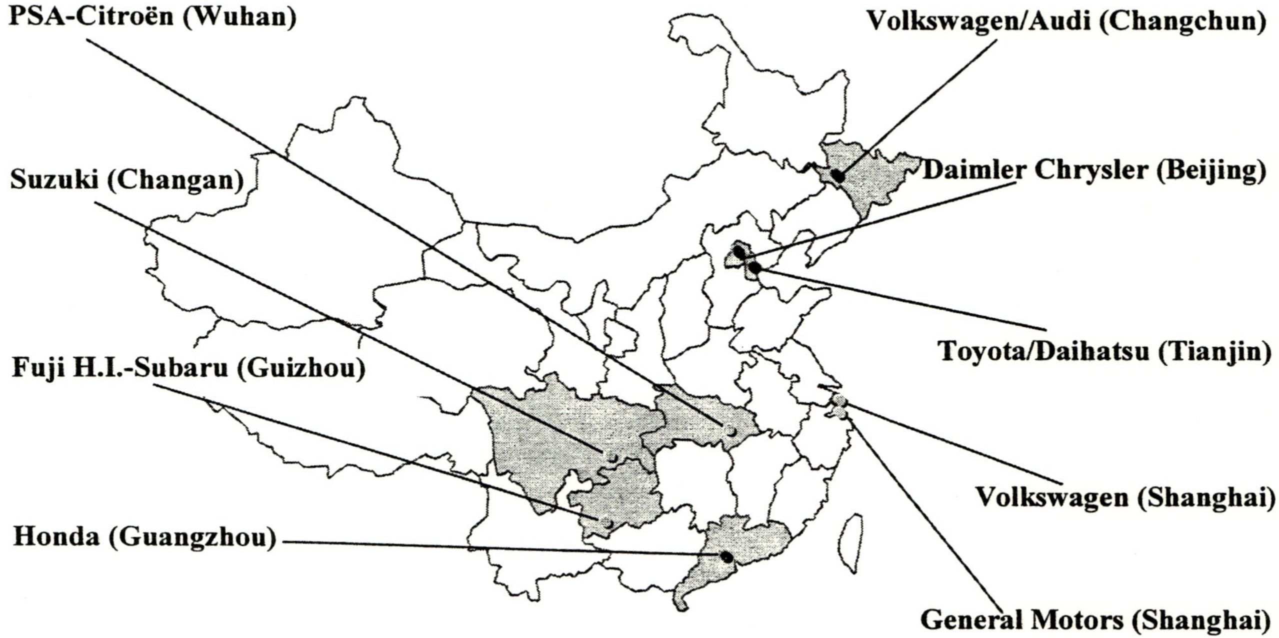

Figure 2: Composition of China's vehicle output

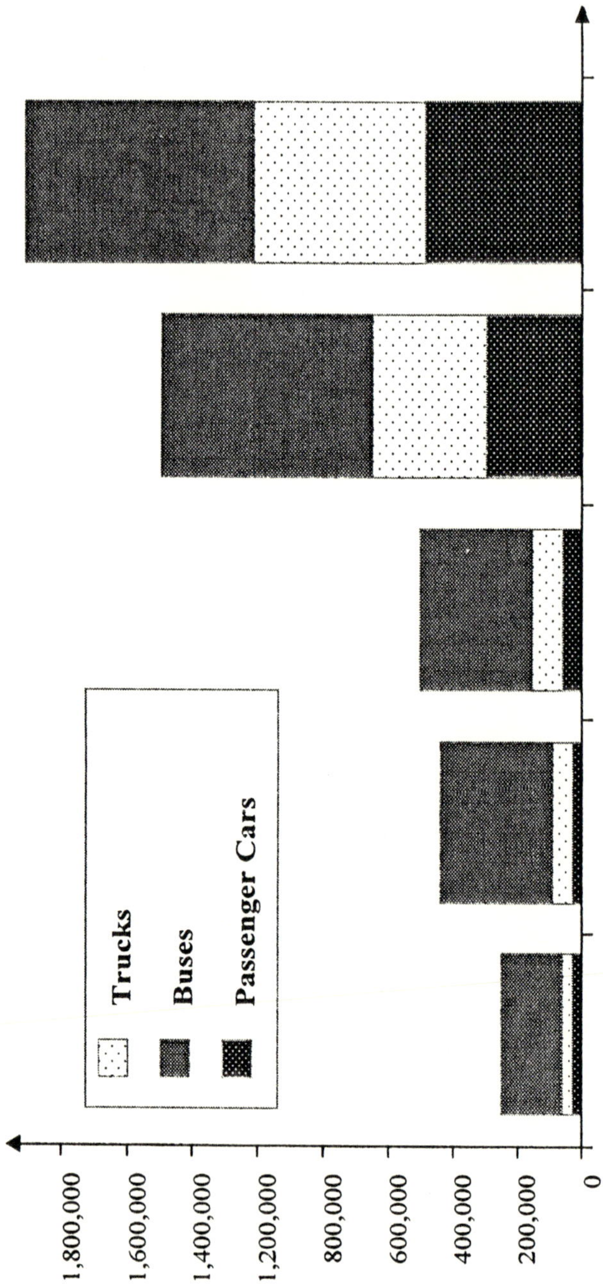

Figure 3: China: Passenger car production 1985–99

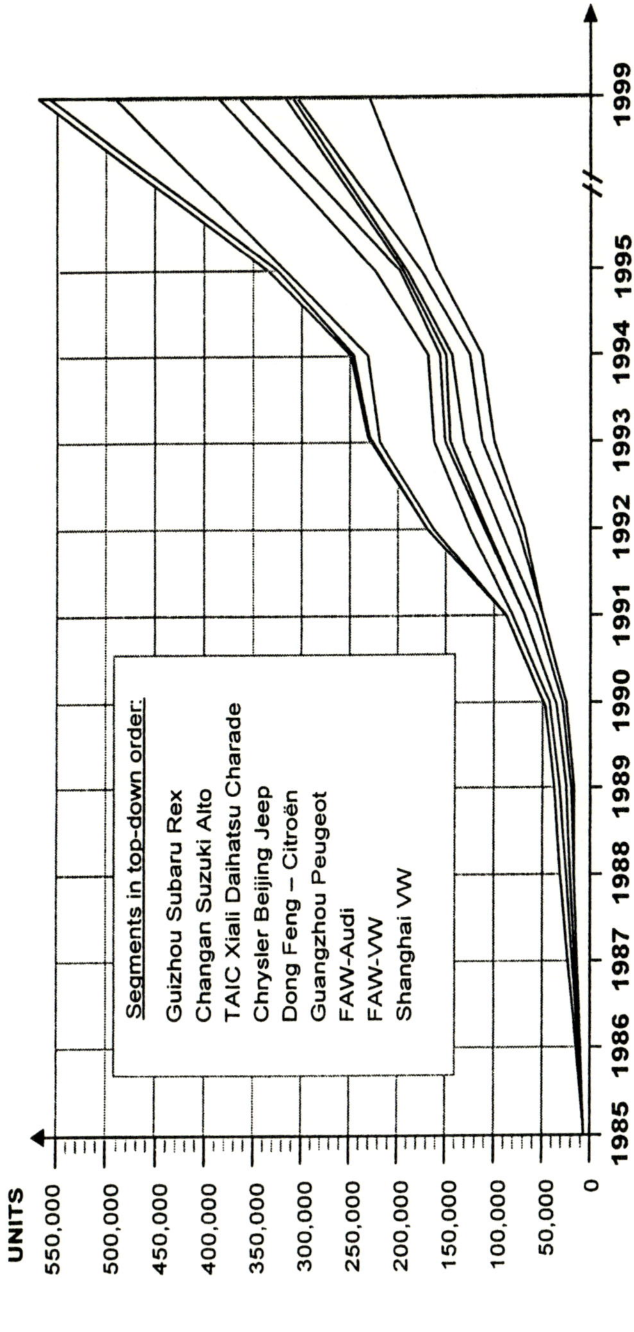

5

The Telecommunications Sector

Jürgen Oberg

The Current Situation

The telecommunications sector is a highly sensitive area in China. Since the sector is regarded as being of strategic importance for the national economy, the Chinese government is only reluctantly opening it – or at least the operator side – to foreign companies.

During the past decade, telecommunications have developed extremely rapidly in China. The sector has become one of the key pillars of the country's economic and technological growth. Over this period, the Chinese government has invested enormous sums in building up a modern telecom network. In doing so, it permitted foreign business partners to set up modern production facilities in the country – in the form of Chinese-foreign joint ventures and wholly foreign owned companies. This development led to extensive technology transfers as well as to the substantial training of Chinese partners in the areas of production and management.

For most foreign manufacturers, it was clear from the beginning that only substantial local presence could ensure an adequate market position over the long term. The situation is quite different in operations and services, where foreign telecoms have not yet succeeded in achieving a breakthrough in China. The current situation in the telecom industry can be roughly described as a structure controlled by the Ministry of Informations Industry (MII) which functions as the regulator that allows 'managed' competition among six local operators: China Telecomm (Fixed Line & Data), China Unicom (Fixed Line & Data), China Mobile (Mobile Services), China NetCom (Data Services), Jitong (Data Services), and China Railway Telecom (with the Ministry of Railways holding the majority of shares) which was added on December 26, 2000. For a while, so-called China-China-foreign operations could circumvent these exclusively local operations, but they have been prohibited again.

In the manufacturing sector, the Telecom Administration Bureau of the MII is responsible for the licensing of all types of telecom equipment. Chinese partners profit from the development of local manufacturing capacity by foreign companies, increasing sales on the domestic market as well as exports. This, in turn, generates the foreign currencies needed to modernize Chinese manufacturing equipment and processes.

The State Development Planning Commission and the MII set quotas for all wholly foreign-owned enterprises as well as Chinese-foreign joint ventures, a practice intended to give local companies the possibility to strengthen their own market positions. This is especially obvious in the production of mobile phones in China, in which Motorola, Nokia, Ericsson and Siemens dominate the market. To enhance the competitiveness of local companies, the Chinese government encourages banks to provide loans to operators who purchase domestic products. Operators are encouraged to purchase from local suppliers.

Consequences of China's WTO Accession

In view of the current status quo in China, it is especially interesting to consider the possible consequences of China's WTO accession on its telecom industry. What kind of impact will China's accession have on foreign telecom manufacturers and operators?

The short term

Looking at the short term first, the most immediate impact will be that trade-related investment measures such as local content and technology transfer requirements will be eliminated upon accession. The same holds true for trade and foreign exchange balancing requirements.

Non-tariff barriers such as quotas will be phased out around 2002. Foreign equipment suppliers will enjoy tariff reduction benefits. The engineering services and systems integration business will profit most from this change. The service sector will gradually open up to foreign operators. 49 per cent foreign ownership will be permitted in value-added services, and 25 to 35 per cent in mobile services.

The medium term

In the medium term – that is, three to four years after China's accession to the WTO – foreign companies will enjoy the following advantages:

- Foreign telecom equipment suppliers will be granted full distribution and trading rights within three years after accession. Tariffs on most telecom products will be cut to zero. Foreign telecom equipment suppliers will further benefit from the reduction and elimination of non-tariff barriers.
- In the service sector, a 50 per cent foreign ownership will be permitted in value-added services, 49 per cent in mobile services and 25–35 per cent in wired services.

The long term

Over the long term – that is, five and more years after accession – the telecom market will have a substantially different appearance.

By 2005, all tariff cuts will be accomplished and foreign telecom equipment suppliers will enjoy zero tariffs on telecom and IT-related products. Foreign operators will be permitted to access 50 per cent in the value added services, 49 per cent in the mobile services, and 49 per cent in the fixed services markets.

In its negotiations with the US and the EU, China quickly saw that telecommunications play a much greater role for Europeans. It is no wonder, then, that they made greater concessions to the Europeans in this area than to the US. The Sino–EU agreement also covers telecommunications services and operations. China will open its mobile telephony market two years ahead of schedule. Maximal foreign ownership will be 25 per cent on accession, 35 per cent after one year, and 49 per cent after three years. Countrywide operations will be allowed. Also, the facility leasing market will be opened within three years.

Three dimensions of opening up

China's commitment as part of its WTO accession includes a complicated threedimensional schedule of market opening.

The first dimension is geographical: the market will first open in Beijing, Shanghai and Guangzhou, and for connections between these cities. At a later point, 14 additional cities will open, and ultimately the entire country.

The second dimension relates to specific telecom sectors. Value-added services will open up first, followed by mobile services and finally by wire line services.

The third dimension involves the percentage of foreign ownership allowed in value-added services. The figure is 49 per cent in the first year of accession and 50 per cent thereafter. For mobile services, the cap is 25 per cent upon accession, increasing to 35 per cent within one year of accession and finally reaching 49 per cent after three years. For wire line services, the cap will reach 49 per cent within six years of accession. Having abandoned its previous weapon of zero tolerance of foreign ownership of telecom services, the MII is now expected to use its power over licensing to exert its influence.

China's WTO accession is expected to ease licensing rules for foreign and domestic firms. However, vaguely worded portions of China's agreements with the US and the EU leave room for special restrictions on the size and nature of domestic partners available to foreign firms. This may effectively leave many of the current restrictions in place. The gradual reduction of imports tariffs on both finished products and components from as high as 14 per cent down to zero to three per cent will leave greater room for price reduction. The impact of China's WTO entry on export quotas and import licenses for raw materials and equipment is unclear. It is generally believed that these two control measures will have to be abandoned eventually, possibly after three years when domestic manufacturers have successfully established a foothold in the local market.

It is assumed that China's government will continue to use non-tariff measures – such as procurement policies and selection of standards – to control imports.

Conclusion

China's WTO accession will not solve all problems and disputes for the telecommunications industry and its players. However, we can assume that international rules of the game will have far greater relevance to China's telecom sector than they had in the past.

Since China will continue to demand open global markets for its own companies and products, it will presumably comply with the signed agreements – though probably later than sooner. It will, therefore, certainly be necessary to call on the country now and again to keep its word. Ultimately, of course, this is in China's own interests in the global market.

6

The Insurance Sector

Hans-Jörg Probst

China's Changing Approach Towards Opening the Insurance Market

The conclusion of bilateral agreements between China and her main trading partners on the terms of WTO accession finally set the scene for China's integration into the world business community. Although some of the terms and commitments are still subject to clarification and technical details need to be settled there is strong confidence that the world's largest emerging market will soon be represented in the World Trade Organization.

In accordance with the general platform for WTO membership, China's accession terms include detailed commitments for broader admission of foreign financial services. The previous 'experimental stage' of market opening for foreign insurers will be superseded by a transitional period of three to five years before domestic and foreign competitors are able to offer insurance services on an equal footing.

From the perspective of foreign investors, China's commitments clearly represent a compromise between the desirable market liberalization and the current capacity of China's domestic market to endure extended competitive pressure amidst an ongoing process of re-engineering the entire sector.

However, foreign investors will also appreciate the positive evolution in China's approach towards opening the insurance sector. In historical perspective there have been various stages of discussing this issue in China with opinions ranging from outright rejection to qualified approval. Today, the implicit advantages of gradual liberalization for the country's insurance market are more or less accepted.

During the first stage of policy discussion, between reintroducing commercial insurance in China's economy in 1980 and the admission of the first foreign competitor in Shanghai (American International Group, AIG) in 1992, the predominant political position assumed that an admission of foreign insurers would have no positive effects on China's foreign economic relations while constituting a threat for the domestic market. At that time foreign investment was generally seen as a mere tool for technical renovation of China's backward industries. Consequently, a training manual published in the 1980s stated that

> [...] during the early developmental stage of the national insurance industry as well as during a relatively long period thereafter [the government] should conduct a protectionist policy towards foreign countries and should not permit foreign insurance capital to intrude into the insurance market of our country.[1]

Even after the first foreign insurer had already been admitted to do business in China a publication by the former monopoly insurer, the People's Insurance Company (PICC), in 1992 still underscored this position:

> As opposed to other commercial activities the insurance sector can fully rely on its own market. Whether or not the insurance market is opened for foreign countries will not have significant influence on foreign trade or the absorption of foreign capital. An opening of our insurance market at this stage would generate more disadvantages than advantages.[2]

The admission of the US insurer AIG in Shanghai in 1992 marked the beginning of the second stage of the discussion. It did not result in a complete abandonment of earlier reservations. During this stage Chinese practitioners and academics critically observed the performance of AIG who had temporarily gained complete control over the Shanghai life insurance sector (with a 91 per cent market share)[3] through distribution of policies by insurance agents – a method previously not used in the PRC. Although the AIG's market share in Shanghai soon dropped to 38 per cent (1996) and 20 per cent (1997), and domestic companies emulated the agents' system during the following three years, there remained a distinct feeling of inability to cope with large foreign competitors.

When the central government licensed more foreign insurers between 1994 and 1997 for business in Shanghai and Guangzhou, it had become obvious that the course of 'opening China's doors' already included admission of foreign financial services – at least as an 'experimental' feature. In this situation, the discussion began to focus on strategic goals, selection criteria, pace and regional scope of opening the market. In essence, it was now recommended continuing the slow pace of market opening, but to confine its purpose to technical know-how transfer. For the selection of companies it was recommended that preference should be given to competitors from Hongkong and Taiwan – or companies otherwise owned by ethnic Chinese – as opposed to international insurance conglomerates. The former were perceived as relatively small, but technically competent companies which could be more easily integrated and controlled due to their Chinese background, their political dependence and the limited capital base.[4] This position clearly displayed narrow and short-term sectoral interests. It largely ignored the fact – which must have influenced governmental thinking in Beijing – that global insurance conglomerates (like AIG) maintain comprehensive networks in world politics and among industrial investors interested in China. Subsequently this approach was quickly overtaken by economic reality.

Nevertheless, some of the proposals entered practical politics of the People's Bank of China (PBoC) in summer 1998. After licensing a wholly foreign-owned life insurer (American International Assurance, AIA) and three joint ventures with 51 per cent foreign shareholding between 1992 and 1997, the government now reversed its position on insurance joint ventures. Future joint ventures would not be approved with a foreign majority shareholding. The People's Bank of China now preferred foreign minority shareholding in domestic insurance companies at the level of 5 per cent for any individual investor and 25 per cent as total foreign investment as the main form of market admission. This was expected to result in transfer of capital and technical know-how without significant influence on domestic management control. It was also generally recommended know-how transfer should be achieved through employment of individual foreign experts in crucial technical assignments (such as actuaries) rather than increasing competitive challenges by admitting more companies.

The conclusion of the Sino–US agreement in November 1999 again created new facts for China's domestic insurers. An editor of the trade magazine 'China Commercial Insurance' probably adequately summarized prevailing emotions at the time by critically noting that 'the asking price fixed in the Sino–US agreement on China's accession to the WTO is too high. It means that the further opening of our insurance market is neither the same as in other developing countries nor does it correspond with our previous opening policy.'[5]

The China Insurance Institute subsequently published a series of articles that served the dual purpose of providing the central government with ammunition for the forthcoming WTO negotiations with the European Commission (May 2000) and developing practical recommendations for how the insurance sector should prepare for the time after WTO accession. Apart from the general request to ensure China's treatment as a developing country, some authors proposed the imposition upper limits on foreign market share at the level of 5 per cent within the next five years and 10 per cent within the next ten years. In their view the central government should ensure an extended protective period for domestic life insurers during which only Chinese-controlled joint ventures are licensed and the current regional as well as product limitations for foreign competitors are upheld.[6] Non-life insurers argued against granting 'national treatment' to foreign competitors which, in their view, entailed 'extreme disadvantages' for a market with a history of state insurance monopoly.[7] However, the majority of authors in this series eventually suggested seeking 'truth from facts' and finding early solutions to the existing problems within the remaining time-window of three years.

Structure, Potential and Issues Surrounding China's Insurance Market

Genesis of China's market players

China's contemporary insurance industry[8] was established shortly after the foundation of the People's Republic as a state monopoly implemented by the PICC. However, after a brief period of only three years, during which the PICC and the PBoC jointly distributed insurance policies throughout the mainland, the sector increasingly fell victim to ideological campaigns. In Maoist economics insurance was considered redundant. Consequently, domestic insurance business was completely terminated in 1959 for almost 20 years, although some activities relating to foreign trade continued.

Following the Third Plenary Session of the CCP Central Committee in December 1978, which marked the beginning of reform and opening politics, the PICC was re-established in 1979 as a division of the PBoC. Its business focused on conventional property and transport insurance for other state-owned companies and reached a total volume of 290 million RMB in 1980. Two years later the PICC expanded its portfolio into life and agricultural insurance. Also in 1982 the PICC was legally separated from the PBoC and restructured into an independent (wholly state-owned) commercial company with a registered capital of 500 million RMB, which was increased to 1 billion in 1998. The PICC's approved product portfolio included property, life, liability, credit, agricultural and reinsurance. Meanwhile, its income from domestic business had quickly grown from 710 million RMB in 1982 to 8.6 billion in 1988.

In 1985 the State Council decided to liberalize the insurance market. This led to the establishment of a specialized state-owned agricultural insurer – the Xinjiang Bingtuan Insurance Corporation (1986) – and two joint stock[9] composite insurance companies, the Shanghai-based China Pacific Insurance Company (CPIC, 1987/1991)[10] and the Shenzhenbased Ping'an Insurance Company (1988). Ping'an was the first domestic insurer with some foreign minority shareholding (Goldman Sachs and Morgan Stanley – each with 6.77 per cent). However, the State Council decision unintentionally also sparked off an unwanted boom in unlicensed insurance undertakings during the second half of the 1980s, many of which were established by local administrations with little or no insurance proficiency. Subsequently, in early 1989, the State Council reiterated the authority of the PBoC as state supervisory authority, and of the PICC as the country's main insurer.

After a two-year period of political uncertainty which followed the events of June 1989, the central government in September 1992 approved the first foreign insurer in Shanghai, thus initiating a new stage in China's insurance history. The AIG, today one of the world's largest financial conglomerates, had originally been established in 1919 in Shanghai, but was forced to terminate business in the early years of the PRC. AIG received permission to establish two wholly foreign-owned branches for the separate local sale of life insurance (registered as AIA) to private citizens and non-life insurance (registered as American International Underwriters, AIU) to foreign-invested corporations operating in or from Shanghai municipality. Both licenses were subsequently extended to Guangzhou – the only other city that was then opened to foreign insurers.

Between 1994 and 1996 several new domestic insurers were established as joint stock companies, some restricted to local business in their registered regions (Shanghai: Tian'an Insurance Co. and Dazhong Insurance Co.; Shenzhen: Hua'an Insurance Co.; Xi'an: Yong'an Insurance Co.; all non-life insurers), others with approval for nation-wide business (Taikang Insurance Co. and Xinhua Insurance Co., both registered in Beijing for life insurance, Huatai Insurance Co., registered in Beijing for non-life insurance).

In view of the increasing number of registered insurers the lack of comprehensive insurance legislation proved to be a genuine deficiency. The previous system of regulation through occasional decrees published by the PBoC was no longer suitable to a market which was composed of companies with different forms of ownership. Consequently, the National People's Congress in 1995 adopted China's first contemporary insurance law. It regulates minimum standards for establishing and operating insurance undertakings and contains a set of rules relating to insurance contracts and consumer protection.

In 1997 the Chinese government began to intensify structural reforms of the country's major economic resources – the state-owned industries and the financial services sector. The reform concept for financial institutions included the separation of supervisory authority for banking, securities and insurance that had previously been concentrated within the People's Bank of China. Whereas the PBoC – as central bank – retained authority for the banking sector, two new commissions were set up as high-ranking governmental bodies reporting directly to the State Council: the China Securities Regulatory Commission and the China Insurance Regulatory Commission (CIRC, formally inaugurated in November 1998).

The establishment of the CIRC finally concluded the transfer of all practical supervisory competence, including product approval and market monitoring, to a specialized professional body which could effectively replace indirect market control through the PICC. In addition, the Chinese insurance law clearly stipulates legal separation of life and non-life business. These two factors subsequently led to the dismantling of the former monopoly insurer. The People's Insurance Company, which had already been structured into three separate sections for property, life and reinsurance managed under a joint executive body ('PICC Group'), was reorganized into four legal entities in 1998. While the property insurance branch retained the name PICC, the other companies were named China Life Insurance Company, China Reinsurance Company and – for international business – China Insurance Company (registered in Hong Kong).

As a result of restructuring the PICC Group there are now thirteen domestic insurance companies registered in China, nine of which are operating nation-wide. This number is likely to increase during the next five years. A five-year development plan for the Chinese insurance industry drafted in 1999 anticipates a total number of approximately fifty insurance companies by 2005, including foreign-invested companies and specialized domestic insurers covering agricultural and credit insurance. The plan also envisages changes in China's reinsurance business which is presently confined to China Re. This company is authorized to manage the 20 per cent compulsory reinsurance which licensed non-life insurers are obliged to place with China Re.

An insurance industry association was established in November 2000. It will act as self-governing body representing the interests of all (member) companies and may assume some market monitoring responsibility, such as the compilation of claims statistics and other vital business data that are indispensable for product design and risk management.

Market volume and potential

The total national gross written premium reached 139 billion RMB (16.8 billion US$) in 1999, representing an average annual growth of more than 30 per cent since 1980. Even though this rate primarily indicates the low business volume in the early 1980s, and actual growth rates declined significantly in recent years, the general dynamics of China's insurance market outpaced many other sectors of the country's economy. For the period from 2000 to 2005, the CIRC projects additional growth of more than 12 per cent per annum to 279 billion RMB (33.8 billion US$).[11] However, in view of the current limited own capital resources of most domestic insurers and the low level of regional penetration[12] the desirable continued fast growth can probably only be achieved by a larger number of nation-wide licensed competitors, a wider range of insurance products, more insurance intermediaries and improved conditions for access to capital markets for premium income investment.

At the current level the PRC is already the fourth largest insurance market in Asia (following Japan, South Korea and Taiwan). Insurance penetration (share of insurance premium income in the total GDP) reached 1.49 per cent (1998), and insurance density (total annual per capita spending on insurance) amounts to 11.4 US$.[13] On national average, these indicators are expected to reach 2 per cent – or 1517 US$ by 2005. In more advanced regional markets these figures have already been exceeded: in Shanghai Municipality insurance penetration reached 2.86 per cent and the annual average per capita insurance spending was 866 RMB (104 US$) in 1999. These figures were achieved by 17 insurers licensed in the city (eight Chinese, nine foreign).[14]

Since the mid-1990s market growth was mainly driven by life insurance business. The relative share of this segment reached 62.6 per cent (37.4 per cent property insurance) in 1999 and is expected to maintain a medium-term growth rate of 14 per cent throughout the period until 2005 (compared to 9 per cent for property insurance). Main regional sources of insurance business are the developed coastal areas in south and central China. In Shanghai, for instance, the market share of life insurance increased from 32 per cent in 1992 to 71 per cent in 1999.

China's non-life insurance market is dominated by conventional property, transportation and motor car insurance – which together constitute 95 per cent of the market. Motor insurance alone has a total national non–life market share of 58.7 per cent and achieved above average growth in recent years (8.96 per cent in 1999). However, only 14.95 million vehicles – i.e. one–third of China's total – were actually covered, which indicates significant future demand when motor vehicle third-party-liability insurance becomes compulsory.

Despite the introduction of a 20 per cent compulsory reinsurance the actual reinsurance business retained in China[15] only amounts to approximately 4 per cent of the total commercial reinsurance market volume. This is partially due to the limited underwriting capacity of China Re – which according to China's solvency regulations can only retain a risk volume of four times its registered capital (officially 33 billion RMB, but only 1.1 billion RMB was actually paid up after establishing China Re's business in 1996). 97 per cent of China Re's income is generated from the 20 per cent compulsory reinsurance and only 3 per cent comes from commercial reinsurance. The remaining non-compulsory business is contracted to foreign reinsurers.[16]

This situation also reflects the tightening domestic insurance competition in the late 1990s which temporarily led to a virtual 'price war' for market share causing wide-spread disregard of financial prudence and profitability. At that time, non-life insurance suffered from the cancellation of insurance programs by debt-burdened state-owned enterprises. Consequently, the non-life insurance market is now based on motor vehicle cover. The growth of life insurance also significantly slowed down following the decline in interest rates from 9 per cent to less than 3 per cent between 1997 and 1999. An increased number of insurance companies newly licensed between 1994 and 1996 now competed in a market with a declining growth rate. The situation was aggravated by the fact that the state-owned insurers of the former PICC Group retained an overall national market share of some 75 per cent. Ping'an and China Pacific, who managed to develop their own nation-wide distribution networks, achieved a combined market share of 23 per cent (13 per cent/ 10 per cent) while all other domestic insurers with fewer own capital resources jointly remained below 1 per cent (foreign market share also 1 per cent).

Subsequently, some domestic insurers sought to improve their own market position by underwriting beyond their own capacity while reinsuring up to 90 per cent of the risk with foreign companies ('fronting') through foreign brokers' representative offices in China. In 1999, the CIRC therefore conducted a 'rectification campaign' aimed at ending this practice. Since then at least 60 per cent of any risk (20 per cent compulsory reinsurance plus 50 per cent of the remaining risk) must be reinsured within China. This apparently prompted some foreign reinsurers to apply for licences in China. The CIRC, in turn, also indicated that China's own reinsurance capacity must be expanded by licensing more reinsurers.

In 1999, the CIRC for the first time approved three domestic insurance brokers. The Commission thereby recognized that the work of professional insurance intermediaries is particularly necessary in a country like China where little insurance awareness among industrial corporations as well as vast ignorance among private individuals constitutes a significant hurdle for avoidance of economic losses. In an international context industrial insurance business is already mainly based on the activities of brokers who can design custom-made insurance programs according to the actual needs of insurance clients. The future activity of brokers – and agencies – will become a significant element of quantitative and qualitative market development during the next decade.

China's future insurance market potential is difficult to quantify for individual business segments. However, current governmental reforms and the ongoing social transformation permit some general assumptions indicating major sources of future insurance demand:

Life, health and pension insurance

- Geographically, the main focus of life and health insurance will remain with developed coastal regions and large urban centres throughout the inner provinces, representing approximately one third of China's population. Governmental efforts to improve economic performance of Western regions may have gradual effects on disposable incomes for life and health insurance[17] in the medium term, but this will not fundamentally change the current regional business distribution for about another decade.

- In terms of customer groups the current business volume generated from private households will probably remain stable, consistently motivated by provision for old age, child education and health care. The high rate of savings (in urban China) and the limited availability of alternative financial products for private investment may encourage private households to invest more into life insurance if the range of products is expanded (e.g. unit-linked policies[18] or profit-sharing concepts). On the other hand, many urban families may be inclined to retain their savings in view of rising unemployment rather than making commitments for long-term premium payments. This marketing problem can be addressed through appropriate policy design (temporary suspension of premium payments).

- The volume of group life insurance is expected to increase as a result of restructuring the state-owned sector, which goes along with a reform of China's social security network. Governmental pension reforms are based on a three-layer concept, according to which the state will only guarantee a broad but basic level, while corporate pension schemes as well as private insurance are supposed to constitute the main part of pension provision. Likewise, responsibility for health care will be shifted towards commercially purchased group insurance and additional individual cover.

- China's fast-growing private sector – which had been completely excluded from the previous social security network – will become increasingly conscious of the need to provide employees with corporate benefit schemes that can be appropriately based on group life and health insurance contracts. Even though the number of private corporations entering the life and health insurance market may initially be limited, their political environment has improved as the government expects this sector of the economy to provide the main source of re-employment for redundant SOE employees. Private enterprises will have easier access to external sources of growth funding and will seek incentives for the recruitment of qualified employees.

- Foreign-invested companies are already obliged to accumulate reserves for corporate pension schemes which have to be professionally managed by insurance carriers.
- Even though governmental pension payments will constitute the smaller part of future old age provision in China, the absolute volume of funds accumulated for this purpose will be too large for direct governmental administration. Their management will require professional pension fund carriers which are not yet available in China.
- Finally, there will be a number of sizeable market niches relating to foreign investments in China or future overseas investments by Chinese companies. One niche is the market introduction of global corporate benefit schemes for expatriates integrated in international insurance programs for globally operating corporations. Other such niches are 24-hour-assistance and private medical services for frequent international travellers. There is already a clear demand for these services in Chinese cities with a high concentration of expatriates. Provision of such services requires specialized know-how as well as excellent local and international networks. This, again, could be provided by multi-national insurance corporations in conjunction with Chinese partners.

Non-life insurance (property, casualty, liability, marine, credit)

- The main future source of non-life insurance can be attributed to the reform of state-owned enterprises as well as the growth of the private sector. In either case professional technical risk handling will have to become a routine occupation of corporate management, especially in connection with external funding through commercial banks. Unofficial estimates assume that currently only about one third of China's manufacturing corporations are covered by any type of commercial insurance – a ratio that will certainly increase in the future.
- In addition to conventional insurance services a number of Chinese companies which are exposed to particular technical hazards may also be interested in preventive risk consulting provided by insurance carriers, because this service will help to contain potential physical and financial losses.
- Foreign direct investments will continue to grow and, as at present, remain a major source of non-life insurance business.

The technological level and financial scope of individual investment projects is likely to increase – as in the case of the Transrapid high-speed train in Shanghai – and previous investments are upgraded – as in the case of Volkswagen.

- Demand for commercial export credit insurance and product liability insurance is expected to emerge as a result of China's drive to expand exports to partner countries in Europe or North America. In view of substantial losses incurred in Asia and the USA during the past decade, the Ministry of Foreign Trade and Economic Co-operation (MoFTEC) and the CIRC have initiated the establishment of a state export credit insurance authority to cover long-term investment risks.[19] As the capacity of this authority is limited and the majority of export risks are short term risks, MoFTEC is also encouraging the introduction of commercial export credit insurance, which in the past has only been utilized by 1 per cent of China's exporters. In addition to credit risks Chinese exporters are also facing quite stringent product liability regulations in their main target markets. Chinese exporters are particularly aware of their high risk exposure in North America.

- Consistently important sources of insurance and reinsurance business are China's infrastructure and energy development programs. Large-scale insurance programs are required for projects like the Three Gorges Dam or nuclear power plants in Southern China that are projected to become operational during the next few years.

- Finally, commercial housing and increased material wealth of Chinese households will lead to an increase of this market segment in property and liability insurance.

China's central government is clearly interested in a commercial insurance sector able to absorb some of the former state obligations in corporate or private risk coverage. However, most of China's domestic insurers are not yet in a position to fully meet all the implicit requirements during the short period of time within which the central government plans to complete economic reforms. This may have contributed to the recent government approval of improved investment conditions and capital sourcing for Chinese insurers. It may also have influenced concessions which the PRC made during WTO accession negotiations.

Current development issues among Chinese insurers

In China's reform program, the development of a modern and professional financial market system has very high priority. Consequently, throughout the two years of its existence China's Insurance Regulatory Commission has been very active in identifying structural market problems as well as corporate management deficiencies existing in many domestic insurance companies. The Commission initiated a number of new regulations based on international standards and actively involved international organizations – such as the OECD Insurance Committee – as well as locally registered foreign insurers and representative offices in improving supervisory efficiency and product design in Chinese life insurance. It took some sweeping steps to eliminate irregular market practices and to tackle the traditional preoccupation with 'quantity' in Chinese economic life which originated from former state-planning methods and harmed risk consciousness among domestic insurers.

Despite these successful efforts, however, China's insurance sector still faces a number of complex developmental problems – which can only be broadly indicated in this paper – that will take time to resolve.

1. In many aspects China's insurers are held back by influences from outside their own sector. This particularly applies to the composition of China's capital markets as well as deficiencies in the country's legal environment – including commercial and liability regulations.

   In addition, specialized insurance supervision itself has only been in existence for two years and is still partially preoccupied with its own internal and regional organization and with supporting regular operational procedures in many of the younger Chinese companies. In more mature insurance markets supervision can largely be confined to controlling solvency and risk management of market competitors. In China, however, the CIRC is still in the midst of a process of establishing all the essential elements of the country's future market supervision. This includes the definition of regional responsibilities within its own network and the necessary extent of involvement in price and product management. Although rates are already permitted to fluctuate by 30 per cent in different regions, some domestic insurers are now suggesting the abolition of centralized control over insurance conditions and rates altogether ('floating rates') and requested the CIRC confine its activity to indirect supervision through solvency and profitability controls instead of 'administering' the market.[20]

Others proposed the transfer of some of the CIRC's current assignments, including market pricing, to an industry association.[21] However, the current level of proficiency in product design leaves the CIRC with little choice but to maintain closer scrutiny on a market without a comprehensive system of consumer protection or specific insurance contract law.

2. Although the companies of the former PICC Group managed to establish a significant number of local branches, there is still no comprehensive regional insurance network in China. The head offices of China's larger insurers sometimes find it difficult to manage their distant local branches and to determine the full extent of total risk exposure. Smaller companies – which are currently operating as regional insurers – cannot expand as fast as they wish to due to their limited own capital base which, in turn, restricts their underwriting capacity. In addition, the CIRC has not yet completely established its own regional supervisory network and therefore hesitates to admit additional local insurance branches.

   In view of China's forthcoming WTO accession some of the smaller regional insurers actually requested the CIRC grant them nationwide licenses – or at least approve additional local branches – before all regions with business potential are opened to foreign insurers. In order to overcome capital shortcomings they propose governmental permission for public listing as well as an 'internationalization' of their own capital funding (i.e. listing at foreign stock exchanges or absorbing additional foreign joint stock shareholders).[22]

   This general approach has also been underscored by China's state-owned insurers, particularly China Re. As they cannot expect further direct state funding (even though China Life requested this)[23] they have proposed a fundamental change in the shareholding structure in favour of joint stock funding or stock exchange listing.[24] In addition, China Re suggested as an alternative way of capital funding opening this company for shareholding by other insurers, thus killing two birds with one stone: generating access to additional capital and promoting business from shareholding investors. This idea comes close to the earlier concept of establishing a reinsurance pool in China, which had not been approved.

3. China's insurance statistics, particularly its claims statistics, are not complete. Although the insurance sector was re-established in 1980, reliable statistics are only available for the period since

1996. According to Chinese sources claims statistics – which are the point of departure for rate calculations – are only meaningful if they extend over a period of at least ten years, which is not the case in China.[25]

4. Until 1999 asset management options for insurers (admitted assets for investment of premium incomes) were confined to domestic bank deposits and treasury bonds. This restriction – designed to protect insurers and their customers from fluctuations on the capital markets and also to retain insurance capital within the country – actually caused serious problems for China's life insurers.

   At a time when bank deposits yielded 9 per cent interest or more in 1996/97 domestic insurers began to compete with banks for customers. Virtually ignoring the protective function of life insurance[26] in their marketing approach, they offered long-term life insurance policies as savings products with the same guaranteed interest rates as clients would have obtained if they deposited their funds with any of China's domestic banks. Subsequently, these policies had to remain in force when the Central Bank lowered interest rates within two years to less than 3 per cent, and when treasury bonds, irregularly available to nominated insurers, only yielded 4.5 per cent. Although the distribution of high interest insurance policies was quickly suspended and newly issued policies were adapted to the new bank interest rate level, there appeared an increasing gap between the high average interest rate level of the policy stock and rates that could actually be achieved in income investment. The problem was soon aggravated by a decreasing growth rate of new business. Policies of this type became less and less attractive as personal investments. Since 1998/99 Chinese life insurers have been facing potentially serious financial problems.

   The narrow limits of admitted assets also affect the financial stability of nonlife insurers. Compared to life insurance their business is short-term, more volatile and subject to potentially very high individual claims in industrial property or liability insurance. In the absence of high-yielding admitted assets, reliance on appropriate pricing as well as conventional risk management methods – such as reinsurance and coinsurance – is particularly necessary. This leaves little room for rapid growth and potentially reduces international competitiveness.[27]

   China's insurance supervisors have clearly recognized these concerns. The bankruptcy of a large Japanese insurer[28] at the time when problems in the Chinese insurance market became evident also contributed to a new thinking. As an initial reaction, the central government in 1999/2000 extended the scope of admitted assets to corporate bonds, indirect access to stock markets (through investment funds with up to 15 per cent of the investment portfolio) and participation in intra-bank lending. In addition, some companies received permission to develop and sell a new product with shared investment risks (low guaranteed interest, profit participation with the remaining investment yield). Unit-linked life insurance policies were also prepared for marketing.

To some domestic life insurers recent improvements have not gone far enough. They demand a further extension of admitted assets to real estate investment (which had already been unofficially utilized as investment in a concealed form) and direct purchase of shares. Additional proposals include permission to float own or joint investment funds at China's stock exchanges, shareholding investments in securities' companies, free negotiation of interest rates for bank deposits, loans to policy holders, cooperation with banks in retail banking or mortgage financing and, finally, establishing nationwide tax incentives for the purchase of life insurance policies.[29]

5. The lack of product diversity is a general problem not only for life insurance. Comparing the product range available outside China, domestic non-life insurers recognized the need to engage in more than a few conventional classes of business and to develop more flexibility towards specific circumstances of industrial clients. More conservative proposals include the introduction of general and motor vehicle liability insurance, credit and guarantee insurance as well as a full range of mega-risk coverage for hightech industries in oil production, aircraft/space technology and nuclear power plants. This approach seems particularly necessary in view of China's dynamic industrial development and export requirements. If Chinese companies did not serve these needs, foreign insurers certainly would. Subsequently, the Deputy Executive General Manager of Ping'an Insurance – a company based in Shenzhen, one of China's special economic zones, thus frequently permitted to venture into unknown territory – indirectly demanded not to cling to the previous method of integrating new technical risks into old standard policies but to design new policies for new risks such as computer viruses, hacker attacks, product liability for drugs, bodily injuries caused by mobile telephones, consequences of economic crime and infringement on intellectual property rights.[30]

6. Insurance distribution in China significantly improved in recent years, particularly after the AIG introduced an agent system in Shanghai in 1992. Problems remain in controlling the agents and in the speed or precision of processing insurance applications. Although agents have to pass an official examination before they receive a license to sell insurance, their commission payments are not clearly regulated. This has caused some concern, because in the highly competitive environment of a buyers' market agents have engaged in irregular, sometimes fraudulent, practices which could potentially lead to extensive bad risk exposure, cost inflation, loss of image or even disciplinary action by governmental authorities. New regulations on agents' administration and commission payments are currently under preparation at the CIRC. At the same time, some Chinese practitioners suggest replacing the current agent system, which is based on exclusive services of an agent for one company, with a system composed of agencies as intermediary businesses representing more than one insurer, and increase the number of licensed brokers or insurance consultants, both of which are new professions in China. In this way companies would be able to replace some of their fixed distribution costs by a flexible amount suiting the business level at the time.

   Some Chinese proposals focus on enlarging the cooperation with domestic banks, which could extend the distribution of life insurance policies to regions where the insurer has no branch or is not licensed for business. This approach also introduces the idea of providing non-insurance financial services to insurance clients, thus providing the company with a long-term option to develop into an all-finance conglomerate. Another current approach focuses on the application of new information technologies in insurance, such as accelerated introduction of e-commerce and call centres.

7. A number of current issues are related to insufficient management experience and technical know-how. The most difficult problem here is the shortage of insurance mathematicians and product designers (actuaries; marketing specialists). Supporting professions – such as specialized lawyers, auditors and analysts – are also difficult to find. Due to the scarcity of adequately trained personnel, salaries of highly qualified executives have experienced inflationary growth in recent years.

   Salary inflation has caused a particularly difficult problem for China's more established state-owned insurers. On the one hand, they are heavily overstaffed and their operating costs are very high. Economically they are forced to maintain a low salary level, but current politics will probably not permit them to shed redundant staff. On the other hand, they need to improve professionalism through external recruitment, which would have to be based on a flexible salary system independent of administrative interference from local labour bureaux.

The problem of rising salaries is also confronting non-state insurers and they, too, must have their salary structures approved by governmental bodies. This led some Jiangsu practitioners to request an 'untying' of the insurance industry from the Labour Ministry and the Ministry of Personnel. They also suggested increasing top level annual salaries to RMB 100,000 to 200,000 (which reflects salary levels of the Shanghai labour market in 1999).[31] Their approach includes the introduction of job rotation schemes – as practised by some foreign competitors in China – for improving exposure of managers to varying business situations and as an element of career planning which could be an incentive against high labour fluctuation.

8. Compared to domestic banks and – more significantly – to foreign direct competitors Chinese insurers are discriminated against through taxation. Whereas the rate of business tax for banks currently stands at 5 per cent, domestic insurers pay 8 per cent. The income tax rate for foreign insurers is 15 per cent, but Chinese insurers pay 33 per cent.

This list of problems is not complete. There are numerous 'smaller' issues standing in the way of improved competitiveness. They include local governmental interference with rates and conditions,[32] lack of co-ordination between various departments within one company to the detriment of customers as well as problems in loss adjustment and claims handling. However, most of them have been identified and addressed in public or during workshops convened by the CIRC. Resulting suggestions for improvement are presented in a pragmatic manner and reflect an awareness of international trends. It can be assumed that in future different Chinese companies will adopt different business strategies – if regulators are able to provide sufficient legal certainty. It also seems that a prolonged trial-and-error period in finding a 'Chinese way of insurance' can be avoided and that the process of adaptation to enlarged foreign competition within China may, indeed, not be longer than the adaptation of newly licensed foreign insurers to business in China.[33]

Foreign Insurers in China – Before and After China's WTO Accession[34]

Foreign representative offices

In 1999, 113 international insurance and broking companies from seventeen countries maintained more than 200 representative offices in the PRC. Most of them are located in Beijing, Shanghai and Guangzhou. A few foreign insurers established a network of representative offices which include regional centres like Wuhan, Changchun and Chongqing. The majority of representative offices were established during the second half of the 1990s when the first foreign insurers had started operation in Shanghai and it had become clear that the central government would open the country for foreign financial services.

Apart from familiarizing themselves with China's market conditions and developing some kind of dialogue with political decisionmakers, some of the representative offices actively engaged in know-how transfer activities for Chinese governmental institutions and domestic insurance companies. They provided information to China's legislators on insurance laws of their home countries and facilitated on-site familiarization with the operation of specific business classes and a wide range of corporate management issues in mature overseas markets for Chinese insurance sector delegations. Also, Chinese insurers did not find the doors closed in Western countries. For foreigners to be conscious 'corporate citizens' in some cases has also meant to invest into educational or other developmental projects in China, thus bearing in mind the public good of the host country.

To the extent permitted by local regulations foreign representative offices assisted Chinese insurers in obtaining international reinsurance cover – most prominently for large infrastructure projects, but also for key projects of foreign industrial investors. Foreign reinsurance engagement significantly extended domestic underwriting capacity and proficiency, thereby indirectly enhancing a constant stream of foreign direct investments over the past two decades.

Licensed admission

During the eight years of 'experimental' market opening a total of fourteen foreign insurers obtained governmental permission for market entry, eight of which have actually started operation. Another eleven European and Asian insurers expect permission in connection with

China's WTO admission. This would bring the total of foreign competitors to more than thirty compared to thirteen domestic carriers. The total market share of foreign insurers in all classes of business is still around 1 per cent, whereas the two state-owned insurers PICC and China Life retain a market share above 70 per cent.

According to current official regulations, foreign insurers qualify for licensing – apart from the minimum two year period of operating a representative office – if they have an uninterrupted corporate history of at least 30 years and assets in excess of 5 billion US$. These criteria were defined in connection with the admission of AIG into the Shanghai market in 1992 within a tentative set of rules for licensing of foreign companies. However, the actual application of these criteria soon became irrelevant in view of the large number of foreign insurers applying for market entry, as most of them could easily fulfil these rather simple criteria.

Subsequently, during the 1990s China's decisions on foreign insurers' market entry became increasingly opaque. Admission seemed to reflect the relative significance of the respective insurer's country of origin in the broader context of China's economic strategy as well as the current political level or climate in bilateral relations. There was also a clear effort to ensure an appropriate political balance among China's main foreign economic partners. Between 1992 and 1999 large companies from North America[35] (six), Europe[36] (six) and the Asia Pacific region[37] (two) received market admission – mostly on the occasion of special events in bilateral relations with the relevant insurer's country of origin. This approach clearly favoured insurance conglomerates with the best political network in their respective home country as well as in China, but not necessarily companies with a specific professional or technical profile. Final decisions on market admission were taken at the highest level of China's political leadership – and skillfully suspended when political clouds temporarily overcast bilateral relations.

After China's WTO accession the formal criteria for market admission of foreign insurers will not change. However, the Chinese government made a commitment that there will be no limitation in the number of licenses and that market admission will be approved on the basis of – yet to be defined – prudential criteria. This approach should guarantee transparency during the process of licence application. Current regulations, which enable the licensing authority to ignore applications,[38] will have to be amended in accordance with the final terms of WTO accession.

Regional scope of business

At present, Shanghai and Guangzhou are opened for foreign-invested insurance business, but market entry is only possible in one of the two cities. Business cannot be conducted outside the licensed city. In 2000, the CIRC adopted a regulation according to which it has become possible to conclude non-life insurance contracts for several locations throughout China if the clients operate their head office in the licensed location of the insurer. Coinsurance outside the licensed city is also permitted now. It has been legally possible to establish a branch of the licensed foreign company in another open city, but this requires a volume of 100 million RMB gross written premium – a level difficult to reach in a relatively limited market of only one city and with an additional confinement to specified market segments.

Among the two cities all current licensees have chosen Shanghai as first location of market entry. Only AIG managed to expand business from Shanghai to Guangzhou, followed by two sub-branches in Shenzhen and Foshan.

This situation will change fundamentally. According to China's WTO accession terms all geographical limitations will be phased out within three to five years as a result of two previous stages of opening more individual cities throughout China.

Admitted classes of business and market segments

At present, licensed foreign insurers may engage in either life or property insurance. The distinction between life and non-life (property) licences is stipulated by China's insurance law, but has also long been common international practice. Most admitted foreign insurers engage or intend to engage in life insurance (ten out of fourteen) and only two companies are or wish to be engaged in both life and non-life business (in two different registered companies) – the AIG (USA) and the Allianz Group (Germany).

Foreign insurance brokers are not permitted to conduct business in the domestic market – although one British-American company holds a licence for international reinsurance broking and insurance consulting services. Foreign reinsurance companies do not have formal access to the domestic market either, but there are no restrictions for their international business out of or into China.

In terms of customer groups, foreign life insurers are currently only permitted to insure private individuals – Chinese or foreign – who are registered citizens of the city for which the insurer is licensed.

They are not permitted to conclude group contracts with domestic or foreign companies or any form of health insurance. This means that the important segment of corporate benefit schemes through life insurance contracts is not accessible to foreign competitors. Non-life insurers, in turn, may only cover foreign-invested companies, but not Chinese individuals or corporations. Both life and non-life insurers are allowed to offer reinsurance in the class of business for which they hold a business licence.

Following China's WTO accession all these limitations will gradually be removed. Foreign insurance brokers will be admitted into the market as joint venture partners of Chinese broking companies. Foreign reinsurers will be able to take part in domestic business, thus complementing their previous engagement in providing international cover for Chinese insurance companies and increasing reinsurance capacities within China. Foreign life insurers will be able to offer group contracts – i.e. to conduct business with Chinese or foreign companies within the licensed region – within a few years after China's WTO accession. This will include an option to conduct pensions insurance. The health insurance market will be opened four years after accession. Non-life insurers may, in the future, also insure Chinese companies and generally enjoy national treatment – with the exception of compulsory motor car insurance (yet to be officially introduced) which will continue to be the exclusive domain of domestic insurance companies.

Legal form of incorporation

At present, foreign non-life insurers are already permitted to operate in China in the legal form of a wholly foreign-owned branch of the parent company, which is the form used by all foreign licensees since 1992.

Life-insurers, however, are obliged to operate in China as joint ventures (with the exception of AIA, a wholly foreign-owned branch). The original intention to force foreign companies to team up with a domestic insurer ('non-banking financial institution') was not always enforced. Only in one of the existing joint ventures are both partners insurance companies. Permanent adherence to this concept would have caused some difficulties, because the number of foreign life insurers admitted into the market already exceeds that of Chinese competitors. In addition, potential joint venture partners would have to share not only the registered capital but also any further capital increase, if necessary, during the course of business development. This consequence may be difficult to accept for many China's insurance companies. Those who decided to team up with a foreign insurer actually had to increase their own capital by finding additional shareholders before they were able to raise sufficient funds for their 49 or 50 per cent shareholding in the joint venture (minimum registered capital of a local insurer: 200 million RMB).

In terms of shareholding proportions within the joint venture the Chinese government previously permitted a majority shareholding of 51 per cent for three foreign insurers[39] who had applied for licences before 1998. All later applicants were already advised that their maximum shareholding would be confined to 50 per cent, while one company even accepted a minority position.

However, regardless of the shareholding ratio all foreign-invested life insurers are governed by the joint venture law which imposes clear limits on foreign management control. The law stipulates that the foreign partner(s) can nominate either the Chairman of the Board of Directors or the Executive General Manager – not both. Most top executive positions would then be 'doubled' through nomination of a Deputy of the other joint venture party. Even in the most harmonious management team these double appointments at the same level clearly inflate costs, delay decisions and potentially frustrate both partners in case of conflicting strategic perceptions of the company's market deployment.

Whereas most other restrictions for foreign insurers will be removed after China's accession to the WTO, the joint venture obligation and the restriction of foreign equity to 50 per cent will remain in force. American and European negotiators devoted a considerable amount of time to discussing this issue with their Chinese counterparts but only succeeded in obtaining a concession with regard to the choice of a joint venture partner: foreign life insurers will henceforth be free to choose their partner from any sector of China's industry – a concession which the Chinese may have agreed upon easily as the previous approach had proven impractical. On the other hand, a free choice of joint venture partners may facilitate partnerships with Chinese companies which have already established own sales outlets or other distribution systems. If these could be utilized for the joint venture, practical market positioning might be accelerated. The more fundamental problem with joint venture operations in life insurance is the fact that any newly established company needs a considerable number of years before the business volume is large enough to distribute profits. This time span might be too long for potential Chinese shareholders whose time horizons for returns on investments are much shorter than those of foreign investors.

Summary – Potential Implications of China's WTO Accession

In the perspective of China's macroeconomic development, a larger number of internationally experienced insurers will clearly benefit the country's insurance clients and improve the commercial environment for ongoing corporate and social reforms. It will not only be advantageous for the volume of foreign industrial investment but could also serve Chinese companies in funding their own growth through bank financing.

For the insurance sector itself competition will certainly intensify. This may cause problems for those domestic competitors who are least flexible in adjusting their structures to new requirements of product design and cost management. However, 'intensified competition' ought to be qualified in terms of a realistic number of competitors, their individual market strategies as well as the probable time frame within which foreign competitors are actually willing or able to enter the market. Continued growth of China's economy will generate new business opportunities and competition will focus on the fastest response to these opportunities. Here, Chinese insurers ought to be able to fully utilize their close affinity to domestic clients.

More specifically, what is likely to happen after China joins the WTO?

1. First of all, it remains to be seen at what rate foreign insurers will actually be admitted into the market. There are two major practical hurdles: first, in life insurance, the selection of a joint venture partner willing and permitted to make a strategic investment into insurance, and second, the definition of the licensed regional scope of business. If the license is only local – as at present – it may be difficult to serve clients in other regions as long as the current prerequisite for establishing branches within China remains in force (annual gross written premium in excess of 100 million RMB).
   The capacity of governmental approval authorities to assess license applications is physically limited and approval procedures will take time. Past experience has shown that it takes a particularly long time to receive approval of a joint venture partner and finalize the relevant contractual documents. This also applies to the approval procedure for new insurance products.

   In addition, during the approval process some competitive advantages of foreign insurers – such as product innovation and introduction of policy processing technologies (IT) – are likely to be transferred to domestic insurers. This practice has been used in the past (suitability testing or 'second opinions') and will probably continue to ensure that at least one domestic company is in a position to offer the same new product at the time of its introduction into the market.

2. In view of current international trends it can be assumed that the eventual number of foreign insurers interested in the Chinese market will not be much larger than the number of currently admitted or applying companies. The world's largest insurers already have a licence in China or are about to be approved either for new market access or for operating additional business classes (cf. Table 1). Even among them only very few wish to conduct all available classes of business – life, health, pension, property and casualty and marine insurance (as well as asset management through own financial group subsidiaries). The majority of foreign insurers will initially confine themselves to individual classes or even individual market segments for a considerable length of time in order to find their own specific market segments and establish branded competence.

   It seems to be a popular political misconception in the Chinese media to envisage a kind of 'closed front' between domestic insurers on one side and foreign competitors on the other. Business reality will certainly look different. Assuming that common international forms of insurance cover are introduced in China, larger projects will be coinsured jointly by domestic and foreign insurers and reinsurance will be spread across the entire market. There will be short or long term cooperation between individual foreign and domestic insurers, and for many foreign insurers competition with their main international adversaries on Chinese soil will be more important than competing with Chinese companies for local business with indigenous clients.

   Domestic insurers will look for allies among domestic or foreign financial institutions to enlarge their distribution networks and product range or to increase their own capital. This will, for instance, include alliances of insurers with banks for enhanced distribution or with other insurers for generating reinsurance business. Eventually, the current composition of the market will change in the direction increasingly dominating international financial services – that is, towards concentration of various financial services under the roof of one provider.

In addition, the introduction of insurance broking will also lead to a mixed involvement of domestic and foreign competitors in specific risks. Brokers are acting on behalf of the insurance customer and thus cannot afford to have national preferences.

3. One of the immediate effects of China's WTO accession will be significant improvements in legislation. Current insurance regulations will be streamlined according to international standards, including a revision of China's insurance law, and separate regulations for foreign insurers will be abandoned in favour of equal national treatment.
4. In the broader perspective of China's national reconstruction, additional underwriting capacity and technical expertise will be available to accompany large-scale national infrastructure projects. This may also have the desirable 'side effect' of ending foreign currency drains resulting from the longtime practice by non-state domestic insurers of placing facultative reinsurance with foreign insurers in order to boost their own underwriting capacity. They may still seek such reinsurance from foreign companies, but if these are licensed in China, a larger proportion of the premium flow will stay in the country.
5. Domestic companies will always remain closer to Chinese customers. This is one of their strategic advantages even if foreign insurers also employ Chinese staff and local marketing advisors. Under these circumstances future competitive pressure will mainly result from the following advantages which foreign insurers bring into the market:

    - Capacity for flexible product innovation based on a focused analysis of market data relevant for product design; appropriate consideration of international experience and standards (especially in life and health insurance), critical consideration of claims/benefits statistics; employment of experienced actuaries who have their own international network assisting in technical calculations;
    - product marketing and distribution systems based on reliable highspeed policy processing; personalized service to private and corporate customers;
    - determined profit orientation and prudent price adjustment to market changes;

- value–added services for corporate insurance clients based on project phase risk consulting, professional claims handling or custom-made policy design;
- service under international programs (local cover with overseas compensation for differences in limits and conditions); this is something Chinese companies cannot offer at all and foreign insurers will probably be able to forcefully increase their market share in business with foreign industrial investors;
- effective investment of premium income;
- human resources development based on regular training, performance-related salaries, appropriate benefit schemes as well as co–operative management training systems which include temporary transfer to assignments with overseas group companies;
- cost management through effective application of contemporary information technologies and maintaining a staff level appropriate to the actual business volume.

In most of these fields Chinese companies still have competitive disadvantages which may initially lead to a loss of market share. Judging from recent developments, it can be expected that the large state-owned insurers will probably find it more difficult to adapt to new market conditions within the transitional period of three years. In contrast, the younger joint stock companies like Ping'an or China Pacific have already reached high professional standards and their competence will probably grow sufficiently fast during the forthcoming years to compete with foreign insurers once the latter have established their operations in China. At the same time, the government may also decide in favour of restructuring the current state-owned insurance companies into smaller, more agile and manageable companies able to respond faster to newly emerging market trends.

6. During the initial period after market opening increased pressure on labour markets may temporarily lead to further increases in salaries and high levels of staff fluctuation. It will be difficult for Chinese companies – and here again particularly for the state-owned insurers – to retain qualified staff unless they adjust their own salary structures or offer other incentives that would reduce fluctuation. However, this should only be a short-term problem as

most newly licensed foreign competitors will not be able to recruit a sufficient number of readily qualified staff for an immediate start. Instead, they will set up their own training courses or cooperate with local education institutions to achieve stability in recruitment over the middle and long term and to guarantee a qualification level suitable to their class of business. Besides, foreign insurers have no interest in creating an artificial cost inflation, and life insurers are also obliged to consider the salary structure of their joint venture partner.

It is still difficult to project the future distribution of market shares between domestic and foreign competitors. The current level of 1 per cent foreign share will certainly increase, particularly through lines of business or products in which Chinese companies are not yet well established or competent. Eventually, however, all market participants will be operating in the same legal and commercial environment, and the mere fact that a foreign company has proven successful outside China does not necessarily mean that it will be equally successful in the Chinese market.

Notes

[1]Cf. *Zhongguo baoxianye de fazhan*, quoted in: Xing, Wei, 'Lun shenhua baoxian shichang kaifang yanjiu', *Baoxian Yanjiu*, Beijing, 1999/5 (Mai), p. 3.

[2]*Ibid.*

[3]Cf. Wei, Hualin, Yu Ziyou and Guo Yang, 'Zhongguo di baoxian jiandu zhidu he Shanghai baoxian shichang kaifang shidian xianzhuang ji pingjia', *Baoxian Yanjiu*, Beijing, 1998/9 (September), p. 12.

[4]Cf. Wei, Hualin, Yu Ziyou and Guo Yang, 'Zhongguo baoxian shichang kaifang zhong di wenti ji qi duice', *Baoxian Yanjiu*, Beijing, 1998/10 (October), pp. 2032.

[5]Xia, Hong, 'Lun woguo kaifang baoxian shichang de duice', *Baoxian Yanjiu*, Beijing, 2000/6 (June), p. 18.

[6]Cf. Han, Yaogen and Wang Xingsong, 'WTO: Zhongguo shouxian congrong miandui', *Baoxian Yanjiu*, 2000/2 (February), pp. 8, 10; Yang, Dazu, 'Jiaru WTO dui woguo shouxianye de yingxiang he duice', *Baoxian Yanjiu*, 2000/3 (March), p. 24.

[7]Cf. Xu, Xingming et al., 'Lun jiaru WTO hou chanxian di kaituo', *Baoxian Yanjiu*, 2000/4 (April), p. 2.

[8]A detailed account of China's insurance history can be found in Kaufmann, Ivo, *Versicherung in der Volksrepublik China – Entwicklung, Organisation, Recht*, Baden-Baden, 1993.

[9]Shareholders of these joint stock companies are mostly state-owned or municipal enterprises whose individual shareholding in the insurance companies is subject to governmental approval. This also applies to the smaller joint stock insurers established in the mid-1990s.

[10]CPIC was initially set up in 1987 as insurance department of the State Communication Bank in Shanghai and reorganized as an independent joint stock company in 1991.

[11]Cf. 'The Chinese Insurance Industry's Drive Towards Liberalization', *Asia Insurance Review*, November 2000, p. 47.

[12]The current share of Shanghai in the national insurance market is 8.3 per cent, whereas the city has only 1.4 per cent of the nation's population; cf. Zhu, Qing, 'Woguo baoxianye ying dui rushi de cuoshi', *Baoxian Yanjiu*, 2000/9 (September), p. 25.

[13]Cf. '1998 nian shijie geguo (huo diqu) baoxian yewu qingkuang tongji', *Baoxian Yanjiu*, 2000/12 (December), p. 4446. In more mature markets insurance penetration is between 7 per cent (Germany) and 12 per cent (Japan) with annual average per capita insurance spending well above 2,000 US$ (3,500 US$ in Japan, 1,030 US$ in South Korea, 774 US$ in Taiwan).

[14]Cf. Zhu, Qing, *op. cit.*, p. 25.

[15]The Chinese insurance law stipulates that risks located within the PRC must be insured by companies licensed for business in China. This requirement can – by nature of the business – not apply to reinsurance.

[16]Cf. Zhang, Baotai and Fang Chunyin, 'Tan Zhongguo zaibaoxianye ruhe yingjie jiaru WTO', *Baoxian Yanjiu*, 2000/3 (March), p. 26.

[17]At present, a typical client purchasing private life insurance would have a monthly disposable income above 3,000 RMB (paying a monthly life insurance premium of approximately RMB 200). In the Shanghai market, for instance, where many foreign investors are contributing to salaries, this sum may not be a very high hurdle, but in provincial cities salaries are not likely to grow as fast as in the coastal regions where foreign investments already have a history of two decades.

[18]The premium payments are directly invested into funds or other admitted assets. The policy holder carries the full investment risk. This model is copied from mature insurance markets.

[19]At present PICC and the China Export Import Bank already have export credit insurance departments. These will be merged into a governmental authority, but it is not yet clear which insurer will offer commercial (short term) export credit cover. Apart from PICC none of the other domestic companies has ever operated credit insurance.

[20]Cf. Chen, Poujian, 'Jiaru WTO dui woguo chanxian shichang di yingxiang he zhengce jianyi', *Baoxian Yanjiu*, 2000/6 (June), p. 17 (Chen Poujian is Chairman of the Board of Directors, General Manager and Party Secretary of Tian'an Insurance Company, Shanghai). The OECD Centre for Cooperation with the economies in transition published 'Twenty Insurance Guidelines' which were also discussed during a joint workshop with CIRC in January 1999 in Beijing. It includes recommendations such as avoiding over-regulation and encouraging stability whilst maintaining the necessary flexibility to meet developments in the market (cf. *Insurance Guidelines for Economies in Transition*, OECD, 1997).

[21]Yang, Dazu, *op.cit.*, p. 24.

[22]Cf. Chen, Poujian, *op.cit.*, p. 17.

[23]Yang, Dazu, *op. cit.*, p. 24.

[24]Cf. Xu, Xingming et al., *op.cit.*, p. 3.

[25]Cf. Zhang, Baotai and Chunyin Fang, *op.cit.*, p. 26.

[26]The mid-1990s brought the first hightide in China's life insurance business and many insurance agents actually sold policies as savings products. According to some observers they consciously avoided mentioning that life insurance policies

are mainly designed to provide cover against death of the policy holder – which is a cost-incurring factor that must be reflected in returns upon maturity.

[27]The rates of Chinese insurers for international transportation, for instance, are twice as high as on international markets; cf. Xu, Xingming et al., *op.cit.*, p. 2.

[28]Nissan Life Insurance went bankrupt because, following the decline in Japan's real estate values and capital markets, neither the company's investment returns nor the declining volume of new business yielded sufficient funds to guarantee contracted benefits payments. This scenario seemed to threaten some Chinese insurers as well.

[29]Xia, Hong, *op.cit.*, p. 19; Han, Yaogen and Xingsong Wang, *op.cit.*, p. 10.

[30]Cf. Zhao, Weixing, 'Lun gao keji shidai baoxianye de fazhan', *Baoxian Yanjiu*, 2000/6 (June), p. 3.

[31]Cf. Xu, Xingming, *op.cit.*, p. 3.

[32]*Ibid.*

[33]This is one of the appeasing arguments put forward in recent discussions preparing China for WTO entry. Han, Yaogen and Xingsong Wang, *op.cit.*, p. 8.

[34]More recent accounts of practical experience gained through representative offices or licensed business include the following titles: Darimont, Barbara, 'Neueste Krankenversicherungsreformen', *Deutsch-Chinesisches Wirtschaftsforum – Zeitschrift der Delegiertenbüros der Deutschen Wirtschaft in China*, vol. 3, no. 4 (Dezember 1999); Dollberg, Heinz, 'Zwar nicht 1,2 Milliarden, aber dennoch ein grosses Potential', *China Contact*, Berlin, no. 8 (August), 1999; Dörwald, Carl-Ludwig, 'Versicherungsmarkt China', *Deutsch-Chinesisches Wirtschaftsforum – Zeitschrift der Delegiertenbüros der Deutschen Wirtschaft in China*, vol. 2, no. 1 (Februar 1998); OECD, ed., *Insurance Guidelines for Economies in Transition*, OECD, Paris, 1997; Kaufmann, Ivo: *Versicherung in der Volksrepublik China – Entwicklung, Organisation, Recht*, Nomos: Baden-Baden, 1993; Miller, Matthew, 'More Barriers Face Latest Licence Victors', *South China Morning Post*, Hongkong, 31.5.2000; Nagel, Christine, 'Know-How Transfer – Was bedeutet dies in der Versicherungsindustrie', *Deutsch-Chinesisches Wirtschaftsforum – Zeitschrift der Delegiertenbüros der Deutschen Wirtschaft in China*, vol. 3, no. 3 (September 1999); Pan, Lufu, 'China's Insurance Law and Policies Need Gradual Improvement', *China Law Bimonthly*, Hongkong, April 2000; Nestmann, Peter, 'Individualversicherung in der Volksrepublik China' (Magisterarbeit an der Albert-Ludwigs-Universität zu Freiburg i.Br., 1999); Probst, Hans-Jörg, 'Ausländische Versicherer – Möglichkeiten und Grenzen', *China Contact*, Berlin, no. 8 (August) 1999; Probst, Hans-Jörg, 'Several Suggestions on China's Insurance Industry after WTO Accession', *China Law Bimonthly*, Hongkong, April 2000; 'The Chinese Insurance Industry's Drive Towards Liberalization', *Asia Insurance Review*, November 2000.

[35]Including Canada.

[36]Including Switzerland.

[37]Japan and Australia.

[38]Applications may be filed once with the CIRC for a certain class of business. However, the CIRC is not obliged to acknowledge receipt of the application. If the CIRC does not explicitly approve the relevant application within a period of six months the applications must be deemed rejected and no second application for the same class of business may be filed within a certain period of time. The CIRC is not obliged to state reasons for not responding to the application.

[39]Manulife (Canada), Allianz (Germany), AXA (France).

Table 1: Foreign insurers in China

Table 1.1: Companies under operation or in preparation for operation

Name of company	Country of origin	Licensed business region	Class of business	Legal form of incorporation
American Int. Assurance (American Int. Group)	USA	Shanghai, Guangzhou, Shenzhen, Foshan	Life insurance	Branch (100% foreign)
American Int. Underwriters (American Int. Group)	USA	Shanghai, Guangzhou, Shenzhen, Foshan	Nonlife insurance	Branch (100% foreign)
Aetna Life	USA	Shanghai	Life insurance	Joint venture (50% foreign)
Chubb Group[1]	USA	Shanghai	Nonlife insurance	Branch (100% foreign)
John Hancock Life[2]	USA	(not finally confirmed)	Life insurance	Joint venture (50% foreign)
Manulife	Canada	Shanghai	Life insurance	Joint venture (51% foreign)
Sun Life[3]	Canada	(not finally confirmed)	Life Insurance	Joint venture (50% foreign)
Tokio Marine and Fire	Japan	Shanghai	Nonlife insurance	Branch (100% foreign)
Winterthur	Switzerland	Shanghai	Nonlife insurance	Branch (100% foreign)
Allianz Group	Germany	Shanghai	Life insurance	Joint venture (51% foreign)
				cont.

[1] Under preparation since 1999.
[2] Ditto.
[3] Ditto.

Name of company	Country of origin	Licensed business region	Class of business	Legal form of incorporation
AXA/UAP (National Mutual)[4]	France (managed by Australian subsidiary)	Shanghai	Life insurance	Joint venture (51% foreign)
Royal & Sun Alliance	United Kingdom	Shanghai	Nonlife insurance	Branch (100% foreign)
Prudential (UK)[5]	United Kingdom	Guangzhou	Life insurance	Joint venture (50% foreign)
Standard Life[6]	United Kingdom	(pending)	Life insurance	(joint venture)
Colonial Mutual[7]	Australia	Shanghai	Life insurance	Joint venture (foreign minority)

[4] Managed by AXA Australian subsidiary National Mutual (AXA Greater China Region).

[5] Ditto.

[6] Ditto.

[7] Joint venture with China Life Insurance Company Ltd. for regional business in Shanghai Municipality. China Life concurrently operates its own Shanghai branch.

Table 1.2: Current EU insurers' licence applications under consideration*

Name of company	Country of origin	Licensed business region	Class of business	Legal form of incorporation
Generali SPA	Italy	(pending)	Life insurance	(joint venture)
ING Group	Netherlands	(pending)	Life insurance	(joint venture)
Commercial and General Union (CGNU)	United Kingdom	(pending)	Life insurance	(joint venture)
Skandia (AEGON Group)	Sweden (Netherlands)	(pending)	Life insurance	(joint venture)
CNP Assurance	France	(pending)	Life insurance	
Gerling Konzern	Germany	(pending)	Non-life	(pending; branch is possible)
Allianz Group	Germany	(pending)	Non-life (second full China-licence)	(pending; branch is possible)
AXA/UAP (National Mutual)	France	(pending)	Life insurance (branch licence for additional business region)	Through existing joint venture registered in Shanghai
Royal & Sun Alliance	United Kingdom	(pending)	Non-life insurance	Through existing
			(branch licence for additional business region)	operating unit registered in Shanghai

* The Chinese Government made a commitment towards the European Commission to the effect that nine more licences would be extended to insurance applicants from EU countries at the advent of China's WTO accession. The names of these companies were never officially published, but media reports from China indicated this selection; cf. *Asian Wall Street Journal*, November 13, 2000; *Reuters English News Service*, November 7, 2000. News reports further indicated that in connection with China's WTO accession licence applications by insurers from other trading regions would be considered. This may apply to Mitsui Marine and Fire Insurance (Japan), Zurich Financial Services Group, Swiss Life, Swiss Re (Switzerland), and Samsung Fire and Marine (South Korea).

7

The Banking and Securities Sector

He Liping

Introduction

This chapter addresses important issues relating to the development of China's banking sector and securities industry in the expectation of its imminent accession to the World Trade Organization (WTO). In November 1999, following difficult and protracted negotiations, a major breakthrough occurred when China reached a bilateral agreement with the United States on membership of the WTO. This event promised to have major implications for the opening up of the banking and securities sectors, and it generated, during the following months, a heated debate among Chinese analysts about the ability of these sectors to survive and compete in an open market. In the wake of such debate, many policy proposals have been put forward – and some have already been adopted – in an effort to combat the supposedly negative impact of WTO accession on banking and securities activities in China. It is against this background that this paper seeks to provide a synthesis of the most important relevant issues in an attempt to give an overview of China's banking and securities industry on the eve of its accession to the WTO.

An Overview of China's Banking and Securities Sector

The banking sector

From the current perspective, domestic banking institutions in China can be categorized under four headings. The first comprises so-called 'wholly state-owned commercial banks, of which there are four, as follows: the Industrial and Commercial Bank of China (ICBC), the Agricultural Bank of China (ABC), the Bank of China (BoC), and the China Construction Bank (CCB). Each of these was formerly a specialized bank, possessing its own distinctive banking function. For example, ICBC targeted the urban economy, while ABC operated in rural areas; BoC handled foreign exchange operations; and CBC provided banking services for long-term investment projects. In the early 1990s, however, the demarcation lines between these institutions became blurred, and thereafter disappeared altogether. Nevertheless, with their national coverage, these four banks have remained the backbone of China's banking network. At the end of 1998, the total value of assets held by them was 7,116.9 billion yuan, equivalent to 90 per cent of China's gross domestic product. Their main activities today are to extend credit to state-owned enterprises (SOEs) and to receive deposits from urban and rural residents. But in other spheres of banking, such as the transfer of money, and credit card and foreign exchange transactions, they are much less well developed than their international counterparts and would-be competitors. Even so, within China itself, they are still the largest sources of loans and receivers of deposits.

The second institutional category is made up of the policy banks that were established in 1994 in the wake of the on-going economic reforms. Three such banks were established in that year: the State Development Bank, the Agricultural Development Bank, and the China Import and Export Bank. The purpose of establishing the policy banks, which have mainly been funded by bond issues, was to reduce and to minimize 'policy-burdens' that had previously been carried by the state-owned commercial banks – in particular, the removal from them of non-profitable essential responsibilities. With their functions following traditional demarcation lines and their activities overwhelmingly orientated towards SOEs or similar networks (for example, the Agricultural Development Bank has sought to facilitate the state's agricultural procurement policy, as well as offering support to its farm product price-support measures), the policy banks have essentially provided the basic banking network in which the continuing remnants of China's economic planning system can be accommodated and serviced. At the end of 1998, their combined assets totalled 1,390 billion yuan.

The third category includes share-holding commercial banks. So far, about ten such banks have been set up, most of them having their origins in regionally-based activities, located in provinces and municipalities, such as Guangdong (especially Shenzhen), Fujian, Shanghai, and Beijing. Contained within their establishment have been important institutional banking initiatives. For example, Shenzhen Development Bank was the first financial institution in China to raise capital from stock markets; China Merchant Bank was the first to require no share subscription from government departments; and Minsheng Banking Group was the first – to date, the only – *private* bank to have been set up in China. These commercial banks have tended to be staffed by younger and better-educated personnel than other Chinese banking institutions. They have also achieved rapid growth in recent years, and have demonstrated a desire to extend their operations into new areas, such as the provision of personal banking and internet banking services, as well as a portfolio service for potential investors. The largest commercial bank is the Shanghai-based Bank of Communications, whose total assets were valued at 500 billion yuan at the end of 1998. Despite their generally buoyant performance, however, two commercial banks have encountered severe difficulties in recent years. The first is Hainan Development Bank, which was dissolved in 1996 as a result of the accumulation of bad debts, leading to runs on its resources; and the China Investment Bank, which, in the wake of similar problems, was forcibly taken over by other banks in 1998.

The final category embraces city commercial banks. At the end of 1998, eighty-eight such banks existed, with total assets of 457 billion *yuan*.[1] These banks also have a geographical focus, in that they are not permitted to extend their operations beyond the boundaries of the city in which they were originally licensed to operate. Most of them have emerged, since 1995, out of former urban credit cooperative unions, or associations of such unions, and largely owe their existence to official efforts to re-organize and consolidate this part of the financial sector.

Credit cooperative unions in China, whether urban or rural, are grass-roots financial institutions, often managed and run by personnel of low quality.[2] At the end of 1998, there were 3,240 urban credit cooperative unions, possessing total assets of 267 billion yuan; in addition, there were 41,508 independent rural credit cooperative unions, with total assets of 1261 billion yuan.[3] In recent years, the number of credit cooperative unions has been in decline, as Chinese government authorities have tried to tighten control and consolidate this sector. In any case, many of the financial organizations are believed not to be truly cooperative and to be carrying a huge volume of non-performing loans. To their clients, they offer few banking services other than the provision of credit loans and the receipt of deposits.

There are other financial institutions in China, such as investment and trust companies (ITCs), that accept deposits from the public. Such institutions usually combine their deposit-taking and loan activities with dealing in securities.

Overall, China's banking sector has witnessed rapid growth in and beyond the 1990s.

The securities sector

In formal terms, the origins of China's securities sector lie in the establishment, in the early 1990s, of two stock exchanges in Shanghai and Shenzhen. Despite its subsequent rapid growth, this remains a young Chinese sector, whose activities have been tightly controlled by a government wanting to use stock exchanges in order to channel funds to debt-ridden SOEs, but simultaneously fearing that fluctuations in stock market prices might come to threaten China's overall financial stability. Accordingly, from the very start, the authorities adopted a cautious approach towards the development of securities firms and activities. Thus, companies seeking to raise capital in stock markets are required to obtain formal approval from various government departments, as well as having to meet the selection criteria of stock exchanges themselves. Those who wish to deal in securities are also subject to strict ownership tests, conducted by the licensing authorities. The outcome is that although there now appear to be a large number of securities firms operating in China, many of them are, in fact, associates or subsidiaries of government agencies (especially fiscal departments, financial authorities or municipal authorities).

At the end of 1998, there were ninety-four securities firms, possessing total assets of 206 billion yuan. In addition, there were 239 ITCs, with total assets of 440 billion yuan. The main activities of these securities firms and ITCs were, and are underwriting, stock dealing on behalf of clients, and – albeit only to a minor extent – advising on investment management. Some firms also conduct market-making business, whether openly or covertly, in search of profits through the manipulation of stock prices. In the mid-1990s, enterprise bond issues were virtually suspended; and in the wake of the subsequent curtailment, during 1998-99, of trading in futures, securities firms in China have concentrated on stock exchange activities.

At the end of 1999, a total of 949 companies were listed on China's two stock exchanges, Shanghai and Shenzhen; and 46 Chinese companies were floated on overseas stock markets, such as those in Hong Kong, London and New York. In all, these companies raised 94 billion yuan on stock markets in 1999, or about 20 per cent less than the peak level recorded in 1997. The market capitalization value of China's domestic stock markets reached 2,647 billion yuan at the end of 1999, the equivalent of 32 per cent of China's GDP in that year. Throughout 2000, China's stock markets continued to expand rapidly, resulting in an increase of more than 40 per cent in market capitalization. But despite such rapid growth, China's stock markets have remained underdeveloped in various respects. For example, regulations require that listed companies' shares still be divided into 'tradable' and 'non-tradable',[4] and the 'tradable' element has accounted, on average, for only one-third of the total share issue. Within the 'non-tradable' category, there is an institutions-holding sub-category which differs from the government-holding category, and can change hands among institutions subject to strict regulatory measures.[5] In addition, stock trading is differentiated according to the currency being used: 'A'-shares are for local currency (Renminbi) markets; 'B'-shares are for foreign currencies (in Shanghai, the US dollar; in Shenzhen, the Hong Kong dollar). Finally, it is noteworthy that most listed companies have their origins in state-owned enterprises, and after flotation, they have remained state-controlled units. All this takes place within the framework of government-appointed regulators.

The presence of foreign financial institutions in China

China's financial sector was completely closed to foreign players throughout the period between the 1950s and the late 1970s. Following the initiation of reforms in the late 1970s, foreign-funded enterprises began to enter China, leading to an associated demand for the services of foreign-banks in China. Formal business operations by foreign banks began in the early 1980s, especially in a number of China's Special Economic Zones (most notably, Shenzhen). Following Deng Xiaoping's 'Southern Tour' (*nanxun*) in 1992 and in the strong expectation that China was about to open domestic banking markets to foreign players, the number of branches of foreign banks increased sharply in 1993. But in 1998 and 1999, in the wake of the increasingly severe Asian financial crisis, operations by foreign banks in China declined to such an extent that the value of their total combined assets had fallen by 16 per cent to US$ 32 billion at the end of 1999.[6] By this time, 170 branches of foreign banks were operating in China, most of them located in large cities and the coastal areas.[7]

The principal activities conducted by foreign banks in China today remain quite limited in scope. They are usually required to conduct banking business denominated in foreign currencies. In other words, they provide credit loans to or take deposits from foreign-funded enterprise clients, expressed in foreign exchanges. Recently, however, there has been some policy relaxation towards foreign banks' use of local currency in doing business. Even so, restrictions are still considerable, and foreign banks are often unable to secure a full license to conduct banking services in China.[8]

In both wholesale and retail banking, a number of joint ventures between Chinese and foreign financial institutions have been set up. The establishment of such ventures is usually conditional on the Chinese side assuming the controlling share. As in China's manufacturing sector, the main policy motivation behind the approval of JVs in the banking and securities sector has been to help domestic financial institutions rapidly acquire international expertise and enjoy a share of the profits with foreign partners. Overall, however, joint ventures in China's financial sector have so far been limited both in the number and scope of their operations.

The operations of foreign securities firms in China are mainly confined to so-called B-share markets. Foreign securities firms and institutional investors may trade the shares of Chinese companies, denominated in US dollars on the Shanghai Stock Exchange, and in Hong Kong dollars (Shenzhen Stock Exchange). Trading in B-shares is not available to Renminbi-holders. In short, there is a dual stock market system in China.

To date, it may be said that foreign financial institutions have become only peripherally integrated with the domestic Chinese economy.

Problems and the Question of Competitiveness in China's Banking and Securities Sector

There are many problems that have faced China's banking and securities industry.[9] In an attempt to address some of the most serious difficulties, for example, recapitalization and the control of non-performing loans (NPLs), the Chinese government has adopted a number of policy measures. But from the current perspective, only partial success has so far been achieved. For purposes of analysis, the problems can be put into one of two categories: balance-sheet problems and issues related to organizational competitiveness. The former can readily be viewed from the account books of the relevant banks; but problems associated with organizational competitiveness demand more careful analysis if they are to be properly identified and addressed. Below is a brief account of these problems, as they exist in China's banking and securities sector.

Non-performing loans, weak capital base, and low profitability

Although NPLs are widely recognized to be one of the most serious balance-sheet problems facing Chinese banks in recent years, the precise level of total NPLs remains unknown. In 1998, the central government issued a special bond, worth 270 billion yuan, in order to recapitalize four state-owned banks. The following year, official authorities proposed initiating debt-to-equity transfers in order to address this issue. This proposal involved the establishment of asset management companies (AMCs) that would take over the existing NPLs of four wholly-state-owned banks, and recover as much of the outstanding NPLs as possible (with the AMCs acting primarily as an owner of equity assets). In 2000, the cut-off line for four AMCs to take over NPLs from the four banks was set at 1.3 trillion yuan, which was equivalent to about 15 per cent of China's GDP. Another estimate indicates that at the end of 1997, the outstanding value of small and medium-sized banks (city commercial banks and share-holding banks) in China was 90 billion yuan, or 14.4 per cent of their total loan-book assets.[10]

The problem of NPLs is not an isolated or self-contained one. It is the product of the rapid expansion of bank lending to poorly-performing SOEs and of low operational profitability by the banks themselves. A consequence of the fast growth of bank lending has been the contraction of banks' capital base relative to their overall operations; and the weakness of the capital base has been further exacerbated by poor profitability or even loss making. It is true that the recapitalization measure of 270 billion yuan in 1998 did generate a sharp rise in the capital to total assets ratio for the four banks (cf. Table 1). Even more recently, official sanctioning of activities to enable smaller share-holding banks to raise equity capital from stock markets has begun to emerge, as with the Shanghai-based Pudong Development Bank in 1999, and the Beijing-based China Minsheng Banking Group in 2000.

Table 1:
Total assets vs. equity capital in China's four largest banks (RMB billion yuan)

	1997			1998		
	A. Total assets	B. Equity capital	B/A (%)	A. Total assets	B. Equity capital	B/A (%)
ICBC	2937.8	96.9	*3.30*	3238.7	183.9	*5.68*
ABC	1573.9	39.8	*2.53*	2022.4	134.8	*6.67*
CBC	1681.8	49.6	*2.95*	1923.6	100.5	*5.22*
BoC	2231.7	87.7	*3.93*	2475.4	139.6	*5.64*

Note: 'Equity capital' includes owners' claims to items such as undistributed profits.

Source: China Finance Society, ed., *Almanac of China's Finance and Banking*, Beijing: China Finance Press, 1, pp. 427–29.

The low profitability of China's major banks is not in dispute. As Table 2 shows, between 1996 and 1998, the absolute level of total pretax profits, earned by the four wholly-state-owned banks, declined (their average rate of return on total assets falling from 0.57 to 0.12 per cent). Meanwhile, during the same period, ten share-holding banks also saw a decline in their average rate of return on total assets. It is likely that many factors have contributed to the low and declining rate of profitability in Chinese banks. They include excessive tax and quasi-tax burdens, insufficient ability to control costs and cost growth, and deficiencies in internal management.[11]

Table 2:
Profitability indicators of Chinese banks (billion yuan)

	1996		1997		1998	
	4 state-owned banks	10 share-holding banks	4 state-owned banks	10 share-holding banks	4 state-owned banks	10 share-holding banks
Total profits, before-tax	34.0	14.2	10.6	24.0	9.5	11.5
Total assets	5947.1	667.3	7213.5	778.1	8259.2	952.5
Return on total assets (%)	0.57	2.13	0.15	3.08	0.12	1.21
Net interest income	517.9	44.8	489.5	46.4	435.8	46.8
Net non-interest income	16.7	10.3	14.4	11.8	14.2	8.7
Net interest income (% of banking income)	96.88	81.31	97.14	79.73	96.84	84.32

Note: 'Banking income' here is the sum of 'net interest income and net non-interest income.' Before 1997, Chinese banks earned significant amounts of non-business (i.e. non-banking) income. But spin-offs from non-banking assets and businesses in 1997 caused such income to fall considerably.

Source: Li, Xuan: 2000 'A Comparative study of competitiveness of state-owned commercial banks', *Finance Studies*, no. 9, pp. 67–75.

Rudimentary banking services

As indicated above, many Chinese banks conduct their business in a mainly traditional manner that focuses on deposit-taking and credit-lending, but leaves many other banking activities underdeveloped. This has resulted in an excessive dependence on a single source of income; thus, net interest income has come to account for over 90 per cent of total banking income for the four largest Chinese banks, and more than 80 per cent for ten medium-sized Chinese banks (cf. Table 2).

This excessive reliance on interest income has also made these banks vulnerable to policy-driven adjustments of interest rates in China's financial sector. Since 1996, interest rates for deposits and loans in China have been reduced on several occasions in order to stimulate the economy. Given that deposit adjustments tend to be slower than loan adjustments, i.e. borrowers are able to change quickly to new (lower-)rate sources of credit, banks face the threat of unexpected declines in net interest income.[12] As Table 2 shows, the four largest Chinese banks all suffered a significant contraction of their net interest income after 1996, even though their total assets continued to grow.

Though 'new' methods of payments, such as credit cards, have developed rapidly in China in recent years, in general, the means of making payments in China remains quite backward. Payments and settlements by cheque have not yet been extended to personal users, and many restrictions still attach to institutional users. Many kinds of credit cards are available but problems of mutual incompatibility (each bank has its own card system for which there is little commonly-shared ATM or POS) have, in practice, inhibited their spread and use. Only since April 2000 has a formal 'real-name' bank account system begun to take effect in China. The fact that China now has the highest cash to GDP ratio in the world (cf. Figure 1) indicates, inter alia, that China's banking services (non-cash payment system) remain underdeveloped, and, in consequence, the public stills use cash to an inordinate extent in order to conduct transactions.

It is, in part, a reflection of the underdeveloped system of payments that China's economy is still implicitly characterized by 'dollarization' (i.e. the frequent use of dollars for purposes of daily domestic transactions). 'Dollarization' practices pose a potential threat to the stability of China's financial system.

Highly-biased client groups

Because China's banking and securities industry has been tightly controlled by the government and its various departments, there has been a high degree of discrimination by them against non-state enterprises and institutions in the operation. As of the end of 1999, of all the outstanding loans extended by Chinese banks (valued at over 9.3 trillion yuan), over 80 per cent were debited to state-owned enterprises. In other words, less than 20 per cent of loans made by Chinese banks had been extended to non-state enterprises.[13]

Figure 1: Cash/GDP ratio (%) (1997 or nearest year)

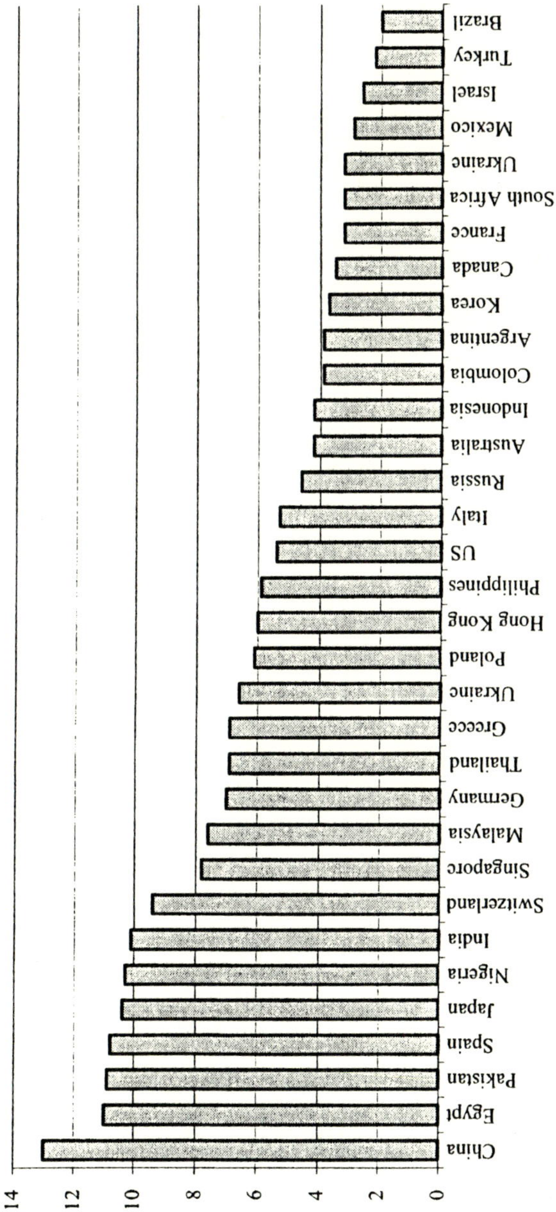

Source: *IMF International Finance Statistics*, 1998.

This bias was even more conspicuous in the state-owned banks. For instance, at the end of 1997, of all the loans made by all Chinese financial institutions, 14 per cent were debited to non-state enterprises; but of all the loans made by China's *state-owned* banks, the corresponding figure was less than 9 per cent.[14]

Such institutional discrimination in lending practices, combined with the underdeveloped state of the payment services system have generated a remarkable profusion of peripheral, informal, and even illegal banking activities in China. The same is also true for the securities sector, where, regardless of their performance, state-owned enterprises comprehensively occupy a dominant role in areas such as initial share offerings, rights issues, and virtually non-withdrawal status of listing.

Liquidity problems

Although funds from the personal sector continue to flow into Chinese banks, it is believed that many banks have suffered from liquidity shortages, as they have encountered problems associated with NPLs and irregular investments. In the mid-1990s, a consolidation campaign in the banking sector sought to eliminate banks' irregular investment activities in order to enable them to focus on more orthodox banking business. The debt-to-equity transfer programme, initiated in 1999, may also enable banks to address the liquidity issue, although a full solution is likely to emerge only in the medium or long term. In the meantime, Chinese banks will continue to face liquidity problems.

Until recently, China sought to address this liquidity issue through the implementation of a high reserve ratio system. This system required banks to place up to 20 per cent of all the deposits they received with the Central Bank in the form of a reserve. Such reserves earned a fairly high rate of interest, but could not be used for settlement purposes.[15] When a bank or branch of a bank encountered a liquidity problem, the Central Bank usually responded quickly through its practice of 're-lending' (this term referring to the special Chinese practice whereby the Central Bank extended loans to a financial institution). This system conferred very considerable powers on the Central Bank in terms of its ability to control banks' lending operations. Reforms in 1998 and 1999 did, however, reduce the ratio of minimum required reserves, as well as cutting the level of interest rates payable on the reserves, thereby transferring responsibility for the liquidity issue to a much greater extent to the banks themselves.

In 1999 and 2000, there were quite a number of small financial institutions (mostly rural and urban credit unions and city commercial banks) that encountered problems of illiquidity and insolvency. In the face of such difficulties, China's Central Bank continued to provide 're-lending' funds to such financial institutions. Meanwhile, inter-bank borrowing and bond trading market transactions in China have grown rapidly in recent years. It may be assumed that such growth assists Chinese banks in their efforts to address the liquidity issue, even if it does not help resolve the insolvency issue.

The competitiveness of Chinese banks

The competitiveness of Chinese banks and securities is, without doubt, a priority issue. In support of this statement, two observations may be made. First, even in China's domestic markets, competition among banks and securities firms has been limited by virtue of the price – interest rate and/or securities pricing – still being subject to tight official regulation, control and determination. Second, foreign financial institutions have so far achieved only a limited presence in China's domestic markets, so that 'head-on' competition between Chinese financial institutions and their foreign counterparts is largely absent. In short, the competitiveness of Chinese financial institutions has yet to be tested.

Several factors impinge on the competitiveness issue. They include the following:

Size: A number of Chinese banks are large in the context of the domestic market, but remain modest by international standards. In addition, many Chinese securities firms are modest, even from a domestic perspective.

Profitability: Many Chinese companies have performed disappointingly in this regard.

Liquidity: A number of small and medium-sized Chinese financial institutions already face a liquidity problem, and the likelihood is that more such financial institutions will be similarly affected in the future.

Access to the market: Chinese firms have obvious advantages in this regard, but the role of exclusive rights is likely to diminish in the wake of Chinese accession to the WTO.

Sophistication in the provision of services: Although there is some evidence that many Chinese firms are catching up with international standards in this respect, inertia and backwardness persist.

Market reputation (brand awareness and credit ratings): The Chinese public formerly made did not discriminate between state-owned financial institutions. More recently, the situation has begun to change, and it is increasingly likely that some Chinese financial institutions will encounter problems of market share shrinkage, if not outright failure.

The following additional observations may also be made in regard to recent changes in the behaviour of Chinese financial institutions:

Profit motivation and cost consciousness: Both have strengthened, as profit criteria have been adopted in order to assess the performance of bank managers and cadres in China's financial institutions.

Risk aversion: Many bank managers and cadres in Chinese financial institutions have demonstrated an increasingly risk-neutral or risk-averse attitude, as measures to reduce and eliminate losses have 'hardened'.

Drive for innovation: Progress in this regard has been slow, but as pressures to improve competitiveness increase, so further progress may well accelerate.

Management capacity: Conflicting anecdotal evidence makes it difficult to offer definitive comment, without further detailed analysis. But it seems clear that for the time being, continuing elements of political intervention in the personnel arrangements of financial institutions will minimize the managerial scope to bring about improvements in financial institutions' competitiveness.

Recent WTO Agreements and China's Banking and Securities Industry

In the recent bilateral negotiations between China and the United States that were thought to provide the key to securing China's membership of the WTO, the Chinese side reportedly undertook to open up the financial sector to foreign – in this case, US – financial institutions.

Thus, China has agreed to commit itself to provide full market access to its banking sector for US banks within a five-year period. The agreement also provides for foreign banks to conduct local currency business with Chinese enterprises, starting two years after China's WTO accession. Five years after accession, foreign banks will also be able to conduct local currency business with Chinese *individuals*. Finally, foreign banks will enjoy the same rights as Chinese domestic banks within designated geographic areas – the principle of national treatment. Both geographical and customer restrictions will be removed after five years.

As for the securities sector, China will permit joint ventures with minority foreign ownership to engage in fund management on the same terms as Chinese firms. As the scope of Chinese firms' business activities expands, foreign joint venture securities companies will be able to enjoy the same degree of expansion in the scale of their business. Minority joint ventures will also be permitted to underwrite domestic securities issues, and underwrite and trade in foreign currency denominated securities (debt and equity).

Subsequent bilateral negotiations between China and the European Union threw further light on China's attitudes towards its banking and securities sector, not least through Beijing's commitment, underlining its determination to open up financial industries. More generally, beyond the scope of purely bilateral negotiations, China has also committed itself to comply with WTO rules and (for example, those relating to transparency and equal national treatment) as they affect the service sector.

The Likely Impact of China's WTO Accession on its Banking and Securities Industry

In line with the commitment undertaken by the Chinese government, following its accession to the WTO, the domestic banking and securities sector will gradually be opened up to foreign financial institutions. We may suppose that in the immediate wake of Chinese membership, several important initiatives will take place in banking and securities activities:

First, China's domestic banks and securities firms will increasingly have to face strong competition from their foreign counterparts (especially in prime locations, such as large cities and the coastal regions) and within some customer groups. In deciding how to allocate their financial resources and from which source to purchase financial service products, Chinese customers will enjoy a greater choice of firms.

Second, government control over banking and securities activities is likely to be weakened. In the pre-WTO world, the Chinese government is still greatly influenced by the ethos of the traditional centrally-planned system in their continuing desire to retain paramount control of the economy, especially in the use and allocation of available funds. The WTO rules and commitments to which China has subscribed will necessarily constrain its ability to control and regulate the economy, including the finance industry. In addition, demands by China's domestic financial institutions for greater autonomy and independence will certainly grow. In such means are embodied the principle that 'opening-up promotes reform.'

Third, accession to the WTO will facilitate the move towards future full convertibility of the Chinese currency. For the time being, there exists partial currency convertibility in China in respect to current-account transactions (i.e. free trade-related monetary flows across the Chinese border). Following WTO accession, more inflows of foreign funds into China's banking and securities industry will be allowed, as will rights to the *withdrawal* of investment funds (albeit subject to certain conditions being fulfilled). In addition, increasing demands by foreign financial institutions for access to China's foreign exchange markets will also encourage the move to increased currency convertibility.

In considering the likely impact of WTO accession upon China's banking and securities industry, two further issues are frequently raised. The first is whether China is likely to experience a damaging 'brain drain'. The second is whether China will suffer a flight of capital.[16]

In addressing the possibility of a 'brain drain', it is indeed likely that China's domestic financial institutions will, in the short term, witness some reallocation of professional expertise between local and foreign financial institutions, as foreign financial institutions seek to employ more local talent. In the long term, however, the supply of local expert personnel is also likely to expand in response to continuing demand by China's domestic financial institutions for such expertise. In short, is seems unlikely that a 'brain drain' will pose a serious threat to China's banking and securities industry in the long run.

As for the second issue, as the economy and the financial sector become more open in the wake of joining the WTO, China may well find itself becoming more vulnerable to financial shocks that are accompanied by capital flight. But again, this should be seen as a long-term issue, the scale of which will depend greatly on the degree of stability of China's macroeconomic management and financial system, as the government seeks to pursue internal and external liberalization. Meanwhile, the very high level of unsolved NPLs and the tight control over interest rates in the banking sector, as well as irregularities in the securities sector, indicate how far China has yet to travel before it achieves a sound and mature modern financial system What is also clear are the potential dangers that could arise out of China's external liberalization in the absence of accelerated reforms to combat the various problems.[17]

The Policy Response

In accordance with the commitments it has already made in advance of joining the WTO, the Chinese government is expected to take steps that will facilitate the further opening of the banking and securities sector to foreign firms. Thus, more foreign banks – and their branches – will secure licenses that will enable them to conduct business in China. At the same time, restrictions on their Renminbi operations will gradually be reduced and eventually entirely removed. In the near future, foreign investment funds and investment banks will also be given access to China's domestic markets, perhaps through the establishment of joint ventures.

As for improving the state of China's own domestic financial institutions, the government has adopted a dual policy approach in its efforts to resolve the outstanding NPL problems. On the one hand, it has established AMCs; on the other hand, it seeks to implement strict rules and criteria, whereby the performance of bank managers can be assessed. There is a strong case for supposing that the AMCs will achieve a degree of success in helping banks to improve their balance sheets by bringing about some reduction in NPLs. But whether they will be able to successfully transform and enhance the basic institutional framework of the state-owned banks and state-owned enterprises remains to be seen.

Fiscal injections or the raising of capital in stock markets are two of the ways whereby the recapitalization of Chinese banks may be continued. It seems likely too that a variety of factors will facilitate the continued rapid rate of expansion of Chinese stock markets. Even so, the danger of serious fluctuations should not be under-estimated.

One final caveat is that as in the past, the government will still face the major challenge of how to reform the regulatory system itself. To date – and perhaps in the foreseeable future too – that has been and is likely to remain the weakest part of China's response to its impending WTO accession.

Notes

[1]Jiao, Junpu, *WTO and The Future of China's Financial Industry*, Beijing: China Finance Press, 2000, p. 27.

[2]Financial Research Institute of the People's Bank of China: 1998. *A Collection of Research Reports on Current Hot Issues in China's Finance*, Beijing: Economic Science Press, 1998, p. 54.

[3]Jiao, Junpu, *op.cit.*, p. 28.

[4]Kanes, Kathryn, 'China', *Euromoney*, July 2000, pp. 56, 58.

[5]For more details see Li, Xiaochun, 'A Study of the liquidity of state-holding shares vs. institution-holding shares', in: Fan, Gang, ed., *Financial Development and Enterprise Reform*, Beijing: Economic Science Press, 2000, Chapter 9, pp. 239–83.

[6]Li, Xiaofeng, and Guang Chen, 'Current developments of foreign banks in China and their future prospects', *International Finance Studies*, 2000, no. 5, pp. 44–7, here p. 45.

[7]Gong, Haocheng, and Guoqiang Dai, eds, *China's Financial Development Report 2000*, Shanghai: Shanghai Finance and Economics University Press, 2000, p. 70.

[8]Moor, Phillip, 'Foreign banks in China: Will WTO open the door?', *Euromoney*, September 2000, pp. 24, 26.

[9]See especially the discussion in Lardy, Nicolas, *China's Unfinished Economic Reform*, Washington, D.C.: The Brookings Institute, 1997.

[10]Gong and Dai, *op.cit.*., p. 120.

[11]See Feng, Zongxian, Tan Yi, and Guo Genglong, 'On International competitiveness of China's banking industry', *Reform*, 2000, no. 4, pp. 84–90; Fu, Fred, 'Reforming China's banking system: A new long march', *International Economic Review*, 2000, no. 4, pp. 5–12; Ketizu, 'An Investigation into various charges on banks in China', *Finance studies*, 2000, no. 11, pp. 67–77; Li, Xuan, 'A comparative study of competitiveness of state-owned commercial banks', *Finance Studies*, 2000, no. 9, pp. 67–75; Li, Yuanxu, Huang Yan, and Zhang Xianqing, 'Comparison of competitiveness between China's state-owned commercial banks and foreign banks', *Finance Studies*, 2000, no. 3, pp. 47–56; Wang, Cong, 'An analysis of tax burdens of Chinese banks', *Finance Studies*, 2000, no. 7, pp. 62–70; Zheng, Liangfang, 'How to stop profit declines in the largest five commercial banks', *Reform*, 2000, no. 5, pp. 95–9.

[12]Cao, Longqi, Zheng Jianming, 'On the effectiveness of interest rate policy in China', *Finance Studies*, 2000, no. 4, pp. 23–33; Wang, Xiaoya, Li Zhenjiang, and Yuan Defa, *Great Breakthroughs: China's Financial Reforms at the Turn of Centuries*, Beijing: China Finance Press, 1999, p. 106.

[13]Gong and Dai, *op.cit.*, p. 103.

[14]Fan, *op.cit.*, p. 31.

[15]Xie, Ping, *Options of China Financial System Reform*, Shanghai: Shanghai Far East Press, 1996, Chapter 3.

[16]Yi, Gang, 'World Financial Integration and China's Finanical Industry', *World Economy and China*, 1999, no. 6, pp. 16–23; Jiao, *op.cit.*

[17]Artus, Patrick, 'The Dangers of opening an economy to the exterior without caution: Poland as an example for China', CDC Marches Research Department *Flash*, no. 2000-218 (16 November 2000).

Part III

Challenges for China's Political, Social and Legal System

8

The Evolution of China's Political System: New Rules for Communist Party Rule?

Heike Holbig

Introduction

China's accession to the World Trade Organization has been seen as a moment of great historical significance. The prospect has not only raised high expectations in the economic but also in the political field. While many people in the West have greeted the resulting new business opportunities with enthusiasm, some have also placed great hopes in China's WTO accession to put the country's political system on a more liberal and democratic path.

Among them, there is no one less than the former US President, Bill Clinton. In May last year, he expressed these hopes in a very catchy manner – which would be hard to imagine coming from high-ranking EU representatives. Of course, one has to see that the Clinton administration, on the one hand, *had to* propagate the prospective benefits of China's WTO accession in a sufficiently stark manner to justify their China policy in the domestic environment and to win over Congress. Congress, as will be remembered, had to pass the permanent normal trade relations bill for China to overcome the last bilateral hurdle. On the other hand, Clinton was *able to* do so because he knew he could claim vis-à-vis Chinese leaders – who must have felt consternation when they heard his words – that this was a necessary tactical maneouvre to secure a positive vote on the trade bill (the bill was indeed passed by the House of Representatives in May and by the Senate in September 2000). Whatever their tactical nature, two of the key phrases formulated by the outgoing US President are cited here for their remarkable prophetic character:

Prophecy A: WTO accession and freer trade with China will 'unleash forces that may hasten the *demise of the mainland's one-party state*'.

Prophecy B: By 'letting our hi-tech companies in to bring the Internet and the *information revolution* to China, we will be unleashing forces that no totalitarian operation can control'.[1] (italics added)

In the following, these two prophecies serve as a starting point for analyzing the implications WTO accession may have for the evolution of China's political system. Will WTO accession really pose such acute challenges to Communist Party rule? Will it accelerate the erosion of the party's grip on political power and bring about a revolution-like transition to a democratic system? Or, will it rather give impetus to a re-centralization of political power as the party-state realizes the challenges and tries to act against them? Will it cause change at all? After presenting various arguments to answer these questions, a set of 'rules' will be suggested which might become relevant 'rules of the game' for Communist Party rule in the wake of WTO accession.

The time horizon of the analysis is limited to a short to medium term of about five years. The analysis is based on new trends in China's political system which have been observed since 1999. It was then that the Chinese side perceived a major breakthrough in the WTO negotiation process and started to prepare itself for accession.

Prophecy A: Demise of the One-Party State?

The functional perspective: Enhanced capacity to rule

Will WTO accession lead to the demise of the one-party state in China? To answer this question, we need to remind ourselves that it has become more and more difficult to conceive of the Communist Party regime as a monolithic power structure with a clear-cut and efficient top-down command hierarchy. This holds especially true for the past two decades of economic reforms. Of course, the central Party leadership still formulates the political guidelines, dominates the decision-making process at the top and supervises the activities of government organs at various levels, most importantly through control of their staff. However, economic de-centralization and the devolution of administrative power has increasingly invigorated local agents, entrepreneurs and other social groups who have learned to pursue their own interests and, if necessary, to defend them against the interests of the central party-state.[2]

In particular, a web of protectionist forces has been formed, consisting of various sectoral and local interest groups: we have on the one hand the state-owned enterprises (SOEs), particularly in the banking, automobile, and telecommunications sectors, which directly lobby the specialized industry departments within the ministerial bureaucracy. On the other hand we have the local governments which are financially dependent on local business and which eventually bear the costs of social welfare when enterprises are not able to do so any more.[3] As is indicated by the most recent impasse reached in WTO negotiations due to China's demands to substantially subsidize its peasants, the articulation of agricultural interests, which used to be largely neglected in the past, has now also gained momentum.[4] Confronted with these protectionist forces, the power of the central party-state to implement national policies and push through reforms has declined considerably since the early 1980s.

With this background in mind, let us now look at the implications of WTO accession. According to conventional wisdom, the dynamics of 'globalization' (put simply as growing economic interdependence between countries and accelerated integration into the world market) are supposed to erode the capacities of the nation-states to regulate their domestic economies and to govern their countries. For China, this would mean that WTO accession, as a strong driving force toward globalization, should further reduce the already weakened grip on power of the central party-state.[5]

However, if the process of globalization, other things being equal, leads to the erosion of state power, other things are rarely equal. Rather, it can be argued that a different outcome seems more plausible in the case of China. This is because, seen from a functional perspective, while WTO accession will increase individual decision-making powers, it can at the same time be expected to increase the leverage of central state agencies vis-à-vis sectoral and local interests. In general, the need for a 'management of globalization' strengthens the position of the central government: Regional actors cannot provide sufficiently well the complex regulatory tasks that are required for the management of international financial transactions, of a stable currency, of technological and educational innovation etc, which have become more and more critical factors of governance. Local and sectoral agents increasingly rely on the centre to deliver these goods. Thus, while the central government will have to withdraw increasingly from social and economic life, its role in regulating the overall economic framework, implementing national and international standards, and checking on local and sectoral self-interests will be enhanced.[6]

The mere prospect of China's entry into the WTO has also already made it easier for the central authorities to push through reforms that seemed to have reached an impasse. By using the constraints of international negotiations and WTO rules as an 'external stick', the leadership has, during the past year or so, already proved able to break crucial deadlocks in the reforms of the state-owned enterprises, of the financial markets, and of the ownership system – three areas of domestic reform which had been entangled in a close web of vested interests.[7]

As elaborated in Wang Yong's cobtribution to this volume, party and government organs are in a continuous process of streamlining. This painful process, which has been intensified in the light of WTO accession, aims at reducing the influence of vested interests and improving policy coordination at the central level.[8] Of course, streamlining the bureaucracy does not guarantee higher efficiency, but it seems to have already improved the chances for the central leadership to assert itself.

The same trend is demonstrated by the fact that a thorough reform of the tax system is on its way, together with more efficient curbs on wide-spread smuggling, tax-evasion, and corruption activities.[9] As a consequence, the central government's share of fiscal revenues, which has been steadily declining since the early 1980s, now seems to be on the rise again. According to official statistics published recently, China's total tax revenue topped 4.7 trillion yuan during the 1996–2000 period, 3.2 times the amount of the period 1991–95; tax revenue is expected to account for 14% of GDP in 2000, compared to 10.2% in 1995. The tax revenue of the central government is reported to account for 59% of the total tax revenue in China in 2000, compared with the ratio of 57% five years ago.[10]

If these numbers reflect real trends accurately, the increasing extractive capacities of the central government bode well for the growing role it will have to play in redistributing benefits and costs resulting from WTO accession. As is acknowledged unequivocally by Chinese and international commentators, gains and losses will not be evenly distributed over society. To avoid sharpening distributive conflicts between winners and losers of WTO accession, the government will have to step up its efforts to compensate the latter through redistributive schemes. If analysts who have warned that the redistributive capacities of the central government, and hence its means to 'buy' social support, have been shrinking over the reform period are right,[11] recent developments seem to indicate that this trend is slowly but steadily being reversed.

Last but not least, WTO accession should cause the balance of power to shift more toward the centre once the WTO requirement of 'uniform administration' is implemented, that is, the elimination of protectionist barriers by uniform application of WTO rules across provinces and sectors. Of course, it would be naive to suppose that the Chinese leadership will be whole-heartedly committed to wiping out protectionism. There are too many economists and bureaucrats who demand that the government take measures to protect domestic industries if it does not want the Chinese economy to fall prey to multinational companies. They rightly point to the fact that WTO rules do indeed allow for limited protection.[12] However, while in the past the degree of protection depended mainly on the creativity of local and sectoral actors, it can be assumed that this will change in the wake of WTO accession: With the menace of the WTO dispute settlement mechanism readily at hand, it will be for the central authorities to determine which industries will enjoy which degree of protection. Thus, the prediction is *not* that WTO accession will put *an end to protectionism* in China, but that the *discretion on how much protection* is granted will gradually be shifted to the centre.

The normative perspective: Enhanced legitimacy to rule

One might object here: If WTO accession will indeed strengthen the leverage of the central party-state to assert itself over local and sectoral interests, does this bode well for political and social stability? Undoubtedly, there is a real danger that the use of WTO accession as an external stick to push through domestic reforms might provoke conflicts or even clashes if systematically disadvantaged groups feel pressured so much that they conquer parts of the public sphere and start to articulate and collectively organize their interests. In contrast to the present situation, where protests are mostly confined to restricted groups of urban workers or peasants directly affected by local hardships, this could lead to widespread unrest across social strata and regions. Yet, the stability of the political system substantially hinges on another critical factor, namely, the moral standing and the social acceptance of state power. It will be argued that WTO accession can be expected to enhance not only the *capacity* but also the *legitimacy* of the central party-state to rule, and thus to enhance its ability to handle potential conflicts which are already latent or might arise in the future.

A first reason that may sound superficial – but in fact is not – is the enormous political capital which is bestowed upon the central leaders through their prominent appearance on the international stage. The series of high-ranking visits to and from foreign countries in close succession, the inflation of toasts and handshakes with the world's top leaders lining up in Beijing, and the new kind of quick-witted humour which President Jiang Zemin seems to have learned in his conversations with foreign guests, create an aura of international prestige and responsibility which should not be underestimated. More specifically, the mere prospect of China joining the WTO as an equal partner with global standing has already increased the acceptance of thorough measures taken by the central leadership among major parts of the bureaucracy and the populace.[13]

There is a dark side to this factor which should be mentioned here: if warnings that there is a crisis looming for the WTO come true, with negotiations reaching an impasse and a new round of liberalization stalling indefinitely, then the newly acquired international prestige of the Chinese leadership might backfire. A WTO crisis could give rise to those voices in China who accuse the leadership of 'betraying' and 'selling out' the country to foreign imperialists, thus severely harming the legitimacy of the central party-state. These voices made themselves heard quite distinctly in 1999, especially after the NATO bombing of the Chinese embassy in Belgrade. Until now, however, they have not been able to drown the general pro-accession consensus.[14]

Short of such a setback in the international standing of the Chinese leadership, the social acceptance of the party-state at home does not seem uncomfortably low. By and large, a patriotically-minded populace seems to be convinced that more or less authoritarian party rule is the best available alternative to defend the country against the challenges of globalization and to safeguard steady development.[15] Hoping to catch up with the world's developed economies in the not too distant future, people seem prepared to temporarily – that is, during an extended period of anticipation – suffer some economic and social hardship (*chi ku*) or, at least, to accept delays in 'getting rich' (*zhi fu*) relative to others. This is not necessarily so because they buy into cheap party propaganda. Instead, the Communist Party has quite successfully projected itself as advocate of social welfare and manager of social risks in a more modern sense than orthodox ideology used to suggest.

This can be illustrated by an example of the public discussion of unemployment. The topic of unemployment had been a long-time taboo of socialist rule. It was only in the early 1990s that the official media started to address the topic. Until recently, however, only the official urban unemployment rate (lately around 3 per cent) was recorded in public statistics, while the much larger numbers of so-called 'administratively discharged' (*xiagang*) workers (who are formally still on the enterprises' pay-roll but are actually unemployed) were not aggregated to form a coherent, nation-wide picture. Nor would the average Chinese citizen find statistical information on the redundant rural labour force which he met daily on the street in the form of poor migrant workers.[16]

Table 1: Estimation of the changes in China's employment structures seven years after WTO accession

Sector	Absolute change of employment (mio. jobs)	Relative change of employment (per cent)
Agriculture	– 9.66	– 3.6
Food processing	+ 0.17	+ 2.1
Textile	+ 0.28	+ 23.6
Garment	+ 0.26	+ 52.3
Automobiles	– 0.50	– 14.5
Machinery	– 0.53	– 2.5
Building & Construction	+ 0.93	+ 2.2
Services	+ 0.27	+ 2.1

Data: Hou, Shusen, *WTO gei Zhongguo baixing dailai shenmo?* (What will WTO Bring for the Chinese?), Beijing: Jingji Ribao chubanshe, 2000, p. 188.

Now, with WTO accession drawing closer, the party propaganda line has changed significantly. What readers of the official media and of popular science publications find is a much more detailed, and sometimes controversial, discussion of the topic. This can be shown by an estimate of changes in employment in various domestic sectors published last year in a best-selling book about the WTO's impact on China (cf. Table 1) (and, similarly, in other publications). Here, official and unofficial unemployment are not longer treated separately; instead, they are lumped together to reflect the real employment effects to be expected in various industries. Also, rural unemployment is now statistically identified and estimated to rise by 10 million in the wake of WTO accession.[17] Of course, these numbers can be doubted as can be any statistics, but, interestingly enough, they are converging with, if not outright duplicating, international statistics that have become available for the Chinese reader, too.

Thus, the author of another best-selling book complains that the Chinese media are using statistics produced by the United Nations Conference on Trade and Development (UNCTAD) and the Asian Development Bank. He argues that these statistics are dangerously underestimating the costs of unemployment resulting from WTO accession. According to data he offers, the real unemployment rate had already reached about 25 per cent by the end of 1999 and will increase even further after WTO accession.[18]

The point to be made here is that a subtle shift has occurred in the image of party rule: unemployment, acknowledged to be the number-one challenge of WTO accession, is now rendered as a 'normal' economic problem which the citizens are expected to deal with reasonably. The new style of discussion signals that the social risks of WTO accession have been calculated well and that the leadership is confident that these risks can and will be handled.[19] One publication even goes so far as to present the following formula: if the inflation rate plus the unemployment rate amount to more than 25 per cent, then social stability will be impaired.[20] As the inflation rate has lately been moving around zero, this formula actually seems to imply that a real unemployment rate of 25 per cent is still in the manageable range. The course of action seems clear – though, of course, it will not solve the problem overnight: in order to enhance labour mobility over sectors and regions, the strict urban-rural divide which has existed for decades will gradually be dissolved. At the same time efforts will be stepped up to secure minimum income levels for the poorest groups and to improve the social security system, which is seen as a critical safeguard of social and political stability and has therefore been declared a top priority of the new five-year plan (for the years 2001–05) announced in March 2001.[21]

To sum up the basic tenet of these arguments: if there has been, as some commentators have found, a gradual decay of party rule over the reform period,[22] the Chinese leadership seems to have embarked on the course of WTO accession in the hope that it will reverse this downward trend and enhance the capacity and legitimacy of party rule.

Prophecy B: Will There Be an Information Revolution?

The role of the internet

Turning now to the second prophecy about the evolution of China's political system cited: will WTO accession bring forth an information revolution in China? Will it, – through the spread of the Internet and other ways of communication, as President Clinton's prophecy goes – 'unleash forces that no totalitarian operation can control'?

At first glance, the answer is no. Of course, China's information borders have become more porous than before, thus not only allowing a larger inflow of external information and the introduction of new media, but also heating competition among traditional media at home. Also, more rapid and efficient flows of information have put pressure on the goverment to open up, consult with the public on important issues, and react more quickly to unexpected events – in a sense, thus, policy-making has become more transparent. Finally, and more generally, as the access to information has increased tremendously over the past years, a gradual pluralization of values, interests and lifestyles, at least among the younger generation, has taken place. The further spread of the Internet and the availablity of more and more 'international goods' in the wake of China's WTO accession will intensify these trends.[23]

However, at the same time, Chinese leaders are fully aware of this process. While they have not yet tried to go against the tide of pluralization per se, they are trying quite resolutely to curb attempts of articulation and organization of social interests that might become politically effective. The case of Falun Gong, which has tried systematically to escape the organizational monopoly of Communist party rule and thus provoked a sustained political conflict, can be seen in this perspective.

Recent examples of state interference into the public sphere illustrate that instruments of authoritarian, if not 'totalitarian' control are still used quite effectively where the leadership deems them necessary to prevent party rule from being challenged. For instance, in August 2000 President Jiang Zemin was reported to have issued a call for tighter controls on the media, warning that 'anti-socialist' and 'decadent' ideas could sweep the country after the mainland was obliged to open up certain media and telecommunication sectors to foreign companies after WTO entry.[24] In November 2000, official media reported that the Chinese government has listed cable TV networks as a prohibited area for foreign investment and that a national cable TV group will be formed.[25]

The internet is the most typical example here. The view that the internet, due to its technical complexity and the sheer volume of information transported through this medium, cannot be controlled effectively by the state or any other agency, does not seem totally convincing. On the contrary, one could argue that, for the common user, the fact of technical complexity and essential lack of oversight of the medium makes it extremely difficult to assess how much control is really possible. As a rule, therefore, control instruments do not have to function perfectly in order to be effective. The mere announcement of control measures to be implemented by various state agencies, as reported in great length in the Chinese press over the last year, heightens the sense of self-censorship.[26] Should a young man or woman have the ambition to articulate sensitive political messages, he or she might think twice before making use of this medium.

In a more positive sense, the Chinese government can be observed to be making active use of the new medium for its own purposes. One of the earliest internet projects was designed to connect government leaders and to give them access to data held by various organizations under the jurisdiction of the Communist Party. After two decades of economic liberalization and devolution of power to lower administrative levels which have created vast pockets of misinformation and fake statistical reporting, the government seems to have discovered the internet as a device to regain information control over these areas and to check on the behavior of local agents.[27]

Party and state agencies have also used cyberspace quite effectively to monitor and manipulate public opinion. Not only have they allegedly used the internet to launch attacks on Falung Gong and to deface Taiwan government web sites during cross-strait tensions, but they also found the internet useful for spreading propaganda and channelling public sentiment. The Belgrade embassy bombing in May 1999 seems to have created a new pattern of interaction between a public articulating their 'innermost', sometimes outrageous, emotions, the state propaganda apparatus filtering, co-ordinating and channelling these utterances into a stream of tempered nationalism serving official ends.[28]

More examples of recent state interference into the public sphere could be given to illustrate that instruments of authoritarian, if not 'totalitarian' control are still used quite effectively where the leadership deems them necessary to prevent party rule from being challenged.

With these kinds of 'totalitarian operations' intact, a direct link between the internet and democracy seems too simplistic. The prospects for the formation of a 'virtual civil society', which some see emerging in chat rooms and bulletin boards across China,[29] seem rather dim, at least over the medium term. In general, internet communication, due to its anonymity and diffuseness, does not seem to offer adequate structures for a public sphere in the sense of an integrated space where the articulation of critical voices is not only stimulated but also held accountable. Also, the internet per se has not yet proved an effective forum for transforming and organizing individual voices into committed civic activities where there is not a pre-set organizational agenda of some kind. As the Chinese authorities have, until now, quite successfully prevented the emergence of autonomous civic organizations, it is difficult to see how a 'virtual' civil society could develop independently from 'real world' civic organizations to become a hotbed for democratization in China.

The role of expertise

Another kind of 'information revolution' seems within closer reach, however. The very process of China's WTO accession, as can be discerned already, creates a real and strong demand for professional information and expertise in various fields. It is this demand for expertise and knowledge of best practices that could lead to a substantial empowerment of new elites who – given the absence of a civil society, real or virtual – could spearhead substantial changes in China's political structure.

To start this argument, a Chinese economist can be cited who, in an article published in summer 1999, aimed to convince his readers that joining the WTO would be a premature step. According to his view, the alleged advantages of WTO accession which have been propagated to the Chinese public have to be questioned. Among these advantages, the claim that China, as a WTO member, will be able to participate in setting the rules of international trade, cannot be upheld. This is, the author argues, because the rules of international trade covered in the WTO process, with all their economic and legal subtleties, are simply a too complex and sophisticated matter to be grasped by the bulk of poorly educated professionals available in China.[30]

This harsh criticism does indeed point to a real scarcity of professional expertise in China which has often been lamented. However, one does not necessarily have to share the author's highly pessimistic assessment of the present and future situation. Rather, one has to see that, first, there is already a 'new breed', albeit small, of highly educated professionals in their thirties and forties in the fields of management, economics, IT and other fields of specialization. Second, there are many more young Chinese in Asian and Western countries who have acquired highly specialized skills and who are are now considering returning home in larger numbers to support their country. According to recently published government sources, more than 20,000 experts have returned in recent years from their studies overseas for work to Beijing alone.[31] As recent personal communications with Chinese living abroad indicate, many more seem ready to return home now in the face of the opportunities opening up through WTO accession. Third, international partners are offering China a vast array of expertise and consultancy for the pre- and the post-accession stages. In fact, the supply of expertise by international companies and, particularly, by international donors, seems so large that the Chinese side can afford to select some offers and politely refuse others.[32]

To illustrate this growing role of expertise, some recent examples from developments in the legal field may be given. As WTO accession requires the adaptation of national laws to WTO rules, the demand for expertise is extremely strong in this field. First of all, the process of legislation, formally vested in the National People's Congress (NPC) and and its Standing Committee, should strengthen the role of legal and other professional experts. While the NPC, as widely criticized, is still heavily dominated by the interests of the Communist Party, a steady growth of legislative output and competence can be observed since the beginning of the 1990s, particularly among members of the NPC's nine specialized committees.[33] In the years to come, this trend of legislative empowerment of the NPC could be reinforced by the sheer complexity of legal matters involved in China's accession to the WTO – even more so in the light of the fact that WTO rules will have precedence over Chinese laws. Among the laws to be drafted or revised by the NPC in the near future are anti-dumping and anti-subsidy rules, joint venture, copyright and trademark laws, regulations on anti-trust, foreign trade, import and export commodities inspections etc.[34] Being a committed member of the Communist Party simply does not suffice any more to cope with these complex tasks.

There will also be growing demand for legal experts outside the field of legislation. Within the short or mid-term, we could see lawyers filling a substantial part of posts not only in the state bureaucracy, but also in consultancy firms and in the boards of directors of larger companies.[35] To meet the growing demand, China has recently welcomed an influx of foreign lawyers in significantly larger numbers than before. More cities will be opened to international law firms in the near future, and foreign lawyers will be allowed to expand their services to include matters of China's national law. Lawyers from Hong Kong are particularly welcomed as they are familiar with both international and Chinese legal norms.[36]

By opening the door to foreign lawyers, Chinese leaders also hope to raise qualification standards among domestic professionals. Since the middle of the 1980s, 110,000 lawyers have been trained in China, and the number is expected to rise significantly after WTO accession.[37] Intensified competition should help to breed a new generation of highly-skilled Chinese lawyers within the next ten years. While the lack of specialists cannot be remedied over night, central and provincial government agencies have made quite some efforts during the past months to train more personnel in matters pertaining to WTO rules, procedures, and practices. As was announced most recently, selected groups of judges will be sent abroad over the next five years to receive systematic training in handling civil suits, intellectual property rights and administrative lawsuits according to international standards.[38]

Similar trends can be found in other professional areas where WTO accession entails an increased demand for expertise. State agenices at the central as well as the provincial level have started to send substantial numbers of civil servants abroad to acquaint themselves with international practices in fields relevant to WTO accession, such as public and business administration, macroeconomics, admininistration of science, education etc.[39] Universities and colleges, among them the prestigious Qinghua University in Beijing and Wuhan University, are offering training courses on WTO rules, free trade, anti-dumping export policies etc. which are taught by domestic and international scholars, experts and business people.[40] The recruitment of Hong Kong professionals into the mainland's financial and economic institutions – such as the recent appointment of Laura Cha, former deputy chairwoman of Hong Kong's Securities and Futures Commission, as deputy chairwoman of the powerful China Securities Regulatory Commission[41] – is another indicator that the need for professional sophistication is indeed acknowledged by the Chinese leadership.

Thus, WTO accession, with its demand for scarce expertise and the opening up of new career prospects, might in the end lead to the empowerment of new elites outside the traditional range of party cadres. In a marked distinction from the Soviet-trained 'revolutionary' generation of elder statesmen as well as from the slightly younger generation of technocrats shaped by the early reform period and pre-occupied with building a 'socialism with Chinese characteristics', members of the incoming professional elite will have learned to benchmark their work against an international set of values and best practices.

This, of course, does not preclude a co-optation of the new elites into the Communist Party. As before, it might be a good career move to become a party member. Nevertheless, the 'incorporation' of new professional elites into the power establishment could – through the impact they will have on the work style and the self-perception of the party itself and on the political culture at large – create an evolutionary, or even revolutionary, potential for political change. In the longer term, the presence of these new elites might thus produce a bias toward an opening up of China's political system – though this will not automatically imply the widening of an avenue toward more democratic participation of the broader populace.

Conclusion

To conclude, let us come back to President Clinton's prophecies. It has been argued that, no, WTO accession is not likely to bring about the demise of the mainland's one-party state in the nearer future. Rather, it might enhance the central party-state's capacity and legitimacy to rule. On the other hand, it was found that, yes, a substantial change could take place among the political and social elites which might amount to something like an 'information revolution'.

If all goes well, there is a chance that this change could, already in the medium term, lead to a transformation of the political system where international values and procedures form a relevant benchmark of political practice and a gateway for democratic options. Over the longer run, the prospects for a democratic empowerment of the broad populace, the emergence of a civil society, and the creation of a full-fledged system of checks and balances seem rather limited. It seems more likely that China will pursue an elite-centred path of political liberalization 'from above', where the Communist Party – perhaps renamed as the 'Socialist' Party – still plays a dominant role but where its power becomes increasingly constrained by a gradual internalization of democratic values.[42]

As promised, the arguments presented above are summarized by offering for discussion a set of 'rules' which could be relevant 'rules of the game' shaping China's Communist Party rule in the course of WTO accession:

New Rules for Communist Party Rule

1. The growing need for a 'management of globalization' shifts the balance of domestic political power toward the central party–state.

2. WTO accession serves as an 'external stick' for the leadership to assert itself against protectionist interests and to break deadlocks in the reform process.

3. International prestige is a crucial asset for the legitimation of party-state rule.

4. The populace will accept Communist Party rule as the best available alternative to safeguard the nation's development – as long as the party is able to communicate with sufficient credibility and transparency that it can manage the social risks reasonably well.

5. The internet and other media will remain under control as important instruments for the party to uphold its power.

6. In order to recruit enough expertise to deliver the goods, the party has to empower new elites.

7. Being 'red', in today's China, means being an expert.

Notes

[1]President Clinton in a speech to Democrats in New York on May 21st, 2000; cited from *South China Morning Post* (SCMP), 22., 23.05.2000.

[2]It has almost become an academic truism that Communist Party rule in China is far from forming a monolithic power structure. A highly insightful analysis and detailed account of how this truism translates in economic and political reality is given from a comparative perspective in: Heilmann, Sebastian, *Die Politik der Wirtschaftsreformen in China und Russland*, Hamburg: Institut für Asienkunde, 1999.

[3]He, Jianming, and Yongzheng Yang, 'The political economy of trade liberalisation in China' (Asia Pacific School of Economics and Management working papers, CEP99-1), Asia Pacific Press at the Australian National University, 1999, via: http://ncdsnet.anu.edu.au. The authors also mention that foreign direct investment companies have incentives to request protection in order to gain an advantage over their competitors outside China; cf. *ibid.*, p. 10–11. For the devolution of powers to local agents, cf. Holbig, Heike, 'Lokalverwaltung in der VR China. Zum Wandel parteistaatlicher Kontrollstrukturen seit 1979', *China aktuell*, 2001/2, pp. 153–168.

[4]SCMP, 23., 27.2.2001; *Asian Wall Street Journal*, 27.2.2001; *Financial Times*, 23.2.2001; *International Herald Tribune* (IHT), 27.2.2001.

[5]On the general impact of globalization on governance, cf. Wessels, Wolfgang, 'An Ever Closer Fusion? A Dynamic Macropolitical View on Integration Processes', *Journal of Common Market Studies*, vol. 35, no. 2 (June 1997), pp. 267–99; Jones, Barry R.J., 'Globalization and change in the international political economy', *Internatiol Affairs*, vol. 75 (1999), no. 2, pp. 357–67; on China, cf. Sandschneider, Eberhard, 'Parteiherrschaft unter Globalisierungsdruck: Probleme und Perspektiven des politischen Systems in der VR China', in Schucher, Günter, ed., *Asien unter Globalisierungsdruck. Politische Kulturen zwischen Tradition und Moderne*, Hamburg: Institut für Asienkunde, 2000, pp. 100–10; Gransow, Bettina, 'Die Politik der VR China zwischen Nationalismus und Globalisierung', *Berliner China-Hefte*, no. 18, March 2000, pp. 40–52.

[6]Cf. Friedman, Edward, 'Globalization, Legitimacy and Post-Communism in China: A Nationalist Potential for Democracy, Prosperity and Peace', 1998 (manuscript from the author). My thanks also go to Wang Yong for his comments on this issue.

[7]Holbig, Heike, 'Chinas WTO-Beitritt in politischer Perspektive – Wechselspiel zwischen nationalen und internationalen Verhandlungsprozessen', *China aktuell*, December 1999, pp. 1251–65. In his theory of 'two-level-games', Putnam has argued that the manoeuvrability of national leaders is enhanced through participation in international negotiations: on the one hand, they can implement otherwise unacceptable domestic policies by refering to external pressures arising from the negotiations with international partners; on the other hand, national leaders can push through their demands at the international level by arguing that a compromise would not be accepted 'at home'; Putnam, Robert D., 'Diplomacy and Domestic Politics, The Logic of Two-Level-Games', in: Evans, P.B. et al., eds, *Double-Edged Diplomacy. International Bargaining and Domestic Politics*, Berkeley: University of California Press, 1993, pp. 431–68.

[8]Cf. Wang Yong's contribution to this volume; see also Wang, Yong, 'Why China Went for WTO', *The China Business Review*, July–August 2000, pp. 42–45.

[9]For recent accounts of China's fiscal reforms cf. Hsu, Szu-chien, 'Central-Local Relations in the PRC under the Tax Assignment System: An Empirical Ecluation, 1994–1997', *Issues & Studies*, vol. 36, no. 2 (March–April 2000), pp. 32–72; Wedemann, Andrew, 'Budgets, Extra-budgets, and Small Treasuries: Illegal monies and local autonomy in China', *Journal of Contemporary China* (November 2000), vol. 9, no. 25, S. 489–511. For recent measures against corruption, smuggling, tax evasion etc., cf. Heilmann, Sebastian, Isabelle Gras, and Kristin Kupfer, 'Chinas politisch-ökonomisches Schattensystem: Schmuggelnetzwerke und der Beitritt zur WTO', *China aktuell*, July 2000, pp. 769–781; Holbig, Heike, '"Grösster Schmuggelskandal" in der Geschichte der Volksrepublik', *China aktuell*, January 2000, pp. 9–11; *Xinhua News Agency News Bulletin* (XNA), 18., 24.11., 15.12.2000; *Wen Wei Po*, 19.08.2000; SCMP, 3., 26., 31.3.2001.

[10]XNA, 18.12.2000.

[11]Cf. Wang, Shaoguang, 'The Social and Political Implications of China's WTO Membership', *Journal of Contemporary China*, vol. 9, no. 25 (November 2000), pp. 373–405; Cheng, Xiaonong, 'Breaking the Social Contract', in: Andrew, Nathan et al., eds, *Dilemmas of Reform in Jiang Zemin's China*, Boulder, London: Lynne Rienner, 1999, pp. 107–126.

[12]Han, Deqiang, *Pengzhuang – quanqiuhua yu Zhongguo xianshi xuanze* (Clash – the trap of globalization and China's real choice), Beijing: Jingji chubanshe (published online: http://www.chinabulletin.com/book/pz/pz.htm); Liu, Guangxi and Hanlin Zhang, eds, *WTO yu Zhongguo jingji (ganbu duben)* (WTO and the Chinese economy (recommended reading for cadres)), Beijing: Zhonggong zhongyang dangxiao chubanshe, 2000; Hou Shusen, *WTO gei Zhonguo baixing dailai shenmo?* (What does WTO bring to the Chinese people?), Beijing: Jingji Ribao Chubanshe, 2000; XNA, 10.01., 27.12.2000; Beijing DRCnet, 31.10.2000, via: *Summary of World Broadcast* FE/W0666/CNS 151100.

[13]Cf. Friedman, *op. cit.*; Fischer, Doris, *Kalkuliertes Risiko? China und die WTO* (Berichte des Bundesinstituts für ostwissenschaftliche und internationale Studien 13–2000), Köln: Bundesinstitut für ostwissenschaftliche und internationale Studien, 2000.

[14]Fewsmith, Joseph, 'China and the WTO: The politics behind the agreement', NBR Analysis (National Bureau of Asian Research online publication), vol. 10, no. 5 (December 1999), via: www.nbr.org/publications/analysis/vol10no5/essay2.html; Fewsmith, Joseph, 'The impact of WTO/PNTR on Chinese politics', NBR Analysis (National Bureau of Asian Research online publication), vol. 11, no. 2 (July 2000), via: www.nbr.org/publications/analysis/vol11no2/essay2.html.; on a possible WTO crisis, cf. Wahl, Peter, 'Zwischen Hegemonialinteressen, Global Governance und Demokratie. Zur Krise der WTO', *Internationale Politik und Gesellschaft*, no. 3 (2000), pp. 235–246; *Neue Zürcher Zeitung*, 12.01.2001.

[15]Cf. Wang, Jianwei, 'Democratization and China's Nation Building', in: Friedman, Edward and Barrett L. McCormick, eds, *What If China Doesn't Democratize? Implications for War and Peace*, Armonk, New York: Sharpe, 2000, pp. 49–73.

[16]For a more detailed discussion of these categories cf. the contribution by Flemming Christiansen to this volume below.

[17]Hou, *op. cit.*, p. 188; for other discussions of employment in the wake of China's WTO accession cf. Qu Dafu (ed.), *WTO yu guoren* (WTO and the Chinese), Beijing: Renmin Ribao chubanshe, 2000, pp. 413–432; Zhang Jianhua (ed.), *Jiejue Zhongguo zaidu mianlin de jinyao wenti* (Solving the most urgent problems repeatedly confronting China), Beijing: Jingji Ribao chubanshe, 2000, pp. 90–93; Jia

Jifeng et al., *Jiaru WTO yihou de xin wenti* (New problems after joining WTO), Shanghai: Shanghai shehuikexueyuan chubanshe, 2000, pp. 60–76.

[18]Han, *op. cit.*, pp. 8–10.

[19]Cf. Fischer, *op. cit.*

[20]Hou, *op. cit.*, p. 193.

[21]Cf. Schueller, Margot, 'Chinas Wirtschaft am Ende des Millenniums – Anzeichen für Überwindung der Wachstumsschwäche im Jahre 2000 und ehrgeizige Ziele im 10. Fünfjahresplan', *China aktuell*, March 2001, pp. 289–298; The detailed Chinese version of the five-year plan can be found in *Renmin Ribao*, 18.3.2001.

[22]E.g., Shambaugh, David, 'The Chinese Leadership: Cracks in the Façade?', in: David Shambaugh (ed.), *Is China Unstable? Assessing the Factors*, Armonk/ London: M.E. Sharpe, 2000, pp. 27–39, here p. 36; Cheng, Xiaonong, *op. cit.*; Wu, Guogang, 'Legitimacy Crisis, Political Economy, and the Fifteenth Party Congress', in: Andrew Nathan et al. (eds), *Dilemmas of Reform in Jiang Zemin's China*, Boulder, London: Lynne Rienner, 1999, pp. 13–32.

[23]My thanks go to Professor Wang Yong for his comments on the use of the Internet in China; cf. Kalthil, Shanthi, 'The Internet and Asia: Broadband or Broad Bans', www.ceip.org/files/Publications/internet_asia.asp?p=5&from=pubdate.

[24]SCMP, 31.8.2000.

[25]XNA, 30.11.2000.

[26]For the details of internet control in China, cf. Giese, Karsten, 'Das gesetzliche Korsett für das Internet ist eng geschnürt', *China aktuell*, October 2000, pp. 1173–1184.; Wacker, Gudrun, *Hinter der virtuellen Mauer. Die VR China und das Internet*, Berichte des Bundesinstituts für ostwissenschaftliche und internationale Studien, 06/2000; Neumann, Lin A., 'The Great Firewall', CPJ Briefings, www.cpj.org/Briefings/2001/China_jan01/China_jan01.html; IHT, 24./25.3.2001; *Asian Wall Street Journal*, 05.12.2000, SCMP, 28.12.2000

[27]Cf. IHT, 24./25.3.2001; Giese, *op. cit.*; Thomas, Simona, 'Das Internet in der VR China' (part I/II), *China aktuell*, May 1999, pp. 500–510, June 1999, pp. 596–606.

[28]Cf. Hughes, Chris Rene, 'Nationalism in Cyberspace', *Cambridge Journal of International Studies*, spring 2000; Fewsmith, Joseph, 'The Impact of the Kosovo Conflict on China's Political Leaders and Prospects for WTO Accession', in: National Bureau of Asian Research (NBR), www.nbr.org/publications/briefing/fewsmith99/index.html;

[29]Cf. David Wall, 'Who's afraid of the WTO? Not me said the CCP', *Japan Times*, 10.2.2001.

[30]Cui Zhiyuan, 'Jiaru shijie maoyi zuzhi bu shi Zhongguo de dangwu zhi ji' (Joining the World Trade Organization is not China's most urgent option), *Zhongguo yu shijie* (China and the World) (online journal), August 1999, via: http://www.chinabulletin.com/99/zs9908c.htm, pp. 1–2. This article is one among various critical articles on the WTO which have been published in the online journal *China and the World* (*Zhongguo yu shijie*). According to the editor, this journal can be accessed throughout China and is widely read among professionals and people in academia (personal Email correspondence with the editor, January 2001).

[31]XNA, 22.12.2000.

[32]Just to name one out of the innumerable activities in this field, the Deutsche Gesellschaft für Technische Zusammenarbeit (GTZ) is offering a series of training and advisory services tailored to the needs of China's WTO accession, among them an advisory service to the Financial and Economic Committee of the Nat-

ional People's Congress, focusing on the reform of commercial laws in China; communication with GTZ representatives, January, March 2001.

[33]These are, in the order of their (re)creation between 1983 and 1998: the Law Committee, the Nationalities Committee, the Financial and Economic Affairs Committee, the Foreign Affairs Committee, the Overseas Chinese Affairs Committee, the Education, Science, Culture and Public Health Committee, the Internal and Judicial Affairs Committee, the Environment and Resources Protection Committee, and the Rural Work Committe; cf. Cabestan, Jean-Pierre, 'The Relationship between the National People's Congress and the State Council in the People's Republic of China: A Few Checks but No Balances' (Centre d'Etudes Français sur la China contemporaine, Working Paper, no. 1, July 2000); for the changing role of the National People's Congress see also Tanner, Murray Scott, 'The National People's Congress', in: Goldman, Merle and Roderick MacFarquhar (eds), *The Paradox of China's Post-Mao Reforms*, Cambridge, M.A., London: Harvard University Press, 1999, pp. 100–128; Holbig, Heike, 'Loyale Ambitionen. Die Jahrestagung des Nationalen Volkskongresses', *China aktuell*, March 2001, pp. 279–288.

[34]XNA, 5.3.2001.

[35]Cf. a speech by Li Yining, a prominent professor of economics and delegate to the National People's Congress; XNA, 19.11.2000.

[36]*Asian Wall Street Journal*, 13.11.2000; XNA, 16.01.2001; SCMP, 21.11.2000.

[37]The huge potential for future developments in this field becomes obvious when one looks at the share of lawyers in society: In China, the present ratio is one lawyer per 11,000 citizens – in the US, the ratio is one lawyer per 300 citizens; *Financial Times*, 21.11.2000; cf. XNA, 18.11.2000.

[38]XNA, 19.11., 06.12.2000, 28.2.2001; SCMP, 5.12.2000.

[39]XNA, 30.3.2001.

[40]SCMP, 2.3.2001.

[41]*Hong Kong iMail* (online version), 9.3.2001.

[42]For a discussion of democratic options in China cf. Friedman, *op. cit.*; Pei, Minxin, 'China's Evolution Toward Soft Authoritarianism', in: Friedman, Edward and Barrett L. McCormick, eds, *What If China Doesn't Democratize? Implications for War and Peace*, Armonk, New York: Sharpe, 2000, pp. 74–98; Bachman, David, 'China's Democratization: What Difference Would it Make for U.S.– China Relations?', in: Friedman and McCormick (eds), *op. cit.*, pp. 195–223.

9

Will WTO Accession Threaten China's Social Stability?

Flemming Christiansen

WTO Accession and Economic Reforms

What does accession to the WTO mean for China's social stability? Some Chinese economists seem to believe that WTO accession will be an instrument with which the Chinese leadership can achieve the aims of the reform policies. According to Wang Hongliang, the WTO can help break down 'local protectionism' and other practices that 'violate the laws of the economy', and will 'strengthen competition' by 'creating a united domestic market'.[1] The vision of a ruthless and quick-fix application of reform measures, using the WTO as a cudgel, does not bode well for social stability, for it is the local protectionism, the gradual and circumspect achievement of partial goals, and the flexibility that have prevented much social harm from arising during the reforms. Will the WTO be a political lever for impatient reformers faced with obstinate locals who refuse to reform? Or will it kindle a competitive spirit strong enough to demolish the last bastions of the planned economy?

The social effects of China's WTO accession will depend on how it helps China's reform policies along, and how the political leadership is able to mediate the large problems that will arise in the further reform process. Many have speculated that WTO accession is a victory for reformers over those reluctant to embrace reforms,[2] while others have emphasized that the Chinese leadership stands rather united when it comes to major reform issues and the WTO.[3] Acharya's remark that the process of entering the international trade and tariffs regime began in 1986 with China's stated wish to participate fully in the GATT, probably reflects the situation best. According to this author,

> [...] many of the domestic economic and political reforms and the changes in its foreign trade regime can be comprehended more thoroughly by contextualising them in the PRC's attempt to engage with the global, multilateral economic and financial institutions [...] the movement has invariably been in the direction of eventual integration into the neo-liberal international economic order.[4]

Thus, we cannot see China's WTO accession as isolated from the reforms. There may be differences in interpretations and preferences among Chinese leaders relating to specific issues, but there is little reason to believe that WTO accession is a separate issue that is used by a faction to reinforce reforms in the face of opposition from other leaders or lower level officials. To the contrary, Chinese economists, political scientists and officials seem to agree that WTO accession is an integrated part of China's socialist economy at the present stage and is fully compatible with the 'laws of the economy' (*jingji guilü*); in their minds, China's problems can only be solved by pursuing the reform policies (and this is the light in which one ought to understand Wang Hongliang's ideas cited above).

Assessing the impact of WTO accession on social stability is thus largely an issue of identifying how the gradual changes in China's political economy cause social transition, and to what extent practices directly linked with foreign trade and investment may influence the situation.

Market 'Mechanism' and Strong State

While the Chinese economy during the last twenty-two years has become increasingly market-driven, the state has, both centrally and locally, played a strong role, delimiting the framework within which the market flourished. The state has used incisive measures and repeatedly shifted the goal posts, thus affecting the economic behaviour of the various players. State intervention, not the withering away of the state, has been a core factor generating growth in the private economy. The political economy of China as it has developed during the reforms has both reflected the rise of market exchange and of market-like exchange mechanisms aimed at nurturing the development of *public choice.* It has also encompassed state intervention and regulation aimed at *manipulating* public choice. The economic self-interest inherent in public choice is an important factor, for it breeds, as many economists and politicians believe, rational distribution of resources in the economy.

The trajectory of the reforms, however, has not been smooth. The legal and regulatory systems were insufficient, and so new *intended* developments proceeded in contravention of formal rules, encouraged or at least condoned by the authorities, but often beyond their control. The notions of legal protection and of the rule of law, therefore, never gained the upper hand in the reform process. Particularistic bonds, favouritism and corruption, to the contrary, dominated the culture of economic and political interaction. What is more, the outcome of government manipulation of the economy during the 1980s and 1990s aimed at directing the utilization of foreign currency incomes through the use of foreign exchange certificates, favouring certain parts of the economy through subsidized allocation of production factors and dual track pricing systems, and protecting the domestic market through import and export tariffs and many other measures, caused *unintended* and *explicitly illegal* practices to proliferate. Large-scale smuggling and corruption scandals of extraordinary dimensions – often involving high-ranking officials – thus arose out of the reform process.[5]

The aim of most reform measures was to break down administrative control over the economy and to invigorate the economy through public choice and 'market mechanisms'[6] aimed at rational distribution of resources. In order to break down the planned economy, the authorities used state intervention, created barriers in the economy, seeking gradually to divest itself of direct management of the economy, and nurturing public choice both in administration and the economy. The side effect of this transitional regime has been predatory behaviour by individuals, authorities and companies, causing venality, uncertainty and high transaction costs. From the perspective of mature market economies with smoothly functioning institutions, the Chinese reform model has appeared irrational and wasteful.

As a part of the reform process, the central state relinquished much of its fiscal and financial control, devolving tax-raising powers to local governments. Decision-making powers were handed down to provincial, city, and county level authorities, while central laws and regulations became less detailed. The centre aimed at binding localities to policy targets through 'administrative contracts' on joint financing of programmes and gross social development policies. The central state, therefore, appeared weakened, while the local state authorities were given leverage to make tough decisions on development priorities, and also to make decisions which the centre did not applaud. The increasing powers at local levels of government have increased the propensity for corrupt behaviour and for local protectionism, thus potentially suffocating reform initiatives. Similarly, inter-departmental competition and work-unit protectionism created obstacles to reform. We may, accordingly, consider the reforms as paradoxical: self-interest as a political engine for reform turned against the reforms. Market forces unleashed as a rational alternative to the planned economy engendered venal behaviour and irrational outcomes. The Chinese leadership was aware of and monitored the adverse effects,[7] but seemed united in the effort to seek long-term solutions to them rather than to use them as an excuse to undo the reforms.

While the priorities of the reforms were to generate growth and restructure the economy and the political administration by creating and using imbalances and barriers in the economy, the priority in the present stage of reform increasingly seems to be to create a level playing field. This is not only a prerequisite for WTO accession, but also for a healthy development of the economy, as it will remove some of the structures which gave rise to corruption, smuggling, foreign currency rackets and so on.

Social Barriers and Projections of Social Development

One of the problems we face when we want to predict the social evolution in the coming years is that the present reforms seem to do away with barriers in the economy which determine China's social make-up. These include the labour and personnel administration, as well as the household registration system. The personnel administration of the Chinese state has reduced the number of official posts in the administrative systems at central and local levels, thus minimizing the number of civil servants. This, to use a public choice term, 'slimming of the state' has redefined whole segments of public administration as economic units responsible for generating their own incomes, and their employees have become part of the general labour market and will gradually be exposed to competition on salaries and labour efficiency. The labour market for graduates from higher education has now for a long period been based on market-like mechanisms, creating competitive mobility across sectors. The labour market for workers and lower-level functionaries has also begun to take shape, albeit slowly and gradually. In the 1980s, workers were encouraged to 'plunge into the sea [of self-employment]' (*xiahai*), some with a golden handshake or other incentives, and from the mid-1990s, redundant workers were 'administratively discharged' (*xiagang*), while labour contracts and implicit provisions for workers were under constant review. The Chinese labour system slowly approaches a 'level playing field' for urban workers.

More importantly, the household registration system that not only regulates within which jurisdiction people are resident, but also designates them as either 'agricultural' or 'urban resident', has since the mid-1980s lost much of its former ability to prevent migration and regulate the use of rural labourers in state-owned enterprises and urban areas. In addition, from the early 1980s to the late 1990s more than 100 million people with an 'agricultural household registration' switched from agriculture to rural non-agricultural work, and perhaps an equal number is occupied on a semi-permanent basis in the urban economy as 'temporary' residents. The household registration system was one of the major politically imposed barriers in the reform economy that helped stimulate growth in the rural non-agricultural sectors and allowed an immense growth rates in urban non-state sectors. To a large extent, it also protected urban residents from competition for resources and jobs.

The fact that these fundamental barriers are in a process of total disintegration makes it impossible for us to use our knowledge of China's social structures for a projection of future developments. Not only is the rural-urban barrier (in the form of the household registration system) about to give way to increasing labour mobility across the former division line, but – as will be argued below – the reform of state-owned enterprises also makes any predictions on employment impossible.

I shall in the following discussion include two policy issues where creating a level playing field has direct implications for social stability. These are the reform of the state-owned enterprises and the gradual abolition of the household registration system that divided the population into urban and rural residents. Based on this discussion, I shall then examine how WTO accession and the present course of reforms are likely to influence social stability in a broader sense.

Social instability arises when groups in society systematically become impoverished or experience relative deprivation in comparison to other groups; for such social instability to have political consequences it must be organized or lead to widespread unrest. In particular, it must have means of mass communication and access to the public sphere outside political control. There are scattered, sometimes large, incidences of unrest in various parts of China each year due to many different issues, but they tend to be localized and single-issue, and the political system is able to deal with most of them through a mixture of repression and concessions.

Who is losing out in the reforms? The four major groups we can identify are redundant urban workers, rural people who mainly rely on farming activities, people who are disenfranchised through poor educational provision, as well as urban pensioners. It is a moral and ideological problem for the Chinese Communist Party that workers and peasants, 'ordinary people' so to say, see their social standing eroded, while the new rich are able to display extravagant and hedonistic lifestyles which contrast with the ideals of frugality and decency propagated for more than half a century by the Communist Party.

The Reform of State-owned Enterprises and its Labour Market Effects

The reform of state-owned enterprises, one of the core issues of economic reform, is associated with mass redundancies. It was estimated that in 1997, of a total urban work force of 147 million, 10 million were administratively discharged (*xiagang*), while almost 12 million were affected by wage stoppages or lowering of wages, and almost 2 million pensioners faced non-payment or lowering of pension payments. About 3 million workers affected by wage stoppages or lowering of wage payments had incomes below the official base line for living expenses. More than 5.5 million urban residents were formally registered as unemployed.[8] These figures amount to a *real* unemployment of 15.5 million,[9] and to almost 30 million people affected by the crisis in the state-owned enterprises. Those most affected seem to be women, middle-aged and poorly educated, who are the first to be marginalized.[10] The situation in 1998 was slightly worse.[11] These observations are in harmony with government estimates of a real unemployment rate of around 20 per cent in urban and rural China.[12]

The urban figures reflect the crisis in the state-owned sector at an aggregate level. However, to assess the longer-term trends, we must not only consider the situation as it presents itself in the form of statistical categories such as 'urban' and 'state-owned' because the underlying divisions are, as already mentioned, poised to give way (at least in their present administrative significance) to a level playing field. The employees of state-owned enterprises are exclusively 'urban residents' (in terms of their administrative status), and so enjoy labour market prerogatives denied to those holding an 'agricultural household registration'.[13] In practice, these distinctions are becoming less important, and within a few years, urban residents and people with agricultural household registration will effectively compete in the same labour market. Already since the mid-1980s, people with agricultural household registration habe been able to change their status in increasing numbers, and they also entered the non-state urban sectors. Thus, the way the statistics are composed do not reflect the real, long-term developments.

The reform of the state-owned enterprises probably can best be seen as the deconstruction of the sector and its integration with other enterprise sectors (e.g. urban collective, rural, private, limited shareholding, partnership) into one economy. State ownership is gradually changing from an administrative relationship between parent departments and enterprises into a separation of formal and managerial ownership. The process, which started with the promulgation of China's Company Law in 1994,[14] has been slow and subject to much debate.[15] There seems to be a general acknowledgement that breaking the link between parent ministries and enterprises is desirable, and the reorganization of the State Council in the late 1990s as well as a spate of laws, regulations and policy statements all support the idea. The obstructions to this reform have largely been of a practical nature, due to the complexity and the many interests involved. Wei Jie has pointed to the fact that the Chinese state does not have a proper system for controlling its assets, thereby harming the reform of the state-owned enterprise system.[16] Few if any state-owned enterprises have yet completed their transition to fully autonomous entities as envisaged by the reform policies and the legislation. This is because the process of asset valuation, decisions on enterprise activity, the ownership of non-core assets, and negotiations with local government agencies on old rights and arrangements can be difficult and tardy. Practical arrangements may include items the value of which has to be assessed separately, such as the transfer of the pension burden to government departments, compensation for relinquishing ownership of residential quarters or renegotiation of contracts on maintaining services. Local governments and parent departments also need time to prepare for the transition. Before the state-owned enterprises become legally fully independent of their parent departments or the local governments, it is, for example, easier to swap assets with them, an issue that may be of great importance for city planning. It may be necessary to find alternatives for redundant workers, setting aside money in the budget to deal with particular expenses, and so on, *before* enterprises are allowed full autonomy.

The process is protracted in order to pre-empt problems, and as a consequence many state-owned enterprises have not yet gained the real independence they need to survive and grow. They are preparing for the new situation, shedding workers and making the most of 'soft' economic constraints, therefore appearing less efficient than they actually might be. Positive status reports from the State Economic and Trade Commission,[17] however, indicate that state-owned enterprises are about to become a sound economic sector.

Labour market effects

The effects of the state-owned enterprise reform on social stability, therefore, depend on the success of the reforms; while they are not complete, the Chinese authorities seem to regard the fundamental issues as settled. Improvements in the economy due to stronger, more dynamic and autonomous state-owned enterprises competing with other enterprises will create more demand for labour and may help some of the administratively discharged workers back into work. The 'level playing field', however, is likely to create a less fragmented labour market where formal distinctions between urban residents and agricultural households no longer determine the right to work in state-owned enterprises. Also, the form of remuneration is likely to shift from a mixture of monetary payments, waivers, subsidies and material fringe benefits to a predominantly monetary wage system, so that the relative market value of a labour contract becomes more visible. Life-long tenure has already disappeared, and salary scales are likely to reflect demand and supply, as employers will have much greater ability to set the terms.

Chinese society has already experienced a growing discrepancy between high and low incomes, clearly visible in lifestyle patterns. Yet, salary scales and management pressures within state-owned enterprises have only allowed for minor wage differences within enterprises. The exposure to labour market pressures and competition will most likely turn skills and efficiency performance into remuneration criteria and widen the income gap between employees within enterprises. State-owned enterprises, which are in general much larger and have a higher capitalization per worker, may soon become able to re-attract many of the highly skilled people they have shed during the last one or two decades and even some of the people who went abroad. The best technical and management staff in private and rural enterprises may be tempted by better conditions and salaries in the state-owned sector. A level playing field among enterprises as a result of the reforms is most likely to engender a wider stratification of the labour market, with highly skilled functionaries at one end and low paid casual workers at the other. Increasing economic activity in the state-owned sector, once its transformation is completed, will spawn demand for services and ancillary activities which the informal private sectors can accommodate due to the surplus of unemployed or partially unemployed people. This is already happening: service sectors can be observed directly reflecting demand created by high-earning self-employed and employees in private and joint venture enterprises.

The opening of the labour market will, in other words, make it irrelevant how large the urban unemployment is in today's terms. The core issue will be how large overall unemployment will be across the rural-urban boundary. Even if the main obstacle to migration in the form of jurisdiction of household registration is formally upheld, it is unlikely to be effective in the informal part of the labour market (covering individual labourers, unregistered enterprises, or mobile labour teams). Accordingly, aggregate unemployment increasingly becomes an issue. Some Chinese economists believe that due to China's regional poverty, around one-fifth of the working population is living in some form of hardship, scarcely interacting with the market, engaging in subsistence farming and petty local trades in rural areas. Perhaps 30 or 35 per cent are part of the formal labour market, which Chinese economists define by the principle the value of the workers' 'marginal productivity exceeds their wage', while between 40 and 50 per cent are self-employed. The latter are not part of the formal labour market, and their income for the same work effort is, by the reverse definition, considered to be lower than what they could expect in the formal labour market. In the urban economies in China, the formal labour market, according to the same economists, constitutes between 60 and 70 per cent of the work force, while the rest is self-employed.[18] Estimating the size of the formal and informal labour markets, they seem to assume that long-term employment in the established sectors such as state-owned and collective enterprises is equal to the formal labour market.

However, this model is flawed, because the decision to work in the formal labour market or to be self-employed is the outcome of calculations of individual risks and gains in response to policy intervention in the economy rather than a function of an economic principle under free market conditions. The formal labour market, as we know it today, provides low remuneration, but was until recently linked with high security and access to social provisions, while incomes in the self-employed sector were often (though not always) much higher, but associated with the perception of high risk and the absence of a social safety net. The privileges and subsidies granted by state-owned enterprises have distorted the labour market and caused the work force to make decisions based on these calculations of risk versus gain.[19] It is most likely, though difficult to substantiate with economic data, that a large proportion of the self-employed sector produces incomes that are not only higher than total remunerations (in cash and kind) for a similar work effort in the formal labour markets, but also equally sustained.

Labour market and social transformation

The bulk of the excess or under-performing work force in state-owned enterprises has, during the last two decades, gradually been encouraged to seek other opportunities. By administratively discharging employees in the last few years before becoming autonomous entities, state-owned companies are able to restructure themselves as profitable enterprises. This means that the informal sector we see today is a mixture of high-earning risk-takers and people dismissed from state-owned enterprises due to low productivity. Although an 'administratively dismissed' person, by definition, is somebody who has not yet found another job, it is well known that many of them are being absorbed into the informal sectors of the economy.

China's labour market is in a phase of transition from fragmentation under the planned economy to a level playing field. As this transition has not been fully realized yet, it is impossible to make straightforward predictions on the labour market composition in the future. Based on my observations above, I suggest that the transition of state-owned enterprises from an administratively managed sector to a sector of autonomous enterprises will cause an invigoration of labour market mobility, where it becomes easier and more attractive for employees to change jobs. It is likely that many administratively discharged persons will be absorbed by the informal sector as self-employed or will re-enter the labour market. Differences in wages and work conditions will increase.

As the social provisions of the work units disappear, and basic provisions like housing, pensions, medical care and so on become commercialized, weak groups in society will experience serious problems. For example, people presently living on small pensions in cheap housing may experience their pension being diminished or cut because their former work unit ceases to be responsible for paying it, leaving them with only local government payments for a minimum income.

They may also find that the property management company in charge of their housing becomes forced to gain a viable income from it, and demands rent increases. The combination of various factors can make life difficult for families, who in some cases will have to rely on poverty relief from the Civil Affairs Administration.

Others may find the transition morally and psychologically destabilizing; many of the values nurtured by the authorities over the last fifty years have centred on the work unit as a paternalistic, all-encompassing small society. Predictability, stability as well as a sense of egalitarianism and comradeship in fixed personal and political relationships have come under great pressure during the last twenty years, and the enterprise reform will deal the final blow to this type of community. Instability, relative deprivation, loss of orientation, and moral confusion experienced during the reforms may thus gain additional momentum with the demise of the work unit.

Public services such as education and medical provisions are now based on fee incomes, and social security, pensions, and unemployment benefits are being converted into insurance systems. The role of insurance and fee payment have already replaced free provision, making it particularly difficult for socially disadvantaged groups to seek medical treatment or receive adequate education. The family is, by law, still the main provider of social aid in China, and socially motivated redistribution through the state is minimal, aimed only at poverty relief.[20]

The social consequences of such changes are hard to evaluate. The main reasons for this are the socio-economic fluctuations over the reform period as well as the absence of broad social destitution or sustained poverty (with the exception of remote rural areas, places afflicted by natural disasters, and some cities hit by mass closures of old factories). Another reason is that the parameters for development have been constantly changing in the process of reform; what seemed to be a problem some years ago, appears to have been solved now. Corruption, repressive management, arbitrariness and injustice in public administration that have exacerbated the feeling of instability have affronted many of the people who formed the backbone of Communist support from the 1950s to the 1970s. The rise of the Falun Gong may be explained by the rise of dissatisfaction in those generations that now feel left behind during the ongoing social transformation.[21] The disenfranchised and disadvantaged, however, have not been capable of organizing themselves to formulate their grievances in a systematic way. The political restrictions imposed on civil society which aim at subduing political resistance and collective action for the improvement of social conditions pose a real problem to social stability. A more open labour market might, for example, entail demands for a much more comprehensive form of labour organization than the one presented by the existing official trade unions.

Social change and WTO accession

How will WTO accession affect social stability? In practical terms, WTO accession will have limited direct effects on social development and the labour market. It will, however, have an indirect impact by guiding the behaviour of enterprises and redefining economic interest.

In general, the imposition of equal treatment of domestic and foreign economic activities in China, the lowering of tariffs, and the incorporation of universal norms in administration and market practice may have positive effects. The self-interest of enterprises as economic players will not only become a strong driving force to realize domestic reforms, but will also promote the development of a culture of fair play. Furthermore, WTO rules will provide a moral justification and legal framework for undermining corruption, infringement on intellectual rights, and smuggling. This is already happening. Chinese companies and individuals, whose copyrights and trademarks are infringed, already bring legal action against the perpetrators. While large-scale smuggling scandals took place because officials were paid to turn a blind eye; legal importers and competitors will have a stronger case under WTO rules. Lowering tariffs and simplifying customs procedures will reduce incentives to smuggle. The evolution of a market culture based on legitimate economic interests, predictability and legality will undoubtedly lead to fairer employment conditions, replacing paternalistic and patronage-based practices with a meritocracy and economic rationality.

Moreover, the market success of some non-Chinese enterprises due to their flexibility, reliability, good management and high technical quality of products indicates that the competitive advantage in the future may not be price, but quality. The Chinese market of the reform era has been dominated by high risks, unreliability and lack of legal protection. The absence of a proper market culture and the authorities' manipulation of the economy created high transaction costs. Here, the sharpening of foreign competition on the Chinese market in the wake of WTO accession may introduce a culture of low transaction costs, i.e. reliability and predictability, which will ultimately be reflected in a higher level of trust. The positive effects for Chinese consumers will be great; it has already been observed that competition in some of the new economic sectors has led to great improvements in service provision and product quality.

In a broader sense, a culture of trust, fairness and legitimate economic dealings may engender better social relationships and percolate into the practices of state authorities.

The Divided Economy

Chinese economists have recently noted that China is experiencing an economic transition from an economy of scarcity to an economy of surplus. The total value of the goods and services in the market exceeds the total purchasing power, a situation that is new to China, where government intervention for the last fifty years has depressed retail prices, while ordinary people were holding large savings. The distribution of goods and services in an economy of scarcity is based on administrative allocation. The advantage is that it should be easier for the less well-off groups in society to sustain a reasonable level of consumption, while the more well-off are barred from excessive consumption (i.e. waste). The disadvantage is that administrative allocation allows state functionaries to confiscate the difference between the scarcity (shadow market) price and the list price for personal purposes, thus creating an endemic source of corruption. While an economy of surplus may help to do away with one root cause of corruption, it also raises the question of whether the state is seeking other ways to intervene in order to secure sufficient levels of consumption for poor groups in society.

In the short term, the groups that will suffer most markedly are the pensioners and the urban unemployed with low skills whose situation will certainly worsen. In the longer term, China's provision of general education will not be able prepare the population for the demands the future will hold for them. Disadvantaged urban strata and large groups in rural areas are presently deprived of adequate schooling. Also, their avenues for pursuing further and lifelong training and education are still much too limited. It would be a pity if China's work force excelled in being cheap rather than skilled. Education thus will be the most critical factor determining China's national competitiveness in the global economy in the long run.

The main future problem rests with the, perhaps, one fifth of the population that does not interact much with the market, producing themselves what they need and buying and selling only marginally. Among these people some are designated as poor, and are given assistance by the state under various schemes. Another issue is agriculture.

Here, WTO accession will, with great certainty, cause the prices of stable agricultural products in the domestic market to decline. As an important proportion of the cash income in agriculture is generated from staple crops, peasant incomes may be affected negatively. We have, however, in the past seen very rapid responses from the peasants to price incentives and market fluctuations and generally very efficient reactions in the form of labour diversification, supported by state initiatives. If any group in Chinese society is able to cope with the market forces it is the peasants, who have been exposed to market fluctuations and changing marketing patterns for two decades already and who have, on a large scale, diversified into industrial production, services and other trades, thus creating a dynamic economy outside agriculture.

The reforms will not only draw this new non-agricultural economy into increasingly formalized frameworks of a regulated level playing field, including pensions and medical insurance schemes, but will also gradually break the link between rural labourers and the soil. By introducing economies of scale by specialist producers, the state is gradually moving towards a situation where peasant family earnings outside agriculture cease to subsidize their loss-making agricultural activities. Such a transition may take several decades, but its contours are already visible, taking into consideration the rural reforms of the 1980s and 1990s and the present trends towards rural-urban convergence.

Migration of rural workers to the coastal areas has already created a buoyant sweatshop labour market, and other opportunities for the adventurous young. Remittances, which these migrant workers send back home, help solve some of the poverty problems in remote parts of the Chinese countryside. The young may either never settle down in their places of origin or, if they do, will bring with them skills and initiatives which may help to invigorate the economy. The sweatshop factories in the coastal areas may soon prove too expensive to run, and in order to undergo a technological transition with a view to competing under the new market conditions they may demand fewer and more sophisticated workers. We may, therefore, see the traditional type of sweatshop processing moving inland to make use of the cheaper labourers and less restrictive government controls there. When the frontier of exploitative capitalism moves deeper into the hinterland, the last subsistence-based one-fifth of the population may eventually be torn out of its vegetative state. On a moral note, all one can hope for is that labour safety legislation and environmental protection will be enforced in such ways that this process does not leave social scars of too great a depth. The WTO will have a role to play in this respect.

Looking into the future, we see the contours of a population which is freed from the last vestiges of the caste-like divisions imposed by the labour administration and household registration system and which will instead be stratified along lines of income. People will become mass consumers in a market that offers more choice than ever before, but they will have to make tougher choices, as the general level of personal savings will decline. The rights of employees will fluctuate with supply and demand on the labour market, as labour becomes more of an economic relation and less of a political and administrative issue. Poor groups will continue to exist, and some people both in China's countryside and the cities will experience hardship. These developments will be due to the reforms, and WTO accession may contribute marginally to them.

Conclusion

Social changes in China following WTO accession will mainly reflect general changes following the reforms. Projections of current social trends into the future are inadequate for the parameters they rest on are in a process of fundamental change. While China's economic reforms aimed at establishing a market economy, the methods applied in this process have been based on the use of non-market policies and strong state intervention in the economy. This has both shielded vulnerable groups in society against hardship and created venal behaviour in the economy. China's reforms aim both at preventing social hardship and at creating a level playing field. China's WTO accession may empower both domestic and foreign players in the Chinese market to remove vestiges of political market interference.

Notes

[1] Wang Hongliang, 'Diba zhang. Zhongguo ruhe "yu lang gongwu"' (Chapter 8: How Can China 'Dance with the Wolves'?), in: Guangdong University for Foreign Languages and Trade (ed.), *Zhongguo de WTO zhi lu* (China's Road to the WTO), Guangzhou: Guangdong jingji chubanshe, 1999, pp. 219–93, here pp. 237–8.

[2] E.g. Prybyla, Jan S., 'China in the WTO: Threat or Promise of Good Things to Come?', *Issues and Studies*, vol. 36, no. 1 (Januray/February 2000), pp. 143–60, here pp. 147–54.

[3] E.g. Heer, Paul, 'A House United', *Foreign Affairs*, vol. 79, no. 4 (July/August 2000), pp.18–24.

[4]Acharaya, Alka, 'The "New Deal": China on the Threshold of WTO', *Economic and Political Weekly*, vol. 34, no. 51 (December 18, 1999), http://www.epw.org.in/3451/comm2.htm.

[5]On dual track systems see Naughton, Barry, *Growing Out of the Plan. Chinese Economic Reform 19781993*, Cambridge: Cambridge University Press, 1996, pp. 228–33; on smuggling see Heilmann, Sebastian, Isabelle Gras, and Kristin Kupfer, 'Chinas politisch-ökonomisches Schattensystem: Schmuggelnetzwerke und der Beitritt zur WTO', *China aktuell*, vol. 29, no. 7 (July 2000), pp. 769–84.

[6]*Shichang jizhi*, a term frequently used by Chinese economists to indicate institutions for commodity exchange that follow marketlike principles.

[7]See for example He Zengke's study of the political economy of corruption, He Zengke, *Zhengzhi zhi aifazhan zhong guojia fuhua wenti yanjiu* (The Cancer of Politics. A Study of Issues of Corruption in Developing Countries), Beijing: Zhongyang bianyi chubanshe, 1995.

[8]Ru, Xin, Xueyi Lu, and Tianlun Shan, eds, *1998 nian: Zhongguo shehui xingshi fenxi yu yuce* (1998: Analysis and Prognosis of Social Trends in China), Beijing: Shehui kexue wenxian chubanshe, 1998, pp. 313–4.

[9]Using the criteria set by Wong, Linda, 'Kapitel 10: Unemployment', in: Hebel, Jutta and Günter Schucher, eds, *Der Chinesische Arbeitsmarkt. Strukturen, Probleme, Perspektiven*, Hamburg: Institut für Asienkunde (*Mitteilungen des Instituts für Asienkunde, Hamburg*, no. 306), pp. 219–35, here pp. 226–8.

[10]Ru, Xin, Xueyi Lu and Tianlun Shan, eds, *op.cit.*, pp. 314-5.

[11]Ru, Xin, Xueyi Lu, and Tianlun Shan, eds, *1999 nian: Zhongguo shehui xingshi fenxi yu yuce* (1999: Analysis and Prognosis of Social Trends in China), Beijing: Shehui kexue wenxian chubanshe, 1999, p. 232.

[12]Sun, Tongqiang, ed., *Zhongguo jingji anquan baogao* (Report on China's Economic Security), Beijing: Zhongguo jingji chubanshe, 2000, p. 85.

[13]On the significance of the household registration system, see Mallee, Hein, 'China's Household Registration System Under Reform', *Development and Change*, vol. 26, no. 1 (1995), p. 129; Christiansen, Flemming, 'Social Division and Peasant Mobility in Mainland China: The Implications of the Huk'ou System', *Issues and Studies*, vol. 26, no. 4 (1990), pp. 22–42.

[14]'Zhonghua Renmin Gongheguo gongsi fa' (Enterprise Law of the People's Republic of China), *Zhonghua Renmin Gongheguo Gongwuyuan gongbao*, no. 2 (20.01.2000), pp. 26–47.

[15]For detailed studies of the policies of structural change of the state enterprise sector towards a market economy see Hebel, Jutta, 'Kapitel 5: Beschäftigung im Staatssektor der VR China', in: Hebel, Jutta, and Günter Schucher, eds, *Der chinesische Arbeitsmarkt. Strukturen. Probleme. Perspektiven*, Hamburg: Institut für Asienkunde (*Mitteilungen des Instituts für Asienkunde, Hamburg*, no. 306), 1999, pp. 113–33; Schucher, Günter, 'Kapitel 1: Chinas Beschäftigungsstrukturen im Wandel', in: Hebel, Jutta and Günter Schucher, eds, *Der chinesische Arbeitsmarkt. Strukturen. Probleme. Perspektiven*, Hamburg: Institut für Asienkunde (*Mitteilungen des Instituts für Asienkunde, Hamburg*, no. 306), 1999, pp. 23–44; Hebel, Jutta and Günter Schucher, *Zwischen Arbeitsplan und Arbeitsmarkt. Strukturen des Arbeitssystems in der VR China*, Hamburg: Institut für Asienkunde (*Mitteilungen des Instituts für Asienkunde, Hamburg,* no. 204), 1992.

[16]Wei, Jie, 'Guoyou qiye gaige de xin silu' (New Thoughts on Stateowned Enterprise Reform), in: Xie, Fuzhan, ed., *Zhongguo jingji zhuanjia xin sixiang nianji: 2000 ban* (Annual Collection of Chinese Economic Specialists' New Thinking: Edition 2000), Beijing: Zhongguo Fazhan Chubanshe, 2000, pp. 203–5.

[17]See for example http://www.setc.gov.cn/zdqy/setc_zdqy_main48.htm, _main49.htm, and _main51.htm.

[18]Ma, Hong and Mengkui Wang, eds, (1999), *Zhongguo fazhan yanjiu. Guowuyuan Fazhan Yanjiu Zhongxin yanjiu baogao xuan* (China's Development Research. A Selection of Research Reports from The Development Research Centre of the State Council), Beijing: Zhongguo fazhan chubanshe, 1999, p. 108.

[19]A strategy adopted by many families was to retain one job in the state sector, and one in the self-employed sector in order to take advantage of both systems; this strategy has jestingly been referred to as 'one family, two systems' (*yi jia liang zhi*), i.e. socialism and capitalism.

[20]There is a substantial redistribution between rich and poor regions through fiscal and financial policies, but the state does not assume a Robin Hood role between social groups. State poverty relief to citizens is normally restricted to families where no members are able work.

[21]Madsen, Richard, 'Understanding Falun Gong,' *Current History,* vol. 99, no. 638 (September 2000), pp. 243–7.

10

Enhancing China's Rule of Law

Sarah Biddulph

Introduction

In this paper I address the question of the effect, if any, China's accession to the World Trade Organization (WTO) will have on the establishment of a system of rule of law in China and, in turn, consequences this may have for the protection of human rights in China. This question is very difficult, as the consequences for China's legal system of her accession to the WTO may be difficult to distinguish from the changes already taking place as a result of the implementation of the Open Door policy and the pursuit of economic reform and modernisation. To an extent, China's accession to the WTO may act as an impetus to continue, or even speed up, reforms that are already taking place. However, there are a number of features of both the structure and the operation of the Chinese legal system that arguably will not be responsive to WTO legal disciplines or affected by China's accession to the WTO. These features exist both in relation to the legal regulation of economic activities and human rights.

In this paper, I first examine issues of the developing legal system and correspondences between this development, legal requirements of the WTO and the rule of law. Next, I use the conclusions drawn from this earlier discussion to examine human rights; in particular those that have been mooted as constituting the subject of possible modifications to the WTO Agreement.[1] I have dealt separately with the question of rule of law and the legal protection for human rights, which are not identical. In the Chinese context at least, it is not accurate to assume that development of a comprehensive legal system will necessarily result in greater definition and protection of individual human rights.

What Are the Demands of the WTO in Relation to Law and Its Operation: Rule of Law?

The WTO has established a comprehensive rule based system governing international trade[2] including new dispute resolution procedures which are intended to assist the enforcement of the substantive agreements entered into by its contracting parties.[3]

The requirement of Article X of the General Agreement on Tariffs and Trade (GATT) Treaty and now the WTO, is that national laws, regulations and rules in relation to designated trade related areas be published,[4] applied in a 'uniform, impartial and reasonable manner'[5] and mechanisms be instituted for independent review of administrative action.[6] Predictability, certainty, transparency and independent review of decision-making are also important elements of what we understand to constitute the rule of law.

The Draft Protocol of Accession[7] that has been negotiated to set the terms for China's accession to the WTO contains a corresponding range of requirements in relation to the structure and operation of the legal system. The Draft Protocol requires that China's laws conform to the obligations undertaken in the Draft Protocol and the WTO Agreement[8] and that her trade regime is administered in a uniform fashion throughout the entire territory, including at the sub-national level.[9] The Draft Protocol goes on to require that China administer in a 'uniform, impartial and reasonable manner all laws, regulations, rules, decrees, directives, administrative guidance, policies and other measures'.[10] China is required to establish a mechanism for reporting of non-uniform implementation of the laws and regulations.[11]

Paragraph 2C of the Draft Protocol requires that only those laws and regulations published and readily available shall be enforced.[12] Paragraph 2D of the Draft Protocol requires establishment of tribunals and procedures for promoting review of administrative decision-making and that these tribunals should be independent of the decision-maker. A party should be able to seek review of an administrative action or decision and appeal, without penalty, from the result of that review.[13]

In all, these obligations in relation to the structure and operation of the legal system are very comprehensive. A number of commentators on Chinese law have questioned the extent to which the Chinese legal system complies with, or can be made to comply with, the basic requirements of the GATT Treaty and the WTO Agreements and the Draft Protocol.[14]

I will now set out the features of the Chinese legal system as it has developed over the last twenty years in order to form some tentative view about whether China can comply with the legal requirements for accession. I will also consider the possible impetus for reform that accession to the WTO may have on the Chinese legal system and the development of the rule of law (and whether this, in turn, will have any impact on human rights). An examination of the substantive regulatory framework relating to customs, trade, investment and intellectual property is not the task of this paper.

What Do We Mean by Rule of Law in China?

Since the decision of the Central Committee of the Chinese Communist Party (CCP) to re-establish the legal system in December 1978,[15] the meaning of the term 'rule of law' has been contested. In the West, the ideal of rule of law includes the idea that the power of government is constrained by the operation of an autonomous legal order.[16] It also contains a requirement that the law protect certain individual rights against incursion by the state.[17]

It would still not be generally correct to assert that the legal system in China is autonomous, or that law can, or is even intended to, constrain the power of the state or the CCP. In China, the relationship of the CCP to law remains fluid despite a clear provision in the Constitution that all organs and individuals are subject to the constitution and law.[18] The Preamble to the Constitution itself spells out the fundamental requirement for leadership of the CCP.[19]

That said, the CCP seeks to use law and the establishment of a comprehensive legal system as a method to legitimate its own rule.[20] Law has been used instrumentally by the CCP not only to entrench and ensure the continuation of the current political system and to ensure social stability and order, but also to structure and carry out the massive institutional and economic reforms of the past twenty years.[21]

It is possible though, to see the growth of law toward having an ideological function, where the law itself, rather than political power, shapes and constrains the exercise of state power.[22] This tendency arguably can be seen in the daily functioning of large economic bureaucracies that have grown to manage different aspects of the economic reform process. As the legal rules and regulations administered by these bureaucracies have become more complex and technical, day to day administration has become more rule bound and professional.[23] It would be a mistake though, to conclude that a transition to a technical and rational application of rules by state organs has occurred consistently or evenly, that the legal standards are now entrenched as the criteria for valid decision-making, or that these bureaucracies are not highly responsive to both broad and specific policy imperatives.

Features of the Chinese Legal System

Legislative form

Despite the massive increase in the volume of laws, regulations and rules and the existence of legislation requiring their publication, significant problems remain with the internal consistency and coherence of the body of laws and rules that comprise the legal system. This influences the degree to which individuals and groups, even with the assistance of lawyers, are able to be confident that they can fully appreciate the legal parameters of their actions.

A brief description of the system of law making will illustrate this point. Under the Constitution,[24] unified power, including legislative power, rests in the National People's Congress (NPC). The NPC Standing Committee exercises this power on a day to day basis.[25] The executive organ of state, the State Council, has power to pass administrative regulations[26] and may receive specific delegations of law making power from the NPC.[27] Ministries and Commissions established under the State Council are empowered to pass ministerial rules, both within their spheres of administrative competence and in order to implement particular legislation. At the local level, the local people's congresses and governments are empowered to pass regional regulations, which are applicable within that local area. Some Special Economic Zones (SEZs) have received delegations of power from the Standing Committee to pass laws relating to economic matters within the SEZ.[28]

Legislation passed by the NPC and its Standing Committee has tended to be drafted in accordance with the principles of generality and flexibility. For these laws to be made operational, they usually require passage of detailed implementing regulations passed by the State Council, or the ministry or ministries responsible for implementation or enforcement of that law. This legislative form also facilitates implementation at the local level, by local congress or local government regulation that is formulated to take into account the specific local situation. Gaps in the legislative regime have tended to be filled by State Council or ministerial regulation. The vast bulk of regulation has been that passed by ministries and local congresses and governments, keen to shape the regulatory framework and to gain some ownership over that area of regulatory competence.

In particular, decentralization of power to the localities making them responsible for local economic development has given local governments and congresses major incentives to pass a large volume of local regulations. The result has been creation of a complex, multi-tiered, and in many cases, incoherent body of laws and rules which overlap and in some cases conflict. Problems have arisen as a result of overlap between rules and regulations, conflicts or partial conflicts between them, rules being superseded in whole or part by other rules, and passage of implementing rules that either extend or limit the scope of the primary legislative instrument. These problems have been most pronounced in respect of ministerial rules and local level rules.

Recently, an attempt has been made in the *Legislation Law* to impose greater order and certainty over law making.[29] It was originally intended by the drafters of this law that the *Legislation Law* would provide greater definition of the limits of rule-making powers of each of the organs of state. In the end, it set out a list of matters about which the NPC and its Standing Committee have exclusive rule-making power,[30] but in other respects failed to specify more clearly the limits of rule-making powers of different state organs. It was also hoped that the *Legislation Law* would be able to establish a detailed, workable mechanism for resolution of conflicts between rules passed by central level ministries and commissions and those passed by local governments and congresses. It did so only to a limited extent.[31]

The *Legislation Law* requires publication of all categories of laws, rules and regulations in accordance with the requirement of GATT Article X and the Draft Protocol.[32] As the legal system develops, an additional requirement is being imposed that, for an administrative action to be valid, it must be based on a published and publicly availability law or rule. For example, the *Administrative Punishments Law* makes void any administrative punishment unless it is imposed on the basis of a rule that has been promulgated.[33] It is anticipated that the draft *Administrative Procedure Law* (*Xingzheng Chengxu Fa*), which it is intended would apply to all administrative actions, will also include a provision to this effect. However, it may be quite some time yet before general support for either the law, or the universal application of such a principle can be obtained.

The remaining shortfall in fully complying with the publication requirement is that there is no requirement for publication of normative documents (*guifanxing wenjian*). This category of documents falls below the categories of laws and rules covered by the *Legislation Law*. Despite claims in some areas that this type of document is no longer used, the use of this form of internal documentary bureaucratic communication is well entrenched. Normative documents often contain detailed directions to officials at all levels on how to carry out their duties and how to implement laws and regulations. So, it is still possible for the contents of normative documents to form the basis for administrative action that affects individuals and enterprises, even though their legal status is the subject of great controversy. It may be that their exclusion from the *Legislation Law* will encourage the conclusion that these documents do not constitute law at all and discourage their continued use, which has been extensive. However, until the principle that an administrative act is void unless based on a promulgated rule is made to be of universal applicability, the continued use of these documents is arguably inconsistent with the publication requirement contained in Article X.

Bureaucratic empowerment

Chinese administrative agencies have always been particularly powerful in all aspects of governance. Their actions permeate all aspects of daily life. Politically, the State Council has always been the strongest of the arms of state.[34]

With the development of the legal system, the institutional power of state administrative agencies has become legally entrenched. The process of empowerment has resulted initially from the institutional strength of the State Council and its important role in legislative drafting. As importantly, the State Council and its ministries and commissions have power to pass detailed rules for the implementation of the legislation they are responsible for enforcing. As much legislation is expressed in vague and general terms, the role of lower level implementing regulations in providing the detail necessary to make the legislation operational is of crucial importance.[35] In the absence of legislation, ministries and commissions also have power to pass other rules necessary for the performance of their responsibilities. Ministerial rules are technically only binding within the same functional hierarchy. However, in practice, other administrative agencies and the courts often defer to them. The courts have no power to determine the lawfulness of an administrative rule.

One of the results of the establishment of a legislative framework such as this has been to concentrate the power to make, interpret and enforce rules and regulations in the hands of the state's administrative organs, thus investing them with broad powers. This fact explains the need for administrative law, and in particular, the importance of the development of rules seeking to better define the scope of powers of administrative agencies, the procedures and principles for exercise of those powers and to constrain their discretionary powers. As yet, no principles of general application, such as reasonableness or proportionality, exist to underpin the exercise of administrative power. Such a body of rules is of fundamental importance to the realization of any degree of transparency in governance.

Procedures

Legal specification of procedures for decision-making is an important component in ensuring application of laws in a uniform, impartial and reasonable manner. Interest in procedural law is comparatively recent.

Since the passage of the *Administrative Litigation Law* (ALL)[36] the courts have been empowered to rescind an administrative decision on the grounds of unlawfulness if the decision is in breach of a lawfully specified procedure.[37] There has been a growing recognition of the need to pass laws specifying mandatory procedures and the role that specifying such mandatory procedures may have in increasing accountability for individual administrative actions.[38] Accountability does not necessarily mean accountability to the individual object of the decision-making, but also means accountability to the state in whose interest it is to ensure efficiency in administration.

In the past, procedures for the exercise of administrative powers were often set out in rules or normative documents and so were not necessarily publicly available. The *Administrative Punishments Law* (APL) was passed in 1996 and represents a first step in establishing a legislative framework of public and mandatory procedural requirements for the valid exercise of administrative powers.

The APL regulates the imposition of administrative punishments such as fines, confiscation of unlawfully obtained income or property, ordering the suspension of production and operations, the suspension or revocation of licences or permits and administrative detention.[39] It is thus directly relevant to China's compliance with the requirement for 'uniform, impartial and reasonable' application of the law in this area.[40]

The APL specifies three mandatory procedures to be applied in giving an administrative punishment. The applicable procedure depends on the severity of the punishment to be given.[41] The hearing procedure set out in this law, which is available in respect of imposition of the most serious administrative punishments, has already been used as a model in other areas of law.[42] Under each of the procedures, before a punishment is given, the administrative agency must inform the party to be punished of the facts, evidence and law upon which the decision is based and give reasons for the decision.[43] That party must also be permitted to respond to the facts and evidence of the accusation, be able to provide other evidence and debate the basis for the decision without penalty.[44]

The APL is intended to be used as a model for drafting a more general law of administrative procedure, the *Administrative Procedure Law*.[45] This legislation remains in the drafting stages. Laws such as the APL and the proposed *Administrative Procedure Law* require a broad cultural change in the attitude toward the exercise of bureaucratic power which can only take place incrementally. Nonetheless, these reforms constitute an important step in seeking to establish a legal basis for requiring a fair and uniform administration.

Scrutiny of decision-making

There are currently several systems in place for externally generated supervision of administrative action. The best known is review of the legality of an administrative decision by the courts under the ALL. Another is administrative review of the decision carried out either by the higher level administrative department in charge of the decision-maker, or the local government at the same level as the decision-maker, under the *Administrative Review Law* (ARL). A citizen is now entitled to claim compensation for losses suffered as the result of an unlawful administrative action under the *State Compensation Law*.[46]

There are also a number of mechanisms for supervision of administrative decision-making that are generated internally, that is, from within the structures of the state and the CCP. I do not consider these here, as the requirements of the GATT and the draft Protocol are that a person dissatisfied with an administrative decision has the capacity to complain about that decision and to challenge it. This type of review is initiated from outside the administrative and political structures of state and in China is reflected by administrative litigation and review.

Administrative litigation

When passed, the ALL represented a major reform in the legal system and constitutes an important development in establishing forms of legal accountability of government officials for their actions. The state has conducted extensive propaganda to inform people of their rights and to encourage them to exercise their rights under this law. The ALL enables courts to review the lawfulness of an administrative act.[47] In administrative litigation, the administrative agency is required to prove that the act was lawful and must supply the documents and rules upon which the particular decision was based.[48] If it refuses to do so, the court is entitled to find that the act was unlawful and quash it.[49]

However, the effectiveness of this legislation in establishing mechanisms for scrutinising administrative conduct, and so making administrative agencies accountable for their actions, is constrained in a number of legal and other ways. The first is that the courts are not empowered to examine the lawfulness of a rule upon which a particular decision was based. The basis for a determination of lawfulness of an act is laws, administrative regulations and local rules.[50] More controversially, courts are also required to 'have regard to' ministerial rules, decisions or orders of the State Council and local rules passed by local people's governments.[51] Courts are not empowered to examine the reasonableness or appropriateness of an administrative decision, the exercise of discretion is also beyond the purview of administrative litigation and the courts have very limited power to amend an administrative decision.[52]

The second is that there are still only comparatively few cases brought under this law.[53] In many cases, people may be reluctant to commence an action, either because of fear of retribution from officials with whom they will be forced to have ongoing contact,[54] lack of confidence in the courts and because of traditional attitudes such as 'officials are high up and the people low down' and that a person suing an official does not know his or her place and is looking for trouble.[55] Rates at which actions are commenced vary throughout the country.

The third is the comparative institutional weakness of the courts and reluctance in some cases to handle difficult cases where the defendant is the local government, or a local government department. Sometimes courts are reluctant to accept cases in the first place, especially where they fear retribution from the defendant, for example, the local government, to which the courts are financially beholden. The rate at which applicants withdraw their case after its acceptance by the court, but before a judgment is given, is high and appears to be increasing.[56] Some reasons for withdrawal of cases are: pressure from the court or from the defendant, the applicant reaches a satisfactory compromise with the defendant (despite the prohibition against mediation of the dispute by the parties),[57] or the applicant finds the claim cannot succeed after obtaining information about the basis for making the original decision.

The institutional weakness of the Chinese courts as well as their vulnerability to local pressures is well documented.[58] The poor quality of adjudication and widespread corruption of judicial personnel[59] has become so serious, and the lack of confidence in the system sufficiently great, that it has prompted the Standing Committee of the NPC to consider introduction of special measures for supervision of judicial decision-making.[60] The Chief of the Supreme People's Court has also introduced a range of measures in an effort to counteract these problems.[61]

Administrative review

The other main form for externally generated supervision of administrative action is administrative review under the ARL. One scholar claims that administrative review constitutes an independent review mechanism of the type required by the draft Protocol of Accession.[62] Under the ARL, a citizen or entity may seek review of any administrative act that he or she believes infringes upon his or her lawful rights and interests.[63] This is a process of internal bureaucratic review, not judicial review. The review agency is required to examine not only the lawfulness, but also the appropriateness of the act in question.[64] The review agency can change the administrative decision[65] and may also amend or overturn the rule on which the decision was based to the extent of its functional power. If the review agency does not have the power to change the rule itself, it may refer the question to a state organ that does have the power to do so.[66] The scope of powers exercised by a review agency under the ARL is significantly broader than those exercised by the courts under the ALL.

The ARL sets out procedures for carrying out review and requires that reasons be given for a review decision. Unless excluded by law, a party may choose either to seek review or commence litigation. Many laws now require a party to seek review of a decision first and, if dissatisfied with the review decision, then commence litigation.[67]

Whilst there is still further to go in the establishment of a legislative infrastructure which ensures the transparency of rules and provides for effective supervision of administrative action, much progress has already been made. The real weakness of the legal system as it is now, lies in enforcement of the laws and in the dominant principles for law enforcement that are currently in place.

Law enforcement policies

The Draft Protocol and Article X require that laws, regulations, decisions and rulings be administered in a 'uniform, impartial and reasonable manner'. A minimum requirement for compliance with these principles is that laws be applied consistently in similar fact situations. Law enforcement and implementation, especially at the local level, often diverges from this aim of consistency and impartiality. Some of the practical problems of law enforcement include lack of understanding and respect for law and lack of faith that the law will deliver a just result. Other, more serious problems include extremely broad discretionary powers coupled with policies that require uneven enforcement of laws and local protectionism.

Discretion

A consequence of China's model of law making is that laws often give both local and central authorities broad discretion in making some decisions. The exercise of discretion is an important part of administration in all countries, though the scope and principles for exercise of such discretion are usually circumscribed in some way. China differs from others in degree, as at present, officials exercise very broad discretion. Many practical problems arise from the unprincipled exercise of administrative and judicial discretion.

Even if all rules were made publicly available, the wide existence of discretion and the overlap and conflict between different rules may result in the party not knowing the basis for a decision and the considerations taken into account when that particular decision is made. The source of discretion may be undefined terms, ambiguous phrases, or powers given in general terms.[68] The Chinese legal system does not yet set out general principles for the exercise of discretion, or provide effective mechanisms for review of the exercise of discretion.

As the legal system develops, some legislation has been passed which seeks to define and constrain the scope of discretion. In legislation such as the ARL and the APL we can see the beginnings of a legislative definition of principles for the exercise of discretion.[69] The APL sets out the basic principles for the exercise of the power to give administrative punishments. A decision to give an administrative punishment must be just, open, based on facts and the penalty must be proportional to the degree of social harm caused.[70] As discussed above, this legislation seeks to establish, for the first time, mandatory basic principles for the exercise of power and discretion for the imposition of administrative punishments.

Constraining the exercise of administrative discretion is a long term ongoing process that requires not only changing the legal structure for the exercise of discretion but will also require a long period of intensive education to change existing attitudes of state officials towards the exercise of their powers.

Controlling the exercise of judicial discretion is more problematic. Procedural rules are set out in the *Civil Procedure Law*, the *Criminal Procedure Law* and to an extent in the *Administrative Litigation Law*. However, in other important areas, especially in relation to evidence, the court has an almost unfettered discretion to determine what matters it will take into account and what weight it will accord to them. This becomes an issue for foreign parties who, for example, may want to prove the existence of international custom in a particular area. What evidence they will be permitted to bring to show the existence of international custom will depend largely on the individual judge and may be particularly problematic when that evidence is case law from foreign, common law, jurisdictions.

Local protectionism

One of the major problems in ensuring uniform implementation of law throughout China is local protectionism. The problem arose largely out of decentralisation of financial control and tax collection. As a result, local governments have much more power to attract foreign investment and to undertake a wide range of activities independent of the centre. There is also fierce competition between provinces and localities for markets and to attract and retain investment. These activities are very hard for economic agencies such as the Ministry of Foreign Trade and Economic Co-operation (MoFTEC) and other central agencies to control. The authority of central agencies is also reduced because of the formation of strong alliances between local business interests, either domestic or foreign, (this is especially so with overseas Chinese, Taiwanese and Hong Kong business) and local government.[71] In addition, the power of local governments and people's congresses to make laws and rules which are appropriate for the local level is fully used and often exceeded. Although the *Legislation Law* seeks to address these problems by instituting a system of supervision over rule-making, it remains to be seen whether this regime will be effective in controlling local level rule-making either in the long or short term.

Local protectionism also creates a particular problem for law enforcement. Local governments exercise a very high degree of power over local organs of state, including courts and procuratorates, because they fund their operation. Local courts are often unwilling to make a finding adverse to a local company, entity, or government agency for this reason. They are also often unwilling to enforce a judgment against a local defendant which has been made in favour of an enterprise or individual from another locality. Courts, in practice, lack effective coercive powers to enforce their judgments.[72]

Administrative controls over the application of law

Remnants of the planning system may still be seen to be operating in the application of laws in particular circumstances. These practices have a great impact on the uniform application of law and specific regulatory regimes and are not readily apparent. An example to illustrate this point relates to recent policy on bankruptcy of enterprises in China. The *Enterprise Bankruptcy Law of the PRC* itself is drafted in broad terms, and there are now many enterprises that would be eligible to be bankrupted in accordance with this law. However, few are.[73] Up to the present, administrative planning mechanisms such as quotas for the numbers of bankruptcies allowed in an area, or to regulate the number of companies permitted to apply for listing on the Shanghai and Shen Zhen stock exchanges have been used in order to preserve the stability of the market. With the exception of GITIC, many other insolvent International Trust and Investment Companies are being wound up on the basis of specific, administratively approved schemes of arrangement rather than the *Bankruptcy Law*. The existence and content of these superadded planning mechanisms are not apparent from an examination of the relevant laws and regulations and undermine the integrity and effectiveness of the legal system.

Conclusion: The Impetus of WTO Accession for the Development of the Rule of Law

Accession to the WTO has been the subject of intense media attention in China and many announcements of legal reforms to bring China's legal system into line with its obligations under the WTO have been made. For example, the Shanghai Municipal Government has announced a review of all its regulations, with a view to abolishing those that do not comply with WTO standards. This type of action illustrates the impact that accession to the WTO is already having on government agencies, spurring them to review their existing raft of laws and rules to ensure they comply with WTO requirements.

It may be that accession to the WTO will provide the impetus to proceed more quickly with the establishment of laws setting out mandatory procedures in the conduct of a broader range of administrative activities. Much preparatory work has already been done. For example, a draft of the *Administrative Licences Law* has been prepared for nearly two years, but the law not yet passed. Laws to provide for stronger NPC supervision of the actions of courts and procuratorates are already under consideration. Concern to improve the standard of judicial performance ahead of accession to the WTO may assist in the expedient passage of law such as this and in the adoption of other complementary measures.

Some other areas of reform to the legal system may be less susceptible to accelerated reform because of WTO membership. For example, the vested institutional interests in preserving powers to pass regulations and rules make difficult any further attempts to rationalize and constrain these powers. The problems I have identified in relation to enforcement of laws and, in particular, local protectionism, are deeply entrenched and will be extremely difficult to change, in the short term at least.

WTO Membership and its Effect on the Protection of Human Rights

Many of the issues raised above about the fundamental operation of the legal system in the economic sphere, as they relate to law making and enforcement, apply to a consideration of human rights. Some considerations, though, are of particular relevance to human rights.

A lot has been said about the abuse by the Chinese regime of the human rights of its citizens.[74] First, in addressing this issue, we must identify which human rights we are talking about. It is natural to assume that human rights means natural rights which are universal, inalienable rights which the individual is entitled to exercise against the interests of the state, society or collective.[75] Discussions about inclusion into the WTO of a social clause or mechanisms to protect human rights tend to frame the nature of such rights in this way.[76] Although all states accept that individual rights may be limited because of public interest,[77] many consider that such limitations should be constrained within the narrowest possible scope. The Chinese authorities have never really talked about individual rights in this way.[78]

The Constitution contains a whole chapter on the rights and duties of citizens guaranteeing a wide range of civil, political, social and economic rights.[79] In theory, rights in China are positive and not inherent in nature. The state grants rights to citizens and has the power to derogate from and amend those rights. The justification for enforcement or enjoyment of these rights exists on more utilitarian grounds, that is the capacity of the individual to enjoy these rights, and is subordinated to the interests of the collective, society and state.[80] Rights have been expressed as being conditional upon fulfilment of corresponding duties. [81] These duties are framed in general terms, such as article 51 which provides that:

> The exercise by citizens of the PRC of their freedoms and rights may not infringe upon the interests of the state, of society or of the collective, or upon the lawful freedoms and rights of other citizens.

These propositions may be understood in the context that traditionally there was a belief, which remains today, that the interests of the individual and the state are not necessarily in conflict and can be brought into harmony.[82] According to this view, strengthening the state will benefit her citizens.[83]

Apart from the conditional nature of rights as set out in the Constitution, there are practical reasons why the rights specified in the Constitution can be viewed only as hortative. Some of the rights patently cannot be realized, such as the right to work, as the state is no longer, if it ever was, in a position to allocate jobs to all of its citizens. In addition, there are currently no specific mechanisms for supervision of acts or laws alleged to be in breach of the Constitution, nor are there any specific channels for bringing a complaint about breach of a right guaranteed in the Constitution.[84]

As a practical matter, for the principles embodied in the Constitution to be given substance, they must first be enacted in specific legislation which would usually set out procedures for the exercise of the right and at the same time empower an organ of state to administer the law.[85] Such legislation may result in the limitation of the exercise of that right.[86]

How can China's accession to the WTO have an impact on the legal protection of human rights? I suggest here two possible mechanisms by which this may happen. The first is that changes in the legal system, its structure and operation will have a 'flow on' effect from the regulatory models adopted in the economic sphere. The second is that the WTO will impose specific obligations relating to human rights in the WTO Constitution along the lines of a social clause. For reasons of space, I have selected an example to illustrate the possibilities of each mechanism.

The 'flow on' effect

Will any improvements in transparency of the legal system in the economic sphere translate into better protection of individual rights? Will there be a 'flow on' effect from economic reform process that will lead to more political tolerance?

Individual autonomy in economic activities

The trend in civil relations has been for legislation to facilitate decentralisation of economic decision-making and to permit greater party autonomy. There has been a gradual increase in legal definition, recognition and protection of private property rights. In 1999 the uniform *Contract Law* was passed, which abolished the legal bifurcation previously in place between domestic and foreign related economic contracts and between economic and civil contracts. The new *Contract Law*, to an extent, enhances the autonomy of parties to a contract.[87] The obligation of the parties in general will be binding upon execution of a contract, subject to the proviso that the contract will be binding only upon obtaining approval where the law otherwise requires approval of the contract,[88] or that only specifically authorized individuals or entities are permitted to enter into certain types of contract.[89]

To an extent, legal reforms to improve transparency of regulations and accountability of government for its actions as discussed above may increasingly provide a legal framework within which individuals are empowered to form and enforce economic relations for their own benefit.

Some argue that the development of a complex legal system and bureaucratic infrastructure to support economic reform will not necessarily translate into increasing political liberalism, or result in the greater protection of individual civil and political rights. They argue that increasingly liberal and permissive regulatory models for economic activity have been depoliticized, thus effectively confining these types of reforms to the economic sphere and separating economic reform from political reform.[90] I will use an examination of the law relating to criminal justice and public order to consider the possibilities for reforms in the legal system as a whole to be translated into greater protection of individual rights under laws relating to crime and public order.

Criminal justice and public order policies

The state has consistently placed great emphasis upon the preservation of social order and political stability. [91] Order and stability have always been seen as essential for ensuring the success of the economic reform program.[92] Leadership of the CCP and preservation of the socialist system are fundamental.[93] There is low tolerance for acts that are seen as jeopardising social stability, or that are seen to be antithetical to continuation of the current political regime.

The state uses the law and legal tools to implement its social order policies and as a method of preventing the establishment of certain organizations, such as independent trades unions and political parties that do not recognize the leadership of the CCP, and for punishing those individuals seeking to do so.[94] The recent criminal conviction of a group seeking to register the Democratic People's Party of China and the heavy sentences given to them for inciting the subversion of state power is seen by many as a cynical use of law to justify what was, in substance, an act of repression of political dissidence.[95] There is every indication that the state will continue to act resolutely to suppress groups and individuals whose acts are seen by the state to be subversive of it and of public order and stability. This attitude is most recently demonstrated by the crackdown on adherents of Falun Gong.

The primary policy relating to public order, the Comprehensive Management of Public Order, has been implemented since its inception in 1981.[96] The policy has as its key link campaigns of 'hard strikes' against targeted activities and groups. The CCP takes a direct interest in the shaping and interpretation of this policy under the leadership of the Politics and Law Committee of the CCP Central Committee. In 1991, a specialist committee, the Comprehensive Management of Public Order Committee, was established under the CCP Central Committee to improve the implementation of this policy.[97]

Legislative regime for criminal justice and public order

The system for exercise of state coercive powers comprises a mixture of both criminal and administrative powers. Administrative measures are employed where the act is not sufficiently serious to warrant a criminal sanction. It is thus necessary to consider both the criminal and administrative regulatory regimes.

The *Criminal Law* and *Criminal Procedure Law* have both recently been substantially amended.[98] These amendments have moved the legislative structure more towards a model of regulation that embodies the principles of uniformity, impartiality and reasonableness. Whilst not seeking to diminish powers of state agencies, these laws have consolidated what had become a highly fragmented regulatory regime. Together, these laws generally provide a more detailed, closer definition of the scope and permitted use of powers and punishments within the criminal justice system. This framework has tended to improve the transparency of criminal justice laws. The amendments to the *Criminal Law* removes politically[99] or vaguely defined offences,[100] removes the principle of crime by analogy and incorporates the principle of proportionality in punishment.[101] The *Criminal Procedure Law* now incorporates a number of safeguards such as: giving an accused access to a lawyer within 24 hours after the first coercive measures have been taken,[102] giving lawyers greater access to prosecution evidence,[103] providing for mandatory legal aid in specified circumstances,[104] and providing for quashing a judgment where the fairness of a judgment was compromised and where the litigation rights of the accused were violated, such as the use of unlawful methods to gather evidence.[105] It has also sought to better define criminal coercive measures that could be taken and at the time of passage of the revisions to the *Criminal Procedure Law*, the notorious administrative detention power of detention for investigation (*shourong shencha*) was abolished.[106]

Despite the reforms to the criminal justice system, the parallel system of administrative sanctions imposed where the offence is not sufficiently serious to warrant a criminal sanction,[107] has not been greatly affected by these legal developments. Examples of administrative powers where a person may be detained without a court order are: re-education through labour, under which a person may be sent to a labour camp for between one and three years, detention for education for prostitutes, under which a prostitute may be sent to a specialist detention centre for a period ranging between six months and two years, and coercive drug rehabilitation under which a drug addict may be sent to a drug rehabilitation centre for between three and six months and up to one year. Contrary to the trend in the criminal justice system, the regulatory regime governing administrative sanctions appears to be becoming, if anything, less transparent.

The legal basis for many administrative sanctions sets out the scope of targeted activity in broad and impressionistic terms[108] and because of the legal form of these powers, supervision on the grounds of either lawfulness or reasonableness of the decision is difficult. The mandatory procedural requirements in the *Administrative Punishments Law*, as well as its requirements that officials exercise their powers to impose punishments in a way that is just, open, based on facts with the penalty proportional to the degree of social harm caused,[109] do not apply to re-education through labour, detention for education, to coercive drug rehabilitation or to detention for repatriation of vagrants. These measures have been categorized as 'administrative coercive measures' and so are outside the purview of this law.[110] There is a lasting reluctance amongst many to challenge decisions to impose such coercive powers, as it may be interpreted as failing to submit to the authority of the state.

Campaigns

One of the dominant strategies of enforcement has been to launch waves of 'hard strikes' against targeted groups or activities. Campaigns have primarily been waged against targeted criminal activity, including violent crime and vice, but are also waged against economic crime, such as smuggling, or less serious infringements of the law, such as customs related offences. The principles for implementing the anticrime campaigns waged during the 1980s and 1990s were to 'strike hard and fast'.[111]

Campaigns encourage widely variable law enforcement practices. They create great uncertainty about the manner in which the regulatory regime will be interpreted and enforced at any particular time and encourage uneven treatment of an act depending on whether it is the target of a campaign.

Often decisions to launch campaigns will be given a legal form. For example, one of the better known was the law and order campaign waged between 1983 and 1986 which was put in legal form by the Standing Committee *Decision Regarding the Severe Punishment of Criminal Elements who Seriously Endanger Public Security.*[112]

During the period of a campaign, the police, courts and procuratorate are required to co-operate in striking hard to achieve the objectives of the campaign. The level of enforcement and the degree of severity of punishment increases during a campaign.[113] Supervision mechanisms that may be exercised by the courts over police conduct under either the *Administrative Litigation Law*, the principles of the

Administrative Punishments Law, or the *Criminal Procedure Law* are impaired during campaigns, as the courts are also responsible for ensuring the success of the hard strike.

There is also some evidence that the use of administrative powers increases during the period of a campaign because they are more flexible and there are less procedural impediments to their use. Campaign style enforcement contradicts the principles of proportionality and uniform application of the law and punishments required under both the *Criminal Law* and the *Administrative Punishments Law*. Despite this, the continuing use of campaigns as an important aspect of law enforcement has been reaffirmed recently at the highest level.[114]

Amending the WTO Constitution

The second possible method by which China's accession to the WTO may affect legal protection of human rights is through inclusion of a social clause or guarantees of protection of individual human rights into the WTO agreements.[115] Even if acceptance could be obtained for inclusion of a social clause, the content of any such proposed clause is far from agreed. One suggestion is that the specific contents of a social clause should be: freedom of association, prohibition of forced labour, prohibition of child labour and guarantees of equality or non-discrimination, especially gender equality.[116] The protection of labour rights has been the subject of much recent publicity and illustrates a number of issues that may arise if proposals to include labour rights within the WTO Constitution are accepted.

Labour related laws

National legislation guarantees the rights and interests of workers and the state encourages workers to join trade unions under the organizational umbrella of the All China Federation of Trades Unions (ACFTU).[117] Workers are not permitted to organize outside the official trade union structure.[118] Detailed standards have been set relating to issues such as working conditions, health and safety conditions, the protection of women workers and prohibiting the use of child labour, amongst others. Chinese law contains an array of provisions that provide both for non-discrimination against women[119] as well as setting out extensive rules providing special protection for women in the workforce.[120] China has also ratified a number of international conventions on these issues. For example, China has ratified the International Labour Organization's Minimum Age Convention No. 138.[121]

The *Labour Law* prohibits employment of juveniles under the age of 16.[122]

As a complement to structural adjustment in the state-owned sector and to address the problems of increasing unemployment, the state is establishing welfare, health and unemployment insurance schemes and directing efforts to re-employment of laid off workers. It is difficult to imagine that Chinese legislation would not comply superficially with most obligations that might be contained in a social clause relating to labour. One notable exception is the prohibition against establishment of independent trade unions. The state has consistently cracked down on those seeking to organize outside the ACFTU structure. Prohibition on the establishment of independent trade unions is an area of great political sensitivity, and if it continues to be seen as having the potential to undermine the existing structure and political organization of the state, will remain so.

Issues of implementation

Despite the existence of legislative provisions guaranteeing the basic rights of workers (with the exception of freedom to form independent trades union), and despite some groups benefiting greatly from economic reform, abuses of workers rights is widespread and well documented. As a result of economic reforms, many workers find themselves either laid off, or their continuing employment vulnerable. The reasons for abuse are complex and many. Even though the legal issues discussed here constitute only part of the problems relating to protection of workers' rights in practice, many of the abuses of workers' rights arise from failure to enforce the laws according to their terms.[123] There is a great disparity between stated legal ideals and practice in terms of gender equality and non-discrimination.[124]

Many of these failures arguably do not arise directly as a result of lack of will at the centre, but arise more immediately out of local political and economic circumstances. In particular, enforcement is influenced by local needs, and problems are exacerbated by the high degree of autonomy of local government that has responsibility for the economic development of that local area.[125] However, the central government cannot claim to be unaware of the general situation at local levels, even if it is not apprised of every breach of the legal standards it has set.

Inspection of work places to ensure that working conditions comply with the legal standard and enforcement of environmental laws is primarily dependent upon the actions of the relevant local government department. Local departments are subject to pressures to favour the privileging of economic investment and development over enforcing legal rules protecting labour and environmental standards, especially where these are seen to conflict.[126] Especially where the local or foreign enterprise in a particular area is the major employer, the political power it is able to wield at the local level is enormous. Failure to prevent abuses of workers' rights arises in part as a result of many particular decisions rather than as the direct result of a general policy. For example, they consist of decisions to turn a blind eye, to notify a factory in advance of a proposed inspection, failure to act on a complaint and enforcement of standards against one enterprise and not another.

The unevenness of enforcement activities at the local level has been well documented.[127] Local unrest has also resulted from a range of dislocations arising as a result of enterprise reform, corruption and exaction of excessive fees and charges by local government.[128] For example, the central government has issued prohibitions on arbitrary imposition of exactions and taxes, but has been unable to effectively prevent this type of activity recurring.[129] Within China there are still no effective legal channels to complain and seek redress in respect of this type of administrative decision-making. The scope of administrative litigation and review does not cover many of these types of administrative actions.

Accession to the WTO will require the Chinese government to reduce subsidization of agriculture and to proceed with structural adjustment and reform of state-owned enterprises. In the short term at least, this is likely to place more strain on public order as workers livelihoods are prejudiced and unemployment in the industrial sector worsens. Already, there is well documented occurrence of industrial violence where workers remain unpaid for long periods, or are put out of work without adequate redundancy pay because of structural adjustment, bad management and depletion of enterprise assets as a result of corruption by management of the enterprise.[130] Although the state has established unemployment insurance and social security systems,[131] and medical insurance, they are still in the process of establishment and many are not in a position to benefit from these schemes.[132]

Given that enforcement of labour standards varies between regions and between enterprises and the causes of abuse of workers rights are many, the difficult question which arises is: how poor must enforcement of published laws be before that failure is laid at the feet of the central government? The answer to that question is political rather than legal.

Also, considering the multitude of different particular reasons and causes for the widespread failure to enforce labour standards, it may be that redress through the formal dispute resolution channels of the WTO are too unwieldy to provide a practical solution to this problem.

Conclusion

From this discussion, we can conclude that in many respects the central government has gone far down the track of implementing a legal system which, formally, contains provisions consistent with the requirements of GATT Article X and the Draft Protocol.

Will accession to the WTO promote the development of rule of law, in so far as it is constituted by the legal requirements of Article X? The picture I have sketched is that of a strong, though not necessarily unified bureaucracy, whose power is increasingly entrenched by laws and rules. Some legal requirements are now in place to encourage the uniform application of laws, for reasonableness and openness in decision-making and to make administrative decision-making more accountable.

Procedural requirements and channels for supervision of administrative action remain fragmented and weak and relate to a portion only of the areas of bureaucratic action. There is potential for them to develop. Both as part of the process of economic reform and modernization and in anticipation of accession to the WTO, it appears that there is political will to continue the development and reforms of the legal system and to encourage continued development toward a more open and accountable bureaucracy.

In the areas touching on human rights, such as the regulation of state powers concerning crime and social order, and even the legal protection of labour rights, the shape of the legislative structure and enforcement policies touch on areas of great sensitivity, that is, the protection of social stability in a time of economic transition and social upheaval and the preservation of the political structure.

Even in these areas, there have been some moves legislatively to introduce a more open legislative framework and to seek a more uniform, reasonable and accountable exercise of powers. These moves are in the preliminary stages. In respect of the group of administrative coercive powers I have identified above, the legislative trend is away from openness, uniformity and accountability. More pronounced in these areas touching on human rights are problems of uneven enforcement of laws and poor accountability for actions. In the area of social order and criminal justice, the continued adherence to campaign style enforcement requires non-uniform law enforcement. In the area of enforcement of labour laws and standards, the precarious economic position of workers coupled with local interest hinders uniform enforcement of laws already in place.

These problems are deeply entrenched in the current social, political, economic and legal systems. Improving the situation will require time, perseverance and attention of those who profess concern about human rights in China.

Notes

[1]Petersmann, E.-U., suggests that these modifications could be made by way of amendment to Article XX of GATT 'The WTO Constitution and Human Rights' (2000), *Journal of International Economic Law*, 19, pp. 20–1.

[2]Peng Shinyi, 'The WTO Legalistic Approach and East Asia: From the Legal Culture Perspective' (June 2000), *Asian-Pacific Law and Policy Journal* 1.

[3]Jackson, J.H., *The World Trading System Law and Policy of International Economic Relations*, 2nd ed., MIT Press, 1997, pp. 1–2.

[4]GATT 1947, Article X(1).

[5]GATT 1947, Article X(3)(a).

[6]GATT 1947, Article X(3)(b).

[7]Copy on file with author.

[8]Paragraph 2A 4, which provides that China's laws, regulations and other measures of government entities at the sub-national level shall conform to the obligations undertaken in this Protocol and the WTO Agreement.

[9]Paragraph 2A 2, which provides that China shall ensure that the provisions of the WTO Agreement and this Protocol are applied uniformly throughout its entire customs territory, including at the sub-national level.

[10]Paragraph 2A 3, which provides that China shall administer in a uniform, impartial and reasonable manner all its laws, regulations, rules, decrees, directives, administrative guidance, policies and other measures (hereinafter referred to as 'laws, regulations and other measures') pertaining to or affecting trade in goods, services, trade-related aspects of intellectual property rights (hereinafter referred to as 'TRIPS') or the control of foreign exchange.

[11]Paragraph 2A 5, which provides China shall establish a mechanism under which individuals and enterprises can bring to the attention of the national authorities cases of non-uniform application of the trade regime.

[12](C) Transparency.

[13](D) Judicial Review.

[14]Lubman S., 'Bird in a Cage: Chinese Law Reform after Twenty Years' (Spring 2000), *Northwestern Journal of International Law and Business*, 383 at 416 citing GATT 1947, Article X and asserting that under the Draft Protocol of Accession China will be required to move toward implementing a more transparent legal system.

[15]Communiqué of the Third Plenum of the Eleventh CCP Central Committee.

[16]Epstein, E., 'Law and Legitimation in Post Mao China', in Potter, P.B., ed., *Domestic Law Reforms in Post Mao China*, Armonk, M.E. Sharpe, 1994, 19–55, p. 22.

[17]Clark, David, 'The Many Meanings of the Rule of Law', in Jayasuriya, K., ed., *Law Capitalism and Power in Asia* Routledge, 1999, 28–44, pp. 28–9.

[18]Constitution, 1982, art. 5 provides that: 'All state organs, the armed forces, all political parties and public organizations and all enterprises and institutions must abide by the Constitution and the law. All acts in violation of the Constitution and law must be investigated. No organization or individual is privileged to be beyond the Constitution or the law'.

[19]One of the Four Cardinal Principles the other three of which are: adherence to the socialist road, adherence to the people's democratic dictatorship and adherence to Marxism, Leninism, and Mao Zedong Thought. The *Legislation Law* at art. 3 added Deng Xiaoping Theory to the principle of adherence to Marxism, Leninism and Mao Zedong Thought.

[20]Epstein, E., *op.cit.*, 19–22. Edward Epstein argues that in many respects the law is still used as an instrument to uphold and preserve the power of the CCP and the socialist system as well as to carry out policies of institutional and economic reform. The instrumental use of law relies on political power rather than the authority of the law itself. The CCP has adopted the Leninist interpretation of law and state in which law is used purely as an expression of political power and as a tool of oppression by one class of another.

[21]Yuan Yuan Sheng, 'Conceptions and Receptions of Legality: Understanding the Complexity of Law Reform in Modern China', in Turner, Feinerman and Guy, eds., *The Limits of the Rule of Law in China*, University of Washington Press, 2000, 27, discusses the instrumental nature of Chinese law generally. See also Yu, Xingzhong, 'Legal Pragmatism in the People's Republic of China' (Summer 1989), *Journal of Chinese Law* 29; Potter, P.B., 'The Chinese Legal System: Continuing Commitment to the Primacy of State Power' (1999), *The China Quarterly*, pp. 673–4, and Epstein, E., *op. cit.*, p. 21.

[22]Epstein, E., *op. cit.*, pp. 25–31.

[23]For a description of this process see Lubman S., *op. cit.*, pp. 383–4.

[24]Article 2.

[25]*Constitution* art. 57, the powers of the Standing Committee are enumerated at art. 67.

[26]*Xingzheng fagui*, *Constitution*, art. 89.

[27]Within the limits set by the *Legislation Law*, art. 9 which prohibits delegation of law making power in respect of crime and punishment, deprivation of political rights and deprivation of personal freedom and the judicial system.

[28]For example the *Resolution of the Standing Committee of the NPC Authorizing the People's Congresses of Guangdong and Fujian Provinces and their Standing Committees to Formulate Separate Economic Regulations for their respective Special Economic Zones*, 26 November 1981.

[29]Passed at the third Session of the Ninth NPC on 15 March 2000 and taking effect on 1 July 2000.

[30]Article 8 provides that the NPC and its Standing Committee have exclusive jurisdiction to pass legislation in relation to matters relating to: state sovereignty, establishment, organizational structure and authority of people's congresses, governments courts and procuratorates, the system of autonomy for minority areas, special administrative regions and grass roots levels, crime and punishment, deprivation of political rights and coercive measures and punishments for the deprivation of personal freedom, expropriation of non state assets, fundamental civil

institutions, the basic economic, tax, customs, fiscal finance and foreign trade systems and systems for litigation and arbitration.

[31]The *Legislation Law* has specified principles by which resolution of conflicts between different legal instruments are to be resolved and has designated the agencies with authority to determine which regulation or rule is to prevail in the event of a conflict between them: arts. 83, 85, 86, 88.

[32]Laws passed by the NPC and its Standing Committee; arts. 23, 41, 52, amendments to those laws; art. 53, administrative regulations; art. 62, local level and autonomous self governing regions' regulations; art. 70, ministerial rules; art. 77 and local level rules; (art. 77 provides that these rules must be published in that locality).

[33]*Administrative Punishments Law*, art. 4 provides that rules governing the imposition of an administrative punishment must be promulgated and rules that are not promulgated will not be the basis for an administrative punishment. Article 3 then provides that administrative punishments are invalid without a legal basis or without following legal procedures.

[34]Keller, P., 'Sources of Order in Chinese Law' (1994), vol. 42, *The American Journal of Comparative Law* 711, a phenomenon Keller describes as bureaucratic dominance, pp. 738–42.

[35]This power may result from an express delegation in the legislation, for example the Foreign Trade Law expressly empowers MoFTEC to pass detailed implementing regulations in relation to licensing of goods subject to import or export controls. For example, art, 19 provides that goods whose import or export is restricted shall be subject to quota and/or licensing control; technologies whose import or export is restricted shall be subject to licensing control. Import or export of any goods and technologies subject to quota and/or licensing control will be effected only with the approval of the authority responsible for foreign trade and economic relations under the State Council or the joint approval of the preceding authorities and other authorities concerned under the State Council in compliance with the provisions of the State Council. Powers to pass ministerial rules may also be exercised in situations where there is no express delegation, out of the functional power of that agency. The Standing Committee *Decision on Strengthening the Interpretation of Law* passed in 1981 partially delegated the power of that institution to interpret legislation. It divided interpretation powers into legislative interpretation, which was to be exercised by the Standing Committee, judicial interpretation, to be exercised by the Supreme People's Court and the Supreme People's Procuratorate and administrative interpretation to be exercised by administrative organs of state. The explanation of the *Legislation Law* indicates that the 1981 *Decision* is revoked upon passage of the *Legislation Law*. The law states that the Standing Committee exercises sole power to interpret national law (Art 42). However this provision does not prevent the Supreme People's Court, the Supreme People's Procuratorate the State Council and its ministries issuing explanations of the meaning and application of a law in the exercise of their functions.

[36]The law came into effect on 1 October 1990.

[37]Article 54(2)(iii).

[38]The *Civil Procedure Law* was amended in 1991 and the *Criminal Procedure Law* substantially amended in 1996. Although there is some support for passage of a comprehensive *Administrative Procedure Law*, attempts to finalize the law have been frustrated. Instead the contents of *an Administrative Procedure Law* have been divided up and passed piece by piece as separate legislation. These include the *Administrative Litigation Law*, *Administrative Review Law*, *State Compensa-*

tion Law, Administrative Punishments Law. Other laws such as *Administrative Licenses Law, Administrative Exactions Law*, and the *Administrative Coercive Measures Law* are all in various stages of drafting.

[39]APL, art. 8.

[40]The APL also specifies the basic principles for decision-making of openness, fairness, and that the punishment must be proportional to the degree of social harm caused, that the decision is based on facts and that reasons be given for a decision; art. 4.

[41]APL, chapter 5. Simple Procedures; arts. 33–5, apply for on the spot fines are applied for a fine to an individual of less than RMB 50 and for an enterprise a fine of less than RMB1,000. Ordinary Procedures are set out at arts. 36–41. A party that is to be subject to a serious administrative punishment, such as revocation of a business license, an order suspending production or a business licenses, or imposition of a relatively large fine may require a hearing procedure; arts. 42–3.

[42]*Pricing Law* 1997, art. 23.

[43]APL, art. 31.

[44]APL, art. 32.

[45]Zhang Chunsheng, 'The Development and Prospect of Administrative Procedure Law of China', unpublished paper given at the *International Symposium of Administrative Procedure Law* in Shanghai, 16 November 1998, p. 6.

[46]The *State Compensation Law*, Chapter III also provides for compensation to be paid where the loss suffered is as the result of designated wrongful acts in the criminal justice process.

[47]ALL, arts. 2 and 5.

[48]ALL art., 32.

[49]ALL, art. 54(2)(a).

[50]ALL, art. 52, this refers to laws passed by the NPC and its Standing Committee, administrative regulations passed by the State Council and local rules passed by local people's congresses or congresses of autonomous regions.

[51]ALL, art. 53. At the time of drafting the *Administrative Litigation Law*, one suggestion made was that the courts should have the power to review the lawfulness of these rules. Instead, the term 'have regard to' requires the courts to use this type of rule as the basis for determining the lawfulness of the act in question. Courts may only ignore these rules where there is a conflict between them and a law or regulation of the type set out in art. 52. Zhang Shuyi, 'Examination of Several Controversial Issues in the Administrative Litigation Law (Draft)' (1992), vol. 24, no. 3, *Chinese Law and Government* 47.

[52]They may only amend a punishment, as opposed to other types of act, if it is 'manifestly unfair'. Explanations of the scope of what is manifestly unfair have been framed very narrowly. The limited nature of orders a court can make is due to the requirement that courts do not interfere in the exercise of administrative functions of the state, ALL, art. 54(4).

[53]Information Office of the State Council of the PRC February 2000, *Fifty Years of Progress in China's Human Rights,* 5. According to this source, there have been nearly 440,000 cases brought under the *Administrative Litigation Law* since its introduction on 1 October 1990 and 2,566 cases claiming compensation under the *State Compensation Law.*

[54]Officials are sometime called the *fumuguan*: mother and father official which is an indication of their perceived status vis–à–vis the object of the decision.

[55]Huang Jie, 'On the Administrative Litigation Law' (1992), vol. 24, no. 3, *Chinese Law and Government*, p. 43.

[56]The officially reported number of administrative litigation cases accepted by the people's courts in 1998 was 98,350 cases, 1.82 per cent of the total number of cases accepted by the courts that year, at 1021. Of the 98,350 cases accepted, 47,817, or 49 per cent were withdrawn by the applicant prior to judgment, at 1023. China Law Yearbook Editorial Committee, *1999 China Law Yearbook*, China Law Yearbook Press, Beijing.

[57]ALL, art. 50.

[58]See for example Clarke D.C., 'What's Law Got to do with it? Legal Institutions and Economic Reform in China', (1991) 10(1), *Pacific Basin Law Journal* 31, Lubman S., *op. cit.*, 383, pp. 392–9, Potter P.B., 'Foreign Investment Law in the People's Republic of China: Dilemmas of State Control' (1995), *The China Quarterly*, p. 155.

[59]Responsibility for investigation of corruption is the responsibility severally of the CCP Discipline Inspection Committee, the procuratorate and, for government departments, the Ministry of Supervision.

[60]Press report 7 July 2000, Xinhua, 'People's Congress considers law governing judges, procurators', reproduced in *BBC Summary of World Broadcasts*, 12 July 2000.

[61]The Civil and Legal Committee, a subcommittee of the NPC, completed a provisional draft on procedures covering the supervision of individual legal cases. Reported as 'China's Parliament May Take Powers To Examine Misjudged Legal Cases', Xinhua news agency, Beijing, 4 February 1999, press report, *Xinhua*, 11 March 2000, 'Chinese courts to promote accountability for verdicts', reproduced in *BBC Summary of World Broadcasts*, 28 March 2000, Work Report of the Supreme People's Court to the NPC, Xinhua, 19 March 2000, reproduced in *BBC Summary of World Broadcasts*, 30 March 2000.

[62]Yu An, 'Several Basic Questions about my Country's Administrative Review Law', *Fazhi Ribao* (Legal Daily), 6 May 1999, p. 7; Yu An, 'Fazhan Fuhe Shijie Maoyi Zhuzhi Guifan de Wo Guo Xingzhengfa' (My Country's Administrative Law Developing Toward Complying with the Norms of the World Trade Organization), http://www.law-star.com, 3 April 2000.

[63]ARL, arts. 6 and 9.

[64]ARL, art. 1 and 28.

[65]ARL, art. 28(3).

[66]ARL, art. 27.

[67]Unless specifically excluded by the law which governs the exercise of a certain power, if a person is dissatisfied with the decision made on review that person has fifteen days within which to appeal to the people's court; ARL, art. 5. The ARL also permits a person to commence litigation from an administrative review decision that the law otherwise provides is final if the review agency fails to accept the application for review within the legally prescribed time limits, or does not provide the decision within the legally prescribed time limits, or if the review decision does not contain a statement of reasons. ARL, art. 19.

[68]Keller argues that the use of vague general and ambiguous language is intentional and the consequential broad scope of discretion that results from this legislative form is also intended. See Keller P., *op. cit.*, 711, pp. 749–52.

[69]For example the ARL at art. 4 specifies the principles of review to be; lawfulness, fairness, timeliness, accuracy and conveniencing citizens, actively correcting mistakes and protecting the accurate implementation of the law and regulations.

[70]APL, art. 4.

[71]Potter, P.B. (1995), *op. cit.*, p. 155.

[72]The problems of poor enforcement of court judgments is discussed at length in Clarke, Donald, 'Power and Politics in the Chinese Court System: the Enforcement of Civil Judgments' (1996), 10, *Columbia Journal of Asian Law* 1.

[73]Joe Studwell, 'Enduring Socialism and the Death of Profit' (2000), Section 2, *China Economic Quarterly* 15, pp. 21–2.

[74]A particular example is the US Congress annual debates about granting China MFN status before amendment of the Jackson Vanick legislation to grant China permanent normal trade relations under the *US–China Relations Act* 2000, see also Lubman S., *op. cit.*, pp. 411–4.

[75]Peerenboom, R., 'What's Wrong with Chinese Rights? Towards a Theory of Rights with Chinese Characteristics', (1993) 6, *Harvard Human Rights Journal*, 29, p. 117.

[76]Petersmann, E.-U., 'The WTO Constitution and Human Rights' (2000), *op. cit.*, 19–25, pp. 23–4, applies the model of universal human rights in the 1993 Vienna Declaration of the UN World Conference on Human Rights as being of a universal nature and 'based on the dignity and worth inherent in the human person'. See also discussion in Garcia, F.J., 'The Global Market and Human Rights: Trading away the Human Rights Principle', (April 1999) 25, *Brooklyn Journal of International Law*, 51.

[77]*Universal Declaration of Human Rights*, 'In the exercise of his rights and freedoms, everyone shall be subject only to such limitations as are determined by law solely for the purpose of securing due recognition and respect for the rights and freedoms of others and of meeting the just requirements of morality, public order and the general welfare in a democratic society.'

[78]For a comprehensive discussion about the meaning of individual rights in China see Peerenboom R.P. (1993), *op. cit.*, 29, pp. 116–48 and Peerenboom R.P., 'Rights Interests and the Interest in Rights in China' (Summer 1995), 31, *Stanford Journal of International Law*, 359.

[79]Chapter Two sets out a wide range of rights including amongst others: the right to vote, stand for election; art. 34, freedom of speech, assembly, association, procession and demonstration; art. 35, freedom of religious belief; art. 36, freedom of the person; art. 37, protection of personal dignity and prohibition of insult, libel, false accusation, or false incrimination; art. 38, inviolability of residence and prohibition of unlawful search of a residence; art. 39, freedom of privacy of correspondence except to meet the needs of state security or criminal investigation; art. 40, right to criticize and make suggestions concerning any state organ or functionary and the right to recover compensation for losses suffered as a result of infringement of their rights; art. 41, the right and duty to work; art. 42, working people have the right to rest; art. 43.

[80]Peerenboom (1995), *op. cit.*, especially pp. 361–4.

[81]Some Chinese scholars now assert there has been an over-emphasis on duties. See, for example, Jiang, Ping, 'State and Society: 'On the Change of Legal Concepts in Modern China', Conference Proceedings on the 1995 Annual Meeting, Research Committee on Sociology of Law', entitled *Legal Culture, Encounters and Transformations.*

[82]For a full discussion of this idea see Peerenboom, R. (1993), *op. cit.*, p. 128.

[83]The Human Rights White Paper issued by the Information Office of the State Council in February 2000 reflects this orientation towards rights.

[84]The NPC Standing Committee is empowered generally to supervise the implementation of the Constitution and there have been attempts made over a number of years to draft a *Supervision Law* to establish a specific body empowered to receive and determine complaints about breaches of the Constitution. To date

there has been no body established whose responsibility it is to receive and hear complaints relating to conduct in breach of the Constitution.

[85]An example is art. 41 which enables a citizen to make suggestions to government institutions , to complain against and report law breaking activities and dereliction of duty of government officials. This article enables citizens to seek compensation if they suffer loss as a result of infringement of their civic rights. The entitlement to claim compensation and the principles and procedures for making such a claim was set out in the ALL art. 67 and then in the *State Compensation Law* 1995. These laws effectively define the limits and scope of operation of this constitutional provision.

[86]One example is the *Law of Assembly, Procession and Demonstrations of the PRC* passed in 1989 which requires that permission be obtained from the public security agencies before a demonstration may lawfully be conducted.

[87]Jiang Ping notes the trend in some areas toward a more permissive regulatory regime, which as apposed to a mandatory regulatory regime under the planning system which required the parties to enter into relations according to a legally prescribed standard. Jiang, Ping, *op. cit.*, *Contract Law*, art. 4.

[88]*Contract Law*, art. 44. An example of the type of contract requiring approval before be coming effective are contracts for the creation of foreign investment enterprises, equity joint ventures, contractual joint ventures and wholly foreign owned enterprises.

[89]Foreign trade contracts may still only be entered into by authorized entities, although increasing numbers of entities are now able to obtain that authorization.

[90]Jayasuriya, K., 'The Rule of Law and Governance in the East Asian State', vol. 1, no. 2, *The Australian Journal of Asian Law* 107, pp. 116–22.

[91]Gao Chuanli, the ex-Minister of Justice in the introduction to the book *Yi Fa Zhi Guo Jiben Fanlue Lunwenji* (trans. Collection of Essays on the Basic Plan for Ruling the Country by Law), Sifa bu Sifa Yanjiu Suo Bian (edited by the Judicial Research Office of the Bureau of Justice), Falu Chubanshe (Law Press) 1998 at 3. He describes party leadership and its sponsorship of the creation of a system of ruling on the basis of law as the way to achieve social stability. At the same time, he juxtaposes this discussion with the pre-reform rhetoric of contradictions amongst the people, which illustrates that the policy of ruling the country by law is not conceived of as a radical departure from pre-reform conceptual referents such as 'contradictions amongst the people'.

[92]Gao Xinting, 'Yong Deng Xiaoping Lilun Zhidao Zhengfa Gongzuo' (trans. Using Deng Xiaoping Theory as a Guide for Political Legal Work), *Yi Fa Zhi Guo Jiben Fanlue Lunwenji* (trans Collection of Essays on the Basic Plan for Ruling the Country by Law), Sifa bu Sifa Yanjiu Suo Bian (edited by the Judicial Research Office of the Bureau of Justice), Falu Chubanshe (Law Press) 1998 states at page 391 that to protect social stability, it is necessary to rely on the comprehensive management of public order and that the key link of public order is to 'strike hard' on the basis of the law.

[93]These are two of the four Cardinal Principles, enunciated in the Preamble to the Constitution, amongst other places.

[94]An example of the instrumental and formalist use of law is illustrated in *Opinion No 21/1999 (China)* of the UN Commission on Human Rights, Working Group on Arbitrary Detention concerns Wang Youcai illustrates the instrumental use of law. Wang was sentenced to three years imprisonment and two years of deprivation of political rights in 1989 for subverting state power. In 1998 he sought to register the Democratic People's Party of China which constituted the crime of incitement to subvert state power and he was sentenced as a recidivist to eleven

years imprisonment and three years deprivation of political rights. The Chinese government argued that the right of freedom of association and speech granted in the Constitution and the International Covenant on Civil and Political Rights (which it has signed but not yet acceded) was constrained in the interests of *inter alia* national security, public safety or public order. The Chinese government argued that it was appropriate to punish Wang as he had instigated subversion of state power.

[95] Potter, P.B. (1999), *op. cit.*, 673, p. 682.

[96] The primary public order policy was instituted in 1981 in the *Summary of the Public Order Meeting of the Five Big Cities of Beijing, Tianjin, Shanghai, Guangzhou and Wuhan* on 14 June 1981 and transmitted by the Central Committee of the CCP in the *Directive on Strengthening Politics and Law Work* and remains in force. The policy is called the Comprehensive Management of Public Order. It includes as its 'key link' striking hard and seriously punishing those committing serious criminal offences.

[97] Wang Zhongfang, ed., *Zhongguo Shehui Zhi'an Zonghe Zhili de Lilun yu Shijian* (Theory and Practice of Comprehensive Management of Public Order in China), Beijing, Qunzhong Chubanshe (Masses Press) 1992, pp. 13–14.

[98] Amendments to the *Criminal Law of the PRC* were approved at the Fifth Session of the Eighth NPC on 14 March 1997 and amendments to the *Criminal Procedure Law* were approved on 17 March 1996.

[99] The crime of counter-revolution was replaced by the crimes of endangering state security, *Criminal Law, Special Section, Chapter* 1.

[100] The crime of 'hooliganism' was abolished from the *Criminal Law*, but still appears as an offence warranting re-education through labour.

[101] *Criminal Law*, art. 5.

[102] *Criminal Procedure Law*, art. 96(1).

[103] *Criminal Procedure Law*, art. 36.

[104] *Criminal Procedure Law*, art. 34.

[105] *Criminal Procedure Law*, art. 191.

[106] See discussion of these revisions in Lawyers Committee for Human Rights, 'Opening to Reform? An Analysis of China's Revised Criminal Procedure Law', October 1996.

[107] The *Criminal Law*, art. 13 provides that 'If the circumstances were clearly minor and the harm is not great, they are not deemed to be crimes'. Corresponding provisions exist in relation to re-education through labour, for example, Jiang Bo Zhan Zhongle, *Gongan Xingzheng Fa* (Public Security Administrative Law) Zhongguo Renshi Chubanshe (China Personnel Press) Beijing 1994, 96, Li Junren, Du Fuzhi 'Lun Laodong Jiaoyang de Xingzhi Wenti' (Discussion of the Nature of Re-education Through Labour, *Laodong Jiaoyang Yanjiu* (Studies in Re-education Through Labour) Qunzhong Chubanshe (Masses Press) 1990 p. 50, 98.

[108] For example, the legal basis for detention under detention for education (for prostitutes) *shourong jiaoyu*, is set out in several documents. In September 1991 the NPC Standing Committee issued the *Decision on Strictly Prohibiting Prostitution* which set out the legal form of the campaign against prostitution and prostitution related activities. The *Decision* consolidated and amended pre-existing laws on prostitution and created detention for education. Criminal law related provisions of this *Decision* were later incorporated into the amended *Criminal Law*. The formal legal basis for the power of detention for education is set out in the *Decision* in the following terms.

[109] APL, art. 4.

[110]Examples of administrative coercive measures are: Re-education through labour, under which a person may be sent to three years in a labour camp, with a possible extension of a year, detention for education (*shourong jiaoyu*) under which a prostitute may be detained for between six months and two years, coercive drug rehabilitation under which a drug addict may be detained for between three months and one year and detention for repatriation (*shourong qiansong*) for vagrants who should be repatriated within either fifteen days for people within the province or one month for people from different provinces after their identity is discovered.

[111]Harold Tanner, *Strike Hard! Anti Crime Campaigns and Chinese Criminal Justice 1979–1985*, Cornell East Asia Series 104, 1999; Bakken, B., 'Crime, Juvenile Delinquency and Deterrence Policy in China' (1993), no. 30, *The Australian Journal of Chinese Affairs* 50.

[112]Passed on 2 September 1983 to give legal form to the law and order campaign also known as the 'yanda', Sun Shengfu, 'Guanyu Jianchi "Yanda" Fanzhen de Yixie Sikao' (Some Reflections on Upholding the 'Heavy Strike' Guiding Principle), in *Zhongguo Renmin Gongan Daxue Xiaoqing Shi Zhou Nian Lunwen Xuanji* (Selection of Essays for the Tenth Anniversary of the China People's Public Security University), Beijing, Zhongguo Renmin Gongan Daxue Chubanshe (China People's Public Security University Press), 1994, pp. 248–54.

[113]Wang Zhongfan, *op. cit.*, 11–14 and see for example, Bakken B., *op. cit.*, 50, at 54–55, Dutton M.R., and Tianfu Li, 'Missing the Target. Policing Strategies in the Period of Economic Reform' (1993), vol. 39, no. 3, *Crime and Delinquency* 318.

[114]For example, in relation to preservation of public order, Gao Xinting, *op. cit.*, 1998, states at page 391 that to protect social stability, it is necessary to rely on the comprehensive management of public order and that the key link of public order is to strike hard on the basis of the law.

[115]Petersmann, E.-U., *op. cit.*, 19–25, p. 23. A note of caution is sounded in Tiefenbrun, S., 'Free Trade and Protectionism: The Semiotics of Seattle' (Spring 2000), *Arizona Journal of International and Comparative Law* 257.

[116]Blackett, A., 'Whither the Social Clause? Human Rights, Trade Theory and Treaty Interpretation' (Fall 1999), *Columbia Human Rights Law Review* 1, pp. 13–26.

[117]Constitution art. 35 includes a guarantee of freedom of association, *Labour Law*, art. 7, *Trade Union Law of the PRC* promulgated 3 April, 1992.

[118]Trade Unions are mass organizations under the leadership of the CCP. After attempts to establish independent trade unions were crushed during the Tiananmen Square crack down, Ni Zhifu, then President of the All–China Federation of Trade Unions (ACFTU), was quoted as saying 'China's trade unions must work under the leadership of the CCP and no trade unions opposed to the CCP are allowed to be established', Peking, 25th July, Xinhua news, reported by *BBC Summary of World Broadcasts, Part 3, The Far East; B. INTERNAL AFFAIRS; 2. CHINA; FE/0520/B2/1.* Since that time, individuals advocating or seeking to establish independent trade unions have been arrested or detained. See also Lehl, A.N., 'China's Trade Union System under the International Covenant on Economic Social and Cultural rights: Is China in compliance with Article 8?' (Summer 1999), *University of Hawaii Law Review* 203.

[119]Constitution arts. 34, 48, *Law for the Protection of the Rights and Interests of Women*, art. 2, which guarantees both the equality of rights and protection of the special rights and interests of women. Chapter IV of this law deals with work

and promises both non discrimination (art. 24) and special protection in light of 'women's differences' (that is to safeguard her reproductive function) art. 25.

[120]Including the *Regulations on Labor Protection for Female Staff Members and Workers, Regulations for Health Care for Women Employees (Trial Implementation)* and which prevent women from carrying out certain types of work during menstruation, pregnancy, purpureum and lactation (*Law for the Protection of the Rights and Interests of Women* art. 25).

[121]From the list of ratifications contained at the ILO website: http://ilolex.ilo.ch:1567/public/english/docs/declworld.htm visited on 9 January 2001.

[122]*Labour Law*, art. 15.

[123]Chan, Anita and Robert Senser, 'China's Troubled Workers', *Foreign Affairs* 3, March 1997.

[124]For a discussion of the gender discrimination that arises in the workplace and its inter-relationship with the disparity between the equality/non discrimination regulatory model and the protection regulatory model see Woo, M.Y.K., 'Biology and Equality: Challenge for Feminism in the Socialist and Liberal State' (1993), vol. 42, *Emory Law Journal*, 134, pp. 175–96; Jordan, Ann 'Women's Rights In The People's Republic Of China: Patriarchal Wine Poured From A Socialist Bottle' (Spring 1994), 8, *Journal of Chinese Law* 47.

[125]The influence of local protectionism on law enforcement is discussed in Clarke D.C., 'What's Law Got to do with it? Legal Institutions and Economic Reform in China' (1991), 10(1), *Pacific Basin Law Journal* 31, Potter P.B. (1995), *op. cit.*

[126]Potter, P.B. (1995), *op. cit.*, Chan, Anita and Robert Senser, *op. cit.*

[127]For example an article in the *China Economic Quarterly* documents discriminatory application of environmental standards where they are applied strictly against a foreign investment enterprise, but not at all against neighbouring state owned enterprises clearly in breach of the same environmental standards. Jim Studwell, *op. cit.*, 15–25, p. 23.

[128]Report issued by the Information Centre for Human Rights and Democracy on 15 November 2000 on *BBC Summary of World Broadcasts*, 17 November 2000. For example a recent press report documents violent demonstrations by peasants in Fujian province against an 80 per cent increase in local taxes on bananas.

[129]Clarke, Donald C. (1991), *op. cit.*, pp. 37–43; Studwell, J., *op. cit.*

[130]Feng, Chen, 'Subsistence Crises, Managerial Corruption and Labour Protests in China' (July 2000), *The China Journal*; Chan, Anita and Robert Senser, *op. cit.*

[131]The Human Rights White paper, *op. cit.*, asserts that three social security systems are currently in place; basic living security system for people laid off by state-owned enterprises, unemployment insurance and the basic living security system for residents of cities and towns. In addition to some people whose pensions are paid by their work unit, the Human Rights White Paper asserts that '94.33 million people participate in the basic retirement insurance policy'. The Human Rights White Paper further asserts that at the end of 1998 there were 5.71 million registered unemployed and at the end of 1999, 'a total of 99.12 million employees were covered by unemployment insurance, more than 15 million unemployed were receiving relief funds and 7.5 million unemployed people had been re-employed'.

[132]For example, the strain of high demand on the health services in Shanghai can be seen from the fact that a person will not be treated in a hospital, not matter how serious the illness or injury, if that person cannot pay upfront, or some other satisfactory arrangement for guaranteeing payment can first be made.

Part IV

Implications for International Trade

11

The Impact of China's WTO Accession on International Trade and Capital Flows

Margot Schüller

Introduction

China's integration with the global economy has contributed to a new pattern of international trade and capital flows. This pattern is characterized by a growing share of developing countries in world trade, which increased to around 28 per cent in 1999. Although global foreign direct investment (FDI) was largely concentrated among developed countries, private net capital flows to *emerging markets* was as high as 150 billion dollars in 1999.[1] China was among those countries benefiting most from the liberalization of the world trading system, which now has the lowest tariffs ever for manufactures. Since the middle of the 1990s, it has also become the second largest recipient of FDI, lying only behind the United States.[2] With accession to the WTO it is expected that China will be able to further expand its exports and absorb more foreign capital. The World Bank projects that by 2020, China's share in world exports will increase to nearly 10 per cent, ahead of Japan, but still behind the United States and the European Union.[3] The issue of whether this rapid integration with the world economy will have a largely favourable effect on the rest of the world – as foreseen by the World Bank – and what exactly the impact on international trade and capital flow will be, are the issues dealt with in this paper.

The paper starts with an overview of China's share in global trade and in the trade of such major economies as those of the European Union, the United States and Japan. It also takes a look at the importance of China as a recipient of global capital. The second part of the paper addresses the issue of the extent to which China's accession to the WTO will influence the direction and structure of global trade and the trade with its major trading partners. In the third and final section, the impact of China's accession to the WTO on global capital flows will be analyzed.

China's Importance in the Global Economy

To show China's importance in the global economy, some basic indicators need to be looked at. Over the last two decades, China has become an important player in the international trade of merchandise products. Between 1980 and 1999, the volume of China's foreign trade increased from US$ 38 billion to 360 billion, while its ratio to GDP doubled to more than 30 per cent.[4] By 1999, China's share in world merchandise exports doubled from 1.8 per cent in 1990 to 3.6 per cent in 1999, and its import share had grown from 1.5 per cent in 1990 compared to 2.9 per cent in 1999 (cf. Figure 1).[5]

Figure 1: China's Share in World Trade 1990 and 1999

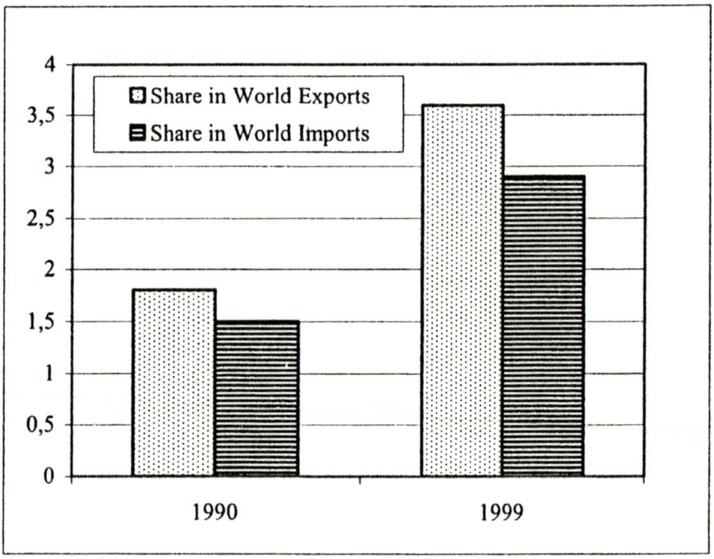

Source: WTO, *International Trade Statistics 2000.*

The successful entry into the world market was marked by a large expansion of the ratio of manufactured goods to total exports, growing from 53 per cent in 1980 to over 90 per cent in 1999. The rapid increase of manufactured exports showed that China was actually able to realize its comparative advantage, which is mainly concentrated in labour-intensive industries.[6]

Two-digit growth characterized the performance of foreign trade in the 1990s, showing an average annual growth rate of 13.5 per cent between 1991 and 1999. However, there was a fluctuation in the export growth in some years. While the expansion of total exports and imports recorded a growth of 19.5 per cent in the first half of the decade, foreign trade expansion slowed down in the latter half of the 1990s. The decline of regional GDP growth in East Asia, which takes a large share of China's exports, contributed to the negative growth in China's exports in 1998.[7]

Figure 2: World Merchandise Exports by Region and Countries, 1999

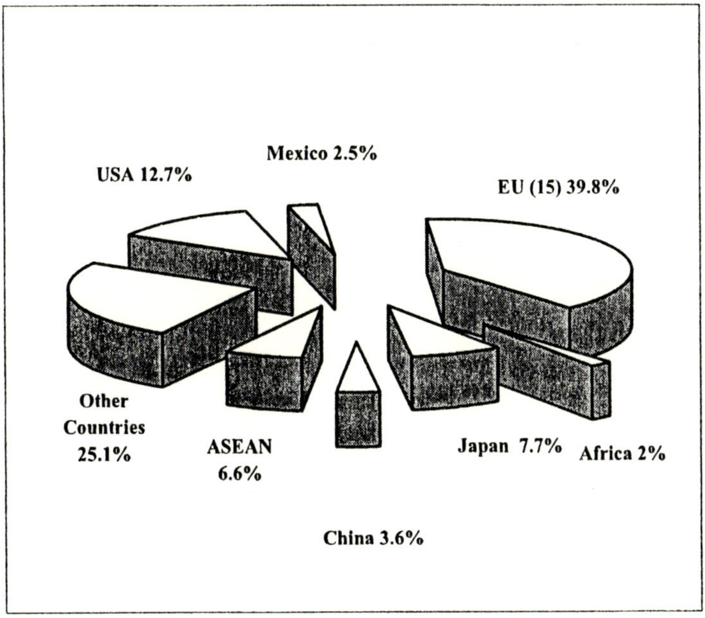

Source: WTO, *International Trade Statistics 2000.*

By the end of the 1990s, China had become the ninth largest exporting country in the world. However, its contribution to global exports of 3.6 per cent is still rather small compared to the shares of many

European countries, especially those of Germany, France, the UK, Italy and even the Netherlands.[8] Looking at the distribution of world merchandise exports by region and countries in 1999, the European Union was the largest exporting region, accounting for a share of 39.8 per cent. Within the EU, Germany was the second most important export country after the United States and even lies ahead of Japan. Within Asia, however, China is the second largest exporting country after Japan (cf. Figure 2).

The picture changes quite remarkably, however, if intra-EU trade is excluded and Hong Kong is regarded statistically as an economic region of China. Without intra-EU trade China's share would account for 4.6 per cent, and including Hong Kong's exports the share would further increase to 8.2 per cent. China's role as a global player becomes much more prominent when applying this concept.[9]

Figure 3: China's Share in Total Merchandise Trade of the United States, Japan and the EU, 1999

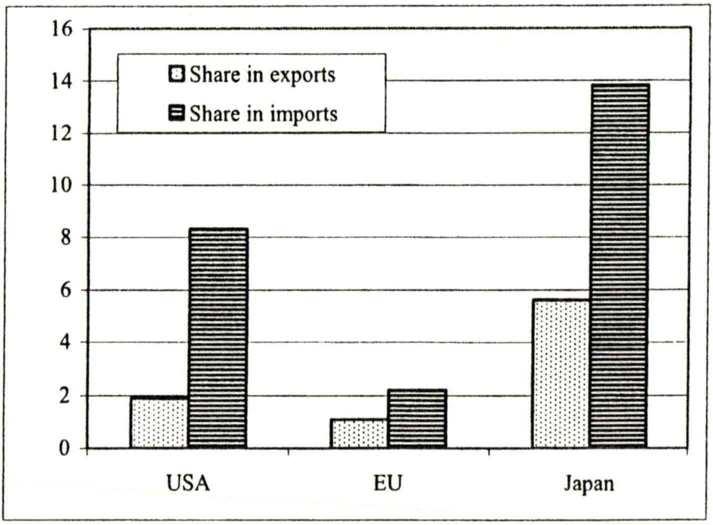

Source: WTO, *International Trade Statistics 2000.*

China's three largest trading partners are Japan, the United States and the European Union, which together make up more than 54 per cent of China's total exports. When exports to Hong Kong are included, which are mostly re-exported to these countries, the share amounts to 74 per cent. For those three countries constituting the economic *triad*, trade with China plays quite a different role. For Japan,

5.6 per cent of its total merchandise exports are directed to China and 13.8 per cent of its total imports come from China. To the United States, China plays an important role as a supplier of 8.3 per cent of its imports, while only 1.9 per cent of its total exports are destined for China. For the EU member countries, trade with China seems to be less important. While China's share of total EU imports accounts for 2.2 per cent, exports to China are even smaller, constituting only 1.1 per cent of the EU's total exports (cf. Figure 3). However, the picture changes, when intra-EU trade is excluded and when looking at some EU countries in more detail.[10]

The structure of exports from Japan, the United States and the EU to China is fairly similar, as around 50 per cent of their exports fall into the category of machinery and transport equipment. Agricultural export products play a minor role in total exports from Japan, but constitute 6.2 per cent of total EU exports and even 9.7 per cent of the total exports of the United States (cf. Figure 4).

Figure 4: Exports of the USA, EU and Japan to China by Major Product, 1999

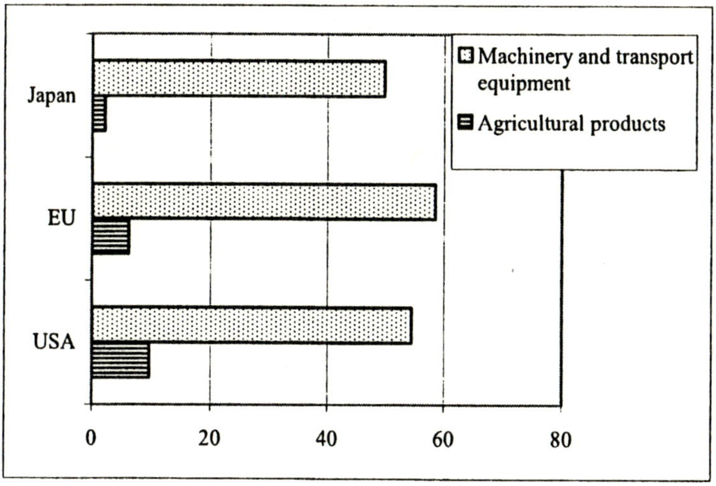

Source: WTO, *International Trade Statistics 2000*

In the Chinese machinery and equipment market, which is the most important export segment for Japan, the United States and the EU, these three countries play a decisive role. With a market share of 31 per cent in 1999, Japan ranks first, followed by Germany with a share of 17 per cent and the United States with a share of 14 per cent. Looking at the development of these countries' market shares during the period from 1992 to 1999, we can observe that no large change in their market shares took place.[11] By contrast, Italy and Hong Kong suffered a substantial loss of their shares in the Chinese market, while South Korea has been able to improve its market position (cf. Figure 5).

Figure 5: Shares of Selected Countries in China's Market for Machinery and Equipment

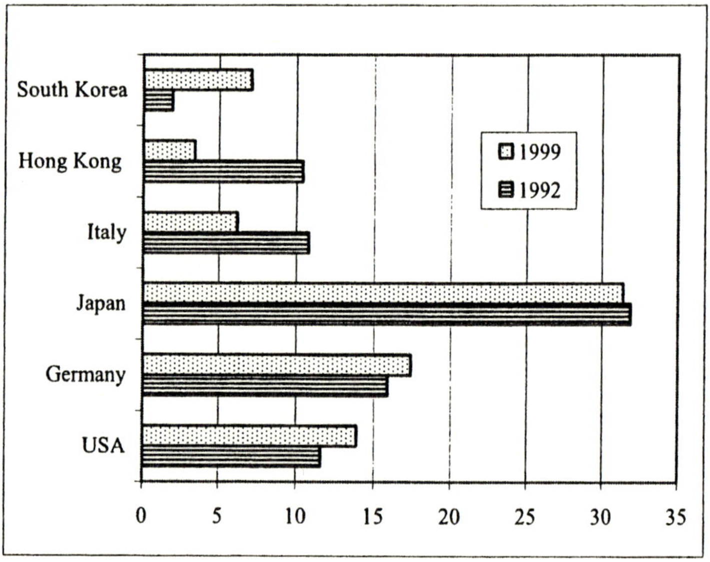

Source: *VDMA Statistics 2000.*

We now turn to China's role as a recipient of foreign capital. Liberalization of markets and privatization of economic activity in most developing countries led to a surge in private capital inflows to those countries in the 1990s. However, in real terms, the increase is less impressive, and if calculated as a proportion of GNP, the aggregate net capital inflow to developing countries averaged only around 5 per cent during the years 1990 to 1998. It is important to note that China accounted for almost one percentage point of this capital inflow.[12]

As part of its 'open door policy', China started to allow private capital inflows at the beginning of the 1980s. At that time, most developing countries shifted the composition of their capital inflow from official capital towards private capital. With the instability of private financial flows, FDI became the preferred source of external financing. China's importance as a host country for FDI increased during the 1990s. On a cumulative basis of FDI inflows, China ranked fourth in the years 1985 to 1995, absorbing a volume of 130 billion dollars (cf. Figure 6). By 1992, China had become the largest recipient of FDI in the developing countries; in 1995, China accounted for one-third of all FDI inflows into non-OECD countries.[13]

Figure 6: Leading Host Economies for FDI Based on Cumulative Inflows, 1985–1995

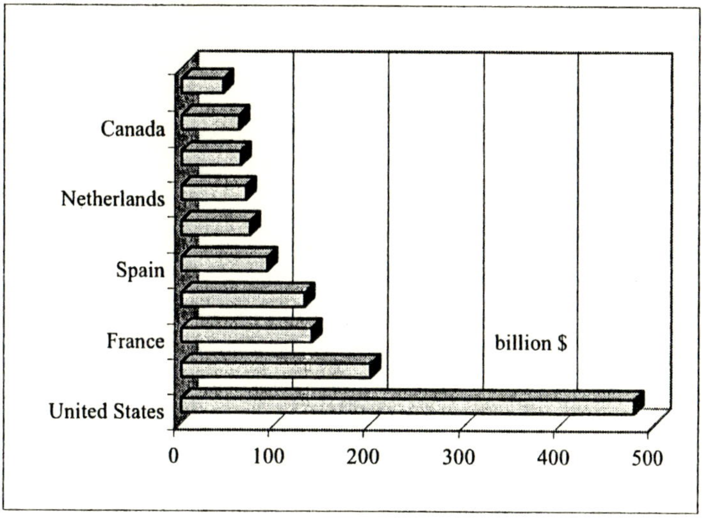

Source: WTO, *Trade and Foreign Direct Investment*, Report by the WTO Secretariat, Press/57, 9.10.1996.

Looking at the period from 1990 to 1997, the ten leading emerging market-countries absorbed more than three-quarters of the FDI inflow to developing countries. China, Brazil and Mexico accounted for almost one half of this. When calculated on a per capita basis, FDI in Malaysia was the highest, amounting to 223 US$, while China absorbed 21 US$ per capita in the years 1990 to 1997.[14] Thus, a great potential for further increases in FDI seems to exist.

Among the Asian developing countries, including the newly industrialized economies (NIEs) of Hong Kong, South Korea, Singapore and Taiwan, China was able to attract around half of total FDI inflows in the years 1993 to 1998 (cf. Figure 7). Most of the FDI inflows to China originated from within East Asia, with the Asian NIEs being the major source of FDI to China, followed by Japan. In analyzing the distribution of FDI within Asia, the Asian Development Bank (ADB) points to a 'flying geese' pattern of FDI. Starting in the 1970s, low wages and openness, the essential factors influencing this FDI pattern, attracted large sums of FDI to labour-intensive industries in Hong Kong, South Korea, Singapore and Taiwan. Due to strong wage increases in the NIEs, flows of FDI in labour-intensive industries shifted in the 1980s to Southeast Asia and later to China.[15]

Figure 7 : FDI in China and Asian Developing Countries, 1993-98

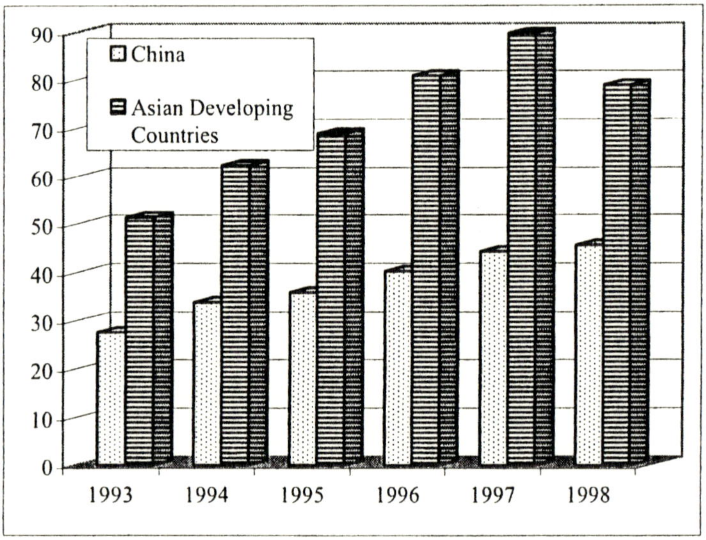

Source: Asian Development Bank, *Asian Development Outlook 2000*, Hong Kong 2000, p. 258.

Short-term capital inflows, consisting mainly of short-term bank loans, portfolio investment, especially short-term government securities and equities, and non-inter-bank deposit holdings can be highly volatile, as the Asian crisis has shown. That China was not affected by this crisis is mainly due to the fact that the Chinese currency is not convertible on the capital account, and that most of the capital inflow took the form of FDI, which means that the exposure to private debt denominated in foreign currency is quite limited.[16] However, foreign commercial lending to China expanded in the 1990s as well. While international commercial loans amounted to US$ 47 billion in 1994, their volume increased to US$ 65 billion by 1999. Nevertheless, the proportion of international commercial loans in total debt only grew from 13.9 per cent to 22.9 per cent in the same period.[17]

Compared to other Asian countries and Latin America, China's outstanding liabilities of international bank lending and outstanding liabilities of net issuance of international debt securities remained limited (cf. Table 1).

Table 1: International Bank and Securities Financing of Emerging Market Economies (in billion US$)

	June 1997	December 1999
International bank lending, outstanding liabilities		
Asia[1]	480	315
- China	**85**	**68**
- Crisis countries[2]	329	190
Latin America	284	280
Russia	54	44
Net issuance of international debt securities, outstanding amount		
Asia	127	139
- China	**17**	**18**
- Crisis countries	98	107
Latin America	136	205
Russia	6	19

[1] Excluding Hong Kong and Singapore.
[2] Indonesia, Korea, Malaysia, the Philippines and Thailand.
Source: Bank for International Settlements, *70th Annual Report*, Basel, 5 June 2000, p. 39.

To summarize, China became a major recipient of foreign capital in the 1990s. Stepped-up reform of the economic system and the large market helped to attract a remarkable inflow of FDI. Short-term capital inflow remained restricted, thus preventing China from playing a larger role in the international capital market.

Impact of China's WTO Accession on Trade Direction

Most studies on the impact of China's accession to the WTO concentrate on domestic industries and on domestic policy issues.[18] There are only a few studies that analyze its influence on international trade and capital flows or question how China's major trading partners will be affected by the country's WTO entry. In his study of the impact of China's WTO entry on international trade, Wang Zhi points to the structure of factor endowments in China and its major trading partners as the basic economic force which shapes the direction of this impact.[19] Wang argues that the decreasing restrictions on imports of labour-intensive manufactures in WTO member countries, especially for textiles and clothing, would allow China to further realize its comparative advantage. For these latter products, the Uruguay Round agreed to replace the quota system of the Multi-Fibre Agreement (MFA) by a new Agreement on Textiles and Clothing (ATC) which, among other policies, requires the restrictions to end in 2005. While China would concentrate on labour-intensive products leading to an increase in these exports, its demand for agricultural and capital- or technology-intensive products from developed economies would grow as well.

Low production costs, especially with regard to labour, give China a comparative advantage over developed countries. According to trade theory, the direction of trade flows is basically determined by the relative factor-intensity of production and the relative factor scarcities among countries, the latter deciding the cost of production.[20] There is a strong correlation between land scarcity and trade flows in food and agricultural products, which explains why the United States and the EU are net exporters of these products but not Japan or South Korea. For the same reason but with regard to the abundance of labour and shortage of capital, China and most other developing countries have become net exporters of labour-intensive manufacturing products such as textiles, clothing, and other light manufactures, while they import capital and skill-intensive products from Japan, the EU and the United States. Different factor endowments make the trade structures of developing and developed countries complementary, but because of similarities in trade structure, China and many developing countries in Asia compete strongly in third markets.[21]

According to Wang Zhi's analysis, when China joins the WTO and obtains the benefits from the phasing-out of MFA quotas for its textiles and clothing, its world market share for these products will rise by more than one percentage point during the MFA phase-out period and increase by four percentage points by the year 2010.[22]

In the textile and clothing market of some of its largest trading partners, China would be able to raise its market share to quite a large extent. In the United States, for example, the increase of China's market share would amount to 15 percentage points by the year 2005 and about a quarter by the year 2010. As a response to China's growing share in the world textile market, production of textile and clothing in developed countries will have to shrink further.

Thus, employment in the textile and clothing sectors in the EU and the United States, which has already declined over the last decade, will fall again.[23] While the Asian NIEs will continue reallocating production facilities to China and become upstream suppliers of intermediate inputs for China, other developing countries will lose part of their world market share. Employment in the Asian NIEs is likely to suffer as well from the reallocation of certain labour-intensive industries to China.[24]

In the coming decade it is expected that the proportion of textile and clothing in China's total exports will further decline, while the share of electronic and machinery exports will rise. At the end of the 1980s, China started accelerating its capital- and technology-intensive exports, forced by quantitative constraints for textiles and clothing in developed countries on the one hand and facilitated by a strong inflow of FDI on the other. Looking at China's export structure in 1999, machinery and equipment already occupy a prominent share of around 30 per cent in total exports.[25] However, a large portion of these exports are produced in foreign-funded enterprises (FFEs) and, as Wang stresses, they have a high import content. This situation corresponds with the general observation that developing countries have been able to increase the proportion of their high-tech products to nearly a quarter of their total exports. Their share in global high-tech exports has grown remarkably from 8 per cent in 1988 to 23 percent in 1998.[26] However, high-tech exports are concentrated in about five developing countries (which do not include China) and 'many high-tech exports by developing countries are based on the relatively simple, labour-intensive assembly of imported components'.[27]

The fact that China's integration with the world economy, accelerated by the accession to the WTO, will have different effects on developed and developing countries is an argument put forward by the World Bank as well. In contrast to Wang Zhi's analysis, the World Bank looks at a longer time period, which is one of the reasons why some of its projections are not identical with Wang Zhi's simulation results. According to the World Bank, exports of capital- and knowledge-intensive products of the developed countries will see faster growth until 2020, and it forecasts that their total exports to China will grow at 8 per cent a year. Because of the rapid growth in demand, prices will increase relative to labour-intensive products and lead to a rise in terms of trade in favour of the developed countries, especially for Japan, the United States and the EU. Assuming a further shift of China's comparative advantage towards intermediate technology manufactures, the World Bank projects that China will gain 10 per cent market share in light manufactures, 8 per cent in transport equipment and other machinery and increase its market share in capital-intensive manufactures by 4 per cent. With regard to clothing, the World Bank projects a long-term loss of China's and Hong Kong's market shares totalling 16 per cent by 2020. While some Asian developing countries will be able to take up China's market share, neither Latin America nor Sub-Saharan Africa would gain from the shift in trade pattern (cf. Table 2).[28]

The impact of China's WTO entry on industrial countries will be largely beneficial to those economies, as they can take advantage of the reduced tariffs for manufactures and non-tariff barriers in China. Only their domestic industries for labour-intensive production will be further challenged by exports from China. The industrial economies' exports of capital- and knowledge-intensive products to China will substantially increase, and their exports of primary goods will grow to some extent as well. With accession to the WTO, imports of agricultural products by China, especially grain, have to be facilitated. As China is a scarce farming resource country on the one hand and due to population growth and changes in diet on the other, we can expect China to become a major net importer of grain in the years ahead. Low-cost and high-quality producers of agricultural products among the WTO members such as the United States and the EU will have better access to China and increase their market share.[29]

The extent to which China's accession to the WTO will influence trade with the EU is analysed in detail by Lemoine and Ünal-Kesenci in their contribution to this volume. They refer to a simulation study by the Development Research Centre (DRC) indicating that both imports from the EU to China as well as Chinese exports to the EU will increase considerably. The composition of EU exports would help exports from the EU to keep up with the growth of China's total imports. However, China's exports to the EU are likely to intensify competition in the EU market of consumer goods, especially textiles.[30] Among the various studies on the impact of China's WTO entry on trade relations with the United States, the US International Trade Commission's (USITC) analysis seems to be the most comprehensive.[31] Based on specific tariff cuts offered by China in April 1999, the USITC found a positive but minor impact on the United States in terms of total exports and imports, GDP, consumption and wages, as China accounts for less than 1 per cent of the United States' GDP. According to the USITC staff estimates for the base year 1998, US exports to China would have been approximately 10 per cent and imports from China almost 7 per cent higher if the 1999 tariff cuts were considered. The

Table 2: World Bank Projections for the Impact of China's Further Integration with the World Economy

	Impact by the year 2020
Exports from developed countries to China - mostly capital- and knowledge-intensive products; partly primary products such as foodgrains	Increase by 8 per cent p.a.
Rapid growth in demand for capital- and knowledge- intensive products from developed countries will raise their prices relative to labour-intensive products	Better terms of trade for developed countries, especially Japan, the USA and EU
Expansion of China's production of light manufactures (such as leather, fabricated metal products, and miscellaneous manufactures)	10 per cent world market share gain
Expansion of China's production of transport equipment and other machinery	8 per cent world market share gain
Expansion of China's capital-intensive heavy manufactures (chemicals, rubber, plastics, paper, iron and steel, non-ferrous metal)	Increase of world market share by 4 per cent
Contraction in clothing production	China and Hong Kong will lose 16 per cent of their world market share by 2020; industrial countries will give up an additional 19 per cent; some developed countries such as India, Indonesia, the Philippines and Thailand will increase their market share.

Source: Author's compilation from World Bank, *China 2020, Development Challenges in the New Century*, Washington, D.C., 1997, pp. 92–4.

sectors in the USA profiting most from China's trade liberalization would be agriculture, paper and pulp, chemicals, rubber, and plastics, other transport equipment (including aircraft), machinery and equipment. In contrast, sectors suffering most from increased Chinese imports would be footwear, garment, wood products, and other light manufactures. China's participation in the ATC is estimated by the USITC to have a positive impact on welfare in the United States, although at the expense of other suppliers to the US market. In line with the World Bank, the USITC expects a higher demand for capital- and skill-intensive manufactured goods due to the expansion of China's labour-intensive manufactures. This would result in an increase of more than US$ 300 million capital-intensive US exports a year to China after the elimination of textile and apparel quota restrictions in 2005. Taking into account non-static effects of trade liberalization such as increases in foreign direct investment, Goldman Sachs estimated that China's WTO entry would translate into US$ 13 billion in additional US exports by 2005.[32]

With regard to Korea and Japan, Cooper expects that in the short to medium term, China's WTO entry will be of benefit to Korean and Japanese companies, as these companies will be able to expand their FDI and exports to China. However, in the long-term, because of China's increased global competitiveness, South Korea will be forced to restructure some of its industries.[33]

Impact of China's WTO Accession on International Capital Flows

China's entry into the WTO will not only require substantial reductions in tariff and non-tariff barriers, but also liberalization of most sectors of its economy, especially the service sector. With more sectors open to foreign companies, FDI flows to China are thus expected to increase considerably. According to the April 1999 report by Goldman Sachs, FDI could reach as much as US$ 100 billion by the year 2005 compared to US$ 40 billion last year.[34] The question of whether FDI flows to China will actually reach such a volume depends on a number of conditions and circumstances which need to be looked at in more detail. With regard to China's position as a host country for portfolio investment and other short-term capital inflow, a rapid liberalization of the capital market is not likely to occur, especially in view of the lessons from the Asian crisis.

In its *Asian Development Outlook* of 1999, the ADB points to the crucial role of FDI in propelling economic globalization characterized by an increasing specialization of production and trade through international networks of production and distribution by multinational companies (MNC).[35] The fact that only a rather small number of developing countries attract most of the FDI shows that FDI-led integration into the world economy is a highly selective process.[36] To be attractive for further investments by MNCs, China will have to open up most sectors and adapt to international rules on FDI which are embodied in the WTO. The integration of investment and cross-border trade in the WTO is represented by the General Agreement on Trade in Services (GATS). It requires that WTO member countries extend Most Favoured Nation (MFN) treatment to all service sectors, i.e. guaranteed conditions of market access, the right to market entry and to national treatment of service suppliers. In the protocol of accession, China will make specific sectoral commitments on market access and national treatment for foreign service providers in banking, insurance, telecommunications, distribution and legal services.[37] The extent to which the service sector is opened up will influence further FDI inflows to China. According to the USITC report, barriers to the service sector resulted in lost sales of US$ 3-5 billion for US service suppliers. In contrast, lifting the barriers would have a significant positive effect on US investment in services.[38]

Although the Agreement on Trade-Related Aspects of Intellectual Property Rights (TRIPS) does not directly address foreign investment, it is an important issue with regard to the legal environment affecting FDI. While the laws for the protection of intellectutal property (IP) are in line with international IP treaties, enforcement of IP law is widely criticized.[39] However, a study on China's compliance with its obligations suggests that China's record is mixed and similar to many emerging countries.[40]

The third agreement related to the global investment mechanism incorporated in the WTO is the Agreement on Trade-Related Investment Measures (TRIMs).[41] It defines certain types of investment measures as inconsistent with WTO rules such as local content, export requirements or transfer of technology.[42] China's foreign investment policies up to now contravene the principles of national treatment and transparency in many aspects. Adjusting to TRIMs, however, requires a member state not only to do away with measures discriminating against foreign-produced goods, but also with preferential treatment for FFEs such as tax and tariff concessions. Such preferential treatment has helped to attract FDI in the past, especially with regard to labour-intensive investment in processing trade.

Whether FDI flows to China will rapidly increase after China's WTO entry depends as well on other factors, especially the estimated potential for further growth and profits in certain sectors by MNCs. In a number of industries such as consumer electrical and electronic products, textiles and clothing, and other light industrial products FDI inflows contributed to excess capacity and strong competition in the last few years. With the weakening of domestic demand and decreasing prices, profitability worsened and thus reduced incentives for MNCs to invest in these sectors. While this situation might change for the better in the medium term, there are estimates that the reallocation of labour-intensive export processing operations from other Asian countries to China may be coming to an end. Wage increases in coastal areas have already eroded profits of some small international companies which have started to move to other low-income countries, despite the new investment incentives by the government to attract MNCs to interior provinces.[43] These developments have worsened the deceleration of FDI inflows to China since 1998, which itself was due to the Asian crisis (cf. Figure 8).

Figure 8: China's Absorption of Foreign Capital from 1989 to 1999 (utilized, billion US$)

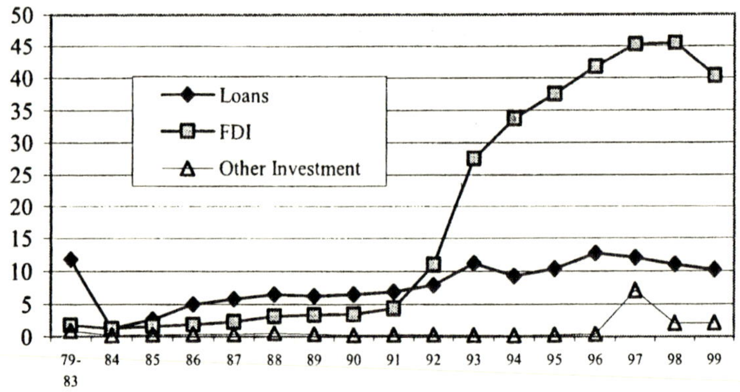

FDI = Foreign Direct Investment
Source: *China Statistical Yearbook 2000,* p. 604.

Although the composition of FDI has changed in favour of a larger share of Japan, the United States and the EU during the 1990s, investment from Asian NIEs still constituted 56 per cent in 1999. Therefore, the two-digit decrease in FDI from Hong Kong, which accounted for around 40 per cent of utilized FDI in 1999, and of Taiwan and Singapore had an important impact on total FDI inflow.[44] Statistics on utilized FDI inflows to September 2000 show that the decreasing trend in FDI could not have been brought to a halt. Compared to the first nine months of 1999, utilized FDI declined by 8.7 per cent. However, contracted investment jumped by around 28 per cent in the period pointing to a more optimistic look at investment opportunities by foreign companies.

To summarize, rapid FDI inflows after China's WTO entry will depend on the extent of the liberalization of the economy and on the enforcement of the investment-related agreements embodied in the WTO. Based on the assumption of high profitability of investment in the industrial and service sector, China's attractiveness to foreign investors will remain strong in the medium and long term. China's position as the second largest recipient of global FDI flows will not change in the coming five years, but it is doubtful whether FDI inflows will more than double by the year 2005 as projected by Goldman Sachs.

Finally, the prospects for short-term capital inflows will be examined. Whether China will play a more important global role as a recipient of short-term capital inflows depends on how quickly existing restrictions on the capital market will be lifted. The extent to which China will be able to absorb foreign short-term capital will also be subject to foreign investors' and creditors' estimations of the stability of the whole financial system.

One of the crucial lessons from the Asian crisis for China was that a weak banking system and an underdeveloped capital market can represent heavy risks to the whole economy. Therefore, banking reform has been accelerated since the end of 1997. Among the most important reform steps were the restructuring of the People's Bank of China, pushing for the commercialization of state banks, rectifying problem banks, including the closure of insolvent financial institutions such as the Guangdong Investment and Trust Corporation (GITIC), addressing the non-performing loan problem and the introduction of more competition through foreign banks' participation in selected locations and selected market segments.[45] Despite some progress made in solving the non-performing loan problem by introducing asset management companies to repackage and sell the problem loans, Chinese banks are still struggling to satisfy capital adequacy requirements.[46]

Control of external debt with regard to size and composition has helped China to maintain its outstanding debt balance at a moderate level and keep its debt indicators below the internationally recognized critical levels. More than 80 per cent of total foreign debt is long-term debt and the debt-service ratio (ratio of repayments of principal and interest on foreign debt to foreign exchange receipts from exports) is less than 10 per cent.[47] However, foreign creditors' concerns over the financial conditions of China's international trust and investment corporations (ITICs), especially the closure of GITIC in January 1999, translated into a reduction in foreign banks' exposure to China and an increasing differentiation between sovereign and non-sovereign entities.

With the first placement of B-shares denominated in foreign currency in 1992, China's securities market began to gradually open up to foreign participation. Although access to China's stock market has been relaxed to some extent, restrictions still exist such as a limit on the number of shares foreigners can hold; access to the larger A-share market for foreigners is not yet permitted.[48] While Hong Kong is still the primary focus for the raising of capital by Chinese companies, a number of large enterprises have turned to other stock exchanges abroad for listing, especially to the New York Stock Exchange. Among those large enterprises receiving a high price for their initial public offering are China Unicom and Sinopec.[49] Placing international bonds abroad has gradually become an instrument for foreign capital inflow as well, but still remains very limited.[50]

Conclusion

China's WTO entry and its accompanying trade liberalization will have a significant impact on international trade direction. Assuming that China will concentrate more on labour-intensive manufactures and, in the medium term, shift towards intermediate technology manufactures, new patterns of comparative advantages among developing and developed economies will emerge. China's further integration with the world economy will have different effects on developed and developing countries. Although projections of changes in trade direction are subject to considerable uncertainties, it can be expected that some countries will face increased competition from China in some current export markets.[51] The impact of China's WTO entry on industrial economies will be largely beneficial, as they can take advantage of the reduced tariffs for manufactures and of the abolition of non-tariff barriers in China. Their domestic industries for labour-intensive production, however, will be further challenged by exports from China. Capital- and knowledge-intensive exports from the industrial economies to China will substantially increase, and their exports of primary goods, especially of some agricultural products such as grain, will grow to some extent as well. While the Asian NIEs will continue to reallocate production facilities to China and become upstream suppliers of intermediate inputs for China, it can be expected that other developing countries will lose part of their world market share. Employment in the Asian NIEs is likely to suffer as well from the reallocation of certain labour-intensive industries to China.

Tariff reduction and the abolition of non-tariff barriers could result in some deterioration of China's external current account, but it is expected that this will be largely offset by higher FDI, especially in the service sector.[52] With more sectors open to foreign companies, FDI flows to China are thus expected to increase considerably. Rapid FDI inflows after China's WTO entry will depend on the extent of the liberalization of the economy and on the enforcement of the investment related agreements embodied in the WTO. Based on the assumption of high profitability of investment in the industrial and service sector, China's attractiveness to foreign investors will remain strong in the medium and long term. It has to be expected that short-term capital inflow and access for foreign financial institutions will be liberalized only gradually. Control of the entry of foreign capital has helped China to preserve a relatively stable financial situation during the Asian crisis. It will take quite a long time for China to build a sound financial system, and it therefore can be expected that liberalization will progress rather slowly during the period of transition.

Notes

[1]World Trade Organisation (WTO), *Developing countries' merchandise exports in 1999 expanded by 8.5% - about twice as fast as the global average*, in: http://www.wto.org.

[2]World Bank, *China 2020, Development Challenges in the New Century*, Washington, D.C., 1997, p. 83.

[3]Ibid., p. 92.

[4]*China Statistical Yearbook 2000*, p. 53; pp. 588–9.

[5]World Trade Organisation, *International Trade Statistics 2000*, table III.1 and table III.2.

[6]See for example the World Bank study on China's 'revealed comparative advantage' (RCA) by Yeats, Alexander J., *China's Foreign Trade and Comparative Advantage. Prospects, Problems, and Policy Implications.* World Bank Discussion Papers No. 141, Washington, D.C., 1991.

[7]Harvie, Charles, 'China's recent macroeconomic developments and policy with implications for trade', in: Tran Van Hoa, ed., *China's Trade and Investment After The Asia Crisis*, Cheltenham, 2000, pp. 123–44; here pp. 131–2.

[8]In 1999, the Netherlands realised an export value of US$ 200 billion, which was slightly higher than the US$ 195 billion China exported in the same year; see endnote 1.

[9]See endnote 1.

[10]With a share of 1.4 per cent in total exports (1999), China does not play an important role for the German export industry either, but imports have recently increased to 3 per cent of total German imports. See Schüller, Margot, 'Überblick über die deutsch-chinesischen Wirtschaftsbeziehungen zu Beginn des 21. Jahrhunderts', in: *China aktuell*, December 2000, pp. 289–298.

[11]The fact that the market shares of Japan, Germany and the United States remained almost the same during the years 1992 to 1999 is regarded by Hansen as a sign of political interference in the import decision of Chinese companies. Interview with Volker Hansen, expert on China at the German Engineering Federation (VDMA), January 2001.

[12]Aggregate net capital inflow includes (1) private capital inflow as non-debt-creating inflows such as FDI and Portfolio equity, as well as bonds and short-term and long-term credit and (2) official inflow such as ODA grants and other official inflow. Net capital inflow refers to capital inflow less capital outflow. See UNCTAD, *Trade and Development Report 1999, Trade, External Financing and Economic Growth in Developing Countries*, New York and Geneva, 2000, pp. 100–2. When China is excluded from the aggregate net capital inflow of all developing countries during this period, the average inflow only amounts to 4.22 per cent. Ibid., pp. 101–2.

[13]WTO, *Trade and Foreign Direct Investment*, Report by the WTO Secretariat, Press/57, 9.10.1996; Asian Development Bank, *PRC Receives Largest Share of Developing World's Foreign Direct Investment*, News Releases, No. 39/96, 11.4.96.

[14]UNCTAD, *Trade and Development Report 1999*, pp. 115–7.

[15]Asian Development Bank, *Foreign Direct Investment Spurs Asia's Development*, News Release, No. 024/99, 19.4.99.

[16]Naughton, Barry, 'Financial Development and Macroeconomic Stability in China', in: Chen, Baizhu, J. Kimball Dietrich and Yi Fang, eds, *Financial Market Reform in China. Progress, Problems, and Prospects*, Boulder, Colorado, 2000, pp. 143–70.

[17]See *Zhongguo Tongji Nianjian 2000*, p. 280.

[18]See for example the comprehensive analysis of major Chinese industries by Yu, Yongding, Zheng, Bingwen and Song, Hong eds, *Zhongguo 'rushi' yanjiu baogao: jinru WTO de zhongguo chanye* (Research Report on China's WTO Entry, Analysis of China's Industries), Beijing 1999; Mo, Tong, *Jiaru shimao yiwei shenmo? Yingxiang Zhongguo jingji yu baixing shenghuo de 22 ge fangmian* (What is the meaning of WTO entry? 22 aspects influencing China's economy and on the livelihood of the people), Beijing 1999; Chen, Yuming, ed., *Zhongguo jiaru WTO ge hangye qianjing fenxi* (Analysis of various industries' prospects when China enters the WTO), Beijing, 2000.

[19]For the following discussion on factor endowment and labour-intensive trade see Wang, Zhi, 'The Impact of China's Entry on the World Labour-intensive Ex-

port Market: A Recursive Dynamic CGE Analysis', in: *The World Economy*, Volume 22, 3, 1999, pp. 379–405. Wang points out that although there are other factors determining trade direction as well such as distance, technical efficiency, prices of intermediate inputs etc., the relative scarcity of factor endowment is the basic determinant; ibid, p. 388.

[20]In the standard Heckscher-Ohlin theorem, the key determinant of trade patterns is international differences in relative factor endowments. This theorem is also applied in the study on export similarities in East Asia. See Xu, Xinpeng and Ligang Song, 'Export similarity and the pattern of East Asian development', in: Lloyd, P.J. and Xiao-Guang Zhang, eds, *China in the Global Economy*, Cheltenham, 2000, pp. 145–64.

[21]Xu and Song perceive increasing export similarities between China and the ASEAN, suggesting that they have narrowed the scope of their export specialisation concentrating on labour-intensive product exports. Ibid., p. 154.

[22]Wang, Zhi, *op. cit.*, p. 392.

[23]According to Wang, the proportion of the US and EU labour force in 1995 was less than two per cent; see Wang, *op. cit.* The World Bank points out that most of the decline in employment in labour-intensive industries of developed countries occurred well before the Chinese exports penetrated these markets. See World Bank, *op. cit.*, p. 93.

[24]See Wang Zhi, *op. cit.*

[25]See *Zhongguo Tongji Nianjian.*

[26]See Mani, Sunil, *Exports of High Technology Products from Developing Countries: Is it Real or a Statistical Artifact?* The United Nations University, INTECH, Institute for New Technologies, Discussion Paper Series, May 2000, p. 20.

[27]Ibid., p. 33.

[28]World Bank, *op. cit.*, pp. 92–4.

[29]Ma, Xiaohe, 'The World Trade Organization and agricultural development', in: Garnaut, Ross, Guo Shutian and Ma Guonan, *The Third Revolution in the Chinese Countryside*, 1999, pp. 167–72. While high-cost and poor-quality producers of agricultural products will be challenged by competition of new entrants to the market, the welfare loss due to agricultural protection will be reduced. See Fang, Cai, 'Comparative advantage and internationalisation of China's agriculture', in: Garnaut, Guo and Ma, *op. cit.*, pp. 173–84; here pp. 177–8.

[30]See the contribution by Françoise Lemoine and Deniz Ünal-Kesenci, 'The Impact of China's WTO Accession on EU Trade' in this volume.

[31]U.S. International Trade Commission, *Assessment of the Economic Effects on the United States of China's Accession to the WTO*, Washington, D.C., Publication 3228, August 1999.

[32]Fred Hu, Goldman Sachs (Hong Kong), *Global Economic Policy Paper No. 14*, April 1999, cited in Rosen, Daniel, H., 'China and the World Trade Organization: An Economic Balance Sheet' in: *International Economics Policy Briefs*, Institute for International Economics, June 1999, in: www.iie.com/NEWSLETR/news99-6.htm.

[33]Cooper, Caroline G., 'China and the WTO: Implications for South Korea and Japan', in: *China Online*. Cooper is the Director of Congressional Affairs and Trade Policy at the Korea Economic Institute (KEI). This paper was originally presented at the National Defense University's annual Pacific Symposium, entitled *Asian Perspectives on the Challenges of China*, held in Washington, D.C., on March 7 and 8, 2000.

[34]The projection by Goldman Sachs is cited in Eugen v. Keller, Nicole Mönter and Hubertus Drinkuth, *China's Accession to the WTO. Strategic Implications for*

Foreign Investors, Roland Berger Study, January 2000; *China Statistical Yearbook 2000.*

[35]Asian Development Bank, *Asian Development Outlook* 1999, Hong Kong, 1999.

[36]See UNCTAD, *Trade and Development Report 1999, Trade, External Financing and Economic Growth in Developing Countries*, New York and Geneva, 2000, p. 116.

[37]See Abbott, Frederick M., 'Reflection Paper on China in the World Trading System: Defining the Principles of Engagement', in: Abbott, Frederick, ed., *China in the World Trading System*, The Hague, London, 1998, pp. 1–46, here pp. 22–3; WTO, *Trade and Foreign Direct Investment*, Report by the WTO Secretariat, Press/57, 9.10.1996.

[38]U.S. International Trade Commission, *op. cit.*, pp. vi–viii.

[39]For an overview of the introduction of IP laws in China see Gao, Lulin, 'China's Intellectual Property Protection System in Progress', in: Abbott, *op. cit.*, pp. 127–37.

[40]See Rosen, *op. cit.*

[41]The discussion on a comprehensive multilateral framework for investment (Multilateral Agreement on Investment = MAI) which should encourage liberalisation of the rules for FDI, provide standards of protection for international investors etc., was going on for three years but collapsed in December 1998. See World Bank, *Global Development Finance, Analysis and Summary Tables*, 1999, p. 49.

[42]See Abbott, *op. cit.*, pp. 12–17.

[43]See Luo, Yadong, *Multinational Corporations in China. Benefiting from Structural Transformation*, Copenhagen, 2000, pp. 20–4.

[44]See MoFTEC; in: www.ahk-china.org/direktinvestitionen-branchen.htm.

[45]For a comprehensive analysis of the banking reform see Lardy, Nicholas R., *China's Unfinishedă Economic Revolution*, Washington, D.C., 1998. For an overview of the latest reform measures see 'China's Banking Reform and WTO', in: *Economic Forum*, December 1999, in: www.tdctrade.com.

[46]See International Monetary Fund, *International Capital Markets. Developments, Prospects and Key Policy Issues, World Economic and Financial Surveys*, Washington, D.C., 1999, p. 48; pp. 160–1.

[47]Zhao, Jinping, 'Management of Capital Inflows in China's Opening Economy' in: Kwan, C.H./Vandenbrink, Donna and Chiao Siow Yue, eds, *Coping with Capital Flow in East Asia*, Tokyo, 1998, pp. 293–319, here pp. 306–7.

[48]Zhao, *op. cit.*, p. 302.

[49]See 'China Unicom notiert an Auslandsbörsen', in: *China aktuell*, June 2000, pp. 634–5.

[50]See *Almanac of China's Finance and Banking 1999*, p. 395.

[51]United Nations, World Economic and Social Survey 2000, *Trends and Policies in the World Economy*, New York, 2000, p. 103.

[52]International Monetary Fund, *World Economic Outlook, October 2000, Focus on Transition Economies*, Washington, D.C., 2000, pp. 27–8.

12

The Impact of China's WTO Accession on EU Trade

Françoise Lemoine & Deniz Ünal-Kesenci

Introduction

For China, the fulfilment of the World Trade Organization (WTO) obligations will lead to substantial cuts in tariff and non-tariff barriers and the opening up of its service sector to foreign direct investment (FDI). WTO accession will induce structural changes in China's foreign trade and capital inflows. In order to investigate how these expected changes may influence the evolution of EU–China relations, this study provides an in-depth analysis of EU–China trade patterns in the 1990s which highlights their current determinants.

Section 1 sketches out the global implications of China's WTO accession according to the studies recently published. Section 2 analyzes first the trends and structures of EU–China trade in the 1990s and then simulates the potential effects of predicted structural changes in China's foreign trade on EU exports to (and imports from) China up to 2005. Section 3 points out the distortions in China's foreign trade pattern resulting from its present trade policy and discusses the implications of a further opening of its domestic market. Section 4 focuses on the potential competition between China and other suppliers in the EU market. Section 5 finally considers the trends towards regional integration both in Asia and in Europe which will continue to underlie EU–China trade.

China's WTO Accession: Global Implications

Several recent studies have estimated the impact on China's economy of its accession to the WTO.[1] Most of these studies use general equilibrium models to provide a quantitative assessment of the expected changes in China's economic growth and foreign trade. They take into account the effects of the reduction of tariffs on China's imports and of the phasing out of MFA quotas on China's exports of textiles and apparel by 2005, but most of them do not consider the effect of the elimination of non-tariff barriers and of removing restrictions on foreign direct investment (for an overview of China's commitments see Box). It is difficult to compare the estimations provided by these studies because they use different models, different assumptions concerning the terms of China's accession, different time periods and also different baseline scenarios to compare the estimations in the case of accession and without accession. However they put forward some similar conclusions. Almost all studies predict that China's WTO accession will have a positive impact on China's long-term economic growth mainly through efficiency gains resulting from trade liberalization. Trade liberalization would lead to a reallocation of domestic resources towards sectors in which China has a comparative advantage (labour-intensive sectors) and away from capital and land-intensive sectors. It would boost China's imports and exports, the latter benefiting from the phasing out of MFA quotas by 2005.

Some of these studies simulated the effects of China's accession on the economy of major regions or countries.[2] They show that in terms of economic growth China would benefit the most from trade liberalization, but that its major partners would also register some gains. The results of these simulations for economic growth in Europe, the US and Japan, differ widely due to the above mentioned reasons, but they tend to indicate that Japan is expected to derive more gains than the other two partners, due to its strong economic links with China. For the same reason the gains would even be larger for Taiwan and Hong Kong, according to the simulations made for these two economies. The studies also suggest that Europe would benefit more than the US from China's WTO accession, a result which seems to be linked with the expected changes in China's foreign trade. The study which predicts the most important impact of the accession scenario, indicates that from 1997 to 2010, the average annual economic growth rate will be up by 1 percentage point in China, by 0.15 percentage points in Japan, by 0.08 in Europe and by 0.04 in the US.[3]

China's Commitments to Liberalize Market Access Under WTO Negotiations*

Industry
Customs duties on imports of industrial products are to be cut from 17.5 per cent (in 1998) to 9–10 per cent by 2005, and quantitative restrictions are to be eliminated.
Customs duties on automobiles are to be cut (presently running at 80–100 per cent) to 25 per cent in 2006 (10 per cent on spare parts). Foreign companies will have the right to provide credit to customers.
Customs duties on telecommunication equipment are to be eliminated in 2005.

Agriculture
Customs duties on agricultural products are to be reduced (in the agreement with the US from 22.1 to 17 per cent by 2004) and a tariff quota system is to be set up for most staple products (wheat, rice, corn and cotton), with import quotas (at low tariffs) rising through to 2005.

Services
• Trade and distribution: foreign companies are to have the right to export, import and sell directly to the domestic market, and may run after-sales and repair services.
• Telecommunications: China is to become a member of the Basic Agreement on telecommunications. Foreign investment is to be authorized, up to 49 or 50 per cent, and within three years, depending on the activity in question.
• Banks: foreign banks will be authorized to carry out operations in local currency with companies, (two years after accession), and with individual clients (after 5 years).
• Insurance: restrictions on foreign companies' activities are to be lifted in five years. Licences will be granted to foreign companies, based on prudential criteria. Foreign equity will be limited to 51 per cent (49 per cent for life insurance).
• Stock markets: Foreign investments in investment funds are to be authorized. Foreign equity in stock-issuing companies is to be limited to 49 per cent.

* Based on China's agreement with the US and the EU.

Potential Impact on EU Trade With China

EU China trade: Trends and structures in the 1990s[4]

Over the last twenty years, China's international trade has increased at an outstanding pace and its share in world trade trebled from less than 1 per cent in 1980 to more than 3 per cent in 1999. Over the last decade this trend has accelerated, as its exports increased at an average rate of 17 per cent a year (against 13 per cent in the 1980s) and its imports at an average rate of 14 per cent a year (8 per cent in the 1980s). China's trade with the EU kept pace with the expansion of its overall trade. From 1990 to 1998, China's exports to the EU increased on average by 16 per cent a year and its imports from the EU by 12 per cent a year. The importance of China, as a supplier and as a market for the EU countries, rose significantly. However, trade with China still represented a small share of EU overall trade. In 1998 China accounted for 0.9 per cent of EU total exports (up from 0.5 per cent in 1990) and for 1.9 per cent of EU total imports (0.8 per cent in 1990). China's trade with the EU was thus almost equivalent to Ireland's trade within the EU. The importance of China was more prominent when measured against EU trade with non-member countries: it accounted for 5.5 per cent of extra-EU imports and 2.3 per cent of extra-EU exports in 1998. China became the most important EU supplier among developing countries, overtaking all Asian industrializing economies. It was the second most important market for the EU among developing countries, after Turkey, ahead of all Asian industrializing economies.

Due to differences in the respective sizes of European and Chinese international trade flows, China's foreign trade was much more dependent on the EU than vice-versa. In 1998, the EU accounted for 15 per cent of China's imports and for 20 per cent of its exports, and kept its share fluctuating around this level over the 1990s.

The effect of this asymmetry in their respective commercial size can be eliminated through calculating an indicator of trade intensity. The indicator measures the ratio between the bilateral trade flows of two partners and their respective weights in world trade.[5] The indicator of China's trade intensity with Japan, the US and the EU-15, for the period 1978–1998, is shown in Figure 1. A first observation is that China's trade intensity with the EU is considerably lower than with Japan and is also slightly lower than with the US at the end of the 1990s. The pattern of China's bilateral trade intensity tends to confirm that, as pointed out by literature on international trade, geographic proximity between partners is an important factor influencing trade

Figure 1: Chinese Trade Intensity with the EU, Japan and the US

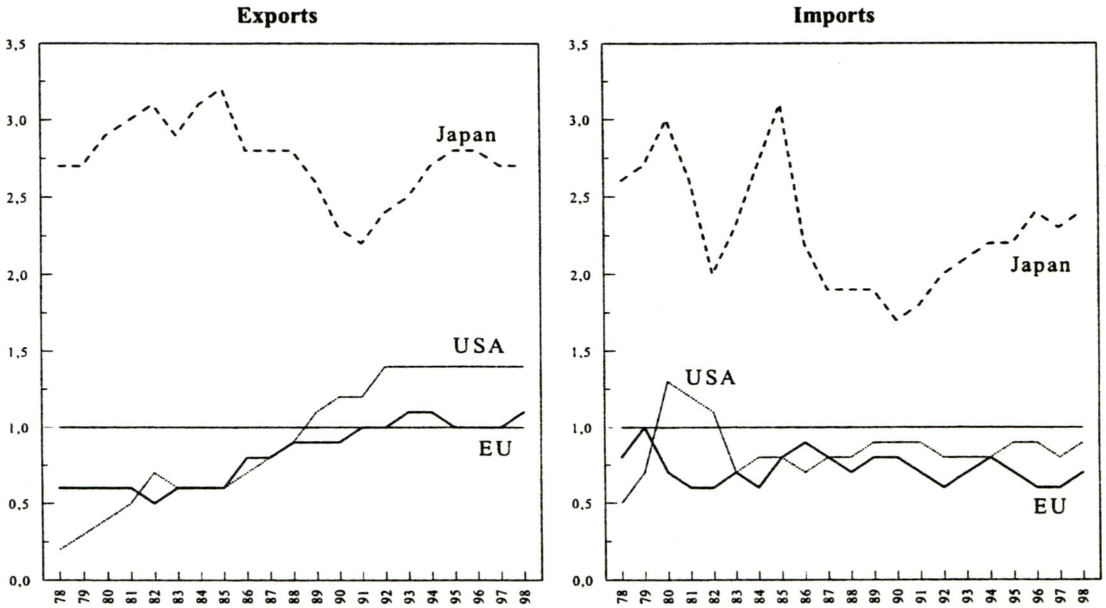

* Intra-EU flows are excluded from EU and world trade.
Source: CEPII, CHELEM database, authors' calculations.

intensity. EU trade intensity with other East Asian industrializing countries is of the same order of magnitude as with China. A second observation is that there is a strong asymmetry in the level of China's export and import intensity with the EU. China's export intensity to the EU has increased dramatically since the mid-1980s and stood around 1 in 1998, indicating that the importance of the EU in China's exports was in line with the respective importance of the two countries in world trade.

By contrast China's import intensity from the EU has remained around 0.7 since the beginning of the 1980s, indicating that the share of the EU in China's imports has been systematically well below the level that would be expected if these imports were proportional to the respective weights of the two partners in world trade. The increase of China's export intensity with the EU and the US since the mid-1980s corresponds to an evolution also observed in Asian countries since the 1970s. As emerging countries have begun liberalizing their foreign trade, they have diversified their partners and reduced the initial concentration of their trade on neighbour countries.[6] However, the low intensity of China's imports from the EU and to a lesser extent from the US suggests that China's trade liberalization has fallen short of eliminating distortions in the access to China's market.[7]

Given the above-mentioned asymmetry of China's export and import intensities with the EU, the latter recorded structural trade deficits. It is well-known that there are large discrepancies between the data reported by China and by the EU concerning their bilateral trade flows, the size and even the sign of their bilateral trade imbalances (cf. Table 1). The major reason for such discrepancies lies in the statistical recording of trade flows transiting through Hong Kong, which represented about 60 per cent of China's exports to the EU. Basically, reporting countries fail to capture the actual origin/destination of trade flows channelled through Hong Kong. In fact, they identify more accurately the actual origin of their imports than the final destination of their exports through Hong Kong. EU statistics thus tend to underestimate EU exports to China, as so do China's statistics for China's exports to the EU. Research work aimed at building up reconciled trade figures came to the conclusion that when trade through Hong Kong is fully taken into account the EU still records a structural trade deficit, although smaller than according to original EU custom statistics.[8]

Table 1: EU* Trade Balance With China and Hong Kong
($ billion)

	1990	1991	1992	1993	1994	1995	1996	1997	1998	1999
EU statistics										
EU trade balance with China	-6.8	-11.6	-12.9	-9.7	-12.1	-15.2	-19.4	-23.8	-27.5	-32.2
EU trade balance with HK	0.9	1.2	3.7	5.8	7.8	11.3	13.0	13.7	8.5	5.3
EU trade balance with China+HK	-5.9	-10.4	-9.2	-3.9	-4.2	-3.9	-6.4	-10.1	-19.0	-26.9
China's statistics										
EU trade balance with China	-2.5	-1.7	-2.2	-2.7	-2.4	2.2	0.0	-4.6	-7.4	-4.8

* 15 EU member countries
Sources: Eurostat and China's Customs Statistics.

There are two main reasons why an important part of China's trade is channelled through Hong Kong. First, the quality of transport infrastructures makes it easier for goods to be transhipped through Hong Kong than from Chinese ports; second, though large parts of the Hong Kong manufacturing industry have been transferred to China over the last twenty years, the final stages of production and marketing services still often take place in the Territory. However as China's transport and industrial capacities have been upgraded, China's direct exports and imports have tended to increase more rapidly than indirect trade through Hong Kong in the second half of the 1990s.

The commodity composition of China's foreign trade reveals that it is determined by sectoral complementarities, reflecting the large disparity in the levels of income between China and its major trade partners (the EU-15, the US, Japan, South Korea, Hong Kong, Taiwan and Singapore account for three quarters of its total trade). China's major comparative advantages are located in labour-intensive goods, and its major comparative disadvantages lie in capital-intensive or technology-intensive goods.[9] Figure 2 reveals that its major comparative advantages with the EU in 1998 were found in traditional industries such as clothing, knitwear, and leather, but also in new industries such as computers, and consumer electronics. Its comparative disadvantages with the EU were concentrated in machinery, telecommunication equipment, and transport equipment. China's entry into the WTO will strengthen its specialization according to its factor endowments and should thus widen its structural surpluses and deficits with the EU.

Figure 2: EU Structural Surpluses and Deficits in Trade with China 1998*

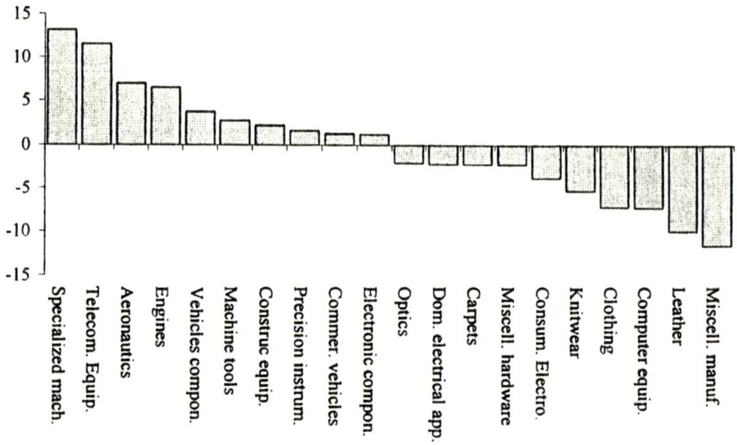

*Share (in %) of a product in EU exports to China less its share (in %) in EU imports from China.
Source: CEPII, CHELEM database, authors' calculations.

China's trade with the EU is thus dominated by inter-industry trade as opposed to intra-industry trade (defined as the simultaneous exports and imports of the same commodity). According to international trade theory, adjustment costs associated with trade liberalization are supposed to be greater in the case of inter-industry trade, as increased specialization means the abandonment of contested, comparatively disadvantaged industries and the displacement of factors towards export-oriented industries.[10]

Trade flows between the EU and China are concentrated in a relatively limited number of products: in 1998, fourteen sectors – out of seventy of CHELEM (Comptes Harmonises sur les Echanges et L'Economie Mondiale) classification – represented almost three–fourths of EU imports, and ten sectors two–thirds of its imports in 1998 (cf. Table 2). China's strong export specialization results in large market shares in several individual sectors, especially compared to other non-EU suppliers (clothing, consumer electronics, domestic appliances, electrical apparatus) (cf. Table 3). Symmetrically, China's market accounts for relatively large shares in EU exports in several sectors, such as specialized machinery and telecommunication equipment. The commodity pattern of trade thus provides evidence that China's trade liberalization may have a substantial impact at the level of individual sectors in the European economy, as well as on EU trade with third countries, even though its macroeconomic impact is expected to be small (as mentioned in Section 1).

Table 2: Commodity Breakdown of EU–China Trade* in 1998 (in %)

EU Exports		EU Imports	
Total exports	100.0	Total imports	100.0
Telecom. equipment	14.6	Miscellan. manuf. art.	12.1
Specialized machines	13.6	Leather	10.6
Aeronautics	7.7	Computer equipment	8.2
Engines	7.0	Clothing	7.2
Electrical apparatus	4.9	Electrical apparatus	5.5
N.e.s. products	4.7	Knitwear	5.4
Vehicles components	3.8	Miscellan. hardware	4.9
Machine tools	3.1	Consumer electronics	3.9
Miscellaneous hardware	2.6	Telecom. equipment	3.1
Precision instruments	2.5	Plastic articles	3.0
Construction equipm.	2.4	Optics	2.6
Basic organic chemicals	2.0	Domes. electrical app.	2.5
Pharmaceuticals	1.8	Carpets	2.3
Electrical equipment	1.8	Electrical equipment	2.3
Total 14 products	72.5	Total 14 products	73.6

* Top 14 products in EU exports/imports.
Source: CEPII, CHELEM database.

Table 3: China's Share in EU Exports and Imports by Product*

	1990	1998	1990	1998
	In % of total EU imports		In % of extra EU imports	
All imports	0.8	1.9	2.3	5.5
Clockmaking	3.4	12.5	4.3	15.2
Leather	4.6	12.0	11.1	24.7
Miscellaneous manuf. articles	5.2	10.9	12.8	26.5
Clothing	5.2	7.5	10.7	12.1
Consumer electronics	4.3	7.0	8.8	15.9
Carpets	4.9	6.9	14.9	16.1
Optics	0.4	6.6	0.8	13.1
Knitwear	2.8	6.6	7.0	12.6
Domestic electrical appliances	1.1	5.8	6.4	26.2
Electrical equipment	0.9	5.4	3.3	13.5
	In % of total EU exports		In % of extra EU exports	
All exports	0.5	0.9	1.5	2.3
Telecommunications equipment	1.5	4.5	3.2	10.0
Specialized machines	2.1	3.9	4.1	6.2
Aeronautics	0.1	2.9	0.2	4.4
Machine tools	1.7	2.7	3.8	4.9
Electrical equipment	2.1	1.7	4.7	3.5
Engines	2.4	1.6	5.4	3.6
Non ferrous ores	0.6	1.6	3.0	5.3
Construction equipment	0.7	1.5	1.8	3.0
Cement	0.0	1.4	0.1	2.9
Tubes	1.3	1.4	3.4	3.2

* Ten products for which the share of China in EU imports/exports is the greatest, in 1998.
Source: CEPII, CHELEM database.

The impact of structural changes in China's foreign trade

As trade liberalization is expected to bring about structural changes in the commodity pattern of China's exports and imports, the first step in analyzing the potential impact of China's WTO accession is to consider what effect these structural changes may have on its trade with the EU. For an estimation of these structural changes we used the results of a study by the Development Research Centre (DRC)[11] which predicted the pattern of China's foreign trade by sectors in 2005, and we compared them to its trade pattern at the end of the 1990s. It was then possible to simulate the effect of these changes on total EU exports to (and imports from) China, under the assumption that the EU would maintain its 1996–1997 share in China's trade, by sector. The results measure the adaptation of EU exports at the end of the 1990s to the expected structural changes in China's demand up to 2005 and the 'exposure' of the EU market to the expected growth of China's exports by sectors. The simulation produced the following findings:

The DRC scenarios indicate that China's imports would rise faster in the case of accession than in the case of non-accession. The simulation implies that China's imports would grow by 10 per cent a year from 1996–1997 to 2005 in the first case, and by 7 per cent in the second case. This means that, even with trade liberalization, China's imports would grow at a slower rate than in the past ten years when imports increased at 13 per cent a year. Table 4 presents the expected changes in China's import structure in the accession scenario and their simulated impact on the position of major suppliers of China's imports. The results of this exercise indicate that the composition of EU exports to China in 1996–1997 should help EU exports to keep up with the pace of China's total imports. EU countries should increase their exports at 10 per cent a year and maintain their share in China's imports at about 15 per cent. This relatively good performance can be explained by the fact that European firms held strong positions in China's imports of machinery and road vehicles (their market shares reached respectively 43 and 33 per cent in 1996–1997) and that these two sectors taken together accounted for almost one fourth of the projected increase of China's imports up to 2005. EU exports thus revealed a higher degree of adaptation to the expected evolution of China's demand than US or Japanese exports. With their market shares by sector being held constant, their exports to China would grow more slowly than China's imports as a whole: Japan's exports would grow at 9.5 per cent a year and US exports at 9 per cent. By contrast, the three Dragons' exports (Hong Kong, Taiwan, South Korea)[12] should benefit from the structural changes in China's demand and especially from the surge in imports of intermediate goods for the textile industry. Their exports would grow at 11 per cent a year allowing for a significant increase of their market share.

Table 4: Structural Changes in China's Trade (1997–2005) Potential Impact on Major Partners

Products	aver. 96-97	2005	aver. 96-97	2005
	Imports		Exports	
All products	100.0	100.0	100.0	100.0
Manufacturing	**88.7**	**90.6**	**91.6**	**95.8**
Processed food	3.2	4.9	4.5	3.4
Textiles	4.8	12.7	4.2	15.9
Apparel	0.8	0.4	17.0	25.1
Leather	2.1	2.9	8.2	4.7
Sawmill and furniture	2.1	0.9	3.0	2.3
Paper and social prod.	1.9	3.1	4.7	5.4
Petroleum rafineries	2.2	1.6	0.7	0.7
Cooking and coal Prod.	0.0	0.0	0.0	0.5
Chemicals	20.1	15.9	10.1	8.6
Building material	0.7	1.1	1.8	3.0
Basic metals	8.6	6.8	5.7	2.8
Metal products	0.4	1.4	1.4	2.9
Machinery	19.5	19.3	7.4	6.3
Road vehicles	1.5	3.0	1.1	0.3
Other transp. equip.	2.4	1.8	1.7	1.3
Electrical machinery	6.0	3.9	5.9	3.7
Electronics	8.6	9.4	7.5	8.2
Instruments	3.3	1.3	3.4	0.3
Other industries	0.7	0.4	3.2	0.2
Partners	Share in China's Imports*		Share in China's Exports*	
EU	15.2	15.1	18.4	17.7
US	11.2	10.3	25.9	24.3
Japan	23	21.9	19.6	20.4
3 Dragons	29.2	31.2	8.2	9.4
Others	21.4	21.57	27.9	28.2

* Assuming that the sectoral market shares in China's imports remain constant from 1996-97 to 2005.
Source: DRC 1998, authors' calculations.

On China's export side, the accession scenario would also lead to a higher growth rate than the non-accession scenario. In the accession scenario its exports should grow by 9 per cent a year from 1998 to 2005 (versus 6 per cent if it stays out), a pace which is however well below the rate recorded by Chinese exports in the 1990s (15 per cent). Entering the WTO would thus make it possible for China to maintain relatively rapid growth of its exports, while staying out would imply a strong deterioration of its export performance compared to the last decade. Expected structural changes in the accession case show that the phasing out of the MFA quota will play a decisive part in China's export prospects as textile and apparel exports are expected to increase 3.7 fold, and to account for more than 60 per cent of China's export growth up to 2005. These structural changes are not likely to affect the geographic pattern of China's total exports. Their mechanical effect implies only a small increase in the share of Chinese exports going to Japan and the three Dragons (after exports passing through Hong Kong have been reallocated to their final destination). China's exports to the EU as well as to other major markets are expected to increase by 9–10 per cent a year.

Trade Liberalization and Trade Distortions[13]

Another approach for analyzing the possible consequences of China's trade liberalization on its trade with the EU is to consider the distortions in China's geographic trade pattern which were created by its current approach to trade liberalization and which should be reduced by China's commitments to improve access to its domestic market.

The effects of current trade policy on trade patterns

To promote foreign trade, the Chinese authorities used different policy instruments which had a strong impact on the commodity and geographic pattern of the country's trade.[14]

The first instrument of trade liberalization was the reduction in tariff and non-tariff barriers. Since 1992 China has substantially lowered its tariff rates which fell from an (unweighted) average of 42.9 per cent in 1992 to 17.5 per cent in 1997. Quota and licences were also reduced.[15] The second instrument was duty exemptions granted to selected categories of imports, which aimed at promoting export-oriented industries and at stimulating the inflows of capital and technology through FDI. Intermediate products used in the production of exports were the most important category of products benefiting from duty exemptions. Concessional import duties were also granted to equipment imported by foreign firms investing in China. These selective tariff exemptions, 'new trade liberalization' instruments,[16] led to accelerated growth of both exports and imports linked to processing activities. The share of imports for processing represented between 35 and 50 per cent of China's total imports over the period 1992–1999 (cf. Table 5). Equipment imported by foreign firm affiliates as part of their initial investment accounted for between 10 and 20 per cent of total imports over the same period. Tariff exemptions thus applied to between 60 and 70 per cent of total imports. At the end of the 1990s, an important part of China's imports was already exempt from custom tariffs and will not be affected by the reduction in tariff rates to be introduced when China enters the WTO.

Table 5: Evolution of China's Trade by Custom Regimes 1992–1998 (in % of total trade)

	1992	1993	1994	1995	1996	1997	1998	1999
Total imports	100.0	100.0	100.0	100.0	100.0	100.0	100.0	100.0
Ordinary imports	41.7	36.6	33.2	32.8	28.2	27.4	31.1	40.5
Concessional imports of which	58.3	63.4	66.8	67.2	71.7	72.6	68.9	59.5
Imports for processing	*39.1*	*35.0*	*41.4*	*44.2*	*44.9*	*49.3*	*48.9*	*44.4*
Imports for FDI	*19.2*	*16.0*	*17.5*	*14.2*	*17.9*	*12.6*	*10.3*	*6.7*
Other imports	*0.0*	*12.4*	*8.2*	*8.8*	*8.9*	*10.7*	*9.6*	*8.5*
Total exports	100.0	100.0	100.0	100.0	100.0	100.0	100.0	100.0
Ordinary exports	51.4	47.1	50.7	47.9	41.6	42.7	40.4	40.6
Exports after processing	46.6	48.2	46.5	49.5	55.8	54.5	56.9	56.9
Other exports	2.0	4.7	2.7	2.6	2.6	2.8	2.7	2.3

Source: *China's Customs Statistics*, authors' calculations.

Normal tariffs rates were applied only to 'ordinary' imports, i.e. to goods imported for domestic use (investment and consumption), so as to ensure the protection of the domestic market from outside competition. From 1992 to 1997 ordinary imports accounted for a declining share of China's imports (from 42 to 27 per cent), an evolution which resulted from the effect of tariff barriers but also from the slowing down of import demand resulting from lower economic growth since 1995 (cf. Table 5). China's commitments to cut its tariff barriers thus concerned between 30 and 40 per cent of its imports. This statement should however be qualified, as it is now well documented that customs statistics underestimate ordinary trade: according to official investigations, illegal imports represented 5–8 per cent of reported imports in 1996–1997 (that is, 15–25 per cent of ordinary imports).[17] These illegal imports have declined recently, following the anti-smuggling measures implemented by the Chinese authorities in 1998, which led to the recovery of ordinary imports in 1998–1999. It must be stressed that the lower tariff and non-tariff barriers to be applied after WTO accession should contribute to bringing down illegal imports.

This segmentation of China's trade regime has to be taken into account when measuring the actual degree of China's trade protection at the end of the 1990s, as tariff rates cannot serve as a relevant indicator. Some of the studies which have estimated the implications of China's WTO accession did take into consideration the pervasive duty exemptions in order to avoid overestimating the impact of reduced tariff barriers on the commodity import structure. However, they have generally overlooked the impact of tariff exemptions on the geographic pattern of China's trade. The following section will investigate how the existing trade regime may have distorted the geographic pattern of China's imports, and how further trade liberalization may influence the position of its major suppliers, depending on their respective involvement in the different trade segments.

The implications of import liberalization

Data available for this study made it possible to analyze the positions of major exporters in the different segments of China's trade during the period 1993–1997, and thus to highlight their 'sensitivity' to the new phase of China's import liberalization.

Table 6: Breakdown of China's Trade by Partner and Custom Regimes (in % of total trade)

1993	World	3 Dragons	Japan	EU 15	USA	ROW
Imports by all customs regimes	100.0	27.6	22.4	15.1	10.3	24.6
China's ordinary imports	36.6	3.2	7.9	7.9	5.1	12.5
Imports for processing	35.0	17.8	7.7	1.7	1.9	5.9
Other customs regimes	28.4	6.7	6.8	5.6	3.3	6.2
1997	World	3 Dragons	Japan	EU 15	USA	ROW
Imports by all custom regimes	100.0	26.9	20.4	13.5	11.4	27.8
China's ordinary imports	27.4	2.4	3.7	5.2	4.6	11.4
Imports for processing	49.3	19.6	12.2	2.5	3.5	11.5
Other customs regimes	23.3	4.9	4.5	5.8	3.3	4.8

Source: China's Customs Statistics and ITC, authors' calculation.

Table 6 shows the geographic pattern of China's imports by partners and by custom regimes. It provides evidence that the weight of Asian countries (Japan and the three Dragons) in China's total imports is strongly linked with their involvement in processing activities. Asian countries already took advantage of China's selective trade liberalization during the 1990s. In 1997, these four countries accounted for almost two thirds of China's imports for processing. More than 70 per cent of the products exported by the three Dragons and 60 per cent of Japan's exports already entered China without import duties. European and American firms contributed only marginally to the supply of goods for processing (they accounted respectively for 5 and 7 per cent of imports for processing in 1997). The presence of European firms in this fastest growing segment of China's imports was thus particularly weak and this can explain the low intensity of EU exports to China mentioned in Section 2.1. China's imports for processing represented respectively 31 and 19 per cent of China's imports from the US and the EU in 1997; moreover they represented the most dynamic component of its imports from both partners.

Reduction in trade barriers will have no direct effect on China's imports for processing, and thus on the largest part of Asian exports. Anyway, as China's economy becomes more open, the propensity of foreign firms to locate stages of their production process in the Mainland may increase and processing trade may thus indirectly benefit from China's trade liberalization.

Cuts in tariff rates should lead to accelerated growth of ordinary imports and alleviate the distortions of China's trade in favour of processing activities. Countries having strong positions in this still protected market should benefit the most from the rise of China's domestic demand for imported products. At the same time these exporters will also face stronger competition as more suppliers will be able to enter the domestic market, since the costs of entry will be lowered.[18]

In 1997 the EU and the US were the most important suppliers of products aimed at the domestic market, accounting for respectively 19 and 17 per cent of China's ordinary imports, well ahead of Japan (13.5 per cent) and the three Dragons (9 per cent). Almost 40 per cent of China's imports from the EU and the US were thus subject to normal tariff regimes in 1997, while the share was below 20 per cent in the case of Japan and 10 per cent in the case of the three Dragons (cf. Table 6). The fact that the EU overtook other suppliers in this segment may have different explanations: one is that European firms had a competitive edge in the categories of products imported within this trade regime and that EU specialization was in line with the pattern of China's domestic demand. Another is that European firms were more willing or able to bear the costs associated with entering this protected market.

During the 1990s China diversified its suppliers and EU share in China's ordinary imports declined, as shown in Table 6. This may indicate that European firms were already suffering from growing competition due to the lowering of China's custom tariffs. But a more in-depth analysis at the commodity level helps to qualify this first conclusion. In fact, the main reason why the share of the EU suppliers in China's ordinary imports declined from 1993 to 1997 was the slowing down of China's imports of machinery and equipment, which represented 25 per cent of China's ordinary imports in 1997, against 30 per cent in 1993 (cf. Table 7). The global export performance of the EU which was by far the major supplier of machinery and equipment was adversely affected by the relative fall of China's demand, resulting from slower economic growth in 1996 and 1997, after a period of overheating in 1993–1995. European exports thus appeared highly dependent on the evolution of China's domestic demand for investment goods.

Table 7: Share of Major Suppliers in China's Ordinary Imports of Machinery*

	1993	1994	1995	1996	1997
EU 15	35.3	43.7	45.9	41.8	39.6
USA	16.8	17.9	17.5	19.1	18.9
Japan	32.0	23.3	21.8	23.7	23.3
3 Dragons	7.2	6.1	5.9	6.9	7.5
Others	8.7	9.0	8.9	8.5	10.7
Machinery in % of Ordinary imports	30.4	36.7	36.5	27.6	26.7

* Machinery and electrical machinery (HS 84+85).
Source: China's Customs Statistics and ITC, author's calculation.

The other category of China's imports in which the EU holds its strongest position corresponds to 'other (concessional) custom regimes' which encompassed barter, entrepot trade, warehouse trade, imports of equipment for processing activities and imports of equipment as investment by foreign firms, the latter being the most important, as shown in Table 5. These concessional regimes represented an important channel for China's imports of capital goods. In 1997, almost 60 per cent of Chinese imports of machinery entered China in this way. The EU accounted for a large share of these concessionnal imports (between 20 and 25 per cent in the 1990s). As the contribution of European firms to total foreign direct investment flows to China was relatively low (5 per cent), this tends to confirm that European direct investment in China was characterized by high capital intensity. Direct investment by European firms thus plays a major role in supporting China's imports from the EU. In 1997, 40 per cent of China's imports from the EU were linked to FDI, while other suppliers were much less dependent on this import segment.

The above analysis underlines that EU exports are dependent on two main factors: China's domestic demand (as opposed to the demand of China's export-oriented sector) and the strategy of European firms investing in China.

The pattern of EU exports to China suggests the following conclusions concerning the impact of China's WTO entry:

- EU exporters should take advantage of their strong positions in the very segment of China's imports which is expected to expand the most rapidly after liberalization, i.e. China's imports for the domestic market. Reduction in tariff rates will stiffen competition in this area as it will attract new suppliers, but will also help more European firms (medium-sized firms) to enter the Chinese market and allow for a diversification of EU exports which were, up to now, heavily concentrated in capital goods.

- FDI will remain an important means for European firms to enter China's domestic market, since specific requirements (local content) will be eliminated and foreign affiliates will be allowed to set up distribution networks for other products than those they produce in China. However the direct links between FDI and trade flows may loosen since discrimination against 'ordinary' imports will be reduced. Moreover, it can be expected that the preferential import regimes granted to foreign firm affiliates will be phased out, in order to level the playing field. Finally, the service sector which will be progressively opened to FDI and may replace manufacturing as the engine for FDI growth is likely to be less intensive in imported capital goods.

- European firms may increase their involvement in processing activities in China. However their production bases in China are likely to source their inputs in the Asian region and these production networks are not expected to be the engine of EU exports to China, as is the case for Asian exports. EU exports to China will rely mainly on 'ordinary' trade, which is more dependent than processing trade on the fluctuations in China's domestic economic activity and on the evolution of the yuan exchange rate.[19]

Competition in EU Markets

This section is intended firstly to identify the countries which are the most exposed to China's competition in the EU market, due to their commodity export structure. Second, it turns to the nature of competition and considers the quality specialization of the major EU suppliers. This investigation was carried using an analytical data base built up by the CEPII from detailed Eurostat statistics for the year 1996.[20]

The similarity of exports structures as an indicator of potential competition

The potential competition between exporters to the EU was first analyzed by measuring the similarity of their commodity export structures (manufacturing sector). The similarity index (finger index, calculated with three digits of the NACE (Nomenclature des Activites economiques des Communautes Europeennes) nomenclature[21]) shows that the countries or regions which faced the highest potential competition with China in the EU market, in 1996, were the three Dragons, ASEAN, India, Central Europe, Mediterranean countries and the EU itself (cf. Table 8). Ranking individual countries according to this similarity index indicates that the exporters most exposed to China's competition (index above 40) were, in Asia, Hong Kong and Thailand, in Central Europe, Hungary and Poland, within the EU, Portugal and Italy, and among Mediterranean countries, Turkey. The following analysis will focus on these regions and countries.

Looking at the commodity composition of EU imports from these different regions and from China, it is possible to identify the sectors which represented important areas of potential competition, that is the sectors which play an important part in both China's and other suppliers' exports (cf. Table 9). This was the case for the three Dragons in office machinery (NACE 300) and electric motors (311), metal products (287); for ASEAN in office machinery (300), TV & radio receivers (323), footwear (193); for India in apparel (182) and other textile articles (174), footwear (193), basic chemicals (241); for Central Europe in apparel (182), basic chemicals (241), metal products (287), electric motors (311); for Mediterranean countries apparel (182), other textile articles (174) and basic chemicals (241).

Table 8: Similarity Index of Exports to the EU (China=100) in 1996*

Similarity index by zones and regions		Similarity index by countries	
Asia-Oceania	55	Hong-Kong	55
3 Dragons	56	Thailand	55
ASEAN	51	Hungary	51
India	48	Portugal	50
Japan	38	Italy	49
Other Asia	35	Poland	48
Australia-N. Zealand	24	Indonesia	48
EU Periphery	51	India	48
Ex-Yougoslavia	53	Taiwan	47
Central Europe	52	S. Korea	45
Mediterranean	47	Philippines	45
Ex-USSR	23	Bulgaria	44
Western Europe	43	Czech Republic	42
EU	43	United Kingdom	42
Other Western Europe	35	Austria	41
America	37	Romania	41
NAFTA	36	Israel	41
Mercosur	23	Turkey	40
Other South America	16		
Gulf	26		
Sub-Sahara Africa	26		
South Africa	24		
Other Africa	23		

* Finger index is calculated to evaluate the similarity of each region/ country's exports to the EU with China's exports to the EU:

$$100\text{–}100\,\frac{\sum_k |X^k_{jEU} - X^k_{China\ EU}|}{2},$$

where k is product j partner and X the share of k in total exports of j towards EU. Thus the index is 100 for China exports. Geographic zones, regions and countries were ranked by the degree of similarity, descending order.

Source: CEPII, *Analytical data base 1996*, authors' calculations.

Table 9: Commodity Breakdown of EU Imports from China and from Other Regions/ Countries in 1996 in %

NACE classification*	China	3 Dragons	ASEAN	India	Central Eur.	Medit.c.	EU
All products	100.0	100.0	100.0	100.0	100.0	100.0	100.0
182 Other wearing apparel	14.6	8.1	6.7	**19.9**	**11.7**	**26.8**	2.1
365 Games and toys	7.2	0.8	1.2	0.1	0.3	0.2	0.3
300 Office machinery and computers	6.4	**22.1**	**22.7**	1.0	1.1	0.7	4.8
323 Television and radio receivers, sound or video rec.	6.2	4.9	**8.1**	0.5	1.8	1.1	1.6
192 Luggage, handbags	5.5	0.9	0.7	2.4	0.3	0.3	0.2
366 Other manufacturing n.e.c.	4.2	1.3	0.5	0.4	0.4	0.2	0.4
193 Footwear	4.0	1.2	**4.8**	**4.5**	3.1	1.4	0.9
252 Plastic products	3.7	1.7	0.9	0.6	1.5	1.3	2.5
297 Domestic appliances n.e.c.	3.4	1.0	0.3	0.1	1.0	0.6	1.1
241 Basic chemicals	3.1	1.9	2.1	**5.4**	**6.0**	**5.8**	**7.3**
287 Other fabricated metal products	2.5	**2.3**	0.5	1.7	**2.7**	0.8	1.5
315 Lighting equipment and electric lamps	2.1	0.7	0.1	0.5	1.1	0.1	0.4
174 Made-up textile art., except apparel	2.0	0.2	0.4	**4.3**	1.2	**1.8**	0.3
311 Electric motors, generators and transformers	1.8	**1.7**	1.4	0.2	**1.8**	0.7	0.8
364 Sports goods	1.7	1.2	0.3	0.4	0.2	0.0	0.1
Total 15 products	68.4	49.9	50.7	42.1	34.2	41.7	24.2

* Selected 15 top products in EU imports from China, descending order.

Bold figures: products with a share in countries' exports similar or larger than in China's exports.

Source: CEPII, Analytical data base 1996, author's calculation.

Price competition and non-price competition

In order to qualify these initial conclusions about potential competition, quality differentiation of exported products has to be taken into account.[22] Products belonging to the same category may be characterized by different qualities and the intensity of competition depends on the position of the goods exported on the quality ladder. Quality differentiation means that competition takes place in different market segments and, moreover, the nature of competition is not the same in the different market segments. Low quality goods are expected to be sensitive to price competition whereas up-market goods and middle-market goods are less sensitive to price competition.

On average, China's exports were heavily biased towards low price/quality products which accounted for 75 per cent of China's exports to the EU, while medium price/quality goods accounted for 15 per cent and high price/quality goods for 10 per cent (cf. Figure 3). This was also the case of the other extra-EU suppliers identified as potential competitors. By contrast intra-EU exports were concentrated in medium and high price/quality range. This quality pattern can be observed in all the sectors selected as sectors of potential competition (cf. Table 10). In almost all these sectors, China's market shares relied mainly on exports of down-market goods, although there were differences across sectors and one exception (up-market goods accounted for one fourth of China's exports of TV & radio).

Figure 3: Breakdown of EU Imports by Quality Range, 1996 Selected Partner Regions/Countries (% Bilateral Imports)

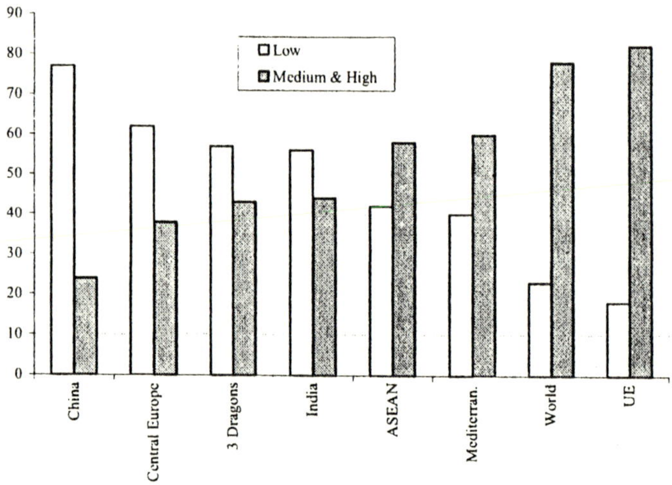

Source: CEPII, Analytical database 1996.

Table 10: Breakdown of EU Imports by Quality Range and Suppliers, 1996 Selected Products (% of total product imports)

174 Made-up textile articles, except apparel	Low	Medium &High	Total	182 Other garment	Low	Medium &High	Total
World	46.3	53.7	100.0	World	55.3	44.7	100.0
EU	11.1	36.2	47.3	EU	10.1	31.7	41.8
China	**7.9**	**3.2**	**11.1**	Mediterranean	10.6	3.6	14.2
Mediterranean	5.8	2.9	8.7	Centr. Europe	6.4	2.8	9.2
Centr. Europe	4.7	3.6	8.2	**China**	**8.1**	**0.9**	**9.0**
India	5.9	0.5	6.4	3 Dragons	4.5	0.7	5.2
ASEAN	1.5	1.1	2.5	ASEAN	4.1	0.7	4.8
3 Dragons	0.6	0.5	1.1	India	2.8	0.4	3.2
192 Luggage, handbags	**Low**	**Medium &High**	**Total**	**193 Footwear**	**Low**	**Medium &High**	**Total**
World	62.2	37.8	100.0	World	42.6	57.4	100.0
China	**36.8**	**1.4**	**38.2**	EU	12.6	46.3	58.9
EU	9.7	25.1	34.7	ASEAN	9.3	2.0	11.2
3 Dragons	4.3	2.5	6.8	**China**	**7.1**	**0.9**	**8.0**
ASEAN	3.3	2.1	5.4	Centr. Europe	5.3	2.5	7.8
India	4.0	0.5	4.5	Mediterranean	1.4	1.1	2.5
Centr. Europe	2.0	0.9	2.9	3 Dragons	1.8	0.7	2.4
Mediterranean	0.7	0.8	1.5	India	1.5	0.9	2.4
300 Office machinery and computers	**Low**	**Medium &High**	**Total**	**315 Lighting equipment**	**Low**	**Medium &High**	**Total**
World	27.5	72.5	100.0	World	27.3	72.7	100.0
EU	12.6	41.9	54.5	EU	12.8	56.4	69.2
ASEAN	2.6	6.9	9.5	**China**	**8.7**	**2.1**	**10.8**
3 Dragons	5.5	2.7	8.2	Centr. Europe	2.7	4.2	6.9
China	**2.0**	**0.3**	**2.3**	3 Dragons	1.4	2.2	3.6
Centr. Europe	0.2	0.3	0.5	ASEAN	0.4	0.4	0.7
Mediterranean	0.0	0.2	0.2	India	0.3	0.4	0.7
India	0.0	0.1	0.1	Mediterranean	0.1	0.1	0.3

cont.

311 Electric motors				323 Television and radio receivers			
	Low	Medium &High	Total		Low	Medium &High	Total
World	32.4	67.6	100.0	World	19.0	81.0	100.0
EU	16.9	42.4	59.2	EU	6.7	48.3	55.0
Centr. Europe	3.5	2.1	5.5	ASEAN	2.4	8.1	10.5
China	**3.3**	**0.9**	**4.1**	**China**	**4.4**	**2.4**	**6.8**
3 Dragons	2.1	1.9	4.1	3 Dragons	3.1	2.5	5.6
ASEAN	1.5	2.3	3.9	Centr. Europe	1.1	1.4	2.5
Mediterranean	0.5	0.9	1.4	Mediterranean	0.1	0.9	1.0
India	0.1	0.1	0.2	India	0.0	0.1	0.1
252 Plastic products				**297 Domestic appliances n.e.c.**			
	Low	Medium &High	Total		Low	Medium &High	Total
World	25.5	74.5	100.0	World	27.4	72.6	100.0
EU	16.7	60.8	77.4	EU	14.5	63.2	77.7
China	**3.1**	**0.5**	**3.6**	**China**	**5.9**	**1.3**	**7.2**
Centr. Europe	1.3	0.5	1.8	Centr. Europe	2.1	0.7	2.8
3 Dragons	1.0	0.8	1.8	3 Dragons	1.5	0.7	2.2
Mediterranean	0.5	0.6	1.1	Mediterranean	0.9	0.3	1.2
ASEAN	0.8	0.2	1.1	ASEAN	0.1	0.6	0.7
India	0.1	0.0	0.2	India	0.0	0.0	0.0
364 Sports gods				**365 Games and toys**			
	Low	Medium &High	Total		Low	Medium &High	Total
World	39.8	60.2	100.0	World	35.7	64.3	100.0
EU	7.7	32.7	40.4	EU	9.4	32.3	41.8
China	**13.9**	**2.6**	**16.5**	**China**	**19.8**	**10.0**	**29.8**
3 Dragons	7.9	4.5	12.4	ASEAN	1.3	4.6	5.9
ASEAN	2.1	1.7	3.8	3 Dragons	1.4	2.1	3.5
Centr. Europe	1.2	1.5	2.7	Centr. Europe	1.0	0.7	1.6
India	0.8	0.2	1.0	Mediterranean	0.1	0.6	0.7
Mediterranean	0.1	0.1	0.2	India	0.0	0.0	0.1

Source: CEPII, Analytical data base 1996, authors' calculations.

Due to their quality specialization, EU suppliers were in fact in different positions with respect to China's competition. In intra-EU trade, which accounted for most EU imports, low price/quality goods had on average a relatively small share (17 per cent). Most EU exports and China's exports in the same product category took place in different market segments. Nevertheless in several sectors, down-market products still accounted for a relatively important part of intra-EU supplies: this quality segment represented more than one fourth of intra-EU exports of wearing apparel and other textile articles (NACE 182 and 174), luggage (192), and about 20 per cent in footwear (193) and games & toys (365), and sports goods (364). In this trade segment, EU exporters will face price competition from China, and presumably the Southern EU countries will be the most concerned. In 1996, Chinese exports had already overtaken EU exporters in the low-quality segment for products such as luggage, games and toys, and sports goods. In the latter sector, China crowded out almost all other suppliers of the down-market segment and got a strong foothold in the medium-quality segment. Increased competition from China will further induce EU exporters to relocate down-market products in low wage countries (Central and Eastern Europe and Mediterranean countries), to upgrade their exports and even move more towards high quality products in order to maintain their market share.

The specialization of other exporters according to quality range indicates that they were more directly and more seriously concerned by China's competition. This holds for countries in the EU periphery (Central Europe and Mediterranean countries) and in Asia.

Central European exports seem to be directly in competition with China's exports in many sectors, as they share similar specialization in the low-quality/price products. In industries in which they hold significant market share (such as footwear, apparel, luggage, domestic appliances) compared to China, they are exposed to price competition. Competition from China is likely to intensify in the textile industry when MFA quotas are removed. However, it should be noted that Central European countries showed relatively better performance than China in medium and up-market products: These segments accounted for 30 per cent of their exports in apparel (182), luggage (192), and for more than 50 per cent in TV & radio (323), lighting equipment (315), and sports-goods (364). One of the reasons explaining their better position in the quality ladder was that Central European exports relied heavily on subcontracting arrangements with Western firms and on the activities of foreign firm affiliates located in these countries.[23] To a lesser extent this was also the case for Mediterranean countries.

Asian industrializing countries (three Dragons and ASEAN) also hold large shares of the EU markets in the same sectors and the same quality range as China. However, except for apparel, their exports are characterized by better position than Chinese exports in the middle and up-market goods segments.

By contrast, Indian exports which were heavily concentrated in apparel and related products were also strongly biased towards down-market products and vulnerable to China's price competition.

In garment, the sector in which China's exports are expected to increase the most rapidly, the countries likely to be most concerned, given their positions in the quality ladder, are identified in Table 11.

Table 11: Breakdown of Imports of Garment (182) by Quality Range and Suppliers

	Quality range			
	Low	Medium	High	Total*
China	90	6	4	9.0
Indonesia	89	7	5	1.6
Hong Kong	88	6	5	4.3
India	87	10	3	3.2
Morocco	84	6	11	3.3
Romania	79	13	8	2.2
Tunisia	78	12	9	3.8
Turkey	70	11	19	5.7
Greece	69	17	13	1.7
Poland	66	26	8	3.3
Netherlands	43	26	31	3.8
United Kingdom	41	33	25	4.1
Portugal	32	34	34	4.1
Belgium–Lux.	31	46	23	4.2

* Total are in % of the EU total product imports. Quality ranges are in % of bilateral imports. Countries are ranked by their share in low-quality range.
Source: CEPII, Analytical data base 1996, authors' calculations.

The two countries which held the largest share in EU imports of low price/quality imports, after China (9 per cent), were Turkey (4 per cent) and Hong Kong (3.8 per cent), followed by Tunisia (3 per cent), Morocco (2.7 per cent) and India (2.8 per cent); then came Poland and Romania. Price competition in the textile industry after the phasing out of MFA will thus concern mainly non-EU suppliers. In Asia, the most industrialized economies have already relocated large parts of this industry to China and EU imports from Hong Kong undoubtedly included products in fact coming from China. To withstand competition textile industries in Central and Mediterranean countries should take advantage of their productive links with EU firms and upgrade their production towards higher price/quality products. The down-market segment of the EU textile industry will be under pressure: For most countries it represented a marginal share of exports, but it was still significant for countries such as Greece, Portugal and also the UK, Netherlands, and Belgium.

Regionalization and globalization

Regional economic integration is an overriding factor determining the foreign trade pattern of both the EU and China. Through its participation in the international segmentation of production processes within Asia, China became an exporter of assembled or processed goods, based on intermediate products and components imported from Asian industrialized countries. This specialization explains the concentration of China's exports to the EU in finished consumption goods (60 per cent of its exports) as well as its huge trade surplus.[24] When China enters the WTO, followed by Taiwan, economic integration within 'Greater China' will be strengthened. Hong Kong and Taiwan are China's partners which will likely benefit most from the further opening up of the Mainland economy. The recent rise of direct investment by Taiwanese firms in China showed that they have anticipated the effects of liberalization, and that they will play a major role in accelerating the modernization of China's manufacturing industries. More generally, following the Asian financial crisis, initiatives have been taken for strengthening regional cooperation in Asia, in which China is taking a growing part.

On the other hand, the prospects for EU Eastward enlargement will intensify the already strong integration of Central and Eastern European countries within the European economy. This integration is reflected in the high trade intensity and in the nature of trade relations between the two parts of Europe.[25] The growing importance of intra-industry trade indicates that the productive structures of the most advanced Central European countries are converging with that of Western Europe, and underlines the contrast with EU–China trade, characterized by strong sectoral complementarities, as evidenced by the dominant share of inter-industry trade. Trade by stages of production also highlights the different specialization patterns of the EU periphery and China: Central and Eastern Europe as well as Mediterranean countries exported many more intermediate goods (around 50 per cent) than consumer goods (20 per cent), suggesting that in some cases they are less in competition with China than the similarity of their export structures would suggest. Through FDI and processing operations, EU firms have established production networks in Central and Eastern Europe, which have played an important part in the restructuring of the manufacturing industries and export capacities of these countries since 1991. The international division of production processes has contributed to increased trade flows between Eastern and Western Europe in the textile industry, the car industry and in electronic goods. In the textile industry, the transfer of the final stages of production to low-wage neighbour countries helped EU firms to withstand world competition and it helped these countries to upgrade their exports and to by-pass MFA quotas.

The geographic pattern of FDI reflects these regional integration processes. According to host country statistics, at the end of the 1990s, Western Europe was responsible for more than 60 per cent of cumulated FDI inflows in Central and Eastern Europe and symmetrically, Asian countries dominated FDI in China as they accounted for 80 per cent of cumulated inflows (Hong Kong alone for 50 per cent). Home country statistics on outward FDI (although they show substantial inconsistencies with host country statistics) tend to confirm that geographic proximity matters: Japan directed about 8 per cent of its total FDI to China, while the EU directed only 0.5 per cent of its FDI to China, but 2.4 per cent to Central and Eastern Europe. However, both China and Central and Eastern Europe took an increasing share in European direct capital outflows in the 1990s, suggesting that they have not been alternative options in European firms' strategies.

Since 1993, European firms have taken part in the wave of FDI in China and they accounted for about 7 per cent of the cumulated capital flows. Since the Asian crisis, FDI in China has slowed down, but the opening up of new sectors to foreign investors, which is laid down in China's WTO agreement, is likely to boost capital inflows. Whereas foreign firm affiliates have already become major players in several industrial manufacturing sectors, FDI in the service sector remained limited due to barriers to entry and should increase rapidly when these are removed. The service sectors in China received around 13 per cent of total FDI, a share which is low by international standards. The sectoral distribution of EU outward FDI shows that services accounted for 42 per cent of the total in 1997–1998. The sectoral distribution of inward FDI stocks in Central and Eastern Europe shows that services accounted for more than 50 per cent of the total.[26] All this shows that there is much room for a substantial increase of FDI into China in these areas, as China will progressively implement its opening up commitments. This explains fears in other emerging countries, especially in Asia, of a diversion of investment flows towards China.

Conclusion

WTO accession will bring structural changes in China's exports and imports. The paper has shown that EU export structure is in line with the expected evolution of China's import demand after accession and that EU firms have strong positions in China's imports aimed at the domestic market, which are likely to increase more rapidly than imports for processing, as a result of trade liberalization. Lower barriers to entry will, however, also increase competition in this trade segment.

The expected growth of China's exports is likely to stiffen competition in the EU market of consumer goods, especially in the textile industry. China is in potential competition mainly with non-EU suppliers, due to similarity in their specialization by commodity and quality range. As China is specialized in low price/quality goods, the countries the most exposed to competition are Asian countries, Central and Eastern Europe, Mediterranean countries and India. However, European exporters which have still kept significant market shares in the down-market segments of several sectors (including clothing) will also be put under pressure to upgrade their production.

There is much room for a substantial increase in capital flows from the EU to China. EU firms should take advantage of new opportunities offered to foreign investors in China's service sector. Given Chinese potential needs, this may divert capital flows away from emerging countries in Eastern Europe and in Asia. However the cautious approach that China is likely to adopt in liberalizing FDI should allay this risk in the short term. The expected rise in trade and capital flows between the EU and China does not seem to challenge the respective patterns of economic relations which remain deeply entrenched in the strong regional economic integration existing within Asia and within Europe. However it should help the level of economic relations between the two partners to reach a level more in line with their respective weights in international trade and capital flows.

Notes

[1]Development Research Center (DRC), 'The Global and Domestic Impact of China Joining the World Trade Organization', People's Republic of China: DRC, December 1998; Fan, M., and Y. Zheng, 'The Impact of China's Trade Liberalization for WTO Accession: A Computable General Equilibrium Analysis', Paper presented at the 'Annual Conference of Global Economic Analysis', Melbourne, Australia, 20.–30. June 2000; Ianchovichina, E., W. Martin, and E. Fukase, 'Comparative study of Trade Liberalization regimes: the case of China's accession to the WTO', Paper presented at the 'Annual Conference of Global Economic Analysis', Melbourne, Australia, 20.–30. June 2000; Lejour, A. 'China and the WTO: the impact on China and the world economy', Paper presented at the 'Annual Conference of Global Economic Analysis', Melbourne, Australia, 20.–30. June 2000; McKibbin, Warwick and Tang2000; McKibbin, J. Warwick, and K.K. Tang, 'Trade and Financial Reform in China: Impacts on the World Economy', *World Economy*, vol. 23, no. 8 (August 2000); Walmsley, T.L., and T.W. Hertel, 'China Accession to the WTO: Timing is Everything', Paper presented at the 'Annual Conference of Global Economic Analysis', Melbourne, Australia, 20.–30. June 2000; Yang, Y., 'China's WTO Accession: The Economics and Politics', *Journal of World Trade*, vol. 34, no. 4 (August 2000).

[2]DRC, *op.cit.*; Lejour, *op.cit.*; Walmsley and Hertel, *op.cit.*

[3]DRC, *op.cit.*

[4]The data used in this section of the study come from the CEPII data base on international trade (CHELEM, Comptes Harmonises sur les Echanges et L'Economie Mondiale) which provides long term series in an harmonized way. In this base, data on the EU trade with China are based on EU countries statistics but exports to China are adjusted to include EU exports transiting through Hong Kong.

[5]

$$\delta_{ij} = \frac{\frac{X_{ij}}{W}}{\frac{X_i M_j}{W^2}}$$

The δ_{ij} coefficient is the 'double–relative' trade intensity ratio. X_{ij} is the observed export flows from country i to j, X_i is the toal exports of i, M_j is the total imports of j, W is total world trade.

[6]Freudenberg, M., G. Gaulier, and D. Ünal-Kesenci, 'La régionalization du commerce international: les déterminants de l'échange bilatéral', *Economie Internationale*, no. 74, 1998.

[7]Gaulier, G., 'Discrimination commerciale: une mesure à partir des flux bilatéraux', *Document de travail du CEPII*, 2001 (forthcoming).

[8]European Commission and CESD, The Customs general Administration of the PRC and the International Trade Center UNCTAD/WTO: 'Comparison of Bilateral Trade Statistics of China and the European Union: Discrepancies and Underlying Factors', Geneva, 4 November 1997.

[9]Lemoine2000.

[10]Freudenberg and Lemoine 1999.

[11]DRC 1998.

[12]The geographic classification used in this study is described in Appendix.

[13]The data used in this section of the study come from China's customs statistics and were provided by the International Trade Center UNCTAD/WTO.

[14]Lemoine, F., 'FDI and the Opening Up of China's Economy', *CEPII Working Paper* 2000–11, June 2000; Lemoine, F., 'Why China Wants to Joint WTO', *La Lettre du CEPII*, no. 189, April 2000. Available on CEPII website: www.cepii.fr.

[15]World Bank, *China Engaged: Integration with the Global Economy*, Washington, D.C.: World Bank, 1997.

[16]Ianchovichina et al., *op.cit.*

[17]OECD, 'Estimation of Illegal Imports through Mirror Statistics', Customs General Administration (CGA), China, *STD/NA/ITS* (2000)13. Paris: OECD, 2000.

[18]Gaulier, *op.cit.*

[19]Dées, S., and F. Lemoine, 'Dévaluation du yuan: une petite impatience peut ruiner un grand projet', *Lettre du CEPII*, no. 178 (April 1999).

[20]Three detailed research studies carried out by the CEPII had already used this data base: CEPII, *Compétitivité des nations*, Rapport du CEPII, Economica, 1998; Freudenberg, M., and F. Lemoine, 'Central and Eastern European Countries in the International Division of Labour in Europe', *CEPII Working Paper*, 1999–05 (April 1999); Fontagné, L., M. Freudenberg, and D. Ünal-Kesenci, 'Trade in Technology and Quality Ladders: Where do EU Countries Stand?', *International Journal of Development Planning Literature*, vol. 14, no. 4 (October–December 1999).

[21]NACE is the General industrial classification of economic activities within the European Communities.

[22]In order to asses quality ranges we assume that differences in prices reflect quality differences. Bilateral trade unit values at the 8 digit level of Harmonized Commodity Classification and Coding System (HS) are used as prices (about 10,000 products). For each product and each partner of the European Union, the unit value of the export or import flow is compared to the intra-European unit value average for this product. Flows are classified in the 'up-market' range when the unit value exceed the Community average by at least 15 per cent, in the 'down-market' range if below the norm by 15 per cent below, in the 'middle-market' range otherwise (for detailed methodology see Fontagné, L., M. Freudenberg, and N. Péridy, 'Trade Patterns inside the Single Market', *The Single Market Review*, Subseries IV, vol. 2, Kogan Page, 1996).

[23]Freudenberg and Lemoine, *op.cit.*

[24]Lemoine, F., 'Les délocalisations au coeur de l'expansion du commerce extérieur chinois', *Economie et Statistique*, no. 326–327, 1999–6/7, 1999.

[25]Freudenberg, Gaulier, and Ünal-Kesenci, *op.cit.*; Freudenberg and Lemoine, *op.cit.*

[26]UNCTAD, *World Investment Report 2000*, Geneva.

Appendix: Geographical Classification

World		
America		
	NAFTA	USA
		Canada
		Mexico
	Mercosur	Argentina
		Brazil
		Paraguay
		Uruguay
	Other South America	Chile
		Colombia
		Equator
		Other America
		Peru
		Venezuela
Asia-Oceania		
	Japan	
	3 Dragons	Hong Kong
		S. Korea
		Taiwan
	ASEAN	Indochina
		Indonesia
		Malaysia
		Philippines
		Singapore
		Thailand
	China	
	India	
	Other Asia	
	Australia–N.Zealand	Australia
		N.Zealand
Western Europe		
	EU	Austria
		Belgium-Lux.
		Denmark
		Finland
		France
		Germany
		Greece
		Ireland
		Italy
		Netherlands
		Portugal
		Spain
		Sweden
		United Kingdom
	Other Western Europe	Norway
		Switzerland
		Other EFTA

13

The Implications of China's WTO Accession for the Economies of Taiwan, Hong Kong and Macau

Newman M.K. Lam

Introduction

The People's Republic of China (PRC) is expected to join the World Trade Organization (WTO) in 2001, with Taiwan to follow as a separate customs territory. The WTO which covers liberalization measures over a broad range of economic activities, including investment, promotes two main principles governing the world trade system. First, the most favoured nation treatment requires trade benefits extended to one trading partner be extended to all. Second, national treatment requires foreign goods and companies to be treated no worse than domestic products and companies. Exceptions to or variations of these principles are allowed only under special circumstances.[1] These and other principles embodied in the WTO regime will have various implications for the economies of Taiwan, Hong Kong and Macau which this paper will outline.

The Taiwan government severed ties with the mainland (the PRC) in 1949 due to political and security reasons. Its economic detachment from the mainland will be difficult to maintain after both have joined the WTO. Taiwan might become economically over-reliant on the mainland, which would give the mainland more bargaining power in their unification negotiations. Furthermore, Taiwan would have difficulty protecting certain sensitive industries, such as telecommunications, transportation, and banking, from being infiltrated by mainland businesses. Joining the WTO, therefore, means both economic benefits and political risks for the Taiwanese government.

China's WTO accession also has serious implications for Hong Kong and Macau. Both Hong Kong and Macau have, in the past, benefited as gateways into China. After its WTO accession, China might not have to rely as much on Hong Kong and Macau as before to be its business intermediaries. On the other hand, China's economic growth and demand for business after its WTO accession would create new businesses for Hong Kong and Macau, and expand certain types of their existing businesses. To them, China's WTO accession means both opportunities and threats. The challenge for them is to minimize the threats and to capitalize on the opportunities.

In this paper, the economic threats and benefits to Taiwan, Hong Kong and Macau are examined (see Appendix for a comparison of their profiles). In the case of Taiwan, it is inevitable that some of the political concerns will be touched upon, although these political concerns are not the focus of this paper.

Implications for Taiwan

Taiwan is one of Asia's newly industrialized economies (NIEs), characterized by rapid economic growth in the 1960s, especially in manufacturing, and a high level of export-oriented industrialization in the final stage of its economic development. Together with South Korea and Hong Kong, they are known as the three dragons (or tigers) of East Asia.[2] Taiwan had a GDP of approximately US$ 288 billion (NT$ 9,290 billion) in 1999,[3] which made it the thirteenth-largest economy in the world. In 1998, Taiwan's international trade totalled more than US$ 216 billion, the twelfth-largest in the world.[4]

The Republic of China (ROC), as which Taiwan is also known, was an original member of the General Agreement on Tariffs and Trade (GATT), the former body of the WTO, when the GATT was established in 1948. The ROC withdrew its membership from the GATT in 1950 after losing control of the mainland to the communist government (the PRC) and moving its government to Taiwan. In the 1960s, Taiwan began to establish itself as a trading power and attended GATT meetings as an observer. Its observer status was lost in 1971 when the PRC began to re-establish relations with western countries, which eventually led to its admission to the United Nations. The PRC gained observer status in the GATT in the early 1980s. In order to avoid a clash with the PRC, Taiwan applied to join the GATT in 1990 as the Separate Customs Territory of Taiwan, Penghu, Kinmen and Matsu. This application was transferred to the WTO after its establishment in 1995. In order to make its application more attractive,

Taiwan agreed to assume all the responsibility of a developed country member, which involved wider market opening.[5] Furthermore, Taiwan has been supporting the PRC in its efforts to gain accession to the WTO.[6] The PRC has refrained from discussing the Taiwan issue in order not to jeopardize its own chance of gaining admission.[7] In addition, the PRC expects better ties with Taiwan when both join the WTO, which will be of advantage in unification negotiations.[8] It has been speculated that Taiwan will join the WTO this year either on the same day as the PRC or shortly afterward.[9]

Nowadays, Taiwan's economy is heavily based on manufacturing industry and the service sector, which accounted for 27 and 64 per cent of the GDP in 1999, respectively. Within the service sector, finance, insurance and business services accounted for 31 per cent of the total, while wholesale and retail trade, combined with restaurants and hotel businesses, accounted for another 31 per cent. In comparison, agriculture, hunting, forestry and fishing accounted for only 2.5 per cent of the GDP in 1999.[10]

By joining the WTO together with the mainland, there is no doubt that Taiwan's economy would benefit as a whole. However, it is unlikely that Taiwan would willingly open its economy to the mainland. Since moving to Taiwan, the ROC government prohibited any direct contact with the mainland under its National Unification Guidelines. Hence, postal, travel and trade links between Taiwan and the mainland had been severed.[11] This would conflict with the membership requirements of the WTO, which demand equal market access for all member states although exceptions can be granted under special circumstances. For example, the United States used national security as the reason to halt trade with and investment in Cuba.[12] It is questionable whether the WTO would allow Taiwan to continue its attempts to sever economic contacts with the mainland.

The 'three links'

Since the 1970s, the PRC has repeatedly called for the resumption of trade, postal services and travel between Taiwan and the mainland. This is referred as the 'three links', ('*santong*' in Chinese). Taiwan has consistently rejected this request on political and security grounds until recently. In spite of the government's efforts to sever economic ties with the mainland, Taiwanese businesses have invested in the mainland through Hong Kong and other avenues. It was estimated that Taiwanese merchants have invested US$ 40 billion in the mainland since the late 1980s, and there has been growing pressure from Taiwanese businesses demanding the government restore the three links.[13] On November 22, a petition urging the government to reopen the three links obtained signatures from 160 of the 221 members in Taiwan's Legislative Yuan. Chiou I-jen, Taiwan's secretary-general, indicated that the government was working to gradually scrap the former 'go slow, be patient' policy of discouraging large-scale cross-strait investment and trade.[14]

As a counter-measure to the PRC's request for opening the three links, the Taiwanese government has been pushing forward a proposal to open a 'small' or 'mini three links'. Under Article 18 of the 'Offshore Island Development Act', direct transportation of local residents, conveyance of local goods, and other related commercial activities are permitted between Kinmen, Matsu, Penghu and the mainland. The Act does not permit the shipment of goods derived from other locations, hence preventing Kinmen, Matsu and Penghu from being gateways for opening up the whole Taiwanese economy to the mainland.[15] On January 2, 2001, the mini-three links were officially opened for the first time when a ship from Matsu arrived at the Mawei Harbour of Fujian province.[16] The reception provided by the mainland side however was unenthusiastic, as the PRC government considers the mini three links a deterrent rather than a prelude to a nation-wide three links. The impact of China's WTO accession on Taiwan obviously depends heavily on the extent and pace of opening the three links.

Trade

In spite of the government's restriction, trade and investment between Taiwan and the mainland has existed by flowing through Hong Kong and other avenues.[17] The exact amount, however, is hard to estimate, due to conflicting figures and statistics. According to Taiwan's 1998 statistics, Hong Kong was Taiwan's second largest export destination, behind only the US, and accounted for 22 per cent of its total exports.[18] A significant portion of the exports to Hong Kong was re-exported into the mainland. One estimate indicates that China is Taiwan's seventh-largest trading partner.[19] According to PRC statistics, Taiwan is China's fifth largest trading partner. It was estimated that almost 20 per cent of Taiwan's exports and 4 per cent of its imports were traded with the mainland and that cross-Strait trade has been growing at more than 7 per cent a year.[20] Due to the imbalance between exports and imports, Taiwan enjoyed a huge surplus trading with the mainland. Putting political concerns aside, opening up the three links would be beneficial to Taiwan's economy.

Increasing trade with the mainland could help Taiwan deal with some of the problems that come with its WTO accession. Although Taiwan has greatly liberalized its trading system in the last decade, high tariffs and non-tariff measures (e.g. import licenses, quotas) are still imposed on a number of imports, including passenger vehicles, automobile parts, food products, and to a smaller extent textiles and apparel. These barriers would have to be reduced or removed after Taiwan has joined the WTO.[21] Joining the WTO would undoubtedly bring overall economic growth to Taiwan. A study conducted by Taiwan's Council for Economic Planning and Development indicates that joining the WTO would increase Taiwan's GDP by an additional 0.9 per cent year-on-year. However, this might come at the expense of turning Taiwan's long-standing trade surplus into a deficit of US$ 5.3 billion. The study suggests that Taiwan should deal with this threat by increasing the exports of high-tech products.[22] Furthermore, Taiwan's exports to Asian markets have declined since the onset of the Asian financial crisis as a result of lower purchasing power in the region.[23]

Increasing trade with China might reduce the potential trade deficit as the mainland would have needs for numerous high-tech and telecommunications products. However, this might also lead to opening Taiwan to a flood of cheap goods and raw materials from the mainland, making Taiwan over-reliant on the mainland, which would be a huge political concern for the Taiwan government. At present, 64 per cent of Taiwan's imports from the mainland are industrial products and 22 per cent are farm products. On the pessimistic side, direct trade with the mainland might reduce rather than increase Taiwan's trade surplus with the mainland, estimated at US$ 16.7 billion in 1999.[24]

Manufacturing

Taiwan has a diversified economy which emphasizes small and medium-sized businesses more than some of its trading partners. Electronics, high-tech products and textiles are significant components of its manufacturing industry, which accounted for 15, 12, and 9 per cent of its total exports in 1998, respectively.[25] Taiwan would see heavy competition from China in the manufacturing industry after both have joined the WTO. Taiwan has already begun restructuring its economy by shifting more of its industrial base to knowledge-intensive, information products. Although Taiwan's labour force was ranked fifth among fourty-nine countries surveyed by the Swiss firm Business Environment Risk Intelligence in 1998 and 1999, behind only Singapore, Switzerland, Belgium, and Japan, its labour force is still considered lacking in creativity and weak in software skills. Its high-tech industry has been concentrating on hardware manufacturing which combined with Taiwanese-invested factories in the mainland, produced between one-third and one half of all the world's PCs. The design of the hardware products however was done by multinationals. In order to diversify its high-tech industry, Taiwan needs to make far-reaching adjustments to its education system as well as its attitude to funding research and development. Taiwan's unemployment rate has been low and went up to only 3.11 per cent after the Asian financial crisis. However, according to the July 1999 statistics, the unemployment rate was a lot higher among the younger generation, 8.8 per cent for the group aged between 15 and 24.[26] Similar to the situations in Hong Kong and Macau, which will be explained later, upgrading high-tech education and emphasizing creativity should be a priority in restructuring Taiwan's economy.

Investment opportunities

If trade and investment were to flow freely between Taiwan and the mainland, the mainland would provide Taiwan with a source of cheaper raw materials as well as numerous investment opportunities. It was estimated that more than 33 per cent of the PCs produced by Taiwanese businesses in 1999, valued at US$ 34 billion, were manufactured by Taiwanese-invested plants on the mainland. This was a huge increase compared to 14 per cent in 1995. In order to discourage Taiwanese investment in the mainland, the Taiwanese government has vigorously pushed forward a 'Going South Strategy' since 1993, which pumped US$ 28 billion into countries such as Thailand, Malaysia, Indonesia and the Philippines.[27] These investments resulted in heavy losses during the Asian financial crisis. The mainland would provide Taiwan with numerous investment opportunities, not only in hardware manufacturing but also in other areas such as textiles and food production. Taiwan's technology and telecommunications companies have already indicated that they are prepared to invest more in the mainland.[28] Although this might hurt Taiwan's manufacturing industry, it would provide profits for further enhancing Taiwan's service sector, as Hong Kong has experienced. The Taiwanese government is also ready to relax restrictions on firms with a mainland interest to invest in Taiwan as long as this would not lead to losing the control of its economy to the mainland. It was reported that the government would allow foreign companies with Chinese holdings to set up subsidiaries in Taiwan. Firms with less than 50 per cent Chinese capital will also be allowed to open branches in Taiwan, compared to the existing 20 per cent limit. [29]

Service sector

Trade, tourism and business-related services have become an important part of Taiwan's economy, accounting for about 40 per cent of Taiwan's GDP. If the three links were to open, the service sector would undoubtedly enjoy further growth. The banking industry is an area deserving more attention. Historically, the Taiwanese government opted for public-over-private banking for reasons of access control. This has changed since 1989 when banks financed by private domestic capital were permitted to open in Taiwan. At the end of 1998, Taiwan had fourty-six foreign banks with seventy-two branches, combining assets of US$ 33.23 billion. The Taiwanese government will be under pressure to further liberalize its financial sector as part of its WTO accession package. In anticipation of this, the Taiwanese government has announced a plan to merge three state-run banks – the Bank of Taiwan, the Land Bank of Taiwan and the Central Trust of China – which would create the world's seventy-fifth-largest bank with assets of US$ 120 billion.[30] The banking industry would grow with increasing trade and investment activities. The same would be true for other business support, trade-related, and restaurant and hotel services. However, the liberalization of the business service sector might weaken the Taiwanese government's control in a number of sensitive areas such as telecommunications, air transportation, and banking, which would make stronger economic ties with the mainland politically more threatening.

In the end, the economic impact of China's WTO accession on Taiwan would depend heavily on the willingness of the Taiwanese government and the pressure that the WTO might apply on Taiwan to open up its economy to the mainland. It is reasonable to predict that Taiwan would open its economy to the mainland only reluctantly and as slowly as it could.

Implications for Hong Kong

Hong Kong, like Taiwan, is also an NIE and one of the four dragons of East Asia. It had tripled its GDP in the ten years between

1988 and 1997. In 1991, a World Bank report classified Hong Kong as a '*high income*' country and placed it in the same category as the developed countries in the Organization for Economic Cooperation and Development.[31] The Economist Intelligence Unit (EIU) ranked Hong Kong the first in the order of business attractiveness among sixty countries for the period between 1993 and 1997.[32] Its projected ranking for 1999-2003 has dropped to the twelfth place at the end of 1998 as a result of the Asian financial crisis.[33]

There are a number of reasons contributing to Hong Kong losing its business attractiveness. The Asian financial crisis was just a catalyst causing some of the accumulated problems to manifest themselves. First, due to the rapidly rising cost of living, Hong Kong has been losing its competitive edge in many areas, especially the labour-intensive manufacturing sector.[34] Secondly, Hong Kong has maintained a linked exchange rate system by pegging 7.8 Hong Kong dollars to one US dollar since October 1983. This system has caused the exchange rates of the Hong Kong dollar to remain arbitrarily high after the Asian financial crisis, since the US economy has been going strong in the last few years. By comparison, Singapore chose not to defend its currency and had dropped from second to only the sixth place in the EIU's ranking of business attractiveness. In addition, Hong Kong's education system is out-dated, with too much emphasis on rote learning rather than creative thinking. Such a system will not produce the necessary human capital for moving Hong Kong into a new era of a high-tech and knowledge-based society. The language ability of the younger generation has also deteriorated in the last decade. The results of a recent survey indicate that 63 per cent of the respondents believed that inadequate English skills have been a barrier to Hong Kong's business development.[35] The Hong Kong government has launched new policies to revamp the education system and to emphasize 'lifelong learning' in order to address this problem. The government's efforts have already encountered resistance from education professionals and its success is still waiting to be seen.[36]

Furthermore, Hong Kong's market is becoming less competitive due to heavy economic control by a few business conglomerates. A European Parliament report on Hong Kong has voiced concerns over the power wielded by a number of tycoons in Hong Kong, exemplified by the Li Kar-shing family, and worried about their undue and dominant influence in certain sectors of Hong Kong's economy. The report estimates that the Li family controls between one quarter and one-third of Hong Kong's stock market capitalization. The report also indicated concerns about the rule of law, the lack of universal suffrage, and incidents of mainland officials apparently interfering with Hong Kong affairs.[37] Although Li Kar-shing denied the extent of his family's influence on the Hong Kong economy and estimated that his family's share of Hong Kong's total market capitalization to be no more than 18 per cent, it is hard to deny the existence of market imperfection in Hong Kong. The high property prices, which are a major contributing factor to Hong Kong's high cost of living, are a prime example of market imperfection. Although property prices have dropped significantly (by about 40 per cent) since the onset of the Asian financial crisis, many economists believe that a further reduction was required to improve Hong Kong's international competitiveness.[38] However, the government has tried to halt sliding property prices by holding off land sales and reducing the government's public housing target.

The above analysis indicates that Hong Kong is already having a lot of problems due to deteriorating international competitiveness. China's WTO accession will quicken the pace of deterioration but at the same time open up new opportunities for Hong Kong.

Trade

China's WTO accession will have severe implications for Hong Kong's import/export trade. Currently, 40 per cent of the mainland's trade goes through Hong Kong. The World Bank projected that China's share in international trade would double within five years after the WTO accession.[39] This means sufficient business to keep Hong Kong busy even if some of this business does not go through Hong Kong. The Chief Executive of the Hong Kong Monetary Authority (HKMA), Joseph Yam Chi-kong, estimated that this would increase Hong Kong's GDP by about 0.5 per centage points.[40] In the long run, China might bypass Hong Kong in trading with foreign countries. This would have severe consequences, since the value of imports and exports amounts to about four times Hong Kong's GDP.[41]

Hong Kong has been an intermediary for trade between Taiwan and the mainland. Since Taiwan will also join the WTO, it is likely that Taiwan and the mainland may trade with each other directly, if the three links open after their WTO accession. The loss of business to Hong Kong would not be too significant in this case. According to 1997 statistics, although 90 per cent of Hong Kong's re-exports either originated from China or were destined for China, only 7.1 per cent of Hong Kong's re-exports were between Taiwan and the mainland.[42]

Manufacturing

Due to the high cost of production, manufacturers in Hong Kong have been moving their production activities into the lower-cost Guangdong Province of China. Hong Kong would be unable to compete with the mainland after China's WTO accession. Currently, 90 per cent of Hong Kong manufacturers have factories in the mainland.[43] The gross output from manufacturing had shrunk from HK$ 348 billion in 1989 to HK$ 284 billion in 1996, reducing its share of Hong Kong's GDP from 19.3 to 7.3 per cent.[44] Due to its high land and labour costs, attempts to revive Hong Kong's manufacturing sector would be futile. The relocation of manufacturing business to the mainland, however, has been bringing benefits to Hong Kong. First, Hong Kong's investment in the mainland has brought huge profits to sustain its economic prosperity. Secondly, the investment in the mainland has created demand for support services in areas such as product development, marketing and financing, all of which have been provided in Hong Kong. This has helped Hong Kong to develop its business services industry. Financing, insurance, real estate and business services had grown from 19.5 per cent of GDP in 1989 to 25.1 per cent in 1996.[45] China's WTO accession would mean more investment opportunities for Hong Kong investors, and would subsequently contribute to further development of Hong Kong's business service industry.

Finance and banking

In order to capitalize on the business opportunities that China's WTO accession may provide, the Hong Kong government has taken steps to strengthen its finance and banking sector. HKMA Chief Executive Joseph Yam Chi-kong expected Hong Kong to become an international financial center for China, with Shanghai serving as a domestic one.[46] Hong Kong's banking industry, however, is not considered competitive enough, due to the large number of family-owned banks. Joseph Yam Chi-kong has been urging these banks to merge or consolidate so that they would have the resources to compete for large syndicate loans. Since the beginning of 2000, the government has already begun to deregulate the interest rate rules. Prior to the deregulation, interest rates for deposits were set by the Hong Kong Association of Banks. The deregulation, expected to be completed in 2001, will allow deposit interest rates to be determined by market forces.[47] The deregulation will reduce the profit margins of banks, hence encouraging the small ones to merge.

The mainland is likely to open up its banking industry after its WTO accession. Currently, the mainland requires foreign banks opening branches in China to have minimum assets of US$ 20 billion. This requirement might be relaxed after its WTO accession. It is expected that China would allow foreign banks to transact business in the Chinese Yuan with mainland enterprises within about two years of accession. Foreign banks will be free to compete with mainland banks for consumer business within about five years.[48] This means that, in the short run, the banks of Hong Kong would continue to enjoy the role of financing mainland business investment.

Many mainland corporations (e.g. China Telecom) have been raising capital through the Hong Kong stock market. The Hong Kong government has introduced a number of measures to strengthen its capital market. The two stock exchanges and three clearing houses in Hong Kong were merged in June 2000 to form the Hong Kong Exchange and Clearing Corporation to strengthen management, supervision and coordination of stock market activities. In addition, the government has introduced a number of debt products, launched an on-line bond trading system, created a US dollar clearing system, and offered dual listing of seven Nasdaq-listed stocks.[49] After China's WTO accession, more mainland companies may come to Hong Kong to raise funds.

High-tech development

There will be increasing pressure on China to upgrade its technology, especially in telecommunications, after WTO accession. The Hong Kong government has already indicated its aspiration to make Hong Kong a high-tech communication hub.[50] Even after WTO accession, China would have difficulty obtaining certain technologies, especially if they have military potential. Furthermore, it would not be in China's interests to have their technological development controlled by foreign firms. Hong Kong would be an attractive intermediary for China to obtain modern technology. When Pacific Century CyberWorks, a Hong Kong company, took over Hong Kong Telecom, there were rumours that CyperWorks was acting according to mainland instructions, because Beijing did not want Hong Kong Telecom to fall into the hands of Singapore Telecom, which was another front runner for taking over Hong Kong Telecom at the time. If Hong Kong has Beijing's blessing, its high-tech development will flourish after China's WTO accession.

Logistics and headquarter business

In the short run, foreign companies would still find Hong Kong an advantageous gateway for doing business with China, even after China's WTO accession. Li Guoguang, vice-president of China's Supreme People's Court, said in October 2000 that when 'handling foreign related cases, courts at all levels should apply WTO rules when there are discrepancies between these rules and the Chinese laws.' However, foreign companies registered on the mainland would be treated as Chinese entities and thus mainland laws should apply. Furthermore, he mentioned that the courts would be flexible with Hong Kong and Macau residents, bear in mind the principle of 'one country, two systems', and that they should not overlook political issues such as possible reunification with Taiwan in their adjudication.[51] This implies that Hong Kong, in addition to having better infrastructure, business expertise, and legal and administrative systems, would offer an additional advantage to foreign firms in case of legal dispute with Chinese firms. Foreign firms may find Hong Kong an attractive place to set up a logistics base or headquarters. Eden Wong Yi-ting, director of the Hong Kong General Chamber of Commerce, has suggested that Hong Kong should position itself as a middleman for small and medium-sized businesses seeking to enter the Chinese market.[52] The Hong Kong government has already planned to conduct a study to examine Hong Kong's position as an international logistics hub in relation to counterparts in Asia, Europe and the US.[53]

Tourism

After China's WTO accession, the purchasing power of mainlanders will undoubtedly increase in time. It is logical to expect that more mainlanders will visit Hong Kong for vacation. Currently, mainlanders account for 30 per cent of all visitors to Hong Kong. However, if the Chinese government relaxed its controls on traveling, Hong Kong might lose the big-spending mainlanders to foreign destinations. Furthermore, mainland cities might also become attractive destinations for foreign vacationers, hence taking business away from Hong Kong.[54] In order to capitalize on the opportunities and avoid the threats, the Hong Kong government has already taken action to improve its tourism industry. A Disneyland theme park is due to be completed in 2005 to increase Hong Kong's attractiveness.

Linked exchange system

Hong Kong's linked exchange rate system may face more threats after China's WTO accession. The Chinese Yuan is fixed within a narrow trading band of between 8.277 and 8.28 to the US dollar.[55] After its WTO accession, China may come under pressure to widen the band or allow the currency to float. Due to the heavy volume of business with the mainland, Hong Kong may find it difficult to maintain its currency peg with the US dollar, should China decide to float the Yuan.

It is obvious that whether the region will be able to capitalize on the opportunities created by China's WTO accession and minimize the negative effects will depend heavily on Hong Kong's ability to restructure its economy. The same is also true for Macau, although the situation for Macau is somewhat different due to its much smaller economy.

Implications for Macau

Macau is a mini-economy characterized by a small population (less than one million), a small volume of domestic economic activities, relatively independent internal economic institutions but dependent internal industrial structure, and an internationally recognized external economic status.[56] Being small does not make Macau poor: in 1998 the World Bank ranked Macau third-highest in terms of per capita income among mini-economies, only behind Luxembourg and Iceland.[57] Within the region, Macau's per capita income was the fourth highest, behind only Japan, Hong Kong and Singapore. In recent years, however, Macau has been suffering from the effects of a declining economy, due to weakening competitiveness and rising criminal activities. [58]

Trade

Entrepot trade is an area where Macau has been losing competitiveness for quite some time. Although Macau was one of the earliest ports facilitating business activities between the East and the West, and was once one of the largest re-exporting centres in the Far East, it lacks the deep-water port necessary to be a commodity trading centre by today's standards.[59] In 1993, import/export trade contributed only 6 per cent of Macau's GDP. China is Macau's largest source of imports. This is because Macau relies heavily on China for food supply. Although China is also Macau's third largest export destination, goods shipped to China accounted to only 9.2 per cent of total exports in 1999, significantly smaller than the exports to the US (47 per cent) and the EU (30 per cent). Potential trade diversion, therefore, is not a major worry for Macau regarding China's WTO accession. On the contrary, Macau could benefit from the WTO accession due to its unique European ties.

In Macau's final years as a Portuguese colony, the Portuguese government tried hard to promote Macau's external relations by signing on the colony's behalf bilateral and multilateral agreements with dozens of countries and international organizations. Macau now maintains consular relations with fifty-seven countries, is a full or associate member of twenty-one governmental and non-governmental organizations, and is signatory to 155 multinational treaties. Portugal and France have promised to defend Macau's commercial interests in the EU.[60] It is expected that China might still be restricted by textile and clothing export quotas for some time after its WTO accession. For example, the US quota of this type might not expire until 2008.[61] Macau's European ties can serve as convenient bridges for China to establish trade with European countries, especially the Latin-speaking ones. Its Portuguese heritage would also make Macau an attractive gateway into China for some South American countries, such as Brazil.

Macau's import/export trade could be further improved if it could solve the problem of lacking a deep-water port. Wang Zhenzhong has explored options for providing Macau with access to a deep-water port,[62] and the Macau government has been entertaining the idea of redeveloping Macau's inner harbour since 1995.[63] There have also been suggestions for Macau to build a deep-water harbour as well as a bridge to connect Macau with Hong Kong and Zhuhai.[64] These plans, if implemented, would revive Macau's trading business and enhance its status as a gateway connecting China and the world. Furthermore, the increasing business activities would help Macau to further develop its banking and business-related industry.

Manufacturing

The biggest threat posed by China's WTO accession is to the manufacturing industry. Similar to the situation in Hong Kong, Macau's cost of living has become quite high in comparison to that of the mainland, causing manufacturing activities to move north. The manufacturing industry, mainly textile, still employed 22 per cent of Macau's workforce in 1999.[65] The government is going to change Macau's industrial base from low-technology, labour-intensive manufacturing to high-technology, value-added industries. Macau, however, has to deal with a number of inherent weaknesses in its industrial modernization. First, the manufacturing sector is crowded with small- and medium-sized enterprises (SMEs). In 1997, only five factories in Macau had the capacity to employ over 500 workers, while 93 per cent of the establishments had fewer than 100 workers each and 61 per cent had less than ten workers. SMEs were not known to have the economic capacity to invest in high value-added product development.

Secondly, Macau's manufacturers have been surviving on 'cross-border subcontracting' in the last three decades, in which Hong Kong provided product design, marketing and distribution functions, while Macau concentrated on production. Under this arrangement, Macau has not developed the expertise and human resources to develop and market its own products. Furthermore, Macau's investment in manufacturing came mainly from Hong Kong. Since China adopted its open-door policy, the special economic zones of Shenzhen and Zhuhai have become better investment options than Macau for Hong Kong investors.[66] Unless the government can find ways to overcome these weaknesses, Macau's economic restructuring will not be easily accomplished.

Logistics and headquarter business

Like Hong Kong, Macau may have the opportunity to become a logistics and headquarter center.[67] Macau has a unique Portuguese heritage, which is quite different from the strong British-American domination in Hong Kong. It was reported that the French have been interested in Macau as a gateway into China because they could not compete with the US and the UK in Hong Kong.[68] In comparison to Hong Kong, Macau offers lower land and labour costs. Hong Kong has already lost some of its international headquarter business to Singapore due to cost considerations. In order to capture this type of business, Macau has to upgrade its management talents, enhance its telecommunication infrastructure, strengthen its banking sector, and improve its commercial law. In recent years, the Macau government has emphasized upgrading human capital through generalizing higher education.[69] Singapore and Japan have recently pledged support to help Macau with its telecommunications and high-tech development.[70]

In addition, the Macau government has granted more licenses to mobile telephone operators[71] and temporary licenses to Internet service providers.[72] These developments will help Macau to move towards becoming an information- and knowledge-based economy. The Macau government has also taken a firm stance on protecting intellectual property rights. The government recently signed an agreement with Microsoft to purchase more than MOP 10 million of software and reaffirmed its commitment to stamp out software piracy.[73]

While Hong Kong is well established as a southeastern gateway into China, Macau can explore the possibility of tailoring itself as the southwestern gateway. President Jiang Zemin announced a 'Go West' programme in June 2000, emphasizing development of the Western region. Geographically, Macau is closer to the southwestern region of China than Hong Kong. In particular, various analysts[74] have examined the feasibility of economic cooperation between Macau and the Guangxi Autonomous Region in Southwest China, which is one of the regions included in the 'Go West' programme. Macau's Secretary for Economic and Finance Francis Tam Pak Yuen has also emphasized developing this economic cooperation.[75] Furthermore, Macau's close proximity to Zhuhai might also facilitate beneficial economic integration between Macau, Hong Kong and other Guangdong cities.[76]

Tourism/gambling industry

Macau is known as the 'Oriental Monte Carlo' where tourism and gambling form a major industry. The tourism industry contributed 38 per cent of Macau's GDP in 1998.[77] Restaurants and hotels employed 26 per cent of Macau's workforce in 1999.[78] In the first ten months of 1999, public revenue generated from the gambling industry accounted for 40 per cent of total government revenue.[79] The gambling industry, however, has been declining in the late 1990s, partly due to increasing criminal activities and the Asian economic crisis. According to the Visitor Expenditure survey of Estatisticas do Turismo, the per centage of visitors coming to Macau for gambling had dropped from 20.2 per cent in 1990 to 10.8 per cent in 1998.[80] Since its unification with the mainland, Macau's law and order have improved tremendously. The Asian economy has shown signs of recovering from the financial crisis. The Macau government has indicated its intention to diversify its tourism industry into culture entertainment. These changes would improve Macau's tourism/gambling industry in the future. In 1999, tourists from the mainland accounted for 22 per cent of all visitor arrivals in Macau, second only to Hong Kong. The wealth created by China's WTO accession in the mainland may bring more tourists to Macau.

Conclusion

The above analysis indicates that China's WTO accession will offer business opportunities as well as pose threats to the economies of Taiwan, Hong Kong and Macau. In the case of Taiwan, its WTO accession will bring economic growth at the expense of economic control. The volume of trade would increase and the service sector will enjoy further growth. The manufacturing sector would need to be restructured to move into software production. China's entry into the WTO will offer numerous investment opportunities to Taiwan. However, increasing flows of trade and investment between Taiwan and the mainland will weaken Taiwan's control of its economy and the Taiwanese economy may become over-reliant on the mainland. This would weaken the Taiwanese government's bargaining power in the unification debate.

In the case of Hong Kong, the major threats are potential diversion of import/export trade originated from or destined for the mainland as well as further decline in its manufacturing sector. The threats to Macau are mainly in the potential loss of textile manufacturing business. The governments of both regions have chosen to restructure their economies by upgrading telecommunications and high-tech expertise. Hong Kong would have a better chance of success due to the financial backing it has. In addition, it would be in China's strategic interests to develop Hong Kong into a high-tech centre. Macau, on the other hand, does not have these advantages. In the short run, both economies would see improvements in commodity trade, tourism, and banking and finance industries. The long-term prospects, however, are less certain and depend in particular on whether they could grow to become knowledge-based societies and logistics hubs for foreign firms doing business with China.

Notes

[1]Mastel, G., *Can China and Taiwan Do Business Together?*, www.intellectualcapital.com/issues359/item8922.asp, March 30, 2000.

[2]Tan, G., *The Newly Industrializing Countries of Asia*, Singapore: Times Academic Press, 1992.

[3]The Republic of China, *Monthly Bulletin of Statistics*, December 2000.

[4]Mastel, G., *Taiwan in the WTO: An Economic and Policy Analysis*, www.taipei.org/un/wto0223.htm, October 6, 1999.

[5]Ibid.

[6]'Taiwan Roots for China's WTO Entry', *Muzi.com News*, dailnews.muzi.com/ll/English/41985.shtml, September 4, 2000. See also 'Taiwan to Push China WTO Entry, as Well as Own', *Muzi.com News*, http://dailnews.muzi.com/ll/English/41989.shtml, September 4, 2000.

[7]'Beijing Plays Down Taiwan Issue in WTO Entry', *Muzi.com News*, http://dailnews.muzi.com/ll/English/88856.shtml, September 16, 2000.

[8]'China Sees Better Ties with Taiwan if Both Join WTO', *Muzi.com News*, http://dailnews.muzi.com/ll/English/50562.shtml, September 4, 2000.

[9]*South China Morning Post* (SCMP), November 21, 2000, Business Post, p. 6.

[10]The Republic of China, *Monthly Bulletin of Statistics*, December 2000.

[11]Qi, L., 'Direct Trading Between Mainland China and Taiwan: Hong Kong's Challenge Ahead,' *American Asian Review*, vol. XVII, no. 3, 1999, pp. 29–58.

[12]Mastel, G., *Can China and Taiwan Do Business Together?*, *op.cit.*

[13]'Taiwan Has Mixed Views on China Ties Inside WTO', *Muzi.com News*, http://dailynews.muzi.com/ll/english/74556.shtml, September 3, 2000.

[14]SCMP, November 23, 2000, p. 10.

[15]Shieh, F.F.Y., *Discussion of the Policy to Decriminalize the 'Small Three Links'*, www.dsis.org.tw/peaceforum/symposium/2000-07/CSR0007003e.htm, November 14, 2000.

[16]SCMP, January 3, 2000, p. 1.

[17]There is a number of ways that cargos found their way across the Taiwan Strait. The most frequently used method was to export goods to Hong Kong first and then re-export the goods to either Taiwan or the mainland. The Ishigaki Island in Japan, Pusan in South Korea, and Singapore have also been used to re-export goods between Taiwan and the mainland. Other approaches include trans-shipment (cargos changing ships in Hong Kong), transit shipment (cargos traveling through Hong Kong without changing ships), and illegal shipment involving chartered ships flying flags of a third country. Since April 1997, a new shipping route has been added to the cross-Strait trade, which is referred to as 'fixed-point direct shipping' or the 'offshore trans-shipment center'. Six shipping companies each from the mainland and Taiwan have been approved to use their foreign-registered vessels to operate a direct freight service between Fuzhou and Xiamen on the mainland and Kaohsiung in Taiwan. This was the first officially-approved direct shipping link between Taiwan and the mainland since 1949. See Qi, *op.cit.*

[18]Mastel,*Taiwan in the WTO: An Economic and Policy Analysis*, *op.cit.*

[19]Prybyla, J.S., 'China and Taiwan: A comparative study of economic problems since the Asian financial crisis,' *American Asian Review*, vol. XVIII, no. 4, 2000.

[20]Mastel, G., *Can China and Taiwan Do Business Together?*, *op.cit.*

[21]Mastel, G.,*Taiwan in the WTO: An Economic and Policy Analysis*, *op.cit.*

[22]'Taiwan WTO Entry to Bring US$ 5.3 Billion Trade Deficit', *Muzi.com News*, http://dailynews.muzi.com/ll/English/50883.shtml, September 4, 2000.

[23]Prybyla, *op.cit.*

[24]'Taiwan Has Mixed View on China Ties Inside WTO', *Muzi.com News*, http://dailynews.muzi.com/ll/English/74556.shtml, September 3, 2000.

[25]Mastel, G.,*Taiwan in the WTO: An Economic and Policy Analysis, op.cit.*

[26]Prybyla, *op.cit.*

[27]Ibid.

[28]*Macau Daily News* (MDN), October 27, 2000, p. A9.

[29]'Taiwan Set to Ease Controls on Chinese-invested Firms', *Muzi.com News*, http://dailynews.muzi.com/ll/English/25174.shtml, September 4, 2000.

[30]'Taiwan to Merge 3 Banks to Help Meet WTO Challenge', *Muzi.com News*, http://dailynews.muzi.com/ll/English/54253.shtml, September 4, 2000.

[31]World Bank, *World Development Report 1991*, New York: Oxford University Press, 1991, p. 207.

[32]Economist Intelligence Unit (EIU), *Country Forecast: Hong Kong*, June 1998.

[33]EIU, *Country Forecast: Hong Kong*, December 1998.

[34]For an analysis of Hong Kong's historical competitive advantages and its forthcoming challenges see Enright, M.J., E.E. Scott, and D. Dodwell, *The Hong Kong Advantage*, Hong Kong: Oxford University Press, 1997; for suggestions for dealing with the challenges see Berger, S., and R.K. Lester, *Made by Hong Kong*, Hong Kong: Oxford University Press, 1997.

[35]SCMP, November 26, 2000, Sunday Money section, p. 2.

[36]Ng, C., 'Quality Education for the 21st Century: A Tortuous Road Ahead in a New Era,' in: Chow, L.C. and Y. Fan, eds., *The Other Hong Kong Report 1998*, Hong Kong: Chinese University Press, 1999, pp. 229–46.

[37]SCMP, October 26, 2000, p. 2.

[38]For example, Paul Krugman is one of the economists who hold this view. See Krugman, P., *Saving Asia*, http://web.mit.edu/krugman/www/, September 7, 1998.

[39]Ibid.

[40]Pritchard, S., 'Threats to "middle-man" role', *Review 2000*, Hong Kong: *South China Morning Post*, October 13, 2000, 7.

[41]EIU, *Country Profile 2000: Hong Kong, Macau*, 2000.

[42]Qi, *op.cit.*

[43]MDN, November 15, 2000, p. B8.

[44]Hong Kong Government, *Estimates of Gross Domestic Product: 1961-1998*, Hong Kong, 1999.

[45]Ibid.

[46]SCMP, September 5, 2000, Business Post, p. 1.

[47]Bickering, L., 'Bank resist consolidation', *Review 2000*, Hong Kong: *South China Morning Post*, October 13, 2000, pp. 16–17.

[48]Bickering, L., 'Finance sector eyes China', *Review 2000*, Hong Kong: *South China Morning Post*, October 13, 2000, pp. 14–15.

[49]Ibid.

[50]Hong Kong Government, *Policy Address 1999: Quality People, Quality Home – Positioning Hong Kong for the 21st Century*, Hong Kong, 1999.

[51]SCMP, October 30, 2000, p.7.

[52]SCMP, November 21, 2000, Business Post, p. 6.

[53]Wong, J.S., 'Logistics under the microscope', *Review 2000*, Hong Kong: *South China Morning Post*, October 13, 2000, p. 25.

[54]Moir, J., 'Tourism chief fight back', *Review 2000*, Hong Kong: *South China Morning Post*, October 12, 2000, p. 12.

[55]SCMP, October 28, 2000, Business Post, p. 1.

[56]Ieong, W.C., and R.C.S. Siu, *Macau: A Model of Mini-Economy*, Macau: University of Macau Publications Center, 1997, pp. 12–13.

[57]Chan, S.S., *The Macau Economy*, Macau: University of Macau Publications Center, 2000, p. 2.

[58]MDN, September 30, 2000, p. A10.

[59]Chao, E. and R. Chan, 'Technology, Work, and the Structure of Employment in Macau,' in: Ramos, R., R. Wilson, J.R. Dinis, and D.Y. Yuan, eds, *Macau and Its Neighbors Toward the 21st Century*, Macau: University of Macau & Macau Foundation, 2000, pp. 91–2.

[60]SCMP, September 30, 2000, p. 15.

[61]MDN, September 21, 2000, p. A10.

[62]Wang, Z., 'Economic Cooperation Between Macau-Zhuhai and Hong Kong-Shenzhen' in Ramos et al., eds, *op.cit.*, pp. 123-128.

[63]MDN, September 10, 2000, p. A1.

[64]MDN, September 24, 2000, p. A10.

[65]EIU,*Country Profile 2000: Hong Kong, Macau*, 2000.

[66]Chan, *op.cit.*, pp. 16, 69-73.

[67]Lui B., 'A Comparison of the Roles Played by Hong Kong and Macau in Sino-European Relations'.

[68]SCMP, September 30, 2000, p. 15.

[69]MDN, September 27, 2000, p. B12.

[70]SCMP, September 30, 2000, p. 15.

[71]MDN, September 2, 2000, p. A1.

[72]MDN, September 29, 2000, p. A10.

[73]MDN, September 5, 2000, p. A1.

[74]Li, X.G. 'Analysis of the Potential Economic Cooperation Between Guangxi and Macau,' in: Wong, H.K and Yuan, S.F., eds, *Proceedings of the Conference on 'Economic Interaction Between Guangxi and Macau'*, Macau: University of Macau, Guangxi: Guangxi University, 1998, pp. 13-18; Chen, D.Q., 'Feasibility Studies of Transferring Macau's Garment and Textile to Guangxi', in: Wong and Yuan, eds, *op.cit.*, pp. 65-70; Guo, X.H., 'Feasibility Study and Choice of Key Projects of Economic and Trade Cooperation Between Guangxi and Macau', in: Wong and Yuan, eds, *op.cit.*, pp. 73-80.

[75]MDN, September 24, 2000, p. A2.

[76]Ieong, W.C., 'The Economic Development of Guangdong, Hong Kong and Macau,' in: Ramos et al., eds, *op.cit.*, pp. 141-146.

[77]Chan, *op.cit.*, pp. 57-60.

[78]EIU, *Country Profile 2000: Hong Kong, Macau*, 2000.

[79]EIU, *Country Report: Hong Kong, Macau*, 2nd quarter, 2000, p. 43.

[80]Chan, *op.cit.*, p. 65.

APPENDIX

Profile Comparison: Taiwan, Hong Kong and Macau (All 1999 estimates unless specified)

	Taiwan	Hong Kong	Macau
Population (million)	22,09	6,80	0,44
GDP (US$ billion)	288,0	158,8	6,1
Exports of Goods and Services (% of GDP)	49%	199%	79%
Imports of Goods and Services (% of GDP)	−47%	−193%	−50%
Main Export Destinations (% of Total Exports)	US (25%) Hong Kong (21%) Japan (10%) Netherlands (4%)	China (33%) US (24%) Japan (5%) UK (4%)	US (47%) EU (30%) China (9%) Hong Kong (7%)
Main Import Origins (% of Total Imports)	Japan (28%) US (18%) S. Korea (7%) Germany (5%)	China (44%) Japan (12%) Taiwan (7%) US (7%)	China (36%) Hong Kong (18%) EU (13%) Taiwan (10%)
Exchange Rate (local currency: US$)	Average NT$32.26:US$1	Fixed HK$7.80:US$1	Fixed MOP8.03:US$1
Main origins of GDP (% of GDP)	Manufacturing (27%) Finance, insurance & business services (20%) Wholesale, retail trade, restaurants & hotel (19%) Government service (10%)	**(1998 statistics)** Finance, insurance, real estate, business services (26%) Wholesale, retail import & export trade (25%) Transport, storage & communications (9%)	**(1993 statistics)** Manufacturing (40%) Tourism (27%) Construction (9%) Trade (6%)

Sources: Hong Kong and Macau estimates are based on the data provided in the Economist Intelligence Unit's (EIU's) *Country Report: Hong Kong, Macau.* Taiwan estimates are based on the data provided in the EIU's *Country Report: Taiwan* and Taiwan Government's *Monthly Bulletin of Statistics.*

14

China's Future Role in the WTO: 'Developing Country', 'Regional Economic Power', 'New Economic Superpower'?

Michael Yahuda

Introduction

China's accession to the WTO is recognized both within and outside the country as a major milestone in the long process of the integration into the modern international system of this 'civilization that pretends to be a state' – to use Lucien Pye's distinctive phrase.[1] This process of integration should be seen within the perspective of the historical experiences of the encounter between the Chinese people and the forces of modernization over the last two hundred years. From the outset the encounter in Chinese eyes has involved a continuing struggle with the Western world as both the bearer and the enforcer of modernity. It has required the Chinese to undergo a painful process of adjustment from seeing themselves as the embodiment of civilization, good governance and central power in world affairs to having become in what the founder of the first Chinese republic once called 'a loose sheet of sand'. Ever since China's leaders and intellectuals have been conscience of the possibility of the 'loss of China' and the disintegration of their state even as they sought to accommodate their country to the modern world without having their identity overwhelmed by it.[2] They have sought in various ways to establish new governance at home, develop the economy along modern lines, strengthen the state and establish a place for China once again at the centre of world affairs. Thus contemporary Chinese intellectuals do not see the rise of their country only in terms of economics or great power politics, they yearn to see China once again become a centre of global distinction in the arts and the sciences. But their pride in pointing to their countrymen having discovered in medieval times the four great foundations of modernity (paper, printing, gunpowder and the magnetic compass) masks a rueful recognition of the absence of any equivalent contributions.

The commitment to join the WTO must be understood within these inherently nationalistic or patriotic perspectives. It is not based on a globalist vision by which all parts of the world should be regulated in the same way to serve the liberal principles that underpin much of the ethos of the WTO. It is instructive to note that what is translated from the Chinese as 'patriotism' is literally 'love stateism'. Hence membership of the WTO is designed to strengthen the Chinese state and to enable 'the Chinese people to make a greater contribution to the world', as the founder of the People's Republic of China, once put it. The problem here is that the China that is joining the WTO is in the process of such complex transitions that neither its leaders nor its intellectuals have been able to articulate a clear vision of its future. The only one available so far is the materialist one of Deng Xiaoping that envisioned China's citizens reaching the average income of the poorer Western countries by the middle of the 21st century. Not surprisingly perhaps, there has been little overt discussion in China about the deeper implications of what entry to the WTO might mean to its society and politics.

Nevertheless it would be greatly surprising if China's leaders did not take notice of the discussion in the West about how much change accession to the WTO will promote in China. Former President Clinton claimed that the relevant American legislation would contribute to the expansion of trade which 'can help bring greater social change to China by spreading the tools, contacts and ideas that promote freedom'.[3] American business people, claiming that China's domestic markets would open up to them at last, reacted to the Sino–American agreement about the terms of China's accession as 'the deal of the century'.[4] More sober evaluations expect change to be slower and more complex. Nevertheless even these anticipate significant change in the longer term.[5] By comparison there has been little discussion as to the impact that China may have on the WTO or what role it may seek to play as a member.

I shall argue that China will not deliberately seek to be obstructive, but its membership will nevertheless raise difficulties for the organization. These will stem from the problems of accommodating such a large country as China, which differs from the WTO in terms of underlying values and practices. China will doubtless seek to promote its interests as these are understood by its current leaders. Despite being among the world's ten largest traders, China will continue to claim the various exemptions and entitlements available to those classified as 'developing countries'. Even though China's leaders have come to depict their country as one of the great powers that seeks to shape the world in a pattern of multi-polarity they still continue to promote the old vision of their country as a victim of Western imperialism that like other third world countries is seeking to develop a backward economy. Although EU and US negotiators have taken the lead in resisting China's entry into the WTO simply as a designated 'developing country' it is the developing world which has most to fear from China's entry. Developing countries will find themselves increasingly at a competitive disadvantage with China. Already China attracts more direct foreign investment (FDI) than the rest of the developing countries put together and it has already eaten into the markets of many developing countries for manufactured products.

Further difficulties will stem from uncertainties about the role that China may wish to play in the organization. China's leaders and intellectuals have often complained about being subject to international rules and laws that were not of their making. But they have yet to identify the principles by which they seek to promote changes, other than asking in effect for the right sometimes to be exempt from their application. Nevertheless it has been argued that where international organizations have shown sensitivity to Chinese concerns China has displayed a good record of adaptation in gradually conforming to their norms and procedures.[6] In this particular case, where the rules being made are supposed to be binding, it will be interesting to see whether China's representatives might interpret the norm of reaching decisions by consensus as allowing them in effect a veto power. Finally, I shall consider the implications that Chinese membership will have for its broader role in world affairs. Will it first contribute to the growing weight of China within its region and then to the world at large, leading it become an 'economic superpower'? How would such developments impact upon the WTO?

The Problem of Values

As the principal international organization that promotes international trade, the WTO is charged with laying down the rules governing international trade so as to promote multilateral global trade. To this end it seeks to remove obstacles erected by individual countries to the free flow of goods and services on a non-discriminatory basis. It is also empowered to settle trade disputes. Because of its commitment to promote trade on the basis of non-discrimination and equal treatment in accordance with the rule of law the WTO, in effect, is the key international institution that embodies what has been called 'the spirit of classical liberalism'.[7] To be sure, the WTO has not always adhered to these principles perfectly and its members have not only complained about their application to themselves, but some have even sought to side step them. Nevertheless, supported by the major OECD countries, the WTO has registered considerable success in applying these principles across the board.[8]

The PRC, by contrast, lacks such a clearly defined philosophical basis for public policy. In the words of the then candidate for president, George W. Bush, which may have implications for America's future China policy, 'China is rising and that is inevitable', but it is a 'power in transition ... and it is difficult to know their intentions when they do not know their own future'.[9] The core of the problem is that the PRC remains under the monopolistic rule of the communist party even as the country continues remorselessly to move away from a command economy in the Stalinist mould towards a more market type economy. The communist leaders claim to uphold communist ideology despite its erosion, not least because of the reform process itself. But it is not only ideology that has been eroded, the instruments of government associated with the former economic system have also been degraded.

Nervous about their hold on power, China's communist rulers regularly use force to prevent the emergence of organized opposition while simultaneously encouraging rapid economic growth and reform. The former is defended in the name of upholding stability and the latter is promoted as a means of increasing prosperity and increasing the strength of the state. Although the top leaders may differ about the pace and the depth of economic reforms, they nevertheless agree that there can be neither a turning back towards the command economy, nor a reversal of the opening to the international economy. Yet it is also important to note that not even the most prominent reformers among the current leaders, such as Premier Zhu Rongji, believes in free choice, free markets, or the privatization of the biggest state owned enterprises. As products of a communist bureaucracy, even the most reform minded of the current leaders, believes in the right and duty of the state to run and directly manage what they regard as the commanding heights of the economy.

Thus the role of the market is seen by China's communist leaders primarily in terms of a mechanism to increase efficiency and productivity rather than as the governing principle of the economy. Although the current generation of leaders have gone beyond the late Chen Yun's depiction of the market as being like a bird in the cage of the state, they nevertheless believe strongly in their role as hands on managers rather than as Adam Smith type regulators.[10] For example, it was only twenty years into the reform process that private ownership of companies was finally recognized in law, and there is still much to be done before private property can be said to be properly defined in law. Part of the problem in tackling many of the loss-making state owned enterprises (SOEs) has arisen from the absence of legal clarity about ownership of and accountability for use of their assets.

The rule of law is also seen by China's rulers in a very different way from the liberal ethos that underpins the WTO perspective. The former see it more in terms of rule by law, that is to say, as an instrument to facilitate their rule, rather than as a system by which their rule should be constrained and held accountable. The strengthening of the legal system may rightly be seen as a major correction to the secretive and arbitrary use of power by officials in the past. It may also be seen as necessary to the operation of the market and to the administration of the country in its new circumstances. But, as the use (or abuse) of the law against the Falun Gong demonstrates, the enhancement of legality under communist party rule does not of itself promote liberal principles or governmental accountability.

The fact that many leaders in the West have openly expressed their belief that China's entry into the WTO will eventually result in political change will probably have the effect of intensifying the alertness of China's rulers to detecting and, if possible, suppressing any harbingers of such change. It is true that the China's economic reforms have led to important social and even political changes, but these have not always been in accordance with expectations in the West. For example, the confident predictions that an independent middle class would emerge in China have not so far been borne out by the evidence. Such is the close correspondence between officials and entrepreneurs that the nascent middle class is enmeshed with the world of officialdom. Arguably, this middle class has been co-opted by the state, rather than it providing the basis for the emergence of an independent civil-society. Beyond which not all of the WTO's 140 members can be said to demonstrate a growing homogeneity in the way they regulate their economies or in the direction they are following in terms of social and political change.

However, given China's growing significance as a world trader, its accession to the WTO is likely sooner or later to bring to the surface the implicit clash in values between the two. These are more likely to be expressed, however, in terms of complaints by the Chinese about infringements of sovereignty by the WTO's dispute procedures or by claims about the lack of sufficient recognition for China's character as a developing country.

Problems of Practice

It is often argued that China's record as a member of international organizations is good and that the Chinese have been able to adapt their practices and procedures to accommodate those required of them as members.[11] This has been particularly true of organizations where the advantages to the Chinese have been clear-cut and commanded considerable support among the top leaders, such as the World Bank. But elsewhere, the picture is more mixed. China has not been the most active of the permanent members of the Security Council of the United Nations, even though membership has certainly been seen as advantageous to the PRC by its leaders. China has grudgingly accepted some of the provisions of the UN human rights regime, but in many respects it remains an obstacle to the operation of the UNHRC [12] China's Membership of the ASEAN Regional Forum and its associated second track diplomacy mechanism, the Council for Security Co-operation in the Asia–Pacific, has familiarized the Chinese side with the diplomacy of multi-lateralism and it has helped to reduce the tension arising from sovereignty disputes in the South China Sea. But privately, other members claim that China has obstructed any substantive attempts to move beyond the declaratory stages to operational measures. On at least one occasion the Chinese side was cautioned that the consensual procedure of the ARF did not mean that it had it could exercise a veto over its activities.[13]

China will have difficulties in accommodating itself to the WTO both because it is fundamentally a rules-based organization and because it necessarily intrudes into the domestic affairs of its members. One of the reasons that President Jiang Zemin and Premier Zhu Rongji overcame the reluctance and perhaps the opposition of other leaders in deciding to join was to promote further economic reform at home. But opposition remains among those conservatives who fear the consequences of increased Western influence and those whose interests are likely to be damaged. The trouble is that whatever immediate benefits may accrue in terms of increased foreign investment and unfettered access to key markets, there will be many clear-cut losers in the short term before the longer term advantages eventually become evident. In particular certain agricultural sectors and many SOEs will be adversely affected. Social unrest could increase with the result that opposition to the WTO might stiffen in the early years rather than gradually diminish. Under such circumstances China could be expected to drag its feet in implementing key aspects of its commitments to the WTO.

In adjudicating aspects of Chinese adherence to its commitments the WTO will end-up being drawn into the murky world of Chinese politics where different leaders often promote their own agendas, where institutions are jealous of their prerogatives and where problems of implementing decisions are legion. In many areas of economic administration decisions are taken and implemented on the basis of bargaining even between ostensibly hierarchical bodies. That characterizes relations between Beijing and the provinces. Inter-provincial relations are so difficult that it is not uncommon for provinces to trade more with foreign countries than with each other.[14]

The Chinese style of negotiation will test WTO patience to the limits. It is a style which, because of its need to be based on consensus within the different domestic interests, is long-drawn out and demanding on the foreign partner from whom much of the internal discord is hidden. Frequently, this entails discerning the final bottom-line of the foreign negotiator which is reached by allowing the negotiations to stretch to the point of failure before an agreement is reached.[15] Meanwhile there will be the usual divisions among China's interlocutors between those who insist on enforcing what are regarded as international rules and laws and those who favour a softer line in order to help perceived reformers against alleged hard-liners. For their part the Chinese can be expected to probe among these divisions for their own advantage.

In practice it will be far from easy for the WTO to adjudicate disputes or to demand effective implementation. There is no doubt that China will be a difficult member to integrate fully into the organization. But much will depend on the standards that will be required of the Chinese. After all the WTO tolerates a wide range of performance by its 140 members. Practices among the OECD countries vary greatly in their adherence to the ostensible rules as may be seen from considering such different cases as Japan, the US, EU countries and say South Korea.

China as a Developing Country

Any assessment of the implications of Chinese membership of the WTO must include discussion of the position that China's leaders claim for their country in the international economy and of the role that they see it playing. For more than forty years China's leaders have claimed that theirs is a developing country. The claim will be considered first with regard to China's dealings with the WTO itself and then in terms of China's position within the developing world.

Throughout the fifteen years of negotiations about the terms of entry to the WTO China's negotiators have consistently claimed the entitlement to join with status of a developing country for whom the requirements of entry would allow greater protectionism. Only at the very end did China's leaders accept implicitly the American and EU arguments that by virtue of size and the magnitude of its part in international trade China could not be treated as a typical developing country. Nevertheless the terms that the Chinese finally offered first to the Americans and then to the Europeans were offered as 'concessions'. This suggests that the matter has not been settled on a once and for all basis, but that the Chinese will return to it perhaps on a case by case basis.

In recent years China's leaders have claimed that their country is one of the big powers that has an important role to play in promoting the emergence of a multi-polar world to counter the overwhelming power and influence of the single superpower. Yet they simultaneously claim to be a 'developing country'. That claim has much merit in view of the relatively low annual per capita income of less than $ 800, with up to 900 million peasant farmers engaged in traditional agriculture and with much of the country still experiencing third world-type economic conditions. So keen are Chinese spokespeople to stress their third world credentials that they prefer to use income statistics based on the market exchange rate for their currency rather than that of purchasing parity which would inflate the previous p.c. figure to over $ 3,000. Even though the latter could be used as a measure of their economic achievement, they prefer the lower figure as it bolsters their claim to be a developing country. But China's position is more complex as there are wide regional variations with the coastal provinces almost reaching the levels of NIEs (newly industrialized economies) and, as already noted, China is no ordinary developing economy. It is among the ten largest trading countries in the world and it attracts FDI to an amount that exceeds the combined total of all the other developing countries.

China is likely, however, to continue to claim that the WTO should treat it as a developing country in all respects other than those it has specifically agreed to discount in the negotiated terms of entry. Apart from such intrinsic merits as may attach to Chinese claims, they are likely to continue to be fuelled by the particularities of Chinese nationalism or patriotism. These include a sense of entitlement to a restitution of China's former greatness that was denied the country as it fell victim to Western and Japanese incursions that inflicted humiliations from which China has not fully recovered. Hence Chinese claims that it is somehow unjust to expect them to abide by rules and laws in which they played no part in making is not shaped by an alternative vision about the principles on which they should be based, but rather they consist of demands for exceptional treatment. But China is heavily enmeshed in 'a complex mix of dependence, autonomy (termed independence by the leadership, and interdependence [...]'[16] Hence it is not well placed to advance alternative general principles for the conduct of international trade.

China can also be expected to try and give voice to many third world issues or to the demands of developing countries as a whole. Indeed, as in the United Nations, the Chinese may implicitly claim a kind of leadership of the developing world. But since the WTO is concerned with the details of the regulations and conduct of trade, the opportunities for rhetorical leadership may be more circumscribed. Moreover China's capacity to offer effective leadership will be constrained, first by its relative isolation as a non-member of any of the third world political or economic institutions. Hence it would be difficult for it to provide a lead for positions on which agreement was reached without its formal participation. Second, China's leaders necessarily distance themselves from most third world countries when they claim great power status and argue that major international developments are shaped principally by the great powers. Thirdly, as a major trading country China has emerged as a damaging competitor to many other developing countries not only in the trade of labour intense products, but also in the next stage of industrial products that involve more capital investment and more skilled labour, such as computer products.[17]

However, in so far as the WTO has become divided into separate, albeit informal groupings China is likely to attach itself to that of the developing countries. Its general rhetoric will probably reflect that and clearly, China will favour the general position of third world countries that seeks to enhance the role of governments at the expense of the free flow of trade across borders. But there will be some important issue areas where China's interests will not coincide with many others in the developing world. As China becomes more integrated into the international economy its foreign investments will increase and it will acquire an ever deepening interest in the reduction of tariff barriers. It will find its interests opposed by selective measures to assist the trade with less well-off developing countries.

Implications for China's Role in the World

China's leaders used to argue that the WTO could not live up to its name without including China with a fifth of the world's population. The implication was that China was already a country of global significance. The corollary, however, was that by joining the WTO China's association with the international community or the international society of states will be complete. I shall consider the implications of this first for China's position within its own region and then for the world at large. I shall argue that this will contribute to China's significance within the region without allowing it dominance and that far from facilitating China's emergence as an economic superpower, it will deepen China's integration into the international economy as a regional economic power with limited global influence.

The region: the economic impact

China's accession to the WTO will significantly increase the economic impact of China in Pacific Asia and that in turn will have a profound impact on China's political role in the region. However China's economic influence in the region will be uneven. In some cases, especially in Southeast Asia, China will become a still more powerful competitor in attracting capital investment and in gaining access to foreign markets, while in others a more complementary relationship will continue to develop.

The key issue turns on production-chains of garments and textiles and of electronics. The former involves low cost intensive labour, flexibility in hiring and firing workers and FDI in which export oriented production has been developed in export processing zones set up in coastal areas. The latter, which may be seen as operating at a higher stage in the technological production process, involves a more complex interaction between the supply of various inputs by adjacent economies for assembly in Chinese facilities. China has already emerged as the world's largest producer and exporter of garments and textiles and, as a member of the WTO, China is poised to increase its market share even more and this will be at the expense of other developing countries. Ministers in ASEAN and other countries have already expressed concern at the plans of garment suppliers to move production to China. They appreciate that even as the current crop of workers in China increase their skills and move up to the next stage of the technological process their shoes will be filled by the enormous reserve of relatively inexpensive labour from the inner provinces. FDI flows into most ASEAN countries have also dropped absolutely and relatively compared to China.[18]

Electronic assembly in the Chinese Mainland is still complementary with the component, sub-assembly and other input production of Japan, South Korea, Taiwan and some of the ASEAN countries. But it has already displaced assembly activities that used to take place in some of the Newly Industrializing Economies (NIEs) such as Singapore, Korea, Taiwan and Hong Kong and it competes directly with Thailand, Malaysia, Indonesia and the Philippines. Even where complementarities currently exist they are likely to be short lived as China's technological sophistication increases and as the government's determination to push China up the value-added ladder has an impact.

In sum China will become an even more effective competitor for the less advanced economies. Moreover as the Chinese economy continues to grow and develop its demand for resources, notably energy will also grow to the befit of some regional economies and to the detriment of others who will find costs rising. China's entry to the WTO is likely to have the effect of accentuating the gap that has re-emerged at the end of the 1990s between Northeast and Southeast Asia. China's entry will also have the effect of increasing the pressure on all the countries in East Asia, but especially in the Southeast to continually move-up the ladder of technology and value-added economic activities. That will reward those with effective governance, good infrastructure and with appropriately trained professional and blue-collar workers.

However, in addition to becoming a more effective competitor, China will also increase aspects of its complementarities with regional economies. This is true even for the Southeast Asian countries though circumstances will vary according to their geographical location, comparative advantage and quality of governance. Thailand and its less developed neighbours Burma, Cambodia and Laos and perhaps even Vietnam may benefit from the export of agricultural products to a growing Chinese market and from the development of the adjacent provinces of Yunnan and Guangxi. The much discussed Mekong River project could well get a boost. Moreover Thailand with its comparatively efficient auto-industry is perhaps better placed than most to continue to move up the value-added ladder. The Philippines and Indonesia, however, are likely to fare less well even though Indonesia stands to gain as an energy producer. In the short term Malaysia will benefit, but much depends on its capacity to keep ahead of the technological trajectory being pursued by China. However, the failure of the ASEAN countries to meet their targets of tariff reduction for their own trade and their difficulties in integrating their economies will increase their problems in accommodating an economically resurgent China.

In Northeast Asia, the impact of China's entry into the WTO will be to enhance the complementarities of China with Japan, South Korea and Taiwan. As the most advanced economy in Asia, Japan is expected to gain most from a growing open Chinese economy. South Korea and Taiwan will also gain, but as more of their manufacturing moves into China they will be under continual pressure to upgrade their value-added economic activities.

Other areas of China's region include Russia, Central and South Asia. These are unlikely to be greatly affected one way or other by China's entry into the WTO. They would be affected if that entry significantly enhanced the growth and development of the Chinese economy. Hence the impact would be medium to long term. With its growing energy needs and its own reserves in Xinjiang, China will be drawn into becoming a more active participant in the geopolitical and geo-economic 'games' being played in Central Asia. Complentarities with Russia are also likely to grow, but these will continue to fail to realize their potential until Russia becomes more effectively governed.

The region: the political dimension

As the above brief survey suggests, the economic impact of China is likely to significant but uneven. In the absence of effective regional organizations for the development of coherent interdependent strategies, China and its neighbours will continue to develop their linkages on bilateral and ad hoc bases. A pattern has emerged of seeking bilateral agreements for economic purposes. The Chinese have also promoted localized networks linking neighbours with adjacent provinces. These include highly effective ones involving Hong Kong, Taiwan, South Korea and even Japan. Elsewhere on China's more inland periphery the results have been relatively ineffective. Thus the regional impact of China's growing pivotal position in the interdependencies of the Asian economies is unlikely to be reflected in organizational terms. In some ways that may be said to suit a major power such as China which would have reason to fear the emergence of a de-facto coalition targeted against it by its smaller neighbours. But even as China may be able to bargain more effectively with individual smaller neighbours, it would nevertheless lack a vehicle with which to promote its regional significance. In effect China would depend on international organizations, where its voice would be less dominant, to set the rules for the conduct of economic relations even among its neighbours.

However, the key question would be how would China be able to use its growing regional significance for political purposes. Since China's leaders seek to assure neighbours about their responsibility and commitment to ensure that they would not be harmed by China's economic growth, they can be expected to try to find ways of mitigating harmful competition and providing means to enhance mutual trade and economic relations. In WTO parlance that would be described as 'managed trade'. But that would be unlikely to deter the parties from carrying out such policies. Indeed such policies would have the effect of integrating China more deeply into the region and raising the costs to it of using military means or coercive diplomacy to try and settle conflicts in Southeast Asia in particular.

Northeast Asia represents a different series of problems that arise in part from the Taiwan problem and in part from the political/strategic divide between China and Japan. With Taiwan's entry due to follow China's into the WTO the two are expected to deepen their economic interactions. That will put even more pressure on Taiwan to push itself up the value-added ladder, but there is no intrinsic reason as to why an even deeper economic interdependency between the two should lead to political integration. Just as it can be argued that Taiwan would have a growing dimension of its economy, society and business communities dependent upon the Chinese Mainland, so it can be argued that for that very reason there would be a demand to emphasize the political separation. In other words, there is no necessary progression from economic to political ties. In the longer term, Chinese society and politics may continue to change in accordance with the economic changes and that would make integration with China more attractive to Taiwan. Similarly, if as a result of WTO entrance China's legal system was significantly improved that too could change the country's image in the view of Taiwanese. But again that is a matter for the longer term and it is not a necessary corollary of WTO membership.

The Sino–Japanese relationship does not seem to have been improved in political or strategic terms as a result of the substantive growth of their economic relations in the 1990s and it seems unlikely to do so just as a consequence of China joining the WTO. The two countries still regard each other as potential strategic competitors or even rivals and they are likely to continue to do so especially as arguments about nuclear missile defence become more salient.

Nevertheless China's significance in Pacific Asia is set to increase as a result of WTO membership both because of growing economic interdependencies and because of the boost it will give to China's GNP and to its technological development. With an economy that is still only a fourth of that of Japan, China will be unable to dominate the regional economy, nor will it be able to compete with Japan as an investor, or as a source of advanced technology and a highly advanced market. But China will become more of a regional hub as the economies of neighbours deepen their ties with it. China will also be able to offer neighbours favourable terms of trade and prospects for joint development. In short, as long as China chooses to act benevolently it will be able to enhance its regional role, especially in Southeast Asia.

Conclusion

I have argued that China will adapt only slowly and unevenly to the requirements of WTO membership because of a clash of values and differences of political and negotiating practice. Nevertheless China may well experience an immediate boost in FDI and in economic growth. However, as China has emerged as a major trading nation it is clear that it has become a serious competitor with other developing countries. It has successfully garnered a share of FDI that exceeds that of all the other developing countries combined and it has reached or is fast reaching a similar position as a manufacturer and exporter of high labour intensity products such as garments and textiles. That can only increase with WTO membership and it will not be much affected even as China moves into the next stage as an assembler of electronic and similar products.

Accordingly, China will find it difficult to promote itself as a defender and promoter of the interests of less developed countries. It can be expected to continue to claim such a status on its own behalf because of the favourable terms of trade and finance and access to aid attached to such a designation. China's leaders may also continue to portray themselves as members and leaders of the third world and others may even formally regard them as such. But the reality is that the interests between China and other members of the third world will increasingly diverge. If China's leader are to go beyond the pretence of rhetorical leadership of the developing countries, they will have to show a willingness to forgo benefits for countries less well situated than their own. On occasions they have made exceptions such as to offer products at 'friendship' prices to particular countries or to make political gestures, for example by offering African countries the abolition of debt (in the context of drawing a distinction between themselves and the West). But on generic issues, the approach of China's leaders in international relations has so far been framed within the language of entitlement rather than that of a provider of public goods.

The impact of the Chinese economy on the world as a whole is still relatively small, and it is unlikely to increase substantively as a consequence of entry to the WTO. But there is no question that its economic significance within Pacific Asia will increase as both a competitor and a complementary partner. However, with GNP that is still but a quarter of the value of that of Japan, China' capacity to become the regional economic leader will be strictly qualified. Its enhanced economic role should deepen its interest in managing conflicts in Southeast Asia by peaceful means, but it will not make a difference – at least in the short run – in Northeast Asia. The main results of WTO membership will be to deepen China's integration into the (liberal) international economy externally and boost the reform process at home. In the longer run they will be of greater significance than any short-term enhancement of an external political role. China will become more integrated into the international economic system, but that in itself seems unlikely to provide a clearer answer to the long-standing question of China's place in the modern world.

Notes

[1]Pye Lucien, 'China: Erratic State, Frustrated Society', *Foreign Affairs*, vol. 69, no. 4 (Fall 1990), p. 58.

[2]For the significance of the fear of 'loss' see Fitzgerald, John, "'Reports of my death have been greatly exaggerated": the history of the death of China', in Goodman, David S.G. and Gerald Segal, eds, *China Deconstructs*, London & New York: Routledge, 1994, pp. 21–58.

[3]Reuters, 28 July 1999.

[4]The title of an article in *Far Eastern Economic Review*, 25 November 1999.

[5]See for example, Prybyla, Jan S., 'China in the WTO: Threat or Promise of good Things to Come?', *Issues and Studies*, vol. 36, no. 1 (January/ February 2000), pp. 143–60.

[6]Oksenberg, Michel and Elizabeth Economy, eds, *China Joins the World: Progress and Prospects*, New York: Council on Foreign Relations Press, 1999; Jacobson, Harold K. and Michel Oksenberg, *China's Participation in the IMF, the World Bank and GATT,* Ann Arbor: University of Michigan Press, 1990.

[7]Prybyla, *op.cit.* pp.147–8.

[8]For a broad view of the place of the WTO in the management of the contemporary international economy see Sampson, Gary, *Trade, environment, and the WTO: the post Seattle agenda*, Washington DC: Baltimore Overseas Development Council, Distributed by the Johns Hopkins University, 2000.

[9]Speech at the Ronald Reagan Presidential Library on Nov. 29, 2000, cited by Moses, Russell Leigh, 'Strategic partner, strategic competitor ... strategic nonentity?', *China Online*, 19 January 2001 (via: www. chinaonline/commentary_anal...relations/currentnews/secure/c01011760.asp).

[10]For a succinct assessment of Zhu Rongji and his strengths and weaknesses as a reformer see, Hutchings, Graham, *Modern China: A Companion to a Rising Power*, London: Penguin books, 2000, pp. 495–7.

[11]See note (4) above.

[12]For a cautiously sympathetic, but thorough account see, Foot, Rosemary, *Rights Beyond Borders*, Oxford: Oxford University Press, 2000.

[13]Djalal, D.P, *Indonesia and Preventive Diplomacy: A study of the workshops on managing potential conflicts in the South China Sea* (University of London PhD dissertation), 2000.

[14]Lieberthal, Kenneth, *Governing China*, Ann Arbor: University of Michigan Press, 1997.

[15]See, Solomons, Richard H., *Chinese Negotiating Behaviour 1967–1984*, Santa Monica, California, 1995; Pye, Lucien, *Chinese Commercial Negotiating Style*, Cambridge, Mass.: Oelggeschlager, Gunn & Hain,1982; Blackman, Carolyn, *Negotiating China: Case studies and Strategies*, Sydney: Allen and Unwin, 1997.

[16]Robinson, Thomas W., '[In][ter]dependence in China's Post-Cold War Foreign Relations', in Kim, Samuel S., ed., *China and the World: Chinese foreign Policy Faces the New Millennium* (Boulder Co.: Westview Press, 1998), p. 211.

[17]See for example the arguments and the statistics in the two papers by Enright, Michael J. and Hung Kai Sun, 'China's Future Economic Roles in the Asian Region', and 'China and its Neighbours: the Economic Interaction', prepared for the Wilton Park Conference 'China and its Neighbours' on 20–3 November 2000.

[18]Enright and Sun, 'China's Future Economic Roles in the Asian Region', *op.cit.*; the following few paragraphs have also drawn on this paper.

Printed in the United Kingdom
by Lightning Source UK Ltd.
113034UKS00001B/13